A Common Bond

History teaches that of all human institutions those that are built on common faith, common traditions, and whose history gives evidence of trustworthy service are the most abiding and will last the longest.

—Thore Eggen, 1929

A Common Bond

The Story of Lutheran Brotherhood

by Hakala Associates Inc.

LUTHERAN BROTHERHOOD · MINNEAPOLIS

History researched, written, and produced by Hakala Associates Inc.
Project director: William T. Hakala
Writer: Philip K. Strand
Designer: David E. Barnard

Scriptural quotations from the King James Version.

International Standard Book Number 0-9621237-0-6

Manufactured in the United States of America

Contents

Acknowledgments and Sources

This book is the result of a research and writing project that spanned nearly three years. It could not have gone forward without the cooperation and assistance of many individuals. Dozens of current and retired employees and field personnel responded promptly to written or phone inquiries and sometimes to unannounced visits. They generously took time away from their duties to answer questions or to seek out information on our behalf. Many individuals, such as Herman Egeberg, Cliff and Ann Thompson, Wayne Hellbusch, and David Zetzman entrusted us with old photographs and personal collections of news clips and memorabilia. To acknowledge them all by name would take more space than we have. (God bless the Savers!)

We are particularly grateful for the foresight and diligence of William G. and Elsie Fisher in preserving over the past fifty years many valuable documents from the early history of Lutheran Brotherhood and for making these available to us. The Fisher collection included materials on the society's fraternal activities, as well as diaries and personal effects of Herman L. Ekern.

Many departments in the home office went out of their way to assist us in our information search. Those we especially leaned upon for help were the Corporate Secretary's office, for early records; Communications, for back issues of society publications, photographs, and overall verification of facts; Human Resources, for employee records; Actuarial, for financial statistics; and Word Processing, for diligently transcribing several hundred hours of taped interviews.

We also wish to acknowledge the help provided us throughout the length of this project by members of the Book Committee: Arley Bjella, Charles De Vries, Richard Hagen, Richard Heins, James Krause, David Larson, E. Clifford Nelson, Roland Seboldt, Clair Strommen, and Lloyd Svendsbye. They gave us their undivided interest and their opinions, without attempting to influence or color the ultimate direction of the story. We thank them for their trust, patience, and candor.

Above all, we want to express our gratitude to the 139 individuals interviewed for this history, some of them two and three times. We appreciate them for sharing their experiences with us. To the interview participants, who are named on page 257, we offer our deepest thanks.

In addition to personal interviews, we relied on a number of books, magazine and newspaper articles, and other written materials, the majority of them from Lutheran Brotherhood, including "Fifty Fraternal Years," an unpublished history of the society written by Willmar Thorkelson for the society's golden anniversary.

Special recognition must be given Albert Erlebacher's doctoral thesis, "Herman L. Ekern: The Quiet Progressive," which supplied numerous facts about, and insights into, the political aspects of Ekern's career. Erlebacher's thesis was also helpful in describing the Progressive movement, as was *History of a Free People*, by Henry W. Bragdon and Samuel P. McCutcheon. *The Farmer from Merna*, by Karl Schriftgiesser, illuminated Ekern's role in the development of State Farm Insurance Companies.

Several books contributed heavily to the discussion of Norwegian immigration, including Odd S. Lovoll's *The Promise of America: A History of the Norwegian-American People* and Lovoll's *A Folk Epic: The Bygdelag in America*, Theodore C. Blegen's *Minnesota: A History of the State*, and William W. Folwell's *A History of Minnesota*.

Our examination of the evolution of the Norwegian Lutheran Church was greatly aided by *Church Roots*, a collection of historical essays edited by Charles Lutz; *All These Lutherans: Three Paths Toward a New Lutheran Church*, by Todd W. Nichol; *The Lutheran Church Among Norwegian-Americans*, by E. Clifford Nelson and Eugene L. Fevold; and *The History of Norwegian Lutherans in America*, by Herman A. Preus. Issues of the *St. Paul Pioneer Press and Dispatch*, from June 9 to June 14, 1917, described the merging convention of the Norwegian Lutheran Church.

Lutheran Men in War and Peace, published by the governing board of the American Federation of

Lutheran Brotherhoods, provided us with much useful information about the history of the Lutheran Brotherhood of America and its connection with Luther Union. This discussion, as well as our profile of P. O. Bersell, was greatly aided by information made available by the Lutheran Church in America Archives in Chicago.

Three books were valuable in helping us develop portraits of Jacob Aall Otteson Preus and his ancestors. They were: *Linka's Diary on Land and Sea*, translated and edited by J.C.K. and Diderikke Preus; *Herman Amberg Preus: A Family History*, compiled by J.C.K. Preus; and *Preus of Missouri*, by James Edward Adams. Also helpful was a magazine article, "Jake and Mrs. Jake—and Jack," written by Frederick Lewis Collins for the June 1924 issue of *Women's Home Companian*.

Several newspaper articles were helpful in describing the campaign for control of the society in 1959, including the *Minneapolis Star*, July 31 and August 15, 1959, and the *Minneapolis Tribune*, October 7 and 29, and November 1, 1959. Reports in the September 27, 1961 *Minneapolis Star* and the October 8, 1961 *Minneapolis Sunday Tribune* contributed to our discussion of the 1961 campaign. The chapter describing the 1967 campaign was aided by articles in the *Minneapolis Star* on September 15, 19, and 22, October 6, and December 25, 1967, and the *Minneapolis Tribune* on October 7, 1967.

Several collections of promotional materials, letters and memoranda also helped us to develop a chronology of events, corroborate information, and provide insights into the structure and intensity of the various leadership battles in 1959, 1961, and 1967. While we reviewed documents from a number of sources, we are particularly indebted to board member James Krause, retired general agent Ole Haroldson, and former superintendent of agencies Herbert Johnson for sharing with us the material in their files.

Our characterization of Carl F. Granrud and the Granrud era was helped immeasurably by reading Don Brostrom's delightful memoir, "The Granrud Years: A few reminiscences from an interesting period."

"The Death of Fixed Rates," from the October 13, 1980 issue of *U.S. News and World Report*, contributed to our description of the insurance revolution of the late 1970s. Reports from the June 5, 1985 issue of the *Youngstown Vindicator* provided valuable information about the tornado that struck Youngstown, Ohio, and nearby communities.

—W.T.H.

Foreword

In May 1986, as Lutheran Brotherhood was approaching the seventieth anniversary of its founding in 1917, members of the board of directors began to consider the value of recording the history of the society. We recognized that many living persons had significant knowledge of Lutheran Brotherhood's early years. Some of these individuals were current, retired, or former employees and field representatives; some were society members; some were church officials or business associates. We thought that their personal recollections of events and experiences could help us to create a better sense of Lutheran Brotherhood's distinctive past. We therefore authorized preparation of a seventieth anniversary book that would provide not only a candid examination of recorded events, but a human story as well.

In reading this monumental history, you will see that now, as in 1917, Lutheran Brotherhood is dedicated to providing services to Lutherans and the Lutheran church. From its earliest beginnings as a society that offered life insurance to people who had no other means of gaining financial security, Lutheran Brotherhood has added a number of services to meet the expanding needs of Lutherans.

We are grateful for the high degree of trust that members have traditionally placed in Lutheran Brotherhood. We are pleased that we are still a fraternal benefit society that can help individuals and institutions of the Lutheran church.

To the thousands of members, employees, field representatives, and directors whose efforts over the years have contributed to Lutheran Brotherhood's great and abiding strength, we dedicate this book.

The Board of Directors

Introduction

"You cannot make a man hear life insurance, but you can make him hear the wind beat around the gables of a house on a winter's evening and the crunch of footsteps in the snow, while inside the house the children are happy and comfortable."

So observed Fred Mueller to a gathering of Lutherans in New York in 1931.

Mueller's purpose, much like ours in preparing this book, was to make real—to bring to life—the background, goals, and experiences of a fraternal benefit society for which he worked. The society was called Lutheran Brotherhood, and it was relatively unknown even in its hometown of Minneapolis.

Today, having completed its seventy-first year in business, Lutheran Brotherhood is far better known than in its early years, yet its identity and purpose still are puzzling to many people. Is the society part of the church? Is it a men's religious organization?

Tough and witty Tony Bouza, when he first arrived in Minneapolis from the Bronx to become chief of police in 1980, was quoted as saying that he thought "the Lutheran Brotherhood" was the name of a street gang.

For church and civic leaders who were invited to the society's annual Christmas luncheons in the old green building during the 1970s, the side dishes of *lutefisk* and *lefse* hinted of yet another identity. Lutheran Brotherhood's Nordic heritage has always been reflected in a host of subtle ways: in its quiet formality, its dedicated work ethic, its methodical and consensus-oriented style, and its tidiness.

Many Twin Citians vividly remember the political turmoil that entangled Lutheran Brotherhood during the late 1950s and 1960s. At the time, the society was in the midst of a headlong surge for growth and national identity, and opposing factions with differing management philosophies battled to see who would lead the society forward. During the campaigns, internal disagreements sometimes were dealt with in less-than-brotherly ways, and local headlines often loomed larger than bottom lines.

In retrospect, these tumultuous years were both cathartic and pivotal for Lutheran Brotherhood. It

was a time in which the society's critical relationships were tested—within its own ranks, with its membership, and with the Lutheran church. It was also an era of considerable growth and a coming of age.

Lutheran Brotherhood survived the period and became the better for it, but the people who witnessed those times still shake their heads in wonderment. How could an organization so intimately identified with the church be so quarrelsome?

In fact, such contentious behavior had its roots in the history of the Lutheran church. Lutherans have been at theological odds with one another for hundreds of years. Their differences seemed to intensify and fracture even further among the immigrant groups who came to America. Between 1846 and 1900, Norwegian immigrants alone formed fourteen distinct Lutheran church bodies. What followed was a gradual coming together that culminated in 1917 with the merging of three Norwegian Lutheran synods to form the Norwegian Lutheran Church of America. It was at this merger convention, on June 13, 1917, that Lutheran Brotherhood was born.

Among many of the delegates assembled at the convention, the concept of life insurance was anathema. It suggested a lack of faith in God's providence. Conservative pastors still spoke out against insurance from their pulpits, and many of the clergy who believed in the value of insurance bought their contracts in secret. Although the new society was approved by the convention, there were other problems to overcome in its early years: harsh economic times, a lack of understanding among the public of the value of insurance, a general mistrust of "big business."

Gradually, that which once had been perceived primarily as aid for widows and orphans gained wider acceptance, and was expanded into forms of saving and retirement planning. Along the way, the society grew larger than its founders ever could have imagined. In 1988, from behind the sloping facade of its striking headquarters in Minneapolis, Lutheran Brotherhood and its subsidiaries managed assets of $6.5 billion, had insurance in force of

$23 billion, and channeled $34 million in fraternal benefits through its members to church and community projects.

The numbers tell a success story. However, Lutheran Brotherhood's success is not built on products or pricing, not on mergers or buyouts, but on the enduring trust of its members. The cautious development and careful stewarding of that trust over seven decades has been the central ingredient in the society's rise to fraternal prominence.

From the beginning, Lutheran Brotherhood has been blessed with able leaders. The society has had the uncanny experience of attracting people with extraordinary convictions and faith whose talents matched the special needs of their times. Not all of them have been saints and diplomats in the execution of their visions for the society, and a few stayed too long, but all have been motivated primarily by a sense of service.

The fascinating people who have shaped Lutheran Brotherhood are the primary focus of *A Common Bond.* You'll read about founders Herman Ekern and Jake Preus, two politicians of contrasting styles who blended their ideas into a common vision. You'll get to know Harold Ingvaldson, a snoose-chewing Norwegian immigrant whose business acumen and generous heart helped pull many struggling farmers and Lutheran congregations through the Great Depression. You'll follow the rise of Carl Granrud, the energetic leader whose contentious, albeit humorous, style became the leading issue in three major political confrontations. You'll follow many of the pioneer field representatives, such as Martin Nelson, Christian Zander, and Carl Rosholt, who rumbled over the dusty back roads of Minnesota and the Dakotas to sell the society's Ordinary Life, Twenty Pay Life, and Brotherhood Specials.

This book is more than a chronology of events that occurred over a period of seventy years. It is the unfolding of a unique cultural past. Lutheran Brotherhood is the product of a time and a set of circumstances that cannot be duplicated. It was the child of a newly united church and was shaped by an eco-nomic and social outlook that was inherent in the times. It was influenced by a Norwegian ancestry whose traditions of self-help and desire for self-governance went back for generations. It was stamped by the grace and humility of immigrants and their children, whose work ethic and simple piety helped imbue the society with a sense of high purpose and keen resolve. Finally, the society is the product of an opportunity presented by the American experience in 1917, an America full of hope and promise.

In telling this story, we occasionally have allowed ourselves the luxury of acting as time travelers, dropping in at the St. Paul Auditorium on June 10, 1917, to overhear Jake Preus argue the merits of a mutual aid society at the merger convention of the Norwegian Lutheran Church of America. We visit Herman Ekern and his daughter, Elsie, as they complete work on the first versions of the new society's insurance contracts. We walk with Carl Granrud as he guides a nervous visitor through the high, open girders of what will become the society's new headquarters in 1956.

We were not there, of course. Our creation of scene and dialogue is a careful reconstruction based on written accounts and the recollections of people who were closely involved with these incidents.

Like most books, ours offers not only facts, but an interpretation of events. We have approached our task more as a storyteller than as a historian. Our selection of material was influenced by space requirements as well as by its thematic content. The decisions not to include certain events or individuals is not a comment on their significance. Rather, out of the vast pool of material at our disposal, we selected experiences that most clearly presented the essential elements and themes important to an understanding of the society's development and those that best moved the story forward. We have endeavored to write an honest story, and a human story, and a story that you would want to read.

—W.T.H.
December 1988

42,012 ...

Total Daily Circulation 144,921

St. Paul Pioneer Press

The Weather Forecast
Generally fair Saturday and Sunday; warmer Saturday; fresh southeast winds.

VOL. LXIV—NO. 139.   ST. PAUL, MINN., SATURDAY, JUNE 9, 1917.   ★   PRICE TWO CENTS ON TRAINS FIVE CENTS

HUNDREDS LOSE LIVES IN SAN SALVADOR DISASTER

LUTHERANS TO CELEBRATE BIG CHURCH UNION

Parade This Morning Will Mark Final Step Bringing Norwegian Bodies Into One Great Religious Organization.

BELLS TO PROCLAIM MERGER

Last Obstacles to Plan Removed at Conferences Yesterday and Way Cleared for Joint Session at Auditorium.

(By Rev. Gustav Stearns.)

GRANDSON OF WEBSTER RAISES FLAG AT SCHOOL

The upper right picture shows Samuel Appleton, grandson of Daniel Webster, who made the presentation at the flag raising exercises yesterday at the Webster school, named in honor of the great statesman. Mildred Tavsch is shown at the right reciting Wilbur D. Nesbit's "Your Flag and My Flag," while below is pictured the crowd that watched the ceremonies.

3 AMERICANS LOST AS DIVERS SINK TWO SHIPS

Two Die When U-Boat Torpedoes British Steamer Manchester Miller — New Yorker and 39 Others Missing.

ENGLISH ORGANIZE GROUND

Every Effort of Germans to Regain Lost Positions in Belgium Fails — Berlin Admits Success of Thursday Attack.

QUAKES CONTINUE THROUGH NIGHT AND VOLCANOES ARE IN ERUPTION, REPORTS REACHING PANAMA SAY

Capital, Santa Tecla and Neighboring Towns and Villages Wiped Out, Fires Adding to Destruction — President of Nicaragua Asks Relief.

(By Associated Press.)

Panama, June 8.—Reports from Managua and San Juan del Sur say that hundreds of lives were lost in San Salvador. Earthquakes continued all through the night and volcanoes are in eruption. Communication between Panama and San Salvador has been broken.

CAPITAL, NEARBY TOWNS RAZED.

San Juan del Sur, Nicaragua, June 8.—San Salvador, Santa Tecla and neighboring towns and villages were destroyed in an earthquake which began at 7 P. M. yesterday and continued throughout the night, according to advices received here from the president of Nicaragua tonight.

ACCOMPANIED BY HEAVY RAINS.

FIRES FOLLOW QUAKES.

ONLY 100 HOUSES STANDING.

JURY TO GET MOORE'S CASE BEFORE NIGHT

Customary Recess Over Saturday Abandoned—Defense May Introduce No Witnesses, Is Intimation Yesterday.

ATTORNEY FEARS OUTCOME

Interference by Accused Man Helps in Evidence Against Him—Hickey Connects Dunn With Case—Ten Are Heard.

STATE'S CASE FINISHED.

CHICKETT A SURPRISE.

MOORE IS COOL.

FEIGNING IS BELIEF.

SUBSCRIPTIONS TO LIBERTY LOAN ARE $700,000,000 SHORT

Secretary M'Adoo Urges Redoubled Efforts to Raise Desired Amount in Next Seven Days.

Favor Army Course

PROGRAM OF SESSION.

LOAN PARADE IN CHICAGO.

MORGAN BUYS $50,000,000.

ALL OBSTACLES REMOVED.

DR. DAHL HONORED.

STUDENTS MAY JOIN AIRPLANE SERVICE

War Department Orders Asks Selections for Such Duty From Men at Fort.

U. S. AROUSED BY GERMAN PLAN TO RESTRICT FIRMS

MILL CITY DOCTOR MADE MAJOR IN MEDICAL CORPS

Flag Raised at Webster School With Ceremony

Colonel Samuel Appleton Gives Chief Address at Ceremonies — Another Talk Is Plea for Bond Issue.

PUPIL BLOWS BUGLE.

DANCE WINS APPLAUSE.

Russ Girls Will Fight at Front

Two Hundred Who Join Regiment Are Urged to Shame Male Strikers.

HOLLAND QUEEN IN WRECK; AIDS INJURED PASSENGERS

17 STATE DRAFT RETURNS ARE IN; BELOW ESTIMATE

BIDS FOR ENTIRE UNION DEPOT TO BE ASKED IN 10 DAYS

Executive Committee Will Call for Prices on Percentage Basis — Track, Grade Work to Be Let.

HOW IT WAS DONE.

AMERICANS MISSING.

FORTY MEN MISSING.

Teuton Counter Attack Put Down by British

THE WAR IN BRIEF.

COUNTIES REFUSED.

BERLIN ADMITS REVERSE.

Hasten Exhaustion of Foes, Kaiser Tells Men

DESTROY ALLIES' FOOD.

Haitian Envoy Presents Passports.

"ANXIOUS TO REACH FRONT," PERSHING SAYS IN LONDON

American Leader Asks That Few Social Affairs Be Held—Party Reaches Capital Unannounced.

(By Associated Press.)

DODGES SOCIAL EVENTS.

PREPARATIONS MADE.

DEFENSE COUNCIL DISCUSSES U. S. RAILWAY CAR BUILDING

AMERICANS MAY LEAVE TURKISH LANDS FREELY

STOCKHOLM SOCIALISTS POSTPONE CONFERENCES

FLOWERS FOR SON BORN TWENTY-SEVEN YEARS AGO

"All Well," Word to Gotham End of Salvador

AREA DEVASTATED BY DISASTER

Faith and Vision

Jacob Aall Otteson Preus rose deliberately from his chair and cast his eyes slowly about the St. Paul Auditorium, which was filled with thousands of people. Preus was a large man, slightly taller than average, and much sturdier, with the barrel chest and wide shoulders of a heavy laborer, and a large, square face that was both aristocratic and pugilistic. His eyes were dark and serious, heavily shaded by thick, bushy brows, yet they twinkled when he smiled or laughed, which was often.

Jake Preus was a politician, accustomed to scanning a crowd for the purpose of quickly assessing its collective mood. The convention floor teemed with activity, yet it was orderly, even quiet. Only a few pockets of delegates were huddled together, talking and gesturing among themselves. Not much fight left in this bunch, thought Preus. It is remarkable to see so many Norwegians and so many Lutherans agreeing on so many things.

But then, Preus remembered, it had been a re-

The St. Paul Pioneer Press *of June 9, 1917, reported earthquakes in El Salvador, news of General Pershing's preparations for America's entry into World War I, and plans for that day's massive parade of Norwegian-Americans to the convention that would merge three synods to form the Norwegian Lutheran Church of America. Reproduced courtesy of the Minnesota Historical Society.*

markable week. Three thousand delegates representing three church bodies that had been at bitter theological odds for decades had gathered in St. Paul, Minnesota, to become one.

It was June 11, 1917, and the world was in conflict. Two months earlier, President Woodrow Wilson had declared war on Germany, a major step that ended America's isolationism and signaled its ascent to world military power. In St. Paul, a newspaper reported that twenty-five thousand young men had registered for the draft, and the virtuous ladies of the local Red Cross labored diligently to remove shameful items of temptation—playing cards and tobacco—from comfort kits issued to soldiers. The war was on everyone's lips. But for the thousands of Norwegian-Americans who descended on St. Paul, the conflict would have to wait a few days. While the rest of the world made war, they would seek to make peace.

Two days before, behind mounted police and flag bearers, church officials, pastors, and lay delegates from three Norwegian Lutheran synods—Hauge's Norwegian Evangelical Lutheran Synod in America, the Norwegian Evangelical Lutheran Church of America, and the United Norwegian Lutheran Church in America—had marched proudly, eight abreast, from the St. Paul Armory to the St. Paul Auditorium, where the merger was to take place. Thousands of Norwegian-Americans lined the streets to cheer the procession. Such was their enthusiasm that police strained to keep them from crowding into the street and interfering with the marchers. Nearly ten thousand people waited inside the auditorium as the procession marched slowly and solemnly through its wide doors, and five thousand more who had been unable to find seats waited outside. As the meeting began, precisely at 10 A.M., bells in three thousand Norwegian Lutheran churches across the country started to ring in unison.

Inside, the massive gathering, led by a chorus of nearly eighteen hundred voices and the Luther College band, sang the first six stanzas of the "Te Deum." "Mighty came its song from the audience," proclaimed one popular account, "which with mouth and heart praised God for the great things which He had done in bringing the divided together and making this day a festive one, a day in which the Lutheran church in America with joy and thanksgiving will long remember." Several speeches and elections later, the Norwegian Lutheran Church of America had been duly organized, blessed by God and Norwegian alike.

The Minneapolis Tribune called the celebration "the greatest and most historic church demonstration ever held by [people of] Norwegian descent," an assessment with which Preus wholeheartedly agreed. What a day that had been, he told himself, full of majesty, drama, joy, reconciliation—he thought of Soren Peterson—and even sadness.

For many years, Peterson, a retired farmer from Minot, North Dakota, and a member of the pietistic Hauge's Synod, had actively opposed the idea of union with other Lutheran churches. But he had suddenly changed his mind at a preliminary meeting of the Hauge's Synod on Friday and stood to voice his agreement with his synod's decision to merge. "Let the Lord rule over this union," he told the gathering. Then he fainted and fell into the arms of friends. The next day, as the procession of delegates made its way through the streets of St. Paul, Soren Peterson died.

The Need for Insurance

As Preus thought of Peterson, he continued to look over the crowd of delegates. His eyes met those of Herman Ekern, an attorney who practiced insurance law in Chicago. Ekern's gaze was steady, and he acknowledged Preus with an almost imperceptible nod. Unlike Preus, Ekern was, at first glance, a physically unimposing man. He was short and wiry, with a stoical yet handsome face and wavy, reddish hair that was beginning to show signs of white. It was Ekern's manner that made a more immediate impression. His bearing was serious and dignified, and his eyes burned with an intensity that reflected his powers of discipline and his noted capacity for detailed work.

Preus and Ekern had met a few years before when they were state insurance commissioners, Preus in Minnesota and Ekern in Wisconsin. Despite their personal and political differences—Preus was an outgoing conservative, Ekern a quiet liberal—the two men got along exceedingly well, for both were prominent Norwegian-American politicians, faithful churchmen, and avowed activists for the cause of insurance.

Ekern and Preus, who was now Minnesota state auditor, frequently met in Chicago to talk about insurance. Early in 1917, some months before the merger convention, Preus had abruptly brought up a subject they often thought about, but rarely discussed. "Why can't we Norwegian Lutherans have a life insurance organization?" he asked.

"The answer to that is easy," Ekern replied. "It is the attitude of your Norwegian Synod."

Preus, grandson of the synod's first president, sighed in agreement. Insurance was not a popular subject among theologically conservative Norwegian Lutherans, no matter what their synodical affiliation. To them, insurance was incompatible with faith in God. Some pastors actively warned church members not to take out insurance policies, and a few congregations barred those who did. Some Lutherans opposed insurance so vehemently that when Preus became insurance commissioner, they openly questioned his Christianity. The Preus family had been somewhat less disapproving, but disapproving nevertheless. None of them had ever owned life insurance, and Preus himself did not own any until his appointment as insurance commissioner.

Yet over the years, Preus said, his family had softened on the subject. They had become well-acquainted with the consequences of not owning insurance, as when Luther College in Decorah, Iowa, which his father had served as president, burned to the ground. Preus also had heard of a congregation that did not insure its church because the pastor and some members opposed insurance. When lightning destroyed the building, the congregation patiently rebuilt. Lightning struck again. When the members next met, the pastor, who still opposed insurance, was conveniently absent, and they voted to insure their third church building. Attitudes about insurance were changing, Preus insisted.

After some discussion, Ekern and Preus determined that the time might be right to propose the idea of a church insurance society, and they decided that the upcoming merger convention, which would unite Lutherans of many theological traditions, might provide the most favorable atmosphere for their plan. Both men were elected as delegates by their home congregations, and met during its early sessions to confirm their proposal. Ekern had done the research, Preus would do the talking. Experienced politicians that they were, Ekern and Preus also took great care to approach Dr. H. G. Stub, who had just been elected president of the new church body, to gauge his reaction to their proposal. Surprisingly, Stub enthusiastically supported the plan. He also admitted a secret to Preus. "I have carried a thousand dollar insurance policy on my life for many years," the renowned leader said, "and I've never told anyone about it." Several influential pastors and laymen also agreed to sign Preus's and Ekern's resolution, clearing the way for its introduction to the convention.

Bear One Another's Burden

The sound of Stub's gavel rang throughout the hall. It was June 11, 1917, and Preus had been called to speak to the convention. Stub, a portly yet handsome man, stood in the middle of the large stage behind a podium, flanked by rows of somber-looking church leaders. "The chair recognizes the Honorable J. A. O. Preus, auditor of the state of Minnesota," he called out.

Jacob Aall Otteson Preus, at right, wearing a bowler hat, served as Minnesota's insurance commissioner from 1910 to 1912 and was state auditor at the time of the convention that merged three synods to form the Norwegian Lutheran Church of America in 1917. Reproduced courtesy of the Minnesota Historical Society.

"Dr. Stub, honored delegates," Preus began, "I would like to move that our convention consider the following resolution." He pulled a sheet of paper from his pocket, drew a breath and began to read in Norwegian:

"Whereas, it is desirable to promote social intercourse among the members of our new church; and whereas, the well-being of our people in the cultural and social realms may be served and the influence of the Church may become further extended, and the temptation, especially among the young people, to become alienated from the principles of the Church may thereby be removed; and whereas, it is advocated by many that there ought to be an aid society composed of the members of the Norwegian Lutheran Church of America only; therefore, be it resolved that the President of the Church appoint a committee of five men to consider this matter and take the necessary steps to form such an organization, if they deem it advisable."

Preus folded the paper and returned it to his pocket. Within seconds, the silence in the hall had turned to whispers. Preus had not once mentioned the word insurance in his resolution, as he and Ekern had intended, for they had decided that the word was still too inflammatory for some delegates. Using such language in their initial resolution might prematurely prejudice theologically conservative members and incite opposition before Preus even had the chance to explain the benefits of the plan. To guard against this potential reaction, Ekern had suggested that the most tactful course would be to couch the proposal within the context of an aid society administered exclusively by and for the members of the Norwegian Lutheran Church.

Despite this strategy, some delegates suspected that Preus had been talking about insurance as part of the proposal, and when Stub opened the floor to questions, several hands shot into the air.

An elderly man stood slowly, his wrinkled, veined hands clutching a frayed Bible. He did not have a question. Instead, he turned to Matthew 6:25 and began to read. "Therefore I say unto you, take no thought for your life, what ye shall eat, or what ye shall drink; nor yet for your body, what ye shall put on. Is not the life more than meat, and the body than raiment?" He turned the page, skipping ahead to Matthew 6:34. "Take therefore no thought for the morrow: for the morrow shall take thought for the things of itself. Sufficient unto the day is the evil thereof." The old man closed his Bible. "The word of God is my only insurance," he declared passionately, and sat down.

"It is also mine," Preus exclaimed without missing a beat. He had heard these verses many times before; they were commonly cited as Biblical authority for the denunciation of insurance. "All of us are dependent on the grace of God and the gift of His Son," he said. "All that we are given comes from God. No insurance policy will ever change that fact. And yet God calls upon us to wisely use the gifts that he has so generously given us, in order that we might help each other to endure our earthy troubles. That

is why I have a favorite Bible verse of my own: Galations 6:2. 'Bear ye one another's burdens, and so fulfill the law of Christ.'

"Fellow delegates, insurance is simply a means by which it is possible to spread risk—not to eliminate it—and prepare prudently for the future. Even Joseph, when he interpreted the Pharoah's dream, called for food to be stored during seven years of plenty for the seven years of famine that were to follow. Thus the Bible itself provides us with one of the first examples of the principle of insurance effectively at work."

"The church already helps those of its flock who are in need," a young minister said. "Why should we get involved with insurance?"

"Because the church has been doing the same basic thing for years," said Preus. "Before aid societies became commonplace, it was a custom in Christian communities, when a man died and left a family without means of support, to raise a fund for their care. Even today, when a man dies and leaves a wife and children without means, this is still done, but more often the widow and children must be cared for by the state or by charity.

"As for insurance, it simply is an agreement between a group of people to the effect that when any one of them dies, the others will pay a specified sum to their survivors for their support. Let us presume that two brothers agree that they will provide for the widow and children of the other if one brother dies. They have in effect entered into an insurance contract."

"We don't need any organized aid society in our church to take care of our own," a thin woman near the front of the auditorium called out. "In my community, we are all happy to bear one another's burdens."

"And God will surely bless your efforts," Preus said kindly. "But where do you live?"

"In a small town in Iowa."

"I myself was raised in a small town in your state," said Preus. "But my work has taken me to the city, as is the case with many Norwegians. The modern industrial society in which we live has made organized insurance a necessity. A mutual aid society, administered through our own church, will simply guarantee that our widows and orphans who live in the midst of strangers in large cities are cared for in the same manner as those who live in the midst of friends in small communities."

A large man with a thick shock of gray hair and a clerical collar asked for the floor. "Is there a precedent for a church aid society?"

"Yes, pastor, the first such group in America was started many years ago by the Presbyterian Synod of Philadelphia," Preus said. "This society has done much good for its people. We Lutherans would do well to emulate such a worthy venture."

"What about the lodges?" Stub asked loudly.

It's about time, pastor, Preus thought to himself, I was beginning to think you weren't going to ask. The delegates had begun to whisper again, for even among conservative Norwegian Lutherans who had accepted the value of insurance, the subject of lodges was still a major source of concern.

"Fellow delegates, we all know that a great deal of insurance is sold by fraternal lodges or societies with secret rituals," Preus said. "This is a practice of which we all disapprove. We know, too, that many people who join these lodges excuse their actions by saying that they joined for the insurance benefits.

The formation of a Lutheran mutual aid society will prove a mighty bulwark against the inroads of these lodges, particularly among our young people. A mutual aid society will not only provide assistance to those who encounter the troubles of this earthly life but will offer many advantages of fellowship and social action among its members, all with the sanction and under the supervision of the Norwegian Lutheran Church of America."

The hall was quiet. Preus searched the room for more questions. When he heard none, he slowly left the stage and returned to his seat. Stub pounded his gavel on the podium. "Let us bring this resolution to a vote," he called out. "All in favor of the resolution, signify by raising your right hand." Hundreds of hands shot into the air.

"All opposed, signify likewise." Preus and Ekern looked about the hall. To their surprise, no hands were raised (although, as some participants recalled years later, more than a few delegates chose to abstain). "The motion is passed," Stub said quickly. "As the resolution provides, I will appoint a committee to consider this matter of a mutual aid society."

Ekern and Preus had passed their first obstacle. Now the real work would begin.

Revival in a New Land

Herman Ekern and Jacob Preus were accustomed to work. It was all they had ever known, and all that their parents had known. Work and the chance to make something of themselves were the reasons their parents and grandparents had emigrated from Norway to America, where people were free, land was cheap, and opportunity, like the horizon, seemed limitless. That was not the case in their homeland. A Norwegian-American once asked his grandmother why she chose to leave her native home, a peaceful village nestled on a fjord of breathtaking beauty. Her matter-of-fact response: "You can't eat fjords."

In 1801, the population of Norway was 880,000. More than 90 percent of its inhabitants lived in rural areas scattered among Norway's inland rivers and lakes or along its narrow coast. The economy was almost totally agrarian. These Norwegians led a quiet,

isolated life, separated from neighboring villages by a series of natural barriers, including mountains, forests, and fjords. God, family, and labor dominated their thinking. They knew little about the outside world, for they resided in self-sufficient communities.

But from 1801 to 1865, a major change took place. The population of Norway doubled to 1.7 million, and land available for agricultural production lagged far behind the population's needs. The economy grew and became more diversified, but the distribution of wealth became increasingly lopsided in favor of the upper class. In rural villages, taxes were high and jobs were scarce. Stomachs growled and children cried, and Norwegians hungry for food and work chose to crowd into the burgeoning cities. Others, divided between a love of homeland and unhappiness with the lack of opportunity she provided, chose to leave for America. "Farewell, Norway, and God bless thee," proclaimed a popular emigrant song. "Stern and severe wert thou always, but as a mother I honor thee, even though thou skimped my bread."

America held the promise of an abundance of loaves. In this land of plenty and prosperity, it was said, the streets were paved with gold, and the pigs somersaulted into one's skillet. Although these tales seemed fanciful to all but the most gullible, they reflected the hope for opportunity that America represented. Between 1825 and 1930, about eight hundred thousand Norwegians emigrated to the United States. Only Ireland sent a higher percentage of its native sons and daughters to America than did Norway.

Although the vast majority of Norwegians emigrated for economic reasons, some left because of religion. They were inspired by the revival of pietism that swept the country in the early 1800s. Mostly poor and rural, used to hard work and meager rewards, these Norwegian Lutherans rejected what they perceived as the cold, intellectual answers of the state church for a simpler, unquestioning faith. The revival also reflected a growing resistance to authority and an increasing class consciousness in a land where the lines between classes had been strictly delineated for generations, a land where the rich did not mingle with the poor. Norway's wealthy landowners and ruling class were not struck with "America fever." But the small farmers and the traders, those with hard lives and limited futures, were.

The first large group of Norwegians to emigrate to America were followers of Hans Nielson Hauge, the fiery lay preacher who had inspired the revival. About a year after his death, on July 4, 1825, fifty-two Haugeans boarded the sailing sloop *Restauration* in the port city of Stavanger and left for America. They arrived three months later in New York, where they were met by their countryman, Cleng Peerson, who had preceded the group to America to prepare for their arrival. Peerson led the group to a region about thirty-five miles northeast of the city of Rochester, New York. Nestled between the shore of Lake Ontario and the newly opened Erie Canal, the colony became known as the Kendall settlement. It was the first Norwegian settlement in America.

The Atlantic Ocean, the money necessary to cross it, and the courage to leave behind their homeland and possessions were all that stood between discontented Norwegians and the opportunity they read about. Most Norwegians financed their journey by selling at auction almost all that they owned: farmland, livestock, homes, furniture, and clothing. In this way, all but the poorest of families could gather enough money to at least pay for a ticket to America, and some had enough cash left for a small nest egg.

The farewells were tearful and heartbreaking, for they carried with them a dreadful finality, the painful knowledge that fathers and mothers might never again see their sons and daughters. One Norwegian-American remembered his mother telling him when he was a child, "I would rather have you dead than see you off to America." Only the hope of someday being reunited, and the sad realization that there was little economic future for them in the homeland, made it possible to say goodbye.

The trip to America by sailing ship was long: two months or more, depending on the wind and weather. Conditions were crowded, and the passengers often were tightly packed in sleeping berths below the main deck. Deaths resulted from outbreaks of contagious diseases, and many makeshift coffins, covered with a Norwegian flag, were lowered into the sea. The wind and the sea could be equally perilous. A few days into her ocean journey, Linka Preus, Jake Preus's grandmother, was standing on deck when she was drenched by a heavy ocean spray. "Isn't this a storm?" she anxiously asked the captain.

"By no means, madam," the captain answered. "In a storm, entire seas wash over the ship."

That's reassuring, she thought. Along with several of her fellow passengers, Linka Preus spent much of the rest of the voyage bent over with seasickness. She was thankful and relieved when, several weeks later, the captain spotted land. At that moment, all hardship and fear were forgotten. Only expectation remained.

Building a New Home

From New York or Quebec, the two primary debarkation points for European immigrants, most

Norwegians traveled by boat through the Erie Canal and across the Great Lakes to growing settlements such as Chicago or Milwaukee. In later years, many rode there by train. From these major centers, the immigrants journeyed by wagon, clearing a path through the brush, building bridges over creeks, and making long detours because of wide and deep rivers. They rested in Norwegian settlements along the way, and most eventually settled in the lush woodlands of Illinois, Wisconsin, Minnesota, and eastern Iowa. By 1860, nearly fifty-five thousand people of Norwegian descent lived in these states, almost 70 percent of whom had been born in Norway.

For these new citizens, America held the promise of work and free land. The Homestead Act of 1862 guaranteed a quarter section of land, 160 acres free and clear, except for a small registration fee, to any man or woman over the age of twenty-one. As a result, the demand for labor was immense. Summer farmhands could expect to earn as much in two months in America as they might in one year in Norway, for there was always work to be done. Before virgin land would produce, farmers had to clear it, often with large plows pulled by a team of eight to ten oxen. The task was especially difficult in forest regions, where, in the first year, it might be necessary to plant crops between the trees. Often, several settlers would jointly purchase a sizable plow, then work together to clear one another's land.

That kind of cooperation—shared labor, barn raisings, husking bees—recalled the sense of community spirit so prevalent in the villages of rural Norway. Immigrants banded together in good times and in bad, and their solidarity gave them the physical and spiritual strength to withstand the hardships of pioneer life. They also sustained each other culturally. Regional Norwegian customs were preserved almost in their entirety; language, food, clothing, religious ceremonies, songs, and holiday traditions remained the same. In many ways, the immigrants lived and worked much as they would have had they remained in the homeland. A subtle feeling of inferiority to more established Americans caused many to cling tightly to old ways, and letters from relatives in Norway kept alive idealized memories of home and childhood and family.

Despite the influence of native traditions, the Norwegian immigrants came to love the freedom of their new land and the riches of the soil they so diligently tilled. Thus, a paradox was created: Norwegians who, despite their ethnic pride, did not desire to return to Norway. A traveling minister once passed by the house of a Norwegian immigrant. "Aren't you homesick for Norway?" asked the pastor.

"Homesick for Norway?" the man replied. "No sir, I should say not. Too many stones over there." He paused, meditated deeply for a few moments, then looked up with wistful eyes. "I'll tell you though, those lingonberries in the fall—I miss them," he exclaimed. "Well sir, they were wholesome berries."

Religious Roots

Faith in God was important to the Norwegian immigrants. God had brought them safely across a wide ocean, led them across an often dangerous land, and bestowed on them the blessings of its generous soil. The Lutheran church became the most dominant institution in the immigrant communities. It exerted a strong social, as well as religious, influence on the settlers. People gathered at the church not only to worship, but to exchange family and village news, to do business, and to reminisce about life in the homeland. Letters from Norway were passed eagerly from settler to settler. Picnics, weddings, conventions, even funerals, served as occasions to see old acquaintances and catch up on the latest news.

However, the Norwegians were less agreeable when it came to doctrine. Congregations regularly disagreed with each other about dogma, and chose to split from those with whom they differed. In many villages, according to historian J.A. Berg, a visitor might see "two or three church steeples point toward the sky, where one would suffice." Husbands and wives sometimes chose to attend different houses of worship, and relatives often met on the street on their way to their respective churches. Between 1846 and 1900, Norwegian immigrants founded fourteen distinct Lutheran church bodies.

However, in the midst of divergence, a desire for unity persisted, and the fourteen denominations eventually merged into three distinct groups. On one end of the theological spectrum was Hauge's Norwegian Evangelical Synod. Better known as Hauge's Synod, it emphasized lay involvement and personal piety. On the other end was the Norwegian Evangelical Lutheran Church of America, better known as the Norwegian Synod. In the tradition of the state church of Norway, it stressed purity of doctrine, scholastic orthodoxy, and adherence to the Lutheran Confessions. Holding the middle ground was the United Norwegian Lutheran Church in America, which composed elements of the other two churches and labored, despite its own turbulence, to unite all three.

Hauge's Synod

The doctrinal differences between the Haugeans and the state church of Norway took their root from the rise of rationalism. The proponents of rationalism held that human reason, not divine guidance, was the only valid basis for moral action, and that human intellect, not God, was the source of all knowledge and spiritual truth. This argument made great inroads among Europe's educated, upper class in the early 1800s. Rationalism was harder for those of simpler faith to accept, especially as they began to believe that it had infiltrated the state church of Norway. In their view, the confessions and sacraments were being pushed aside, and sermons were becoming more concerned with defining acceptable behavior than proclaiming the message of the Gospel. The state church had become comfortable, far too comfortable for those accustomed to a faith that demanded more. Strong voices protested, and the strongest belonged to Hans Nielson Hauge.

Hauge, a farmer's son, was expected to quietly assume his place among other peasants in the lower class. But like the young Martin Luther, he ached from the intense spiritual struggles that raged inside him. His deep sense of sin and unworthiness placed a stamp of zealous sobriety on his Christianity, and his concern for personal piety led him to share his message with others. As he traveled through the rural villages of Norway, Hauge's thunderous voice called out to the peasants, warning them not to depend on church attendance without personal repentance, admonishing them to bear daily witness to their faith. His message soon captured the hearts of the lower classes.

Hauge's message also captured the attention of the authorities. Lay preaching was thought presumptuous by the state church; it was also illegal. Norwegian statutes prohibited its citizens from traveling from place to place, alone or in company with others, or from holding public meetings. Over a period of nine years, Hauge was arrested ten times and was always released after a hearing or a short time in jail. But after his final arrest, he was brought to Oslo in chains, denied bail, and placed in solitary confinement. For the next seven years, while the authorities built a case against him and confiscated his writings from houses throughout Norway, Hauge remained in prison. Although he was later released, his health had been broken, and he died in 1824.

His imprisonment served to fan the flames of the revival he had created, and his message began to reach beyond religion into the very class structure that controlled Norwegian life. Hauge may not have been aware of his influence, historian Ivar Welle observed, "but his movement was the first blow in the battle between officialdom and common folk, between city culture and rural culture. . . ."

Hauge's example also inspired many Norwegians to seek spiritual freedom in America. Thirteen years after the first Haugeans landed in America, the first Haugean denomination was organized in 1846 by Elling Eielsen, a fiery preacher with a scorching tongue. The group was known as Eielsen's Synod. Its members practiced a Christianity of the heart (a joyless piety, critics said) and demanded of each other personal testimony of their conversion. Eielsen's fervor and energy did much to bring the scattered Norwegian settlers into the same fold, but he was not the kind of leader who could hold a movement together. Unlike Hauge, who had called for reform within the framework of the established church, the legalistic Eielsen feared organization so much that he was openly antagonistic to the idea of clerical authority, or indeed, to almost any form of organization. His desire for freedom encouraged doctrinal anarchy, and his synod divided several times. In 1876, the majority of its members left to form a more mainstream body known as Hauge's Synod. Eielsen's Synod continued on its own and slowly dwindled; by 1983, it was composed of two congregations, fifty members, and no clergy.

In marked contrast to other Norwegian settlers, who often gathered to dance and sing as a respite from the labors of prairie life, the Haugeans were a more subdued lot. Like other immigrants, they cared for one another, but they denounced festivals, alcohol, and luxuries. Instead, they put all their energy into hard work. The Haugeans, it was said, rarely smiled, and their demeanor became a symbol for the new land on which they staked an existence—harsh and unyielding, yet providing and constant.

The Norwegian Synod

The vast majority of early settlers identified strongly with Hauge's message. However, state church authorities in Norway did not approve of immigration, and they declined to respond to the spiritual needs of the immigrants by sending ordained ministers to America. Thus, many of the first Norwegian immigrants who were not Haugeans organized their own congregations. Lay preachers conducted prayer meetings in barns, gave sermons in log cabins, and baptized children in whatever water was handy. But they could not, under the auspices of the organized Lutheran church, administer the sacrament of holy communion. This led to a widespread desire for a formal church organization and ordained ministers.

Because the state church in Norway was not particularly interested in its Lutheran expatriates, the pastors with university training who responded to calls from their brethren in America acted on their own. These men were skilled theologians, most of them graduates of the University of Christiania (Oslo). They traveled throughout the wild country, preaching and organizing congregations of settlers. In 1853, the missionaries organized a denomination of seventeen congregations that became known as the Norwegian Synod.

Despite their affiliation with the state church back in Norway, the leaders of the Norwegian Synod generally respected the Haugean message, which had gained many proponents in the upper class. But they were also passionately committed to the tenets of their own theological training. They were orthodox to the core and devoted to doctrinal purity. Their goal was to build a highly ordered, traditional, disciplined, and strictly confessional Lutheran church. Thus, they clashed early with the Haugeans, who considered the clergy of the Norwegian Synod to be aristocratic elitists with a stagnant theology.

Relations between the Norwegian Synod and other Norwegian-American denominations also languished because of the Synod's close ties with the Germans of the Missouri Synod. Their alliance was natural, for the two groups shared a commitment to the same orthodox confessional theology. The Missouri Synod lent aid to the Norwegian Synod and even trained its pastors for a time. But the coalition was never really popular among the widespread membership of the Norwegian Synod and sometimes caused deep schisms within its constituency.

The Middle Ground

It was not long before Norwegian-American Lutherans sought a middle ground between the Norwegian Synod and the Haugeans, a balance between high church and low church, between orthodoxy and personal piety. Two new centrist denominations were created in 1870. The Norwegian Augustana Synod was formed when a small group of Norwegians parted amicably from the Swedes of the Scandinavian Augustana Synod. A second denomination, the Conference for the Norwegian-Danish Evangelical Lutheran Church, was specifically organized to provide a central option for Lutherans uncomfortable with the extremities of the Haugeans and of the Norwegian Synod.

The Conference was an ambitious and utopian undertaking. Its creators envisioned a church in which Christians of differing thought could freely mingle, challenge, and learn from one another, yet worship God together. But factionalism overcame compromise, and the Conference became embroiled in controversy. Adherents of the New School, who considered theology a free and evolving exposition of Scripture, clashed with proponents of the Old School, who favored a more defined and settled doctrine. It was essentially a moderate version of the old debate between the Haugeans and the Norwegian Synod. The two sides argued for years, and, eventually, the students of the New School left to form their own body, the Lutheran Free Church.

A third centrist denomination was formed in 1887 when a large group of pastors and congregations withdrew from the Norwegian Synod, citing their opposition to the Synod's dogmatic alliance with the Missouri Synod. The group called itself the Anti-Missourian Brotherhood, and its departure was spurred by the question of election to salvation, or predestination. Election became one of the leading Lutheran controversies of the times and, perhaps more than any another issue, prevented Norwegian-American Lutherans from uniting.

The question of election centered on the relationship between grace and faith. Since the Reformation, Lutherans have believed that they are saved by the grace of God, accepted by faith. This theology maintains that because humans are innately mortal and sinful, God's grace alone is capable of saving them, but faith is the only way to receive that grace. In the election controversy, two conflicting questions arose. First, if grace alone is responsible for redemption, then what is the value of personal faith? Second, if faith is necessary for salvation, then what is the value of grace? In other words, does God choose people, or do people choose God?

Two different views emerged on this subject in the late nineteenth century. One group, the Missouri and Norwegian Synods prominent among its members, argued that God simply elects people unto salvation. Another group, including the Anti-Missourians, contended that God saves people in view of the faith He knows they will someday have. These conflicting views caused dissension among Norwegian-American

The lives of most Norwegian immigrants revolved around the Lutheran church. Members of the congregation of St. Lucas, a Norwegian Lutheran church located about nine miles northwest of Cottonwood in Minnesota's Yellow Medicine County, are pictured in this photograph, taken beween 1910 and 1915 by Carl Graff. Reproduced courtesy of the Minnesota Historical Society.

church members, making enemies of friends and splitting congregations. On several occasions, Norwegian Synod pastors were physically carried out of the churches they served by members who opposed their views on election.

Yet even as the election controversy raged, the desire for unity persisted among the moderate synods, and three denominations chose to unite in 1890. After a long series of negotiations, the Norwegian Augustana Synod, the Conference of the Norwegian-Danish Evangelical Lutheran Church, and the Anti-Missourian Brotherhood became the United Norwegian Lutheran Church (UNLC) in America. This church was built to include rather than exclude, and it kept alive expectations that Norwegian-American Lutherans might someday worship together.

As the UNLC pushed hard for unity, the idea began to gain support in the Norwegian Synod and Hauge's Synod. The years had taken the edge off old arguments, and except for arcane theological distinctions, it was difficult to find any significant differences between the churches. All three shared a common heritage of catechism and hymns. Interest in merging was especially keen among newer church members, many of whom were recent immigrants unaware of past arguments and uninterested in the theological hairsplitting of their leaders. Slowly and methodically, over several years, the three synods settled almost every doctrinal point of contention.

Finally, only the disagreement over election stood in the way of solidarity. In 1912, the UNLC and the Norwegian Synod put their arguments in the hands of two pastors and locked them together in a room. "Don't try to come out until you thrash this thing out," they were told. The negotiators emerged with an agreement called an *Opgjor* (or settlement) that recognized both views as valid Lutheran positions on the question of election to salvation. The *Opgjor* became known as an agreement to disagree, and it set the stage for the creation of the Norwegian Lutheran Church of America in 1917.

A Clerical Lineage

Jacob Aall Otteson Preus was a child of the church, for his own growth was concurrent with that of Norwegian-American Lutheranism. The church's preoccupation with dogmatic details and tendencies toward factionalism fostered in Preus a skepticism about church affairs and a stubborn streak of synodical independence. "Let's just say my membership's in the Communion of Saints," he once told an inquiring pastor. But Preus was also deeply pious, a reverent and moral man, who felt a deep need for the Word and the sacraments. Preus came to his dual opinions of the church by way of close observation. He was the son of a distinguished family whose name had, by virtue of its energetic leadership, become synonymous with the development of Norwegian Lutheranism in America. If there was such a thing as Lutheran royalty, the Preuses were it.

The Preus family traced its lineage to Hans Preus, a wealthy German landowner, and his three sons, who emigrated to Norway around the turn of the eighteenth century. The Preuses flourished in various professions in their new land, and several descendants became prominent pastors. One of them, Herman Amberg Preus, was accused of heresy by some members of the state church because he desired to preach among Norwegian immigrants in America, and, for a time, the bishop of Christiania (Oslo) refused to ordain him. But the bishop eventually relented, and in 1851, Herman and his wife, Linka, bade farewell to Norway and boarded a schooner bound for America.

They arrived in the New World that summer and traveled to Spring Prairie, Wisconsin, where Herman had received a call. He immediately began the Lord's work, preaching to and organizing seven congregations within a twenty-mile radius of Spring Prairie. He became one of the leaders of the new Norwegian Synod and was named its president in 1862. He occupied the post for the next three decades.

It was a turbulent time, an era of theological warfare and dogmatic combat. Orthodox Lutheranism was constantly under attack, and Herman Preus took his place in the front lines, defending his synod against the Haugeans and Anti-Missourians. One contemporary compared Preus's willingness to engage his doctrinal foes to that of the Biblical builders of Zion: ". . . *every one* with one of his hands wrought in the work, and with the other hand held a weapon" (Nehemiah 4:17). His enthusiasm no doubt proceeded, in part, from the vivid memory of being removed from his church and evicted from his parsonage, his family's clothes tossed out the window and strewn about the yard, by an Anti-Missourian group in his congregation.

Preus devoted most of his waking hours to the church, and when his beloved wife died in 1880, he plunged even more deeply into his work. When the last of his children grew up and moved away, he moved in with his eldest son, Christian Keyser Preus, and his family in Spring Prairie. In this large and busy household, Herman Preus generally could be found at his living room table, stacked high with books and papers, near a hard coal heater. It was his habit to study into the wee hours of the night, and he found it difficult to hide his annoyance when visitors showed signs of sleepiness just because the clock had slipped past midnight. "To him those were the very best hours of prolonged and earnest discussion," his grandson, Johan, remembered.

Like his father, Christian Keyser Preus was devoted to the ministry. But unlike the serious Herman, he possessed a sunny disposition, a trait undoubtedly endowed on him by his mother, Linka. As a young boy, he had been all play and pranks, more inclined to tend to the horses than to study. A graduate of Luther College and Concordia Seminary in St. Louis, he was also a skilled speaker with a resonant voice and the ability to use everyday illustrations to bring alive the Gospel message. He was also known for his concern for the sick. Although one seriously ill man lived several miles from the parsonage, Christian visited him every day, no matter what the weather. When heavy snow made the roads impassable, Christian strapped on his skis. He sometimes skied ten to twenty miles each day to complete his calls, and occasionally suffered frostbite on his face and feet.

Christian Preus married Louise (Lulla) Augusta Hjort in 1877. She gave birth to eleven children, four of whom died of illness: Herman at age thirteen, Linka at age twenty-two, Christiane at age eight, and Christiane, namesake of her late sister, at birth. The remaining Preus children were Ove, Johan, Jacob, Paul, Henriette, Cathinka, and Herman, named for his late brother.

Life inside the Preus home was alternately hectic, with hordes of children racing about its confines, and calm, in deference to the study habits of their father. The books and papers that concealed his study table were considered sacred and not to be touched by any of the children. However, by contrast with many other parsonages, the Preus home was not overly strict, especially as the children grew older. As long as the boys attended church on Sunday morning, they were permitted to play baseball on Sunday afternoon, and minor forms of mischief were generally accepted as the natural result of active youth. "You see, the Preus family is liberal," Jake Preus once said of the relaxed style of his otherwise conservative parents.

A Politician, not a Pastor

Christian and Lulla Preus named their fourth son after the famed Reverend Jacob Aall Otteson, a close associate of Herman Amberg Preus. Young Jacob was husky and athletic, a student with an affinity for mythology, a polished social conversationalist, and an unpretentious young man who preferred to be called "Jake."

Jake attended Luther College in Decorah, Iowa, where his father had become professor of religion and now served as president. He excelled as an oboe player in the concert band, which also featured him as a whistler. "That wasn't an artistic accomplishment," Preus said years later of his talent, "It was self-defense. I learned to whistle while milking father's cows. It soothed 'em." Yet such was his ability to whistle that in later years, when he attended band concerts at Luther, he was occasionally called upon by band director Carlo Sperati to share his gift with the audience. "Come on, Jake, let's have the old whistle," Sperati would call out as the band struck up the old melody, "Listen to the Mockingbird."

Jake's two older brothers, Ove (father of David W. Preus, later president of the American Lutheran Church) and Johan, had chosen to become ministers, and his younger brother, Herman, became a pastor years later. When Jake graduated from Luther College in 1903, his father leaned heavily on him to do likewise. He entered the seminary grudgingly, but stayed only a few months before dropping out, for he was more interested in the law and politics. Jake attended the University of Minnesota Law School, simultaneously working as a shoe clerk in a Minneapolis department store, and graduated in 1906. He moved to Washington, D.C., and became a messenger in the United States Senate.

Two years later, Jake married Idella Haugen, his college sweetheart, whom he had known because his family purchased milk from her father, a Decorah merchant. Even as a young woman, Idella was accustomed to responsibility, for she had been in charge of raising her five brothers and sisters since her mother's death in 1901. She was calm and disciplined, and acted as a thermostat to her husband's dynamic nature. Idella gave birth to twin sons in 1910, but they died of an illness two months later. Jake and Idella mourned their deaths for years, and when their sons, Jack (later president of Lutheran Church-Missouri Synod) and Robert, were born ten and fourteen years later, their parents showered them with constant attention.

Jake was back in Minnesota, having just married Idella, when he received a call from Senator Knute Nelson of Minnesota. The Republican senator, one of the most beloved and picturesque political figures of his generation, was having difficulty with his Norwegian correspondence and sent a telegraph from his Washington office to friends back home. "Send me a Scandinavian who knows shorthand," he wired.

"Why don't you try Jake Preus?" they wired back.

So the senator sent a telegraph to the young bridegroom, asking if he knew shorthand and, if so, would he take the job? Preus immediately went out and bought a book on shorthand. He read it cover to cover, decided that he knew its contents and wired Nelson his answer: Yes. Jake and his bride then spent a good portion of their honeymoon honing his newfound skill. "I spent those first weeks giving dictation," Idella remembered. "I'm always glad I did, for I've had to take it ever since."

Jake became a trusted confidant of Senator Nelson over the next two years, as he watched and learned the art of Washington politics. As part of his tutelage, he also listened for hours to the aged senator reminisce about all things Norwegian. He stayed at the Senate office as long as Nelson stayed, then walked him home, pausing to converse some more in front of Nelson's house. When Jake arrived at his own home, he inevitably encountered a cold supper. Idella was understanding. "He'd never complain," she recalled. "He'd just say: 'I couldn't bear to ask the old gentleman to finish his story.'"

With Nelson's blessing, Preus returned to Minnesota to begin his own law career. But not long after he had obtained his first client, the governor offered him a job as executive clerk, then appointed him Minnesota's commissioner of insurance in 1910. Preus knew little more about insurance than he had once known about shorthand, but he studied the subject diligently and eventually became a national authority on insurance law. He also became one of its most eloquent supporters. "What nobler institution than one which protects the widows and orphans from poverty and need?" said Preus of insurance. "It needs no defender for its existence; it needs no advocate for its virtue. Every good citizen, who understands insurance, will purchase it to the same extent that his dependents require, and his resources allow."

As commissioner, Preus favored not only legislation of insurance, but educating the public about its benefits. "The citizen who most needs fire, life or health and accident insurance is the man who has but little property and small income, and comparatively large obligations," he once told his fellow commissioners. "This citizen is usually the man who has not had the advantages of more than a public school training. If he is the individual most in need of insurance, ought he not be the man who should be most diligently and uniformly taught as to the merits and virtues of insurance?"

Preus learned insurance well enough that when he finished his term as commissioner, an eastern insurance company offered him a position that paid a sizable salary. But he was still committed to public service, so he turned down the offer, and was named state auditor in 1912. His political star was rising.

Like many of his ancestors, Jake Preus had become a successful and influential man. But unlike his father and grandfather, he was not a pastor, and he never really allowed himself to forget that fact. He often referred to himself jokingly as the black sheep of the family, but the remark always carried with it a slight edge, for Jake's failure to become a minister had always disappointed his father. In early 1921, a few months before Christian Preus's death, Jake was inaugurated governor of Minnesota. On the same day, a celebration was held in Decorah. The Luther College band played patriotic songs in front of the Preus home, and a spokesman congratulated Christian on his son's accomplishments.

Yes, the eldest Preus responded, it was a great day, and he was proud. But he would be truly happy if Jake were instead being ordained a Lutheran minister.

For the Common Good

The Norwegian word *bygd* comes from the Old Norse verb *bygge*, which means "to build or settle." It was common in nineteenth century Norway to refer to a village in the mountains, along a river, or on the coast as a *bygd*. But the word was also used to denote a sense of sharing and living together, a community of customs and traditions.

The Norwegian immigrants shared many things, foremost among them a strong yearning to work together for the common good. Rural communities in the homeland were segregated by such natural barriers as mountains, forests, and fjords, and cooperation was critical to survival. Most immigrant settlements in America were likewise rural and isolated, and many of the newest arrivals were penniless.

The settlers went out of their way to help each other in matters large and small. They supplied new arrivals with milk until they could earn enough to buy a cow, watched each other's children, and helped one another to build log cabins. Shared labor enabled most members of the village to prosper economically, and shared cultural customs helped them to overcome homesickness. The church, especially, helped to care for those in need, the elderly, and the sick. Rural Norwegian settlements in America thus took on the likeness of extended families.

As the economic face of America began to change from agricultural to industrial, however, more and more immigrants moved to large cities. There they found work and opportunity, but they did not easily find the family spirit and ethnic traditions that had existed among their rural counterparts. Partly in answer to this lack of community and as a substitute for family and neighbors, Norwegian-Americans organized mutual aid societies. The Sons of Norway, for example, was formed in Minneapolis in 1895. It was established primarily for the economic protection of its members, but developed into a movement that encouraged social interaction between Norwegian-Americans and the continuation of Norwegian customs.

Regional organizations called the *bygdelag* also sought to strengthen ethnic pride by bringing together immigrants who hailed from the same regions in Norway. Each year, after spring plowing or fall harvesting, they would meet to celebrate in the manner of the old traditions. The church, so influential in the rural villages, at first viewed the *bygdelag*, which was essentially an urban phenomenon, with suspicion. But pastors soon warmed to the idea and joined the *bygdelag* in great numbers.

Yet the church found itself in conflict with other Norwegian aid societies, especially those that modeled themselves after American lodges. Church authorities condemned the secret ceremonies conducted by these societies. The resulting tension between the two groups was an important factor in Preus's and Ekern's assertion, at the 1917 convention, that a church-sponsored aid society might dissuade young people from joining secret societies and lodges.

Norwegian aid societies and the *bygdelag* were formed for many reasons: to seek solutions to common social problems; to promote certain causes such as temperance; to advance political views; to share special interests such as music, literature, or sport; or simply to socialize. Some aid societies were concerned primarily with economic support, usually in the form of life and health insurance, and others were organized to help preserve the Norwegian language, customs, and traditions. But whatever their reason for existence, all of these societies grew out of a tradition shared by other ethnic groups in America: the desire to unite with others of similar backgrounds.

The Age of Progressivism

The cooperative spirit that inspired mutual aid societies also found its way into America's political arena. Norwegian immigrants, most of whom were farmers, joined those with similar opinions to fight against political and economic forces that, in their minds, threatened to enslave them, much as the old authorities in Norway had tried to do. Their primary opponents were corrupt businessmen and politicians.

The rise of big business, especially oil, steel, and the railroads, helped to create vast new wealth and improved the lives of many Americans. But the widespread corruption associated with this phenomenon alienated the common people. Some large companies bribed public officials to pass laws advantageous to their interests and not to enforce regulations unfavorable to them. Municipal and state politics were rife with kickbacks. Railroad tycoon Jay Gould is reputed to have spent half a million dollars in bribes during one session of the New York state legislature. Observers began to note cynically that business had become a game in which the biggest players got ahead by cheating while the referees looked the other way. Voices of protest arose, and many of them belonged to the farmers.

American farmers had long been perceived as independent survivors, beholden to no one but God and the weather. They farmed on a subsistence basis, making little cash, but providing their families with almost everything they needed to live. But as large urban markets became predominant, more and more farmers turned to single cash crops, such as wheat, corn, cattle, or milk. Farm income from these crops rose, but at the price of independence. To buy machinery and additional land necessary to make a profit, many farmers mortgaged their land. If prices dropped or the crops failed, they could not pay the interest due on the mortgage, and they lost their land. The American farmer had become dependent.

Farmers were especially dependent on the railroad companies that shipped crops to market, the grain elevators that stored their crops, and the merchants who marketed them. Because many of these groups colluded to keep their prices high, farmers were forced to pay exorbitant prices for their services. The only alternative was bankruptcy. Powerless alone, many farmers decided to organize to fight back. The Patrons of Husbandry, better known as the Grange, was a national organization of farmers. Its goal was to influence legislation that would curb the power and abuses of the railroad companies. By 1874, seven years afters its founding, the Grange was 1.5 million members strong and had convinced several states to pass laws prohibiting railroad price fixing and monopolies.

The Grange helped give birth to the Populist party, also known as the People's party. Populism was a direct expression of rising agrarian protests. Its platform called for free silver, more paper money, cheaper credit, and government ownership of the railroads. Like the Grange, the Populists were particularly strong in the rural farmland of the Midwest, especially among Norwegian immigrants (who may have recalled stories of Haugeism and the resulting class consciousness in Norway that brought them to America). The Populists were inspired by fiery national leaders such as Ignatius Donnelly of Minnesota and Mary Elizabeth Lease of Kansas, who urged farmers "to raise less corn and more hell."

Populism eventually gave rise to Progressivism, a political movement that reached its peak during the first fifteen years of the twentieth century. Progressivism, which operated as an insurgent wing of the Republican Party, influenced nearly every aspect of American life. It was dedicated to the concept of equal opportunity and inspired by the widespread feeling that that was no longer the case in America. Wages were ridiculously low. Some women garment workers received only fifty cents for twelve hours of work. Children were forced to work in factories. Industrial accident rates were astronomical, with little or no compensation for those injured on the job. Relief systems for the unemployed were nonexistent. Meanwhile, the barons of shady business and their political cronies prospered, seemingly beyond the grasp of rules and regulations, controlling public affairs to the detriment of honest businessmen and the public.

Theodore Roosevelt, who had left political life

after having served two terms as president, returned to Republican politics as a Progressive in 1910 and became one of the movement's most eloquent spokesmen. "We are face to face with new conceptions of the relations of property to human welfare," he proclaimed. "The man who wrongly holds that every human right is secondary to his profit must now give way to the advocate of human welfare, who rightly maintains that every man holds his property subject to the general right of the community to regulate its use to whatever degree the public welfare may require it."

The Progressives believed that the cure for America's ills was more democracy, and they pushed through many state and federal legislative reforms designed to give more power to the average voter, such as the direct primary; direct election of senators; and the right of initiative, referendum, and recall. They passed laws that limited the amount of money that political candidates could spend. Progressives advanced the causes of conservation and women's suffrage, passed laws to protect consumers and child laborers, and established commissions to regulate public utilities.

The Progressive party eventually faded from political view. Yet, as with all successful reform movements, its effects long outlived its popularity. The movement's crowning achievement was not that it changed capitalism, as the Socialists had proposed to do, but that it reformed and improved it. Like the Norwegian settlers who worked together for the good of the community, the Progressives attempted to prove that common people who united for a common cause could effect change for the better.

A Man for the People

Herman Lewis Ekern was a Progressive to his core. He was committed to the interests of the public and the protection of the downtrodden, but strongly opposed the idea of handouts. "People ought to feel some dignity in their work," he said, "and should be given the opportunity of becoming self-reliant." In Ekern's mind, one of the best roads to self-reliance, besides a lifetime of hard, honest labor, was insurance. Ekern believed in insurance as strongly as he believed in Progressivism, and he devoted most of his life to its advancement and refinement. Insurance meant protection, and Ekern zealously clung to that precept throughout his life.

There had been no insurance for Even Ekern, his father, whose family had farmed near Birid, a community north of Oslo. Even's father had died when he was young, and his mother had remarried. The family was poor, as was the soil on which they farmed. When they decided to seek a better life in America, the family had to borrow money to make the trip. The last of his family to come to America, Even arrived in 1872 with his wife, Elizabeth.

The Ekerns settled in southwestern Wisconsin, in Trempealeau County, near the little Norwegian valley community of Pigeon Falls. Even purchased 120 acres of farmland for $150 and, the next year, purchased eighty acres more. Herman and his seven brothers and sisters were born on the Ekern farm. The work was hard but the land provided, and life in Pigeon Falls was good, despite the fact that the easygoing, pipe-smoking Even was not a particularly successful farmer.

Elizabeth, a hardworking woman, pushed her children harder than did her husband. It was from her, said relatives, that Herman derived his will to succeed. Herman was also influenced by his uncle, Peter Ekern, the most important Norwegian in the valley. Peter operated a number of lucrative businesses and served in several public offices, including the Wisconsin state assembly in 1881.

Herman began to develop his lifelong love of learning in a schoolhouse so small that half the class had to stand against the wall while the other half worked at their desks. After graduating from high school in nearby Whitehall, where his father had opened a general store, Ekern decided to become a lawyer and entered the University of Wisconsin Law College. Although most of his classmates had more education than he, Ekern excelled in the classroom. Fellow students remembered him as "a studious boy with bright red hair who led a very exemplary life, avoiding drinking, smoking or chewing, and seldom dating girls." He spent most of his waking hours attending classes, reading at the library, and preparing briefs for cases. On Sundays, Ekern satisfied his theological curiosity by attending a variety of churches, from strict orthodox Lutheran to liberal Unitarian congregations.

After graduation, Ekern returned to Whitehall, where he formed a law partnership with Hans Anderson. Much older than Ekern, Anderson was a dreamer whose idealism was complemented by Ekern's tireless energy and attentiveness to detail. He made a lasting impression on his young partner, as did his daughter, Lily. Ekern eventually married her.

The Political Life

In 1894, soon after forming his partnership with Anderson, Ekern ran for district attorney. The job paid little, but it was an effective way for a novice lawyer to gain legal experience and make contacts that might prove valuable in furthering his career. Like almost everyone else in Trempealeau County, Ekern was a Republican, and he defeated his Democratic opponent easily. During his years in office, Ekern built a reputation as a thorough and competent attorney. He was reelected in 1896 by an even higher margin than in his first victory.

While he was district attorney, Ekern's private practice grew steadily. He also sold insurance and lent money for farm mortgages. His professional successes enabled him to help his stricken family, who had sold the general store in Whitehall after a series of financial setbacks and had moved to Superior, Wisconsin. With Herman's help, however, all of his brothers and sisters were educated at the state university or at the normal school in Superior.

By the time Ekern's first child was born, he had become a follower of Governor Robert LaFollette, a Progressive who was popular among the Scandinavians in Wisconsin, and among graduates of the University of Wisconsin. Ekern was both, and in 1902 he announced his candidacy for state assemblyman. He campaigned on the Progressive platform: popular primary elections and taxation of the railroads. The great threat to this generation, Ekern told the voters, was "unlimited power in the hands of centralized wealth and the great combination of capital."

That Ekern won the election easily attested to the popularity of his message and his commitment to it, for he generally disliked campaigning. Campaigns

meant smiling when one did not feel like smiling and relying on catchphrases and humor to captivate the audience. Ekern relied on facts. Although he possessed a dry wit, he was unwilling to joke with large crowds. Nor was he a gifted orator. His speeches were serious and dry, and filled with statistics that were rarely of interest to the average voter.

Ekern's first term in Madison, during which he was paid the modest sum of five hundred dollars, was not particularly noteworthy. He worked tirelessly but quietly, paying close attention to workings of the assembly. When he was reelected two years later, he was ready to take a leading role in its affairs. More important, he was named to a committee investigating insurance activities in Wisconsin. It was an assignment that would encourage him to devote most of the rest of his public and private career to insurance.

Opposition from conservative church leaders aside, insurance had become a significant industry in America. Insurance became popular not only because it protected widows and orphans, but because it made possible the rapid accumulation of large sums of capital for investment. Unfettered by the demands of legislation and regulation, some insurance companies became more concerned with their investments than with providing safety for families at the lowest possible cost.

Spurred by several muckraking magazine articles, an investigation by New York's Armstrong Committee in 1905 revealed that the officers and directors of some of the state's largest insurance companies were not nearly as beneficent as they wanted the public to think. They voted themselves exorbitant salaries, appointed family members to lucrative jobs, gave lavish balls at company expense, purchased securities from companies in which they held an interest, and spent hundreds of thousands of dollars a year to influence state legislators. As a result, New York passed legislation to protect policyholders by regulating the activities of insurance managers.

In the wake of the Armstrong Committee's work, LaFollette appointed an investigative committee to look into the practices of Wisconsin's insurance companies. As secretary of the committee, Ekern enthusiastically sank his teeth into the investigation. Insurance was a complicated business. Detailed study would be required to understand it, and detail was

Ekern's forte. He pored over every document and every piece of correspondence that came his way. He tenaciously probed witnesses. By the time the investigation closed in 1906, Ekern was the committee's most knowledgeable and influential member.

Although it did not uncover nearly the level of corruption that had existed in New York, the insurance investigation was big news in Wisconsin, and Ekern rode its wave to his third assembly term in 1906. He was gaining a reputation for his extraordinary command of facts, and his belief that there was "something of right and wrong" on each side of every political question earned him the respect of even his staunchest opponents. The Norwegian from Trempealeau County had become a proven leader, and he was elected speaker of the 1907 state assembly.

The *Evening Wisconsin*, a conservative opposition newspaper, said of his victory, "It's no small thing for a little cuss like Ekern to come down from some outlandish place up in the woods, a man without any special prepossessing charm, in fact, a cold, icy, serious sort of a chap to defy most all the political forces in the state and win out for one of the most important places in the state. Much as anyone may dislike him he cannot but acknowledge that he has ability."

The 1907 session was, for many years thereafter, the longest in the history of the state legislature. Governor LaFollette had been elected to the U.S. Senate, and his absence set off a wild scramble among Progressives for state control of the movement. It was Ekern's task to direct the assembly's agenda amid the chaos.

The session was also notable for the spirited opposition that it raised from Wisconsin insurance interests. Ekern made insurance reform his personal fight, and he was instrumental, one observer wrote, "in placing some of the best insurance laws on the statute books of Wisconsin that have been written." While his reforms earned him respect, they also earned him the hatred of some insurance companies.

Their bitter opposition took its toll during Ekern's campaign in 1908 for a fourth assembly term, as did the vicious fight between the temperance movement and the supporters of legalized alcohol. Ekern was

a teetotaler, and his opposition to alcohol did not endear him to many Wisconsin voters and the state's liquor interests. Yet he did not favor prohibition and, thus, failed to satisfy those in the temperance movement. Caught in the middle, Ekern lost in the primary. It was his first political defeat. Urged on by LaFollette, Ekern decided to run as an independent in the general election. He fell 152 votes short of victory.

Commissioner of Insurance

Ekern might have returned exclusively to private law practice but for his reputation as an insurance expert. Instead, he was appointed Wisconsin's deputy commissioner of insurance in 1909. The job so intrigued him that he decided to run for commissioner of insurance two years later, and won in a landslide. As a Progressive, Ekern was not content merely to shuffle papers in his position. He used the office to execute needed reforms, promoting several revolutionary ideas that eventually became standard practice.

For example, he fathered the first system of state life insurance in the country. By offering insurance at rates that average workers could afford, he reasoned, the state fund would serve as a yardstick for comparison with private insurance companies and cause them to lower excessive rates. At the same time, he took care to see that strict legal limitations kept the state fund from competing too heavily with private firms.

As commissioner, Ekern also devoted extensive study to fraternal insurance societies. He liked the idea of fraternals, and recalled with some fondness the Norwegians in Pigeon Falls who had founded a fraternal society. Ekern believed that fraternals encouraged community spirit and should, therefore, be encouraged by the state. However, for all their good intentions, many fraternal insurance societies had fallen into financial straits.

These societies operated on an assessment basis. They charged members only after one member died, and they often maintained only a small reserve of funds. If the reserve was not sufficient to pay all obligations, which was often the case, the society was forced to increase the assessments to its living members. The situation quickly became a vicious circle. If the members were unable to pay the assessments, which became increasingly excessive as they grew older and more members died, the society could not pay any death claims, and eventually folded.

Ekern attempted to solve the problem by calling for legislation that required fraternal insurance societies to charge their members higher rates and to maintain minimum amounts of funds (called legal reserves) adequate to pay death claims. Before this law passed in 1913, fraternal societies had maintained a solvency rate of little more than 40 percent. By 1925, the solvency rate of fraternals had increased by 30 percent.

Ekern served as commissioner of insurance for four years, until a conservative won the governorship and declined to reappoint him. He left office having done more than any insurance commissioner in Wisconsin's history to put the insurance industry's house in order. "Not even the most bitter foe can charge you," an opponent told Ekern, "with unworthy motives in the conduct of the department or in what you stood for."

Ekern had maintained his law practice in Whitehall and, later, in Madison while he practiced politics,

and his reputation promised him plenty of private work. He quickly occupied himself with several projects, among them the rewriting of the insurance codes of Kentucky and the Territory of Hawaii. In 1916, he decided to set up a law practice in Chicago with a young attorney named Erwin A. Meyers. The firm specialized in insurance law, but Ekern and Meyers decided to limit their clientele to mutual and fraternal companies. The stock insurance companies respected Ekern's expertise, but because of his background as a reformer, an uneasy feeling always existed between them and Ekern.

In the following years, Ekern's name became almost synonymous with insurance law. His Progressive commitment never waned, and he became one of LaFollette's most trusted advisors. Ekern even made an occasional foray into politics himself, but his attempts became fewer and fewer, and they were, for the most part, unsuccessful, for he still lacked sufficient enthusiasm to campaign effectively.

Insurance was his life now. Ekern had found a private career in which he could put his great mental skills to work for the common good. Ekern believed in Progressivism and he believed in insurance. In his mind, they had become one and the same.

A Mutual Aid Society

The desire for religious unity had brought Norwegian-American Lutherans together, and Progressive reforms had helped convince many of them of the value of insurance. Now, as the hall of the St. Paul Auditorium came alive this morning, Ekern and Preus would attempt to weave those two seemingly disparate elements into one common thread: a church aid society.

It was June 13, 1917, and the convention of the new Norwegian Lutheran Church of America had entered its fifth daily session. Preus and Ekern had finished their work on a committee appointed two days earlier to study the advisability of a mutual aid society. Stub had appointed five men to the committee, including Ekern and Preus; the Rev. Thore Eggen, a pastor and editor of *Lutheraneren*, a Norwegian church publication; and two area pastors, the

Rev. S. T. Reque and the Rev. C. J. Eastvold. A. G. Anderson, a banker in Fergus Falls, Minnesota, had originally been appointed to the committee, but when he had to leave the convention, Eastvold was named to replace him.

Following its appointment, the committee had prepared a report outlining several recommendations. As chairman of the committee, Eggen would present those recommendations to the convention today. The group also had considered the question of a fire insurance society, but, after some discussion, the subject had been dropped.

The mood in the auditorium on June 13 was cordial. The convention had not solved all of its members' doctrinal disagreements, but it had brought together Lutherans who agreed on many more things than not. A quiet feeling of good will permeated the convention, the kind that follows when old friends have settled their differences with a warm handshake.

The week had been one of hard work. Thousands of reports had been read and hundreds of votes taken. There were scores of organizational concerns to be ironed out, one of which had been the matter of a church-sponsored mutual aid society. Ekern had been sure that the motion would pass its first test— Ekern's solid facts and Preus's eloquent testimony had seen to that—but he was somewhat less confident about today's report. Surely a few conservative delegates still opposed the idea of insurance. They had been silent when the motion was passed two days before, choosing only to grumble among themselves and abstain from voting, but they might not be so quiet today.

On the other hand, Ekern reminded himself, who would have believed that all these Norwegians would ever be able to join hands in a single prayer, let alone a single church body? If that was possible, why should they not approve of the idea of an aid society? As Preus had told Ekern months before, attitudes were changing. Even pastors in the Missouri Synod, those most orthodox of churchmen, had conceded that life insurance, when properly administered, was not sinful. Harsh economic conditions, which had sparked Populism and Progressivism, had also convinced working people of the value of insurance. Legislative reforms had helped bring regulatory stability to the insurance industry and cleaned its nest of cheats and swindlers. Yes, attitudes about insurance had changed.

Feeling confident, Ekern turned his attention back to the convention. Eggen was preparing to read the committee's report. Eggen was a short, balding man who wore round, black-rimmed glasses. His face was soft and delicate, almost angelic, and his manner was humble and gracious. If ever there was an honest soul, thought Ekern, this is the man.

"Dr. Stub, honored delegates, our committee has thoroughly discussed the merit and propriety of a mutual aid society," Eggen said slowly and evenly in Norwegian. "It is our opinion that the idea meets both of these criteria and we most enthusiastically endorse its approval, subject to four recommendations.

"First, we recommend that there be established within the Norwegian Lutheran Church of America an aid society, the purpose of which shall be to promote better fellowship, brotherly cooperation, and mutual aid in case of sickness, accident, and death.

"Second, the statutes, by-laws and working plans of this society shall be approved by the Church Convention and its Board of Directors shall annually report to the Church Council concerning its progress. Three, the society shall by incorporation be placed under the control of the insurance department of the state of Minnesota. Four, the activity of the society shall be founded on an actuarially sound basis."

Stub peered into the mass of delegates. "The floor is now open to discussion," he said. "Are there any questions?"

The floor was strangely silent. The whispers of two days ago began again, quietly, but no one stood or called to be recognized. Stub waited, some surprise beginning to show in his eyes. Ekern and Preus sat stiffly. "Are there any questions?" asked Stub, more sharply this time. No response. Stub pounded his gavel on the podium. "The question of a mutual aid society stands before us," he called out. "All in favor, signify by raising your right hand."

Many hands quickly went skyward, followed by less confident, yet approving, hands. Preus turned to Ekern, his eyebrows arched in surprise. Ekern's thin smile betrayed his immense pleasure.

"All opposed, signify likewise," said Stub. A few arms rose slowly, more, it seemed, in scattered protest than in united disagreement. Stub's gavel met the podium one last time. "The 'ayes' have it. The report of the committee is hereby accepted. We have a mutual aid society."

To Aid the Lutheran Church

Following the vote, Ekern, Preus, and the other committee members met in a small room adjacent to the convention hall. Ekern laid out nine articles of incorporation and a preamble. As was typical of his work, the articles were brief yet comprehensive, and from them a preliminary sketch of the fledgling organization emerged.

The society was to be a not-for-profit corporation, organized for the mutual benefit of its members. Any person who had been baptized in the Lutheran faith and who was a member of the Norwegian Lutheran Church was entitled to membership. The society would be based in Minneapolis, and would be governed by a board of directors. The directors would be elected by a general convention of delegates who had been elected by local society branches; the delegates would thus be the supreme governing body of the society. Until the society's first election, in June 1920, the board would be composed of Ekern, Preus, Eggen, Eastvold, and Reque. Eggen would serve as president, Eastvold as vice president, and Preus as secretary-treasurer.

The most important article was the first, for it stated the society's purpose in no uncertain terms, namely "to aid the Lutheran Church in extending the Lutheran faith, to foster patriotism, loyalty, justice, charity, and benevolence, to provide education, instruction, proper entertainments and amusements, to encourage industry, saving, thrift, and development on the part of its members, to give aid in case of poverty, sickness, accident, or other misfortunes, and own and operate homes, hospitals and sanatoria, and to furnish protection and issue of benefit certificates, and the payment of benefits thereon in case of death, or disability by sickness, accident or old age, and otherwise to promote the spiritual, intellectual and physical welfare of its members." (The society's bylaws later were amended to read "Christian faith," rather than "Lutheran faith.")

The articles were signed by Ekern, Preus, Eggen, Eastvold, Reque, Stub, and three others: T. H. Dahl of Minneapolis, former president of the UNLC; and J. N. Kildahl of St. Paul and G. M. Bruce of Red Wing, both professors at Luther Theological Seminary. Witnessing was L.W. Boe, president of St. Olaf College, who had been in charge of arranging the convention and was serving as master of ceremonies for several sessions.

The next day, June 14, 1917, was the final session of the convention. With Stub presiding and Eggen speaking for the committee, the society's articles were approved and its board of directors elected. As Stub shuffled a stack of papers, preparing to move on to other business, he suddenly caught himself and stopped.

"One last thing, Pastor Eggen," said Stub. "What is to be the name of this mutual aid society?"

"Doctor Stub, this week we have put aside our differences and have become united in God's name," said Eggen. "With that in mind, our committee has chosen a name that we feel to be appropriate to this occasion and to our purpose. We recommend that our mutual aid society be named 'Luther Union.'"

"It has been a blessed occasion," Stub said, "and the committee's suggestion seems fitting." He looked out among the delegates. "Does the convention agree?" The sound of affirmation was strong and clear, and it echoed through the hall.

The day's final business went rapidly, as did the closing prayers. Unity had proved tiring, and the delegates were ready to go home. Near the back of the hall, Ekern and Preus shook hands with delegates, many of whom expressed their desire to join the new mutual aid society. When they had gone, Preus turned to Ekern. "A historic week, my friend," he said brightly. "I am optimistic about this society. It should help many Lutherans."

"Yes," said Ekern dryly. "Now we only have to find several hundred willing to be helped."

Preus laughed out loud. "I assume that you will determine in the next few months how we are to do that," he said. Ekern nodded, and the two men shook hands and parted.

THE BOND

OFFICIAL PUBLICATION OF THE
LUTHERAN BROTHERHOOD

LOYALTY TO HOME CHURCH AND COUNTRY

Vol. 1 MAY, 1924 No. 1

A Fraternal Society

EMBRACING THE ENTIRE LUTHERAN CHURCH OF AMERICA

A Clearing House for Lutheran Societies

* * *

OUR AIMS AND PURPOSES

As set forth in the Articles of Incorporation

ARTICLE 1. The purpose and object of this corporation shall be to aid the Lutheran Church in extending the Lutheran faith, to foster patriotism, loyalty, justice, charity, and benevolence, to provide education, instruction, proper entertainments and amusements, to encourage industry, saving, thrift, and development on the part of its members, to give aid in case of poverty, sickness, accident, or other misfortunes, and own and operate homes, hospitals and sanatoria, and to furnish protection, and issue of benefit certificates, and the payment of benefits thereon in case of death, or disability by sickness, accident or old age, and otherwise to promote the spiritual, intellectual and physical welfare of its members.

Come and Join Us!

Establishing Trust

"Elsie! Come in here! I need you."

Elsie Ekern reluctantly closed the book she had been reading. Time to get back to work, and just when the story was getting interesting.

As she got up from her chair, the teenager looked out the living room window. It was February 1918. A soft snow was falling, and the flakes were gently painting the streets of Madison. Elsie brightened as she gazed into the blanket of white. Maybe her father would take the family skating later on nearby Lake Mendota.

"Elsie! Please!"

"I'm coming!" she answered, a little startled. Reading and skating would have to wait today, she thought, as she hurried into the dining room.

Herman Ekern was seated at the table there, surrounded by several piles of official-looking papers. "I want you to type something for Luther Union," he said. "Is it snowing?"

"Yes, it's so pretty."

Ekern smiled. "Too bad we have so much work to do."

In May 1924, when many rural members of Lutheran Brotherhood received no other magazines or newspapers, the society introduced its first monthly publication. The BOND aimed "to foster and strengthen the feeling of fellowship" among the society's members.

Elsie sighed and nodded. Her father always had work to do. Whether at his law office in downtown Chicago, or in the dining room of the family's white frame house on the east side of Madison, he always seemed to be working on some piece of business, new or old. One of his newest projects concerned a fledgling organization called Luther Union. Since the Norwegian Lutheran Church convention, Ekern had been attending to the organizational and legal details necessary to start a mutual benefit society. He had even drafted his seventeen-year-old daughter, whose secretarial experience consisted of a two-week typing course, to type the initial versions of Luther Union's contracts.

Elsie had been working for her father throughout the winter of 1917-1918, but she had little interest in his latest venture. All this talk of life insurance and premiums and mortality tables was not nearly as interesting as the car he had promised her when she turned eighteen. But she was happy to have any chance to spend time with him, for he had been home only on weekends and holidays since opening his law office in Chicago almost two years before.

Although Elsie had been chosen for the job primarily because of her typing skills, some family members jokingly speculated that she had been selected because she was the only Ekern with enough patience to work with her father, an incessant tinkerer whose attention constantly shifted from one project to another. Typically, he would call Elsie into the dining room, dictate to her as she typed for several minutes, then suddenly start on a completely different project, leaving his daughter with nothing to do. It might be fifteen minutes before he asked for her help again, and it might be two hours. In the meantime, all she could do was wait.

Rose Anderson, Elsie's aunt, who had been Ekern's secretary at the Wisconsin state capitol, had warned her about the frustrations of working for her father. "He's a wonderful and considerate man," she had said. "But he's very difficult to work for because he has so many irons in the fire. He's always jumping from one thing to another."

Sure enough, today, fifteen minutes after working on the Luther Union contract, Ekern had excused his daughter, and started working on something else. As usual, Elsie patiently retreated into her chair in the living room, where she resumed reading. Occasionally, she looked outside. It had stopped snowing, and her younger brothers, John and George, were joyously hurling snowballs at each other across the white lawn. She wished she could join them.

Suddenly, her father stuck his head into the living room. "I need your help again."

"Still working on Luther Union?"

"No," Ekern said. "I'm done with that for today. I need you to help me find my skates. Mother is getting Irene and Dorothy ready now, and the boys are outside. You did want to skate, didn't you?"

Elsie brightened and nodded enthusiastically. Luther Union would have to wait. There would be no more work today.

Starting the Organization

There had been few opportunities for recreation since the Norwegian Lutheran Church merger convention. Several people, primarily Ekern, had been working long hours finishing the preliminary work required to qualify Luther Union as a legal mutual aid society.

The new board of directors of Luther Union had held its first regular meeting at Augsburg Publishing House in Minneapolis on July 6, 1917. The board's agenda had contained just one item. To be licensed as an insurance society by the state of Minnesota, Luther Union had to obtain a minimum of five hundred paid applications for life insurance coverage of not less than one thousand dollars each.

The society had made a good start toward that goal during the last days of the merger convention. Nearly half of the required applications had been secured from pastors and lay delegates. Most of them had signed ten-dollar notes to be paid when their contracts were issued, and the rest paid cash.

In October, the Minnesota commissioner of insurance gave the society one year to solicit the remainder of its applications. Progress was slow. Operating funds were almost nonexistent, and the directors were occupied with other full-time jobs. Ekern was assembling a national base of clients for his new law practice in Chicago, and Jake Preus was polishing his political reputation in Minnesota. Though their interest in Luther Union never waned, the two men communicated only occasionally about society business. Luther Union's membership goal was further delayed because many applicants had entered the armed forces before completing their applications.

To help Luther Union reach its quota of paid applicants, the directors had hired Peter Olai Holland, business manager of St. Olaf College in Northfield, Minnesota, to be its first manager. Holland was a trustworthy financial steward whose extensive knowledge of investments and land values had helped his alma mater to build a solid fiscal foundation. He was also an influential community leader, who was serving at the time as the mayor of Northfield, and a prominent churchman active in local and national church affairs.

An immigrant with a thick Norwegian accent, Holland had a simple appearance that belied his financial acumen. P. O., as he was known, was tall, with a conspicuous midriff. His face was round, his cheeks plump, and his eyes placid, even shy. He was an almost unnervingly pleasant man, never so occupied with his work that he forgot to smile or to talk politely with others. He had a special affinity for children and teenagers, for he had no children of his own, and he had long been known to take a fatherly interest in the St. Olaf students who needed financial assistance.

At the request of Luther Union's directors, Holland took a leave of absence from his job at St. Olaf to lend Luther Union a hand. During that time, he and Thore Eggen were headquartered at Augsburg Publishing House, where Holland shared a cramped office with Augsburg employees Henrietta Aunness and K. Marie Sperati. Company funds were so low that Holland frequently had to use his own money just to purchase stamps.

It was Holland's job to spread the word about Luther Union. He visited with Lutherans in the Twin Cities area and wrote to others throughout the Midwest, establishing a network of impromptu volunteers who convinced family and friends to purchase insurance contracts with the society. Although some Lutherans did not understand the concept of insurance, others welcomed the opportunity to join. Hugo Walter had been married just a few months when he signed an application. The Iowa farmhand had little money, and thought that the contract would at least pay for his funeral.

Eva Worden had just completed nurses training and had started work in St. James. As a young, single working woman, Worden decided that she was solely responsible for herself. When a member of her church told her about Luther Union, she signed up immediately.

Martin Hermanson, a young farmer from Winona, took out insurance with Luther Union along with his neighbor, because he felt that any group made up of Lutheran churchmen must be trustworthy. Besides, times were hard, and Hermanson was getting just a few cents each for his hogs. Insurance would help protect his family in case of tragedy.

Peder Konsterlie, a young pastor, had just married when he heard about the new mutual aid society. Because he was planning to travel to China soon as a missionary, he signed an application for insurance.

Several charter members joined Luther Union because of their family connections. Elsie Ekern was signed up by her father, and Jake Preus signed up several of his brothers, cousins, and other relatives. Even Ellertson, who was helping to organize the society, purchased contracts for his sons, Oscar and Selmer.

The charter members included Lutherans from across the Midwest: country folk and city dwellers, farmers and merchants, doctors and pastors. The society's charter members also included a then unknown St. Olaf College professor and part-time author, O. E. Rolvaag, whose *Giants in the Earth* later became one of the most critically acclaimed books of its time.

By the summer of 1918, primarily through Holland's efforts, Luther Union had acquired more than five hundred applicants, more than enough to qualify for an insurance license. Obtaining the necessary capital was more difficult. The officers of Luther Union attempted to take out a loan for six thousand dollars but were turned down by the first bank they visited. The second bank finally approved the loan. Its officers must have been extremely trusting, because they authorized an unconventional method of repayment. The bank was to be repaid from the society's expense fund—not according to a schedule, but whenever money was available.

On September 18, 1918, Luther Union received its life insurance license from the Minnesota insurance commissioner, Louis C. Weeks. The society issued 506 contracts that day, the first to Emma J. Aaberg of Glenwood City, Wisconsin. Preus and Ekern originally had intended to hold the first two Luther Union contracts, but their plan was discarded to avoid any indication of preference. Instead, the names of all the charter members were drawn from a pan. Ekern's name was the fourth one drawn, and Preus's was the 361st.

The premiums represented by the charter contracts totaled less than five thousand dollars, only about half of it in cash. By the end of the year, Luther Union had insurance in force of $676,000 and assets of $6,735.09. To protect itself, the society began to reinsure all contracts over one thousand dollars.

During the fall of 1918, a flu epidemic spread across America and killed thousands. The epidemic placed heavy demands on many insurance companies, especially beginning organizations whose reserves had not yet had time to build up. Early employees of Luther Union were constantly worried that the young

LUTHER UNION
1917

INCORPORATORS   DIRECTORS   OFFICERS

T. EGGEN
President

H. L. EKERN
Director

J. A. O. PREUS
Secretary-Treasurer

C. J. EASTVOLD
Vice President

H. G. STUB
Incorporator

J. N. KILDAHL
Incorporator

S. T. REQUE
Director

T. H. DAHL
Incorporator

G. M. BRUCE
Incorporator

society would fold, but it was more fortunate than most insurance groups. Luther Union had only one death claim—a young woman from Grand Forks, North Dakota—during that terrible autumn.

An Act of Separation

The resolution that created Luther Union required that its officers report annually to the church council of the Norwegian Lutheran Church of America. Thore Eggen dutifully made his first report in 1918. It was noted with approval at the church's annual convention by Dr. H. G. Stub, president of the church, and seconded by a convention committee. "Luther Union has made a promising beginning," the committee said, "in recognition of which the

Above: Seven prominent Lutheran pastors and two former insurance commissioners served as the first incorporators, directors, and officers of Luther Union. They included the Rev. Thore Eggen, Herman Ekern, J.A.O. Preus, the Rev. C.J. Eastvold, the Rev. S.T. Reque, the Rev. H.G. Stub, the Rev. J.N. Kildahl, the Rev. T.H. Dahl, and the Rev. G.M. Bruce.

Right: Martin Rostad, who operated a general store and small coal mine in Montana, was issued this life insurance contract by Luther Union on December 11, 1919.

convention expresses its joy. This association and its work is hereby recommended to the congregations of the church."

When the committee's report came to the convention floor, however, some delegates balked at approving it, and a lively argument ensued. Several old objections against insurance resurfaced, inspired in

Luther Union

Accepts and insures .... Martin L. Rostad, ...

of .... Comertown, Montana, ...

a member of .... Luther Union, as a beneficial member,

and agrees to pay to ... Hannah P. Rostad - wife ....

....

of said member, beneficiary, subject to the right of the member to change the beneficiary, the sum of

Three thousand Dollars, less any indebtedness hereon, upon due proof of death of said member while this insurance is in force.

This certificate shall continue during the life of said member, unless terminated earlier as herein provided, and is made in consideration of all the conditions and agreements of this contract, including the payment by said member in advance of regular assessments as required by the within table.

At age 70 or after, the reserve hereon shall be payable as an old age disability benefit at the option of the member on written request and surrender of this certificate.

The application for membership and medical examination and the conditions and agreements recited herein or endorsed hereon or contained in the articles of organization and by-laws now or hereafter in force, are made a part hereof to the same effect and extent as if incorporated herein over the signatures hereto, and constitute the entire contract. No change in such articles or by-laws shall effect any increase or decrease in the rates of assessment, the reserves, or the benefits of this certificate.

IN WITNESS WHEREOF, The LUTHER UNION has caused this certificate to be signed by its President and Secretary and its corporate seal to be hereto affixed at Minneapolis, Minnesota, this

... 6th ... day of .... January ...., 19 20 ...

Age 38 .... Amount, $3,000.00 ...

Number 898 ....

LUTHER UNION,

....
President.

....
Secretary.

ORDINARY LIFE.

part by the fear that a church-sponsored insurance organization might ultimately prove a financial burden to the church. As a conciliatory gesture to insurance opponents, the section of the report that dealt with approval of Luther Union was referred to a special committee.

After deliberation, the special committee presented several resolutions intended to place some distance between the church and Luther Union. Although the Norwegian Lutheran Church wished the society much success, the committee said, "it must not be construed to mean that it places it on an equal footing with other branches of the activities of the Church, such as missions, the training of pastors, Christian education, and the like. No one is required, as a matter of duty, to become a member of the society, but the individual is free to choose for himself whether he wishes to become a member or not."

Although the committee's resolutions, which were passed by the church convention, marked the beginning of the end of the brief relationship between Luther Union and its parent, the church asked that the society report annually to the trustees of the church "concerning its progress, success and financial status." As instructed, Eggen reported on May 1, 1919 that Luther Union had been licensed to sell insurance in Minnesota, North Dakota, Illinois, and Iowa. The society had issued 628 contracts, and the total insurance in force as of April 30 was $793,500. In addition, the society had established several local branches, and the board of directors had held four meetings during the year.

"The first general convention of the Luther Union will take place in connection with the general convention of the Norwegian Lutheran Church in the summer of 1920," Eggen said in his report. "This convention will be made up of delegates from the various local organizations and will elect directors and adopt such legislation as may be found necessary."

Eggen's report was the only one ever filed with the board of trustees. It was published in the church's annual report but was not recognized by the church. Official ties between the young society and its parent continued to weaken and soon faded away. Luther Union was on its own.

Expanding the Horizon

The termination of official ties with the church was not particularly distressing to the leaders of Luther Union. The church had helped the society to get under way, and several prominent leaders, like Stub, continued to lend their support in its behalf.

Besides, it was becoming clear that by limiting its membership to the Norwegian Lutheran Church, the society was severely limiting its chances for success. Ekern, for one, had always believed in a fraternal benefit society for all Lutherans. Aware of the conservative ways of his peers, he had been content with the approval of the merger convention as a starting point. Now the time had come for Luther Union to expand its horizons.

In September 1919, the society began negotiating with the Lutheran Brotherhood of America "with a view to securing some form of cooperation" between the two. The Lutheran Brotherhood of America, also known as the LBA, was a national organization that, in its own words, consisted of "all men's societies, clubs or brotherhoods who are members in good standing in the Lutheran Church in the United States of America regardless of language or synodical connections."

The LBA had been established in 1917 at Camp Dodge, Iowa, where several thousand Lutherans were among the soldiers training for World War I. That there was no religious center for these soldiers concerned several church leaders. They decided to start their own inter-synodical organization and sent a letter to Camp Dodge. It said: "The Lutheran Brotherhood of America, realizing the need of providing every comfort and convenience to the men in our training camps so that they will feel at home and be contented, asks the privilege of erecting a building in Camp Dodge where the men of our Church may find the literature with which they are familiar in their homes and meet socially with those of their own faith and consult with their pastors.... We believe that we can in this way cheer and encourage our young men in preparing themselves for the defense of our country and the extension of American ideals."

The request was quickly granted, and the Lutheran Brotherhood of America became a huge success.

Society Snapshot: 1918

Home office: 939 Security Building, Minneapolis

Number of members: 530

Number of employees: 3

Insurance in force: $676,500

Assets: $6,735

Life insurance death benefits: $1,000

Society officers

President: Thore Eggen

Office manager: P. O. Holland and S. H. Holstad

Resolutions from the founding convention of the Norwegian Lutheran Church of America in 1917 were printed in Norwegian in the church's first annual report. Among them was the recommendation that a committee of five, including Herman Ekern, J.A.O. Preus, and the Rev. Thore Eggen, the Rev. S. T. Reque, and the Rev. C.J. Eastvold, organize a mutual benefit society called Luther Union.

The Board of Trustees of The Norwegian Lutheran Church in America has been requested to recommend that the committee of five appointed by the chairman to organize a mutual benefit society, have its powers so extended to permit it to organize a fire insurance arrangement for insuring property whenever a plan may be approved by the above mentioned Board.

The Board has also been requested to recommend that once each year the two mentioned insurance organizations make report of their financial condition to the Board of Trustees.

The Board of Trustees respectfully recommend the adoption of a resolution authorizing the above.

S. H. HOLSTAD, chairman.

Within a few months, it had gained sixty thousand members, raised more than $1 million, and established LBA centers at military sites and Lutheran colleges across the country. After World War I ended on November 11, 1918, the organization continued to prosper, inspiring such enthusiasm among its leaders that some spoke with prophetic zeal of a quick merger of all the Lutheran bodies.

That hope was not fulfilled. Nevertheless, considering Ekern's hope for an insurance organization that would serve all Lutherans, it seemed natural that Luther Union should desire a closer relationship with the LBA. In December 1919, the Brotherhood appointed a committee "to take up the whole matter of insurance as part of the LBA program and after a thorough consideration, report back a definite program as a basis for a department of insurance in our Lutheran Brotherhood of America."

On April 6, 1920, Luther Union and the Lutheran Brotherhood of America reached an agreement by which Luther Union would become the insurance auxiliary of the LBA. The agreement effected four major changes in the bylaws of Luther Union. First, it expanded its membership from the "members of the Norwegian Lutheran Church of America" to "any person who has been baptized in the Lutheran faith (later this phrase was changed to Christian faith) or is affiliated with a Lutheran Church organization." Second, the insurance society's board was expanded to include at least one new director from each of the following Lutheran synods: Augustana, Iowa, Ohio, United Church, Danish, and Free Lutheran.

Third, the members of the LBA automatically became social members of the insurance society, and local LBA brotherhoods became its branches. That this move was significant is evident by comparing the memberships of the two organizations. In 1920, Luther Union had about thirteen hundred members. The Lutheran Brotherhood of America had about sixty thousand members—each of whom was now eligible for insurance.

Fourth, Luther Union took a new name. The committee that had pursued the merger had recommended that the society's name remain the same, and that "'in all printed matter an explanation be made that the association is an organization of the Lutheran Brotherhood of America." But that opinion apparently changed, probably because the directors of Luther Union hoped to reap the benefits of the LBA's widespread name recognition. In any case, by the time the final merger accord was signed, Luther Union's official name had been changed to Lutheran Brotherhood.

Despite its new directors, its new name, and the merger agreement, Lutheran Brotherhood never became the insurance auxiliary of the Lutheran Brotherhood of America, as the LBA had envisioned. Instead, the two agreed to continue to operate as separate corporations. The LBA did, however, contribute much to Lutheran Brotherhood's growth. It advanced $8,500 to the struggling insurance society for organizational work and promotion. (The loan was repaid in 1926.) It gave advertising space to Lutheran Brotherhood in the *LBA Bulletin*, its national publication, and encouraged its members to take out contracts in the insurance society.

"Lutheran Brotherhood is open to any man or woman between the ages of sixteen and sixty who is a Lutheran or is affiliated with any Lutheran organization," Ekern explained in the August 1920 issue of the *Bulletin*. "Anyone desiring insurance may apply to the local representative or may write direct to the Lutheran Brotherhood."

The *Bulletin* gave Lutheran Brotherhood a national forum from which to espouse its goals. No longer fettered by the need to tiptoe gently around Norwegian pastors who opposed insurance, the society defined its philosophy in a manner that left no doubt as to its certainty of divine and evangelical purpose. "No heathen...cares for his family as does a true Christian," Eggen wrote in February 1921. "Thrift is a Christian virtue. Encouraging and promoting thrift is a Christian mission. But thrift can be fostered only by curbing extravagance and encouraging frugality and saving. Right here the insurance plan offers itself as a ready and efficient medium. It serves automatically as a check on extravagance."

"What the Knights of Columbus is for the Catholic Church, Lutheran Brotherhood aims to be for the Lutheran Church, and more. We have a fuller measure of light, and should be able to make this advantage count in better service. Ignorance as to what insurance is prevents many from securing protection. An educational campaign conducted by local brotherhoods cannot fail to produce results. The time will come when every Lutheran community will want an active organization in its midst that can look after the material interests of Church members."

That time was not yet at hand. Despite national advertising access to the membership of the LBA, Lutheran Brotherhood made only moderate gains in the next few years. By 1923, the society had 2,211 contracts, only 325 more than the previous year, and its insurance in force was nearly $3.7 million, only $550,000 more than the year before.

One of the main problems was that the names of the organizations were so similar. J. E. Hegg, Lutheran Brotherhood's general field supervisor, told the board of directors that prospective insurance clients often mistook Lutheran Brotherhood for the Lutheran Brotherhood of America, and he advocated a new name for the insurance society. "'It is generally considered, even by those who do not think it advisable to change names, that it is unfortunate and confusing to have a name so similar to that of the LBA. To get the best results from advertising, the company or sales object should have a distinctive name which automatically classifies itself in the minds of the public.

"The whole Lutheran field is our sales field. The LBA is only a small part of that field. Unless we want to definitely limit our activities, we can with no more reason allow ourselves to be identified with the LBA than with any definite synod. As I see it, one of the best advertising stunts we could put on would be to advertise that we were not the LBA."

Others thought that the name *Lutheran Brotherhood* was too limiting a title for an insurance organization that was beginning to write contracts for women and children. "'The Society is young enough so that a change of name would not seriously hamper production,' a member wrote in 1925. "It is strong and influential enough to stand on its own legs. It is an insurance society for Lutherans and a short name expressing this condition would in my opinion preclude further changes for all time to come. It would be a name that could include all Lutherans, Danish, Swedish, English, German, Finnish and Norwegian. I hereby respectfully suggest to the Board of Directors the following name: 'The Lutheran Insurance Society of America.'"

This suggestion, and several others, were considered but declined by the board. By 1927, the confusion with the Lutheran Brotherhood of America had ceased. That year the LBA dissolved itself, and formed a restructured organization called the American Federation of Lutheran Brotherhoods, better known as the AFLB.

Its only recognizable link with insurance was a tiny fraternal benefit society that had taken part of its name.

The Operating Philosophy

The founders of Lutheran Brotherhood shared the opinion that it should be a fraternal benefit society. Ekern was unwavering on that point.

Fraternalism was founded on the universal belief that people are responsible for their fellow men and women. Throughout history, human beings had organized themselves into associations specifically for that purpose. Informal societies that provided for members and their families during sickness and death flourished in ancient Greece and Rome. In early Christian communities, when a man died and left his family without means of support, it was customary to raise funds to care for his family.

Centuries later, the fraternal movement prospered in America, especially after the Civil War, when hundreds of thousands of immigrants seeking a better life streamed into the country's urban centers. Fraternal societies flourished during this period, as immigrants and rural refugees joined with others of similar backgrounds to promote the common good. Ethnic fraternals were organized to help immigrants learn the English language, as well as customs and trades that would help them to assimilate more easily into American society, and religious fraternals were organized to provide inexpensive insurance protection and fellowship for parishioners.

The first fraternal benefit society in America was founded by a railroad mechanic named John Jordan Upchurch. Upchurch had been raised in poverty, and he had personally witnessed the economic adversity that befell many families whose breadwinner had died prematurely. Insurance was available from a few commercial companies, but at rates much too expensive for most average workers, and the government provided few, if any, benefits for survivors. In America, the land of the free, the free were expected to take care of themselves and their own.

In 1868, Upchurch assembled fourteen railroad workers in Meadville, Pennsylvania, and formed the Ancient Order of United Workmen. Under his plan, the workers agreed to pay an assessment of one dollar whenever any member of the society died, to be distributed to his spouse. Although several fraternal societies were already in existence, they were primarily social in nature. Upchurch's was the first American fraternal organization that offered truly affordable insurance protection to its members. By the turn of the twentieth century, fraternal benefit societies accounted for a major portion of the total life insurance issued in the United States. The first insurance group to attain $1 billion of insurance in force was a fraternal, the Modern Woodmen of America.

Like his friend Jake Preus, Ekern had seen from his position as state insurance commissioner all types of insurance organizations in operation, including stock companies, mutual companies, and fraternal benefit societies. As he mulled over the idea of an insurance society for Lutherans, he took into consideration the merits of all three.

Stock companies were in business for profit, he emphasized, and their earnings were passed on to a few stockholders, not to the policyholders whose premiums supported the company. In his view, mutual insurance was a more equitable option. Mutual companies were nonprofit, cooperative associations organized solely for the benefit of their members, who shared on an equal basis both the profits and losses of the companies. Ekern had great regard for mutuals, and he would someday work closely with several of them. But mutuals tended to be secular in nature, and he knew that it would be difficult to convince Lutherans who were already skeptical of the need for insurance protection to join a mutual company.

Because Ekern was a passionate advocate of Progressivism, his decision that the insurance organization he envisioned could best serve Lutherans as a fraternal benefit society was not surprising. According to statute, fraternals operated without stock, not for profit, but for the benefit of members and their beneficiaries, and they were ruled by a representative form of government. Voting by proxy generally was not practiced by fraternals, as it was by mutuals. Because the members of fraternals voted in person at their local branches, electing delegates from among their ranks who were eligible to elect directors and pass bylaws at conventions, it was difficult for management to control the results of elections.

The only drawback of attempting to organize as a fraternal, Ekern knew, was that some church leaders were still highly suspicious of fraternal organizations. They disliked the idea of insurance anyway, and they disapproved of the local lodges that made up the framework of fraternals. Some congregations so mistrusted fraternals that they expressly prohibited their members from joining lodges. Despite threats of expulsion, a growing number of Lutherans (as well as Catholics and other Protestants) joined fraternals, citing their desire for inexpensive insurance benefits.

Recognizing that bans on fraternal membership might cause many church members to leave their congregations, some church leaders decided to compromise. They encouraged the formation of religious fraternals that would provide a sanctioned alternative to secular lodges. One of the most successful of these fraternals was Aid Association for Lutherans, organized by laymen of the Wisconsin Synod in Appleton, Wisconsin, in 1902. Like other religious fraternals, Aid Association was a compelling example for Norwegian-American Lutherans who still doubted that religion and insurance were compatible.

While Ekern looked to religious fraternals as models for the insurance organization he was planning, he did not look to them as examples of fiscal

First Biennial Convention of the Lutheran Brotherhood of America Morrison Hotel Chicago Nov. 5th 1919

reliability. Many fraternal societies still operated on an assessment basis, compensating for inadequate premium rates by assessing their membership when one of their members died. These plans worked well enough when members were young and deaths few, and they offered insurance protection at a low cost. But as the membership grew smaller and older, and more and more members died, the assessments became increasingly frequent and burdensome. Eventually some members became unable to pay, and when those members died, their families received nothing.

"If all who enter an association of this kind understand that if they live long they may get nothing from the insurance for their families, and enter

In an effort to attract more members, tiny Luther Union decided to affiliate with the Lutheran Brotherhood of America (LBA), a national intersynodical organization of Lutheran men's societies. Pictured is the first biennial convention of the LBA in 1919.

merely for the purpose of getting low-cost insurance at the period of life when it is most needed, well and good," Preus said. "But if they expect to get their policies paid in full regardless of how long they live, they are likely to be disappointed."

The fundamental weakness of assessment plans had spurred Ekern, when he was insurance commissioner of Wisconsin, to encourage legislation that required fraternal benefit societies to charge their members premium rates based on sound actuarial principles, and to maintain legal reserves adequate to pay all death claims. The legal reserve system brought financial stability to fraternal benefit societies, and enabled them to support their good works with proven business practices.

Because Ekern knew that Lutheran Brotherhood could not flourish, much less survive, as a vital fraternal organization without a solid fiscal foundation, he insisted at the 1917 merger convention that the proposed mutual aid society be organized "on an actuarially solvent basis." To delegates who were unfamiliar with insurance, those words probably had little meaning. Indeed, many of them still regarded insurance as a complicated patchwork of mysterious mathematical manipulations, full of risk and uncertainty.

But Ekern and Preus understood that life insurance was based on established mathematical principles. They believed that insurance was no more incompatible with faith in God than was building a home, living a frugal life, making a will, or seeking the help of a physician in time of illness or accident. Above all, the founders of Lutheran Brotherhood understood that faithful stewardship and fraternal service demanded the sound business practices that had enabled stock insurance companies to grow and flourish. They insisted that the society establish its operations on that basis—as a level premium, legal reserve society.

Eliminating the Guesswork

Before there were reliable statistics on the length of the average person's life, no satisfactory method existed for collecting insurance premiums. Eventually, the records of millions of lives were compiled, which made it possible to predict accurately how many people in a large group would die each year.

These records became the basis for mortality tables, which listed the number of expected deaths per year and the death rate per thousand from all age categories. The larger the statistical group, the more accurate the death rate. Commonly used in England since the middle of the nineteenth century, mortality tables gave insurance companies a reliable base from which to determine how much to charge their members in order to protect them.

The first table based strictly on the lives of insured Americans was known as the *American Experience Table*. Based on the mortality experience of the Mutual Life Insurance Company of New York over twenty years, the table became the standard mortality guide for most commercial insurance companies. Despite its fraternal status, Lutheran Brotherhood followed the lead of these companies by adopting the *American Experience Table* as its mortality table and the level premium as its method of collecting premiums.

A level premium remained the same during each year of the contract. Because the chance of death increased with age, so did the annual cost of insurance. But level premiums alleviated this rising cost by mathematically calculating the amount of fund reserves that must be built up during the early years of the member's contract, when the chance of death is low, to compensate for the later years of the member's contract, when the chance of death is high. These premiums were totaled, then divided by the number of years of the contract. The result was an average, or level, premium.

The introduction of level premiums meant that the owner of an insurance contract no longer needed to be in doubt, as were the members of assessment societies, about the cost of future premium payments. Nor did the member have to worry that the premium payments were inadequate to fulfill the obligations of his or her contract, for the level premium plan allowed insurance companies to systematically build up a reserve of funds adequate to meet those obligations.

Before mortality tables and level premiums existed, the business of calculating the cash reserve had been largely a matter of guesswork. If a company guessed wrong and its reserve was too low, it inevitably failed to pay all of its death claims and was forced to declare bankruptcy. As a result, state insurance commissioners began to require that insurance companies maintain a reserve that would, at minimum, pay its contract obligations. This became known as the legal reserve, and it went hand in hand with level premium payments.

During Lutheran Brotherhood's early years, Ekern reminded members continually that the society was based on a level premium, legal reserve system. To him, this fact was not merely a source of pride, but proof of the stability of the society. "The legal reserve principle is the basis of all sound life insurance of all kinds, whether issued by the Lutheran Brotherhood or any old line company," he explained. "There need be no mystery about life insurance, and the Lutheran Brotherhood has no secrets from its members."

The society was further strengthened because of its fraternal system of representative government. "The statement that Lutheran Brotherhood is owned and controlled by its members is not a mere phrase," Thore Eggen noted. "It expresses an actual and real condition. The members, organized by local branches, by means of representation at the general convention, enact laws and elect directors. We want this idea of ownership to sink into the consciousness of our members. It will help them to a higher appreciation of their membership. The members are the real owners. The officers and other workers in the organization are their servants."

Democracy must have appealed strongly to the immigrants who founded the society. They had left behind a Norwegian hierarchy that tried to box them in economic and cultural classes, and had moved to a new land in which it was proudly proclaimed (if not always practiced) that all men were created equal. It stood to reason that if Norwegian-American Lutherans formed an insurance society, it must be controlled by its members.

Lutheran Brotherhood's operating philosophies—fraternalism, legal reserve, member-owned—were set firmly in place from the beginning of its existence. During the early 1920s, when Lutheran Brotherhood struggled to gain new members, these philosophies served as the solid rock upon which it built its future. The society might not be large, but it was trustworthy.

"Of course, we want LB to grow big," Eggen said in 1925. "If possible, we want all Lutherans to buy their own insurance; but mere size is not the deciding factor in any business enterprise. What we want is absolute solvency. A man may hold title to one thousand acres of land and be dead broke. Another may own a small forty-acre farm and have unquestioned credit. It is all a question of assets to liabilities.

"When anyone asks you about the solvency of the Lutheran Brotherhood, you may state that we could close our doors right now, never write another policy, keep the necessary office help to conduct routine business, liquidate every obligation we have till the last death claim is paid, and have a nice balance left."

The First Employees

In the summer of 1925, Eleanor Buck answered an advertisement in a Minneapolis newspaper for an office worker at Lutheran Brotherhood. Buck was seventeen and a recent graduate of Minneapolis West High School, where she had studied business. She wanted to work, she told the society, because her father had just died and her family needed the money. That Buck applied to a fraternal organization for Lutherans was surprising, because she was a Methodist, but the subject of her religion never came up during the interview, and she was hired.

Buck joined a home office staff that was small in number, cramped for working space, and used to few frills. P. O. Holland, Lutheran Brotherhood's first business manager, had worked out of a tiny corner office at Augsburg Publishing House. His replacement, S. H. Holstad, fared somewhat better for elbow room. Shortly after he took over for Holland in the summer of 1918, the society acquired its own quarters, leasing Suite 939 of the Security Building at Fourth Street and Second Avenue in downtown Minneapolis. Rent was eighty-five dollars per month.

Eggen took over as full-time president and home office manager in 1920. He supervised a staff of three full-time employees. Inga Holm wrote contracts, Ruth Lee kept the books, and Florence Sifferlie did stenography. The staff shared two small, sparsely furnished offices and a reception room with two lawyers. One of the attorneys, Elias Rachie, worked on abstracts and routine legal matters for the society (although Ekern still held the title of legal counsel).

Lutheran Brotherhood eventually outgrew its office space in the McKnight Building in downtown Minneapolis and, in 1929, confident of its future, leased the entire twelfth floor of the Metropolitan Bank Building (later the Pillsbury Building) for the next ten years. The Metropolitan Bank Building is shown here, circa 1917.

In those days, it was cause for celebration whenever the society received more than two hundred dollars in premiums in a single day. Holm deposited the money in the bank, then on the same trip delivered contract applications to Dr. John R. Peterson, the society's part-time medical director. A cautious man, Peterson demanded that every applicant for insurance, no matter what the size of the contract, have a medical examination, and he performed every one of them himself.

By 1925, when Buck joined Lutheran Brotherhood, the home office had moved into more spacious quarters, the old offices of the Minneapolis Civic & Commerce Association in the McKnight Building. Eggen was still the office manager by official title, and he occasionally presided at meetings in the home office, but he spent the majority of his time on board business and promotional writing for the society. The real daily supervisor was Lewis L. Johnson.

Johnson was a former member of the Wisconsin state legislature, where he had served on an investigative committee on insurance with Ekern. He had taken a great interest in the progress of Lutheran Brotherhood since its creation, and even when he was employed by other companies, he had provided actuarial advice to the society. He joined Lutheran Brotherhood full time in the early 1920s and was named its treasurer in 1925.

Johnson supervised a staff that was entirely female. Holm headed the policy department, Betty Wold was cashier, Lee and Laura Sleizer worked in accounting, and Alice Vraalsted worked in the actuarial department, then known as statistics. Buck typed contracts and checked those that had already been typed for accuracy; she also did stenography for Johnson.

As Lutheran Brotherhood's business grew, so did the home office staff, increasing from six full-time employees in 1925 to thirty-two by 1929. That year, Lutheran Brotherhood leased the twelfth floor of the Metropolitan Bank Building. Located on Second Avenue and Sixth Street, the structure was later renamed the Pillsbury Building. Only half of the floor was needed by the staff, but the leaders of the society must have been confident that it would prosper, because they signed a ten-year lease for the space.

Expanding the Field Force

About the only job requirement for Lutheran Brotherhood's first district representatives was that they have a coat or pants pocket in which to keep a book of insurance rates. Despite the lack of job qualifications, the society's first representatives were few, as were the number of contracts they sold. For most of them, ministers, teachers, farmers, or college students, selling insurance was a part-time effort at best, an after-hours job that might reward them with a few dollars on a good day.

One of the first full-time salesmen was Lars Oyo, a young Norwegian immigrant, who represented Lutheran Brotherhood during the first six months of 1918. Oyo traveled from farm to farm throughout southeastern Minnesota, using horses and sleigh during the winter, explaining the new society to local pastors and congregations. Oyo signed up a number of charter members, but eventually returned to Norway to join his father's business.

For the next several years, the society attracted most of its salespeople by word-of-mouth. "We want someone to represent us in every Lutheran community," the society told its members. "In order to accomplish this, we must secure representatives. If you value your own membership in our organization, and the insurance that goes with it, don't keep mum about it. Speak of it to your friends and neighbors. Spread information about Lutheran Brotherhood as far as possible. And if you should chance to find someone who, in your judgment, possesses the qualifications necessary for field work, talk to him about it, and if he shows interest send us his name and address."

This strategy succeeded in attracting many eager candidates, but few of them were willing to commit to more than part-time work. By 1924, Lutheran Brotherhood had only two full-time representatives.

Even when the society did attract a full-time sales representative, the relationship did not always blossom. One salesman with a commercial insurance company received an agency contract with Lutheran Brotherhood on the condition that he sever his connection with the stock company. Some months later, an inquiry from an interested prospect in his territory reached the home office. It was forwarded to the representative, who then sold a contract to the prospect, but it was not a Lutheran Brotherhood contract. "Incidents of this kind," Eggen observed, "tempt us to make the historic prayer our own: God save us from our friends! We can handle our enemies ourselves."

In 1924, Eggen asked his nephew, N. K. ("Kelly") Neprud, to review the society's operations and to see what he could do to improve them. A native of Coon Valley, Wisconsin, where it was said that even the dogs barked in Norwegian, Neprud had worked as a barber and sold commercial insurance on the side. He agreed to take a sales job with Lutheran Brotherhood on the condition that he could continue to sell commercial insurance.

Neprud's appearance was well-suited to his new profession. Thin and full of nervous energy, he was obviously accustomed to moving quickly. His long face was open and friendly, and he loved an easy conversation. Neprud was also something of a fashion plate. He often sported a bow tie and suspenders, and his wavy hair was always trimmed short and parted smartly down the middle. He looked and acted confident, and he backed his appearance with results.

Shortly after examining Lutheran Brotherhood's sales department while Eggen was on sick leave, Neprud launched an impromptu sales drive. Upon his return, the president was so impressed by the results that he urged the salesman to join the society as its full-time field supervisor. Neprud had seen enough to convince him that Lutheran Brotherhood had potential, and he accepted. He served as the entire agency department for the next several years, directing, assisting, and recruiting field personnel.

Recruiting full-time salespeople was not an easy job. The decision to leave one's career behind completely for Lutheran Brotherhood was a true leap of faith. Jobs were not easy to come by, and life insurance offered no guarantee of success. After Ralph

Christian Zander, who sold insurance in eastern Nebraska, was Lutheran Brotherhood's leading producer during the late 1920s, in part, because he knew how to advertise effectively.

Undem of Sioux Falls, South Dakota, joined the society in January 1925, Neprud reported that Undem had "left a good position as school superintendent and burned all bridges behind him."

One of Neprud's primary jobs was to teach these fledgling salespeople how to succeed. In his mind, psychology was critical to good salesmanship. Because insurance terminology was foreign to most prospects, Neprud taught his representatives that they must speak in terms that the prospect could easily understand. Since most of the society's prospects farmed or lived in rural areas, that meant speaking in agricultural terms, as one representative found out.

He had been trying to convince a farmer to purchase insurance for nearly an hour, and seemed to be making no progress. The farmer seemed interested, but could not grasp the obscure terminology being used by the salesman. In his mind, insurance seemed too expensive. Finally, the salesman decided to direct the conversation toward more general topics. As he was talking, a brood of chickens walked by.

"Say, those are fine-looking chickens," the salesman said, suddenly thinking of a new sales strategy. "I guess they must lay a lot of eggs."

"About a hundred a day."

"What price do you get for eggs?"

"About thirty cents a dozen."

"You know, for about four eggs a day, I can give you a thousand-dollar insurance contract," the salesman said. "For eighteen eggs a day, I can give you a five thousand-dollar contract."

The farmer thought about the offer for several seconds. "Okay, I can afford that," he said finally. "I'll take the eighteen-egg contract."

Bolstered by such sales techniques, Lutheran Brotherhood's district representatives sold almost $5 million worth of life insurance in 1925. Of the total, which was produced by 348 salespeople, about two-thirds was written by just thirty-five district representatives.

Following its merger with the Lutheran Brotherhood of America, the newly named Lutheran Brotherhood added several directors who had served on the board of the LBA. One of the first post-merger boards included, front row, from left: C.H. Boyer, Thore Eggen, Herman Ekern, J.A.O. Preus, and Dr. C.M. Roan. Back row: Dr. Otto Mees, Dr. P.O. Bersell, P.O. Holland, P.S. Peterson, and Alva Davis.

The society's leading producer during the next few years was Christian Zander of Omaha, Nebraska. A jovial man with thick, black hair and glasses, Zander always seemed to be selling. When he drove from Nebraska to the home office in Minneapolis in a big car with a Lutheran Brotherhood sign stenciled prominently on the door, he often brought with him a special line of jewelry. Most of the women who worked at the home office occasionally bought a pair of earrings or a decorative pin from him.

Led by representatives such as Zander, Lutheran Brotherhood increased its insurance in force at a rate of about $6 million per year, until, by 1929, the society had insurance in force of $32 million.

Life on the Road

Flamboyant salesmen like Zander made the business of insurance seem almost glamorous. It was a harder existence for the representatives who worked the sparsely populated regions, where towns were small and the distances between them wide, where the wind blew hard and the view consisted of miles of dusty roads, fields of corn and wheat, pastures of cattle, and, occasionally, a solitary house or barn.

Carl Rosholt was one of Lutheran Brotherhood's first full-time sales representatives. He grew up in Pelican Rapids, Minnesota, where his father ministered to a traditional Norwegian Lutheran congregation in which the men sat on one side of the church and the women on the other. Carl's father died when he was young, and his mother moved the family to northeastern Montana, north of Glasgow, near the Canadian border. They homesteaded, then borrowed on the land, and some members of the family moved on, but Carl and his brother, T.L., stayed.

Carl attended Luther College, which his grandfather had helped found, then returned home to Montana to run a general store, which also served as a regional post office and blacksmith shop. He married, but his wife died a few years later, leaving him with two boys, ages four and two. Faced with an uncertain future, Rosholt gave up the store, which did not seem especially promising, and took a chance selling insurance for Lutheran Brotherhood in 1926. His brother, T.L., who was now a pastor, was already selling Lutheran Brotherhood insurance when Carl joined the society.

Carl's territory included western North Dakota and the entire state of Montana, an area about eight hundred miles wide. In his early days, he lived out of his Model A, in which he loved to sing, usually off key, as he drove from appointment to appointment. Even after he remarried, several years after his first wife's death, he retained his love of the open road. He worked western North Dakota and eastern Montana during the winter; then hitched a house trailer to his car, and worked central and western Montana with his wife during the summer.

The Rosholts would pull into a town and stop by the church to visit the pastor, with whom Carl usually was acquainted and from whom he picked up most of his leads. Carl would then park the trailer,

Society Snapshot: 1927

Home office: 1254 McKnight Building, Minneapolis

Number of members: 14,300

Number of employees: 23

Insurance in force: $20,551,205

Assets: $907,627

Life insurance death benefits: $43,145

Dividends paid: $23,728

Society officers

Chairman of the board: J.A.O. Preus

President: Thore Eggen

Counsel: Herman L. Ekern

Secretary: C. M. Roan

Treasurer and actuary: L. L. Johnson

Agency manager: N. Kelly Neprud

Medical director: J. R. Petersen, M.D.

General field supervisor: J. E. Hegg

"One Hundred Percent Lutheran Brotherhood Families," or families in which all of the members, adult and juvenile, owned Lutheran Brotherhood insurance, were pictured regularly in The BOND *during the 1920s and 1930s. One of them was the Nels Mikkelson family of Hawley, Minnesota.*

4

A FINE LOOKING GROUP.

Six adults and five juveniles, all members of the same family, and every one of them carrying Brotherhood insurance! Can you beat it? Just take a look at this picture! Every member of this family will from now on be a booster for Lutheran Brotherhood—a living advertisement of Brotherhood insurance. Following are the names of the parties shown in the above picture: Parents: Nels and Grete Mikkelson, children: Lauritz, Joseph, Marie, Gerhard, Esther, Agnes, Lars, Hartvig and Ellen. Residence: Hawley, Minn.

Statistics Fraternal Societies is a volume of 240 pages giving detailed information relative to practically every fraternal society of the United States and Canada. The membership and lodges in good standing, officers, plans, rates, average age, mortality, losses paid, increase or decrease in membership during 1925, amount collected, assets, liabilities, members and insurance written, benefits paid since organization and many other items of pertinent information appear in the 1926 edition. In addition it contains many other mortality and special tables

the benefits paid by the fraternal system amount to $3,521,926,498.

Woman (in radio-supply store): "I want to buy one of those radio fans I read so much about. My room is awfully stuffy."—New York American.

If a man keeps his face toward the sunshine, the shadows will fall behind him.—Church Management.

Doggie Ellis—"Say, Wallace, did you hear what the Doctor said to Claude Sander?"

"Mother's health was always delicate, though she was always hard-working and uncomplaining. People nowadays can hardly understand what scanty means a small farmer had fifty years ago, and how much toil and planning and scrimping were required to keep a family of four clothed and fed. Saturday nights mother often sat up until the stroke of twelve, patching and mending our clothes so that we could go to church the next day. Father used to remonstrate with her, but she always had much the same answer: 'The children can't go to church without clothes, William, an they mustn't get into the habit of stay ing at home. If they don't learn to g when they're young, they'll never tak to it when they're older.'

"My eleventh birthday I spent Uncle Sidney Fletcher's. A day Uncle Sidney's was a rare treat and returned, happy and excited, except one disquieting accident. I had to the knee of my new gray Sunday tro ers. I can remember just how mot said, 'Why, Joey, dear!' as she drew frayed edges together between slim white fingers, planning no d how best to mend the rent.

"How little I suspected what next few hours would bring! was a Saturday night, and mother suddenly in the gray dawn of the r ing following. For hours I co believe it. It seemed like an terrifying dream, and I kept thi I should wake up presently an everything as it had been before first thing that brought me out daze was that pair of gray t hanging on a hook behind the s turned them around and looked neatly mended knee—mother work. My eyes burned with One so near dying must feel weak, I thought in my boyi but she had stitched and stitc stitched, so that I could go t Sunday morning! That was est wish, and I resolved that not be disappointed.

"Apparently no one no when I stole out of the fr arrayed in my Sunday best off across the fields on foot five miles to the little count and the day was hot, but I

unhitch the car, and spend the next week or so searching the area for possible sales. Then they drove to the next town.

The Rosholts did their best to make life on the road as normal as possible. While Carl was making sales, his wife canned fruit at the trailer. Sunday was a day of rest, and no matter where they were encamped, the couple went to church, then spent the rest of the day visiting prospects.

Trying to make enough money to support his family was not easy. His boys lived with relatives until they reached high school age, when the family moved to Williston, North Dakota. There Carl became a general agent, but he continued to travel and sell. His sons did not see him often. Sometimes he would drive in, son Norm would wash his car, and he would be gone again.

Montana was a wild, harsh country, hard on ranchers and farmers, and even harder on insurance representatives. Rosholt's prospects were few and far between, and he never became rich at his trade, but he did his best with his territory. Not many of his prospects had telephones, so he became an experienced practitioner of the cold call, the industry term for an unannounced visit. Rosholt often timed his cold calls to coincide with coffee breaks, lunch, or

dinner. After eating, Rosholt would launch into his sales pitch. He grabbed salt and pepper shakers, creamers and sugar containers, and in his hands they became cash values, reserves, and dividends. When he began moving items around the table, some customers were so impressed that even if they didn't completely understand what he had said, they often bought the contract.

For men like Carl Rosholt, selling Lutheran Brotherhood insurance was more than a profession. It was a calling, a form of missionary work that demanded a durable automobile, an appreciation for broad horizons, a resolute optimism, and an unyielding commitment to make converts for the cause of insurance.

Rosholt eventually made enough of a name for himself that Neprud offered him a job at the home office in Minneapolis. It was his chance for a more reliable and less wearisome existence, but Rosholt turned down the offer. The open country was all that he had ever known, and there was still Lutheran Brotherhood work to be done out there. If he left, who would take his place? Besides, a man couldn't drive all day and sing off-key in the city. Folks would think he was crazy.

Selling Trust

Thore Eggen was a seemingly placid man, but underneath his calm exterior beat the heart of an energetic promoter. In early 1924, the pastor, then sixty-five years of age, determined that Lutheran Brotherhood needed a publication that would help to build greater unity among its members. An appropriate title, he decided, was *The BOND.*

"You may ask: "What does this name signify?" Eggen wrote in the first issue in May 1924. "The answer is not difficult. A bond is something that binds. There are bonds of friendship, of love, of mutual interests. Our *BOND* will be all of this and more. There is no bond stronger than that of common faith and love. *The BOND* aims to foster and strengthen the feeling of fellowship among those who profess the Lutheran faith."

In Eggen's opinion, the need for a society magazine had become a necessity. Most of Lutheran Brotherhood's members lived on isolated farms in the Midwest, and the media did not have nearly the connective influence on American life as today. "Our members are scattered over the entire continent, from coast to coast. While belonging to the same fraternal family, the relationship is to a large extent merely nominal, and there has been very little feeling of solidarity. *The BOND* aims to remedy this defect. It will serve as a medium through which one member can get in touch with others—a medium for interchange of thoughts and ideas."

Few men were as capable of fostering such an exchange as Eggen. As the editor of *Lutheraneren*, a church news and issues magazine for Lutherans, published in the Norwegian language, he had guided the publication through a period of great doctrinal turbulence by consistently pushing for unity among Norwegian-American Lutherans and avoiding articles that addressed doctrinal issues or synodical differences. As a result, he had managed not to offend any of the various synodical factions, and was well regarded by all sides. It was this reputation that had led Ekern, who had attended Eggen's church in Madison before the pastor moved to Minneapolis to work on *Lutheraneren*, to seek his support during the 1917 merger convention.

(Later, after Eggen was named president of Lutheran Brotherhood, he kept in close touch with Ekern, who visited the Minneapolis home office only every few weeks. Because Eggen still had some roots in Madison, they often met at the Ekern home, where Eggen brought material from the home office for Ekern's inspection.)

Much of Eggen's editorial focus was aimed directly at countering objections to life insurance and extolling the virtues of fraternalism. "Our work is, to a considerable extent, pioneer work," he wrote in January 1925. "We find it necessary to educate people and disabuse their minds of false and dangerous notions. We meet objections like the following: 'You should not mix religion with business.' If this were true, what would become of business? If religion does not touch and influence everyday life, it is not worth having. 'Show me thy faith by thy works.'

"Another criticism: 'The church should not engage in insurance work.' We might with equal right urge that the church should not build schools or homes for orphans and old people. The state takes care of this business. Again: 'The church should not have anything to do with investment of funds, buying mortgages, bonds or real estate. Why enter into competition with regular business?' As a matter of fact, we find that the church cannot divorce itself from these various activities. Religion, if it be true, enters into every phase of human life and wherever religion goes the church must follow."

As a relatively new and struggling organization, Lutheran Brotherhood had little to sell in the way of meaningful accomplishments. Its history was

brief and its sales were few. What set Lutheran Brotherhood apart was trust, and the organization succeeded, in large measure, because *The BOND* effectively communicated that message to its members and prospects. Eggen understood that Lutheran Brotherhood's members were often less concerned

Much of the prose and art in early issues of The BOND, *like this somber cartoon in the September 1924 issue, emphasized the potentially dire consequences of not owning life insurance.*

with the details in a contract than with the character of those from whom they purchased the contract. Therefore, he often emphasized the fact that church leaders, such as the Rev. C. J. Eastvold, the former president of Hauge's Synod, would not lend their names to Lutheran Brotherhood unless the

The umbrella of fraternalism protected Lutheran families from "the stormy future." From The BOND, *November 1926.*

society were capable of meriting their confidence.

The BOND even took its campaign to the children of its members, as exemplified by an article describing Ekern on its junior page. "Mr. Ekern is a husband and father," said *The BOND*. "He loves children. If you children were on a picnic in the woods and there were hundreds of other men there, I dare say that you would pick out Mr. Ekern as one that you would like. You'd even like to play with him, and I know that he would play with you. Now you know what kind of man he is. Look at his picture and tell me if you think I'm right or not."

The BOND also published testimonials from satisfied charter members, editorials that claimed that the profession of selling life insurance was second only to preaching of the Gospel, and articles that explained why Lutherans were better insurance risks. "As a rule Lutherans are people of clean habits. Their mortality rate is low as compared with other classes [about 25 percent of the expected mortality rate]. This means safety. You need never fear that an epidemic is going to wreck Lutheran Brotherhood."

But the final proof of the trustworthiness of Lutheran Brotherhood was evidence that it fulfilled its financial promises. In August 1929, *The BOND* published a chart of the society's death claims for the first six months of the year. Prominently displayed were numbers that illustrated that the death payment to the beneficiary was much larger than the insurance premium paid by the deceased.

Besides selling insurance, the pages of *The BOND* also gave Eggen a chance to advance the frugal economic values that, in great measure, shaped the society's philosophy for several decades.

On thrift: "The trouble with most people in this fevered age is that they are not satisfied with slow progress. They are looking for shortcuts to wealth. These shortcuts often lead to insolvency and sometimes lead to the penitentiary. If you want to play safe, live within your means and be satisfied with small profits."

On the relationship between religion and economy: "Religion is the greatest factor in causing business conditions to be good or bad. Every period of prosperity is the result of the thrift, industry and righteousness generated by the preceding period of depression and the result of the extravagance, inefficiency and unrighteousness developed during a period of prosperity."

On credit: "Credit does not raise your earnings, but it most generally adds to your expenses. Credit means making drafts on the future, which is a book not yet opened. Credit most generally tempts people to live beyond their means. Conclusion: Live within your means! Buy for cash!"

A New President

The Rev. Thore Eggen's quiet leadership had helped Lutheran Brotherhood to make great progress during its first ten years, and his eloquent pen helped to illuminate the society's guiding principles. But on December 1, 1928, Eggen informed the society's board of directors that he wished to step down as president and general manager. "My main reason for this step is my age with consequent loss of strength, mental and physical. Only a few months more, and I shall reach the seventy mark."

"Allow me to assure you that stepping out of the front line shall in no way signify loss of interest in the Brotherhood cause. I consider my connection with Lutheran Brotherhood a logical rounding out of a life dedicated to service in the Lutheran Church. I applied for my first life policy at a time when life insurance was by most Lutherans looked upon as an invention of the evil one. I kept quiet about the move, not wishing to worry anybody's conscience. But I soon discovered that I was not alone, other pastors having learned that life insurance offered, not only the best, but practically the only opportunity to provide for their families as God himself had directed.

"A wonderful change of sentiment has taken place within the last quarter century. Ignorance and prejudice are fast disappearing. As a natural consequence, competition is becoming more keen. But the future of Lutheran Brotherhood is secure."

The BOND of March 1929 announced the election of Herman Ekern as the society's new president. "We congratulate Lutheran Brotherhood with the good fortune of securing the services of so able a man. As we view the situation, Lutheran Brotherhood is on the verge of a prosperous period, and we will be in better shape to take advantage of opportunities offered."

But elsewhere in the same issue, *The BOND* also pondered the future with less optimism. "We hear and read so much about money lost in wild speculation that we begin to fear that there will not be enough left to keep the human family alive. And there are other alarming signs: Installment buying is increasing all over the country, filling the minds of timorous economists with dark forebodings. Preachers are warning their flocks to be on the lookout, lest they be carried away by the present tide of extravagance."

The preachers and timorous economists were right. In October 1929, the stock market crashed. The Great Depression had begun.

Building Blocks

It was a cloudy October day in Iowa. The crops were in, the fields were bare, and the horizon seemed endless, except for a small Lutheran church with a gold cross on its steeple.

It was warm inside the church, and the Sunday School room was crowded with young boys in baggy overalls who tugged uncomfortably at their ties, and with attentive girls in starched, homespun dresses. At the front of the room, a woman with graying hair read from the Bible. Today's lesson was the parable of the talents, she explained, and its message was that God expects us to be good stewards of all that we have been given.

A man sitting at the back of the room nodded in agreement. Husky and gruff looking, with glaring eyes, Harold Ingvaldson appeared out of place in the Sunday School class. But he listened intently to all the teacher said, making notes. After several minutes of writing, he stood quietly, thanked the teacher, and left the room.

Ingvaldson made his way deliberately through the small church and stopped at the pastor's office. There

Few men better exemplified the Lutheran Brotherhood work ethic than Harold Ingvaldson, the society's first investment manager, at left, and P.O. Holland, the society's first office manager.

he introduced himself as Lutheran Brotherhood's investment manager and inquired about the church's financial records. While the secretary pulled ledgers from a high shelf, Ingvaldson spent several minutes poring over the church's contributions to the mission activities of its synod.

By the time he was finished, the church service was starting. Ingvaldson hurried to the sanctuary, which was full, and took a seat at the back. While he listened to the pastor's sermon, he studied the congregation. When the service was over, he made a few final notes, shook hands with several members, and talked briefly with the pastor. Then he drove back to Minneapolis.

On the way, Ingvaldson mentally reviewed his notes: The Sunday School was active. That was a promising sign; the church would still be going strong thirty years from now. And the congregation had a good record of contributions to missions. A church that gives generously to others can usually be counted on to keep its own fiscal affairs in order. The pastor's sermon had been pretty good, and the congregation sang loudly, the way Lutherans are supposed to sing. This was a thriving congregation.

By the time Ingvaldson reached the Minnesota border, he had made up his mind. As investment manager, he would recommend that the society approve the church's application for a three thousand-dollar building loan.

Surviving the Depression

In l929, an unprecedented wave of speculation broke the back of the stock market, and thousands of small investors lost their lifetime savings. People who had been considered rich before the stock market collapsed were now heavily in debt. Newspapers were full of reports of suicides, and one columnist advised people to look skyward as they walked down Wall Street, lest they be hit by a falling banker. The Great Depression had begun.

By the summer of 1932, the American economy was at its lowest point ever. National income had been reduced by one-half. Up to one-third of all industrial laborers were unemployed. Businesses frequently went bankrupt, and thousands of banks failed, taking with them the life savings of their customers. In the cities, people stood for hours in bread lines and at soup kitchens, waiting for a free meal. In the country, many farmers had been victimized by drought, and others were able to sell far less than they grew; their incomes fell even more rapidly than did stock prices.

The stock market crash and the depression that followed did not immediately affect Lutheran Brotherhood. In 1930, new business grew by about $6 million, increasing the society's insurance in force to nearly $37 million. "I cannot get away from the idea that just now is the time to stress the value of life insurance as a safe investment, or call it protection if you like that word better," said Thore Eggen, the society's recently retired president, in the February 1930 issue of *The BOND*. "I am satisfied that the recent scare will have a beneficial effect and prove to be a blessing in disguise. People will begin to study values, and that is the very thing we life insurance people want them to do. I am satisfied that when the excitement is over, and people again begin to think rationally, the Lutheran Brotherhood field will be found more fertile than ever."

Eggen was correct—eventually. The effects of the depression hit the society hard. In 1931, new insurance business dropped by $3 million. New business plunged to only $200,000 the next year, the lowest amount in the society's history. But it increased to $1.5 million the next year, and by 1935 the society had resumed its annual insurance contract increases of $5 million to $6 million per year, a pace that prevailed through 1940.

While Lutheran Brotherhood was confident that its new business would grow, it was less confident about the management of its own money. The total assets of the society had grown from a few thousand dollars in 1918 to nearly $2.5 million in 1930. The society needed to invest wisely, prudently, and above all, safely. But the stock market crash had caused mass fear among money managers, and even investments that had been considered safe had become risky. One never knew whether the values that applied one month might hold to the next. Lutheran Brotherhood faced a turning point. How well the society managed its assets would determine whether or not it would remain in business.

Thus, in 1931, amid national economic uncertainty, Lutheran Brotherhood hired its first investment manager, Harold Ingvaldson, and went into the business of lending money.

Ingvaldson was born in Norway in 1886 and came to the United States in 1907. He lived with his uncle in Minnesota, where he worked as a farm laborer and attended college to sharpen his command of English. Eventually, he went to work for Harold Thorson, the owner of twenty-seven banks in Minnesota and the Dakotas. Based in Fessendon, North Dakota, Ingvaldson started as an assistant cashier and became the primary inspector and auditor of Thorson's banks.

When Thorson died in 1920, he left the bulk of his estate, including his banks, to St. Olaf College, which he had helped found. Ingvaldson was named executor and trustee of Thorson's estate, and worked closely with St. Olaf officials in the next few years, especially with P. O. Holland, the college's business manager. Holland was also a director of Lutheran Brotherhood, and when the society decided to hire

This headline in the September 1929 issue of The BOND *was prophetic. The next month, the stock market crashed and the Great Depression began.*

You Cannot Insure Too Soon Because You Do Not Know How Soon It Will Be Too Late

Looking Ahead

LET us not forget that about two out of every three who enter the working period at age 25 live to the retirement age of 65, whereas only one dies prematurely.

Let us visualize the fact that to-day not one family head out of ten has a reasonable estate at that retirement age sufficient to keep body and soul together decently.

Let us bear in mind the concept that it is best for the present generation to provide adequately for old-age support and not to blast the normal opportunities of children by compelling them to assume the heavy burden of parental financial support.

As I have explained so frequently, life insurance is a great thrift promoter, and an ideal investment, one that embodies every attribute of a perfect investment—absolute safety of principal, certainty and reasonableness of income, stability of value, ideal spread of risk, avoidance of the dangers of individual selection, avoidance of managerial care, convertability into cash.—Dr. S. S. Huebner.

A Sound Argument

ONLY one man in one hundred lives to be 50 and leaves anything except insurance at death. Are you certain you will be the man? It takes time to accumulate wealth. Suppose you die early? Only life insurance can eliminate that time element and change uncertainty to certainty.

Your place as provider for your wife and children must be filled when you are gone. Will the provider by an adequate life insurance policy, or must it be your widow who struggles to take your place?

Last year 25,000 men waited sixty days too long.

Looking Forward

WISE is he who provides against that day, who will set aside a small sum of his earnings in youth that will come to him surely when the old age milestone shows up in the path of life. It can do no harm if the party is rich and it is a godsend if they are poor. It is one thing that is good under all circumstances and it is one thing that is almost a crime not to do in a great majority of circumstances.

If you would have that feeling of contentment that comes with the knowledge your family is safe from want and poverty, fully protect them with life insurance. Then your yesterdays will be happily remembered, your to-days will be cheerful, your to-morrows confident.

HE WHO pays for life insurance makes a contribution to the needs of many and at the same time protects himself and those dependent upon him at the time when a great tragedy comes into the home. Modern life insurance is the most far-reaching institution in the world of helpfulness to human beings bereft of father and husband.
—Rev. Dr. R. G. Smith.

"I Am Insurance"

SHOULD an insurance policy be endowed with the gift of speech it would say something like this:

I protect the home when he who founded it has passed away.

I give to the widow financial relief in that dark hour when it is most needed.

I help the orphan to obtain an education.

I bring a ray of light and hope into the home when the shadows are the heaviest.

I am the best evidence of the goodness of the home founder when he is gone.

I am a bank that never fails, a bank note always worth its face value.—Yeoman Shield.

There's an Old Man Coming to Your House!

THERE is going to be an old man dependent on you some day. He is not your father, nor your wife's father, nor an uncle, nor an elder brother, but you yourself. What are you laying by for his happiness, comfort and sustenance during the sunset days of life? The time to make provision for him is now while you are young and strong and prosperous. Later on it may be too late.

Can You Afford It?

CAN you afford to give your wife comforts only when you can share them?

Can you afford to spend all you do on your living now and take a chance on your wife's having to live on the interest of what will be left?

Can you afford to leave that all where inefficient or careless advisors or changing conditions may wipe it out and leave her penniless?

Can you afford luxuries to-day if they may mean that she will have to earn her own living to-morrow, when years of domestic duties have dimmed her former training?

Can you afford to take from your children their mother's care that she may earn them bread?

Can you afford to deny your children that education which ever grows more essential, or can you afford to cast upon them that double burden as they strive to learn?

Can you afford even to live if your earning powers become crippled by accident or weakened by disease, or when they are lessened by time itself, as some day they surely will be?

Can you afford to shift to other shoulders that responsibility which should rest upon your own?

Do not worry about how much your life insurance costs you. The real thing to worry about is how much it will cost your wife and children, or you in your old age, if you don't carry a goodly amount.

Unity Is Strength

SOME people do not understand life insurance.

It is a great social plan, which merges the individual into the mass and places behind the frailty of man standing alone the immeasureable strength of men standing together.

Abraham Lincoln expressed the idea when he said, "In unity there is strength." You can take one stick and break it easily, but if you take a bundle of them and try to break them, you have a different proposition on your hands. So it is in financing programs of life. It pays to have cooperation of others.

Life insurance is the only system known to the world of economics which begins to function where everything else leaves off.—The Royal Highlander.

It was Theodore Roosevelt who said that only those are fit to live who do not fear to die; and no man is fit to die who has not provided for the future of the girl who gave up all to stand by his side, or for the helpless children he has given life.—Yeoman Shield.

KABLE BROTHERS COMPANY, PRINTERS, MOUNT MORRIS, ILL.

someone to manage its investments, Holland suggested Ingvaldson.

When Ingvaldson came to Lutheran Brotherhood, the society had no investment department. It had several bonds with such diverse groups as the U.S. government, the states of Minnesota, North Dakota, and South Dakota, and the countries of Canada, Australia, Chile, Denmark, and Panama. The society had made a few loans, but they were often the result of requests from pastors for their rural parishioners; some of the loans were of dubious merit and were more a matter of church relations than good business.

Ingvaldson instituted a strict lending system. For many years, he inspected every loan application personally. If the loan was over a certain amount, he took along a member of the board's executive committee. Then, once the loan had been approved, he kept a watchful eye on its progress.

Although Ingvaldson was careful with Lutheran Brotherhood's money, he was not tight-fisted. He lent money on land when few banks or insurance companies were willing to do so. When it came to real estate, he believed strongly in the necessities of life, such as farms and homes and churches. Almost all Lutheran Brotherhood mortgages were written on single-family homes of modest value, moderate-sized farms operated by the owner, or Lutheran churches. Only a few mortgages were secured on commercial buildings.

By 1939, Lutheran Brotherhood had made more than fourteen hundred loans with a total value of $5.5 million (an average of $3,900) in nineteen states from California to Florida, but predominantly in Wisconsin, Minnesota, Illinois, and North Dakota. Eventually, the number of loans grew to nearly seven thousand. Because the mortgages were small and spread across a large territory, the society was ensured a consistent flow of investment returns that were scarcely affected by market fluctuations.

Ingvaldson was particular about those to whom Lutheran Brotherhood loaned money. When he arrived at a farm, he seldom went inside the house. Instead, he walked out to the barn. If it was painted better than the house, then the farmer had his priorities in order. As Ingvaldson was fond of saying,

the barn produced income, not the house. Then he went inside the barn and looked for a pile of manure there. If he saw one, that was a bad sign: Manure should be out in the field.

Ingvaldson also spent time talking to the farmer. He freely dispensed financial advice to anyone who asked for it. Ingvaldson believed in the family farm, just as he believed in the rich Midwest soil. "No farmer ever went broke just farming," he often said, and he helped several of them become rich by convincing them to hang onto their land when they felt like quitting. "If you can just pay the interest," he would say, "we'll carry you for another year until you get squared around."

One bitter winter day in North Dakota, Invaldson and his son, Welden, who often accompanied him on long trips, sat shivering in a car. They were trying to convince an old farmer and his son, who could not make their mortgage payment, not to sell the farm. "Look," said Ingvaldson, "just give me fifty dollars. I'll hold the farm until next year for you until you get another crop." The old man was willing to listen, but his son was dead set against it. "No, Dad," he said. "It's time to quit. We just can't keep going like this." Finally, after arguing with his son for several minutes, the old man walked into the house, reached into an old cream container, and dug out fifty dollars. "We'd like to go for another year," he said. Several years later, the farmer's son stopped in at the home office of Lutheran Brotherhood. He had just hauled a truckload of cattle to South St. Paul, and his overshoes were covered with manure. He walked up to Harold Ingvaldson and pulled a wad of bills out of his pocket. "Ingvaldson, here's $25,000," he said with a big smile. "Do something with it for me, will you?"

Besides making farm loans, Ingvaldson inaugurated the policy of lending money to churches at a time when Lutheran congregations found it difficult to borrow.

The loans were at a low rate of interest, usually 6 percent, but Ingvaldson granted no favors. He insisted that all church loans be made on a sound, businesslike basis. To qualify for a Lutheran Brotherhood loan, the church had to be an established congregation that was building a new church, an addition, or a parsonage. As with the farms, Ingvaldson usually made a personal investigation of its Sunday morning work. He also devised strict formulas based on membership for determining maximum loan limits.

Ingvaldson's system worked well. Over the next two decades under his management, Lutheran Brotherhood granted more than $15 million in loans for construction of new churches and parsonages. About $2 million of that total went to Lutheran churches on the West Coast, lending credence to the statement that "Lutheran Brotherhood helped build the Lutheran Church on the Pacific Coast." On all those loans, not one penny of principal or interest was ever lost.

There were moments when Ingvaldson found it necessary to lay down the law, however. One prosperous Lutheran congregation, located in one of the richest farming communities in North Dakota, had a five thousand-dollar loan with Lutheran Brotherhood. The annual interest due was three hundred dollars, and the church was in default. Ingvaldson waited and waited for the payment. Finally, he drove to the church. He found the pastor, who was attending a ladies' aid meeting, introduced himself, and asked if he could say a few words to the ladies. He walked before the group and said, "I'm Mr. Ingvaldson from Lutheran Brotherhood. We have a mortgage on your church. There are three hundred dollars due. You won't pay it. We have an application here from a Missouri Synod congregation that wants to build a church in this town. Why don't you sell your church to them?" Then he turned and walked out. By the time Ingvaldson arrived back in Minneapolis, the interest on the loan had been paid.

Such incidents were few and far between, and Lutheran Brotherhood's church loans helped to place the society's name prominently before many congregations. It did not hurt a district representative's business when he was able to say to a pastor, "I'm bringing you some people from the home office to help you with that loan." Ingvaldson generally co-operated with Neprud and the society's agencies in that regard. But he insisted that church loans be treated the same as any others, and he resisted any interference, perceived or otherwise, from society personnel in other departments.

Ingvaldson and His Boys

Ingvaldson usually got his way when it came to the investments of Lutheran Brotherhood. The board rarely objected to his opinions, except when he made the dubious suggestion that they begin to buy expensive real estate in downtown Minneapolis for a future home office site. They fought him on that issue, but he ultimately convinced them. That kind of influence made Ingvaldson a powerful man in the society.

Around the home office, it was tacitly understood that the investment department operated under a different set of rules than did the rest of the society. "We don't do it that way," Ingvaldson would say grumpily. "We do it this way." And that was all there was to it. When the rest of the society went to a five-day work week, Ingvaldson's boys—"boyce" in his Norwegian accent—continued to work five days plus Saturday morning, sometimes all weekend if Ingvaldson decided to hit the road to inspect loan applications. The "boys"—Dave Zetzman, Herb Mohr, Sheldon Kingstad, Harold Falls, and Welden Ingvaldson—were young and eager, and Ingvaldson expected much of them. Since no telephone operator worked at the home office on weekends, the boys had to know how to run the switchboard. They also typed and took shorthand. Most of all, they knew how to follow orders, for Ingvaldson was not the kind of man to ask twice. He often marched out of his office and handed a sheet of paper to one of the boys. "I just got this letter," he would announce sharply. "You know how to answer it."

But if Ingvaldson was a demanding boss, he was also fair. He earned his employees' respect by working harder than they did, and he amazed them with his intellect and his memory. Not only did he remember the name of nearly everyone to whom he had granted a loan, he also remembered the file number of each loan at the home office. Once he had visited a farm, he could always recall its location. That was a gift he shared with his good friend, Governor Preus, who often accompanied him on loan inspections.

Ingvaldson and Preus sometimes dozed in the back seat while one of the investment department employees drove them from farm to farm. They always

An Influential Voice

Folks do not always mean exactly what they say. There was the talkative automobile salesman who said: "Within a year I hope to see this old world on its feet again."

Dr. P.O. Bersell, who wrote those words at the height of the Great Depression in 1932, always said exactly what he meant. For more than twenty years, Bersell was one of the most influential voices of Lutheran Brotherhood, dispensing often pungent observations about the state of the world from his monthly column, "Peter's Observatory," in *The BOND*.

Bersell did much more than observe. A director of the society from 1927 to 1943, he was one of the leading Lutherans of his time and a major force for ecumenism among world Protestants. During his long tenure as president, and later as president emeritus, of the Augustana Lutheran Church, he played a key role in uniting that synod and three other bodies into the

Lutheran Church in America in 1962. He also was one of the architects of the World Council of Churches and the National Council of Churches. During World War II, he made a dangerous secret journey aboard an army transport plane to coordinate a national Lutheran relief effort for the devastated churches of Europe.

A native of Rock Island, Illinois, where he graduated from Augustana College and Augustana Seminary, Bersell became involved with Lutheran Brotherhood through his work with the Lutheran Brotherhood of America, the intersynodical organization that gave a newly formed fraternal benefit society named Luther Union its present name. His subsequent work as director of the society also helped to legitimize its fraternal mission among the many Swedish-American Lutherans who were members of the Augustana Synod.

Bersell died in 1967, five days before his eighty-fifth birthday.

seemed to wake up just as the car pulled into the drive, and then routinely conducted their inspection. As soon as the car left, they fell asleep again. At the end of the day, when they reviewed where they had been, Ingvaldson and Preus remembered every detail about each farm. The boys just shook their heads in amazement.

Ingvaldson was something of a legend in the home office, for he used snuff incessantly. In deference to his habit, spittoons were placed strategically about the home office. However, Ingvaldson also spit into other containers, and Lutheran Brotherhood workers learned the hard way never to reach into a wastebasket! When Ingvaldson walked down the aisles, alert workers would grab their wastebaskets and hide them under their desks until he had passed by.

Ingvaldson was a devoted family man and a caring Norwegian provider. During his first winter in Minneapolis, he not only provided a home for his wife and seven children, but he opened his home to four other relatives. Family was important to Ingvaldson, and he always took time at the office to ask workers how their families were.

By 1953, Ingvaldson, who now was a member of the board of directors, had headed the investment department of Lutheran Brotherhood for twenty-two years. In that time, the society's assets had grown from $3 million to $72 million, and its annual investments had risen from $750,000 to $20 million. Early that year, at age sixty-six, Ingvaldson suffered a heart attack and was forced to take some time away from work. He even made plans to visit Norway for the first time since he had left as a young man. His son, Welden, delivered the tickets to him on a Friday evening. But Ingvaldson had been restless. There was much work that needed to be done before the trip, so he decided to make several loan inspections over the weekend. On Sunday, he put in an especially long day. That night, in a restaurant in Beloit, Wisconsin, he slumped over his table, dead from a heart attack.

Developing the Field

Martin Nelson had been skeptical. His friend, P. O. Holland, had been trying for nearly ten years to convince him to sell insurance for a new fraternal benefit society called Lutheran Brotherhood, but Nelson had thus far resisted. He was sympathetic to its cause, and he respected its leaders, especially Holland and Herman Ekern, but he had doubts that it would ever amount to anything.

Holland's desire to convert his friend was understandable, for Nelson had been a successful businessman. A South Dakota native, he had learned the general store trade and eventually purchased several stores in Wisconsin and Minnesota, one of them in Northfield. But shortly after he moved his family there in 1929, Nelson began to experience severe pain in one leg. He spent several months at the Mayo Clinic in nearby Rochester, where doctors tested his knee for tuberculosis and cancer, among other things. But they could not diagnose the problem and decided to alleviate his pain by making the leg permanently stiff. Nelson limped for the rest of his life.

Convinced that he could no longer personally take care of his businesses, Nelson began to look for another job. Holland repeated his offer of employment at Lutheran Brotherhood, and Nelson began to sell part-time for the society in May 1929. A few months later, the stock market crashed, and Nelson lost a sizable chunk of his savings. In March 1930, he attended a regional sales meeting in Minneapolis, where he visited the home office for the first time. He was impressed, so he sold his remaining business interests and became the society's general agent in Northfield, Minnesota.

Nelson eased into the insurance business slowly, but he soon grew to love it. He took insurance courses by correspondence and bought every book he could find on the subject, building a formidable insurance library in the process. Nelson's children thought his books dull and plodding—no plot, no heroes—but Nelson pored over them as would any diligent student.

His approach to insurance was academic, but his

approach to selling was natural and spontaneous. Nelson was a small man, with an open, almost child-like face. His manner was relaxed, and he did his most effective selling at the kitchen table over a cup of coffee. No other approach would have been acceptable in quiet Northfield. Nelson never forgot that he was selling to his neighbors, and he rarely pushed a potential client. He was too shy for that; he became embarrassed when his children teasingly asked him if he had been looking for new prospects during church services. Nelson used no gimmicks. "Here's what I'm selling and here's what it can do for you," he would say. "Do you want it?"

Many people did. Covering southern and western Minnesota, Nelson was Lutheran Brotherhood's top producer during the 1930s and early 1940s, and he established a record of consistency that has not since been matched in the society. For twenty years straight, Martin Nelson sold at least one application each week.

Among Lutheran Brotherhood's top general agents and sales representatives during the 1930s and 1940s were, from left, Woodrow Langhaug, Martin Nelson, Richard Falck, and Levi Jesperson. Lutheran Brotherhood never had sold much insurance in Chicago, Illinois, until Langhaug moved there. Within five years, Langhaug had become one of the society's top general agents. Nelson, of Northfield, Minnesota, was the society's leading personal producer during the 1930s. Falck, a former school superintendent from Northfield, established a society record by selling 485 applications for insurance in 1947. Levi Jesperson of Minneapolis was one of the first general agents in the society's history to concentrate more on building a productive sales organization than on his own personal production.

In the minds of the society's leaders, selling one application every week was a goal second only to total sales volume, and App-A-Week Club members were held in high esteem. Striving for an application every week eliminated slumps and lessened the tendency to procrastinate. It generated regular income and ensured that a representative was always looking for a prospect. The representative who garnered a new application every week was sure to pick up others along the way, as evidenced by the fact that almost all of the leading members of the App-A-Week Club were also leaders for the year in personal production.

During Nelson's career, which included the worst years of the Great Depression, he personally sold more than $5 million worth of insurance, and representatives from his general agency sold several million more.

One of Nelson's most promising representatives was a teacher and principal in Northfield. Richard Falck, a graduate of Gustavus Adolphus College, had been an educator for several years when Nelson approached him in 1939 about selling Lutheran Brotherhood insurance during the summer. Like many teachers of that era, Falck was struggling to make ends meet, and he eagerly accepted Nelson's offer.

Falck's first summer as an insurance representative was not especially encouraging, however. He earned eighty-one dollars, not enough to cover his

expenses. He did better the next year, and even better in 1941. That year the United States entered World War II, and rationing went into effect. To save gas when he was prospecting away from home, Falck left his car in Zumbrota, located about thirty miles from Northfield, then took the bus back and forth from home. Despite the lean times, Falck progressed until he was the society's leading seller in the summer of 1945. The next year, Falck, then forty years old and with a wife and one son, decided to quit his job as principal and join Lutheran Brotherhood full time.

Falck made an immediate impression as an outstanding producer. During the last seven months of 1946, he sold $460,000 worth of insurance, finishing in second place in personal production for the year. "There is no stopping that man Falck," said *The Go-Getter*, Lutheran Brotherhood's publication for sales personnel. "He reminds us of the great [Bronko] Nagurski on our Minnesota football team—the All-American fullback who could always be counted on to tear through the line and make the yardage and the touchdowns."

Falck scored more than his share of touchdowns in 1947. That year he wrote 485 life insurance contracts totaling nearly $805,000, almost all of them $1,000 or $2,000 contracts, and he earned $7,000. Both the number of contracts sold and the total amount of insurance sold were new Lutheran Brotherhood records, and the contract record remained unbroken for the next forty years. Falck was easily the top producer for the year. His nearest competitor had an excellent year, with $413,000 in sales, yet that total was little more than half of Falck's.

Like his mentor, Nelson, Falck was knowledgeable, thorough, and disciplined. He studied Lutheran Brotherhood's products and its fraternal history, so that he would be ready to answer any question that might arise. But the comparisons with Nelson ended there. Falck was by nature aggressive, even relentless, and he did not easily give up on his prospects. If they were sometimes convinced that they did not need insurance, Falck was equally sure that they did, and set about teaching them why. His tenacity was sometimes unnerving, but more often than not he made the sale.

Falck was Lutheran Brotherhood's leading producer again in 1948 and 1949, and one of its top sellers in 1950 and 1951. The next year, Martin Nelson retired, and Falck was named general agent in Northfield.

New Territory

Top sellers like Nelson and Falck helped Lutheran Brotherhood to increase its insurance in force from $31 million in 1929 to $366 million in 1951. During this period of growth, Lutheran Brotherhood maintained a relatively unsophisticated approach to recruiting and selling. Throughout the 1930s and 1940s, new district representatives were simply handed a book that illustrated insurance rates, were tutored for a few days by traveling sales supervisors, and were then expected to begin selling. Expenses were kept as low as possible. When Harold Hoel, the society's assistant superintendent of agencies, took Ole Haroldson, a new district representative, on his first selling trip in 1940, the pair subsisted on hamburgers and shared the same hotel bed.

Hoel traveled the country searching for prospective representatives, and he recruited most of the men and women who began selling for Lutheran Brotherhood in the 1930s and 1940s. Tall and heavyset, with a long and expressive face, Hoel was an emotional man whose oratorical skill rivaled that of the best traveling evangelists. Such was Hoel's enthusiasm for life that he was known around the home office as one of the few men who could break a sweat while calling for the invocation.

Most Lutheran Brotherhood field personnel received much of their initial sales training simply by watching Hoel work to persuade potential members to buy insurance contracts. During a trip to North Dakota in 1941, Hoel accompanied Don Lommen on a few of his calls to demonstrate how to make sales presentations. The first prospect was a farmer. He met the salesmen at his barnyard fence, and Hoel immediately launched into his sales talk. It became quickly apparent that this prospect was in no mood to purchase insurance, yet Hoel, intent on showing Lommen the art of selling, persisted. "I don't want to buy insurance," the farmer finally shouted, but Hoel kept after him. In desperation, he kicked at Hoel through the fence, missing him and striking his toe on the fence. Only when the farmer limped away, cursing, did Hoel abandon his pitch.

Hoel's performances at the home office were equally renowned. At each training school for new district representatives, Hoel delivered the closing speech. His impassioned tones quickly carried beyond the confines of the classroom, and employees from nearby rooms often gathered in the hallway outside to listen. By the time he finished his talk, Hoel would be trembling with emotion, and he would inevitably light up a cigar, which seemed to calm him.

Although Hoel was a master salesman, his main talent was creating enthusiasm among the field force, not teaching them specific sales skills. Besides, he was so busy seeking new recruits for the society that he rarely had time to spend more than a day or two with new representatives. The result of this lack of training was that when Hoel or one of his sales supervisors left, many of the recruits floundered.

Albert Ebbert, a former teacher in Lititz, Pennsylvania, was hired by Lutheran Brotherhood in the spring of 1949. Hoel signed him up, and he spent two evenings with Herman Bergeth, a training supervisor, learning the basics of selling insurance, before Bergeth had to return to Minneapolis. Ebbert was well-received by pastors in his area, and he sold a few contracts to family and friends, but he soon discovered that he did not really know how to sell to strangers.

By late fall, Ebbert's meager sales commissions amounted to far less than his expenses, and he received a letter from the home office informing him that his negative balance was growing so large that it might be difficult for him to pay the money back. Perhaps Ebbert should go back to teaching, the letter suggested, and gradually pay back his debt.

Ebbert immediately wrote back: "I left teaching for good and I joined Lutheran Brotherhood for good. I've seen the potential out there and I know I can sell these people. I'm meeting them and talking to them, but I'm just not able to close the sales. I just need more training."

A few months later, the society sent E. A. Anderson, a sales consultant from Chicago, to work with Ebbert. They spent nearly ten days together, and when Anderson left, the struggling representative finally understood the basics of selling. Anderson taught Ebbert several simple techniques for illustrating the long-term value of insurance, one of which involved a marble and a baseball. He would start by offering the marble to the prospect. "You wouldn't mind carrying this around in your pocket all day, would you?"

"No, that wouldn't be much of a problem."

Then Anderson would hand the baseball over. "How would you like to carry this around all day?"

"I wouldn't like it."

"Well, that's what you'd be doing if you became sick, and didn't have insurance. You'd be carrying a baseball around in your pocket, because that's what it would take to pay for insurance then. By purchasing insurance now, you only have to pay a small amount of money every month in order to protect your family. By carrying around the marble, which is easy, you can keep from having to carry the baseball."

Bolstered by such techniques, Ebbert quickly wiped out his debt and began to prosper as a district representative for Lutheran Brotherhood. He was later named a general agent in Pennsylvania.

Although Pennsylvania was densely populated with Lutherans, many of them of German origin, Lutheran Brotherhood had only recently begun to penetrate the market there. Several men had pioneered the territory, including Charles Boyer, a former commercial agent from Boalsburg who served as a society director and its Eastern sales manager; Alva Davis of Altoona and Stephen Wach of Pittsburgh, two of the society's early agents; and George Sowers, a leading producer during the 1940s.

Despite their valuable work, the name Lutheran Brotherhood was not nearly as recognizable among most Pennsylvania Lutherans during the 1940s as among their Midwest brethren. Some weeks after Ebbert joined the society, a prominent member of his local congregation stopped him in the Lititz post office. He looked concerned. "Al, can I talk to you for a minute?"

"Sure," Ebbert said. "What's on your mind?"

"Did you investigate Lutheran Brotherhood before

Society Snapshot: 1937

Home office: 608 Second Avenue South, Minneapolis

Number of members: 48,500

Number of employees: 91

Insurance in force: $61,097,084

Assets: $7,523,062

Life insurance death benefits: $130,740

Dividends paid: $171,690

Church loans: $636,123

Society officers:

Chairman of the board: J.A.O. Preus

President: Herman L. Ekern

Executive vice president: L. L. Johnson

Secretary: C. M. Roan

Extension vice president: C. O. Teisberg

Medical director: J. R. Petersen, M.D.

Assistant secretary: Fred C. Mueller

Assistant treasurer: Ingolf Lee

Superintendent of agencies: N. Kelly Neprud

Assistant superintendent
  of agencies: William G. Fisher

Investment manager: Harold Ingvaldson

Auditor: Roy W. Haugen

Cashier: Elizabeth I. Wold

Registrar: Inga E. Holm

A group of pastors, members, and field representatives met in Allentown, Pennsylvania, with society officer William G. Fisher. The 1937 meeting was sponsored by George M. Sowers of Allentown, one of the society's leading producers during the 1930s and 1940s. Pictured at the speakers' table in front of the group are, from left: C. H. Boyer, eastern sales manager and director; Sowers; and Fisher.

Just out of college, Ken Severud joined Lutheran Brotherhood in 1934 and, like several other young employees hired during the depression, stayed with the society for more than four decades. Severud, who served as longtime corporate secretary and later as a director, was one of the select few who came to be known as Mr. Lutheran Brotherhood during their careers. Severud also served as president of the National Fraternal Congress of America in 1972-73. He retired in 1977.

you started selling for them?"

"No, not really. There were some good men who talked to me about joining up, and my pastor was the one who recommended me to them, and what I have learned about them has been terrific."

"Well, I just don't want you to get hurt. Nobody around here seems to know much about this outfit."

Ebbert, who worked for Lutheran Brotherhood for the next three decades, encountered less skepticism among other local residents, but they lacked knowledge about the society. Some thought that Ebbert was representing a men's religious organization, until he mentioned that the fraternal society sold insurance.

A few local residents had been sold Lutheran Brotherhood contracts by representatives from other cities, but not all of them were pleased. When Ebbert introduced himself to a mill owner as a representative of Lutheran Brotherhood, the man launched into a denunciation of the society. Ebbert was shocked by his reaction; maybe his friend had been right about these people.

Some weeks later, Ebbert was driving by the mill, when the man waved and pulled him over. "I'm sorry about the way I reacted the other day," he said. "A while back, a Lutheran Brotherhood agent came through town and wrote an application on each of my two daughters. I paid the premiums, but I never received a policy or heard from the guy since."

"Do you mind if I look at the policies?"

"Sure," the man said. He went inside, and pulled them out of his desk. Ebbert inspected the applications for about ten seconds, then frowned.

"Where were you living when you bought these contracts?"

"In rural Lititz," the man said.

"Well, this application says rural Lancaster. The agent must have written down the wrong address."

Upon further investigation, Ebbert found that the home office had indeed sent the policies and premium notices to Lancaster, which was located a few miles away. The policies had already lapsed, but the man at least felt good about Lutheran Brotherhood.

In uncharted territory such as Lititz, it was critical to share the story of Lutheran Brotherhood's fraternal activities. Ebbert began each interview by talking about student scholarships and branch activities and donations to the Lutheran church. This information convinced many prospects of the society's mission. One businessman was so impressed that after purchasing three contracts, he decided to pay the annual premiums all at once, in effect investing the money in his insurance contract.

Going to his wall safe, the client returned with six thousand dollars—in cash.

It was Friday afternoon, and the banks had closed. Although district representatives were discouraged from collecting premiums in cash, Ebbert was not about to turn down the money. He did not let the money out of his sight during the entire weekend, and placed it under his pillow at night. On Monday, he deposited the money in the bank and wrote a personal check for six thousand dollars to the home office.

As Lutheran Brotherhood expanded into newer territories far from the comfortable lap of the Midwest, such as Pennsylvania (which eventually became Lutheran Brotherhood's second largest state in total membership, behind Minnesota), the society began to increase the number of sales tools it provided for its representatives. Kelly Neprud, the superintendent of agencies, established numerous training programs and materials for the society's representatives in the field. He also started *The Go-Getter*, a monthly sales publication. Through the publication, Neprud and the home office maintained an essential link with the field, honoring top performers, inspiring representatives with success stories from their peers, and teaching the latest sales approaches, such as using the phone more effectively and looking for leads in metropolitan areas.

The January 1944 *Go-Getter* pointed out that most Lutheran Brotherhood members were farmers, and it passed on advice for dealing successfully with rural prospects. "Be sincere," said the field editor. "The farmer detects lack of sincerity at once. Have humility. Know all about life insurance, but don't pretend to know all the answers to everything else. Watch your clothes. Don't affect what you think is a 'hayseed' appearance, but don't dress as though you just stepped off Broadway. It won't hurt if your shoes are unshined."

As training increased, Lutheran Brotherhood's basic organizational sales structure began to change, and general agencies began to exert a much stronger influence over what previously had been an individualistic and nomadic field force. The general agent was assigned a sales territory, then was supposed to recruit representatives to sell in that territory. It was the general agent's job to direct the representatives; in exchange, the general agent received an overwriting commission. Although the position had existed for many years, most general agents directed only themselves. Rather than spend time recruiting, a difficult task in rural areas, they continued to spend most of their time selling.

Levi Jesperson was one of Lutheran Brotherhood's first true general agents. A former salesman for the Singer Sewing Machine Company, he joined the society in 1943 and was subsequently assigned the Minneapolis general agency. Jesperson did not try to sell contracts himself. Instead, he began to recruit representatives and build a sales organization from the ground up. He devoted his time to training his field personnel, supervising them, and cajoling them and picking up their spirits, when necessary.

Jesperson was combative. He stood up for his men and for himself and was willing to argue with the home office over any decision with which he disagreed. Yet any argument with Jesperson was sure to end on a friendly note. He was respected for his abilities, and, above all, he produced. In the fourteen years that he led Lutheran Brotherhood's Minneapolis agency, Jesperson's representatives wrote nearly $29 million worth of insurance contracts, and his agency led the society twice in yearly production.

Other general agents were inspired by Jesperson's example, and the society's insurance sales began to accelerate.

A Chance Encounter

Woody Langhaug shivered as he walked, watching his breath float away in the freezing air. It was a bitter February morning, ten degrees below zero with a biting wind. Just a few more calls, Langhaug told himself, then you can take a break. He knocked on a door. No one home. As he hurried down the sidewalk to the next house, he noticed a car pulling up beside him. Two men were inside, and they motioned for him to come over. Langhaug hesitated, then approached the car. "Can I help you fellows with something?" he asked cautiously.

"We noticed you out knocking on doors," the driver said. "You're a salesman, aren't you?" Langhaug nodded, still puzzled.

"We're salesmen too," said the man on the passenger side. "Why don't you step inside and warm up?" Langhaug quickly accepted the offer.

"We couldn't help but notice somebody crazy enough to be out selling on a day like today," said the driver. "We just wondered if you might be crazy enough to work for us." Langhaug laughed, and listened as the man began to tell him about his company. Several minutes later, when Langhaug left the car, he had a new job with the Singer Sewing Machine Company, at the promising salary of one dollar per day plus commissions.

Langhaug worked for Singer two years, then took a job with the *Minneapolis Star Journal* as its district circulation supervisor. He had done well in sales, and he thought his father, Ole, who had recently sold the family farm near Evansville, Minnesota, and retired in Alexandria, Minnesota, might also thrive in sales. So, in 1944, he called Levi Jesperson, the man who had been driving the car on that frozen February morning four years earlier.

Jesperson was no longer with Singer. He was now a general agent in Minneapolis for Lutheran Brotherhood. He did not have responsibility for the Alexandria territory, he told Langhaug, but he would put him in touch with men who would arrange something for his father. In the meantime, the general agent invited Langhaug to lunch, where he informed the young man that he had no business at the newspaper, but instead belonged at Lutheran Brotherhood.

Jesperson coaxed a reluctant Langhaug to the home office, introduced him to Neprud and Hoel, and then gave him a peptalk that lasted for more than an hour. "Think of the commissions," he said, "Think of the possibilities. You know, I've done well. You can do well, too." Langhaug was convinced. A day later, he gave the paper his two-week notice. He was going to learn how to sell insurance for Lutheran Brotherhood.

Langhaug had grown up in western Minnesota, where his parents, both Norwegian immigrants, operated a grain, poultry, and dairy farm. The farm was good to the Langhaugs, but young Woody discovered that he had a talent for selling. While still in junior high school, he answered an ad in a farm magazine to sell neckties, and he made the rounds to neighboring farms on his bicycle until he had sold every tie.

Langhaug left the farm in 1937 to attend St. Olaf College in Northfield, Minnesota. During the summers, he helped on the farm and continued to hone his selling skills. In the summer of 1939, Langhaug, then twenty, earned $250 per month selling

popular magazines. At a time when $85 was considered a fair salary, $250 was big money. Langhaug earned his salary by working harder than other salespeople and by being more adaptable. Not everyone to whom he sold magazines in the rural countryside had the ready cash to pay for their subscriptions. No matter. In its place, Langhaug accepted non-laying chickens. He placed the chickens in a wooden crate attached to the back of his car and headed for the poultry company in Alexandria to sell them.

Langhaug's ability to adapt also served him well during his early days with Lutheran Brotherhood.

Several home office employees played important leadership roles during the 1920s and 1930s when Lutheran Brotherhood was developing. Among them were, from left: Fred C. Mueller, secretary, 1939 to 1955; Elizabeth Wold, who joined Lutheran Brotherhood in 1922 and eventually headed personnel, becoming the first woman to head a society department; William G. Fisher, executive vice president, 1941 to 1951; L. L. Johnson, executive vice president, 1935 to 1941; Dr. John R. Petersen, medical director, 1918 to 1951; and N. Kelly Neprud, superintendent of agencies, 1925 to 1959.

One of his first sales was to an elevator operator at the Sheraton Hotel in Minneapolis, where the young agent lived. It was difficult to interview the operator while the elevator was moving, but Langhaug eventually wrote her a contract—somewhere between the top floor and the lobby.

A few months later, Langhaug was out making sales calls. It was a sweltering August afternoon, too hot to stop for a visit, he thought, as he drove by the house of Dr. Norval Peterson, one of his agency's clients. But by the time he had reached the end of the block, he had changed his mind and turned around. Mrs. Peterson welcomed Langhaug inside. During the course of their conversation, she mentioned that her niece, Eunice Tande, who was working as a receptionist in her husband's medical office,

was fishing with Jesperson. "How can I get a date with this lovely lady?" Langhaug kept thinking. Finally, he determined to go to Dr. Peterson's office to see if the paperwork on her medical examination was complete.

As Langhaug had hoped, Eunice was at the office. It was almost closing time, and he asked her if she would like to have a Coke with him after work in the cafe downstairs. Eunice consented. As they were talking, Langhaug said, "I'm going to south Minneapolis later. Would you like a ride home?" Eunice was hesitant; she hadn't known this young man very

had no insurance. Would Woody like to return later that day to talk with her about insurance?

Langhaug returned to the Peterson home that evening. As he was sitting in the living room, a pretty young lady came walking down the stairs. Langhaug was instantly smitten. "Oh my gosh," he thought, "is this my prospect?" Mrs. Peterson introduced Eunice and Woody, excused herself, and left the two to talk about insurance. Langhaug managed to sell her a two thousand-dollar contract, but he had a difficult time keeping his mind on the work. That was true all weekend long, especially when he

long. Langhaug reassured her. "I think it will be okay," he said. "And I'm sure your aunt will think it's fine." As they drove to the Peterson home, Langhaug became a little bolder and asked Eunice if she would like to go to the state fair that night. "Oh, I'll have to definitely ask my aunt about that," she said firmly. But Mrs. Peterson gave her blessing to the impromptu date, and Woody and Eunice dated practically every night thereafter.

When Langhaug finally delivered Eunice's Lutheran Brotherhood contract, he said to her, "I hope I can pay the next premium on this." They

The home office statistical department, circa 1948.

were married in December of 1945.

Langhaug's powers of persuasion extended to his prospects, as well. In 1944, after only ten months on the job, he became Lutheran Brotherhood's leading district representative for the year. Langhaug was asked to become the general agent in Albert Lea, Minnesota. He signed up several full-time representatives and pushed the tiny agency to fourteenth place in society production for 1946. Impressed with his efforts, Neprud asked Langhaug to start an agency in an even larger city, Chicago.

The society had never done well in the Windy City. Several general agents had tried there and given up, and only three Lutheran Brotherhood representatives were left in Chicago, all of them part-time. When Langhaug and his wife traveled to Chicago to scout the territory, they were met by the society's regional field director. He was honest with Langhaug. "You know, Woody, we like you and want the best for you, but you've got a great thing back in Albert

Lea," he said. "Chicago is a white elephant. We've never been able to get it started, and I'd hate to see you lose your shirt down here."

Discouraged, the Langhaugs decided to call Jake Preus, who worked in Chicago. "Governor, I'm in the city, looking it over," said Langhaug. "Is it possible to have a visit with you?"

"Get down here right now," Preus bellowed. They went to lunch, where Langhaug explained his reservations about the job and asked the former governor of Minnesota what he thought. "Langhaug, you can make it here," said Preus. "This is a great city. I came here in the depression, and I made it. There's lots of business here. You'll have to work hard, but you can do it." Buoyed by Preus' peptalk, the Langhaugs decided to accept the challenge.

Langhaug set a lofty goal for his new territory, pledging to Neprud that his new agency would be Lutheran Brotherhood's leading producer in five years. Yet he was unsure where to begin. Chicago was a large city, replete with insurance companies, and Lutheran Brotherhood was starting at the bottom. Langhaug knew that he had to come up with a sales tool that would at least capture the attention of area Lutherans. He was particularly interested in an approach he had seen in an insurance industry booklet. The publication clearly outlined three basic scenarios for the owners of insurance contracts: "If You Live, If You Die, If You Quit." Impressed with the clarity of this approach, Langhaug prepared his own plan that applied the same principles to a Lutheran Brotherhood contract. Then he took a new sales representative with him and tested the technique. On their first call, the representative sold a ten thousand-dollar contract.

To most people, life insurance was a complicated subject, full of fine print and unintelligible terminology. Langhaug's brochure, called the *Money Plan Book*, worked because it was easy to understand. If you quit the contract in ten years, here's what you get; if you die, here's what your survivors get; if you live, here's what you get. In just a few minutes, without launching into a lengthy discourse, the representative was able to show the prospect exactly what life insurance is and what it does. The *Money Plan Book* worked so effectively in Chicago that the home office adopted it for the society's entire field force, and it was used for two decades.

Langhaug also became interested in using audio-visual sales aids. In 1937, the society had considered using "moving pictures" to tell members about Lutheran Brotherhood and its involvement with the church. Langhaug eventually applied the same idea to sales. He and a friend wrote a script that adapted the *Money Plan Book* to the screen, and Langhaug had a filmstrip made in Chicago and had his representatives test the technique. The agency achieved its most productive month ever, and the use of sales filmstrips became standard practice among Lutheran Brotherhood's agencies.

These new sales tools helped the Chicago agency to become the society's leading producer in 1950, beating by one year Langhaug's promise to Neprud. The agency ranked among the society's top five producers for the next decade, and was ranked first four more times.

The Home Office

In December 1934, twenty-two-year-old Ken Severud received a telephone call from a Minneapolis employment agency. The agent told him about a job opening at Lutheran Brotherhood. Severud thanked the agent for the information, hung up the phone, and scratched his head. Who or what was a Lutheran Brotherhood?

Despite his lack of knowledge about the society, Severud, who had a degree in economics from Macalester College and experience as a vacuum cleaner salesman, quickly applied for the job. It was a temporary position in the actuarial department. He was interviewed by Ingolf Lee, one of the heads of the department. During the interview, Severud mentioned that he was from Rushford, Minnesota. Lee's eyes lighted up; he had good friends from Rushford. Severud was hired.

Severud had been working at the home office for several days when he was handed a calculator and told to start to add numbers. "You do know how to run one of these things, don't you?" he was asked. Severud's mind said no, but his mouth said yes, and he spent the next hour nervously calculating his fate. Finally, he approached Evelyn Hille, another employee in the actuarial department. "How much do they pay an hour for overtime here?" he asked.

"Gee, I don't know."

Severud cleared his throat. "If I paid you, would you be willing to stay after work some night and show me how to run the calculator?" he asked sheepishly. Hille said yes. After a few hours of instruction, Severud felt confident enough about the calculator to get by. He reached into his pocket for payment, but Hille stopped him. "Keep it," she said. "You'll need it."

Severud did. Seven months after he had been hired as a temporary employee, L. L. Johnson, the executive vice president of the society, asked Severud to stop at his office. "You've done a good job for us," Johnson said. "We've decided that you'll be a good employee on a permanent basis. You've been getting $15 per week, is that right?" Severud nodded. "Your salary now will be $65 per month, less the five percent needed for your retirement plan. Agreed?" Severud nodded again and went back to his desk. He was elated, until he figured out that he would now be taking home $3.25 per month less than before.

Severud sighed. "I'm not making much progress at this place," he thought. "Oh well, at least I have a steady job."

In 1935, not everyone did. America was still recovering from the effects of the Great Depression. Jobs were scarce, and they did not pay much. New employees at Lutheran Brotherhood started at sixty-five dollars per month, and most of the others earned less than one hundred dollars per month.

Lutheran Brotherhood's employees liked the society. It was still small, only about sixty employees, but it was growing steadily. Cliff Thompson, a business student, was told at his interview in 1934 that the society believed in helping young people get a start because jobs were so scarce. Many of the newer employees, such as Thompson, came in for an interview and were hired on the spot.

Al Konigson visited Lutheran Brotherhood because one of his friends was interviewing for a job there, and he had nothing better to do that day. During the interview, it was learned that Konigson's friend was related to a home office worker. His friend was told that the current policy was not to hire relatives (even though the society's roster of employees included a number of sons and daughters and cousins of employees). Konigson was asked to apply for the job and was later hired.

Employees found the home office to be warm and friendly, almost cozy. There were few secrets. They knew what the board of directors, their superiors, and each other were doing. When a wedding or funeral was held for an employee, everyone in the company attended. Home office parties and picnics were common. Lutheran Brotherhood felt like family to home office employees, and its fraternal philosophy seemed to set the society apart from other business organizations.

The society's young employees, almost all of whom were Lutheran, liked that feeling, especially those just starting out, such as Ken Severud, Al Konigson, and Cliff Thompson. It engendered in them feelings of deep loyalty and made them work harder. Many of them liked Lutheran Brotherhood so much that they stayed for forty years and longer. A few, such as Dave Zetzman and Sophie Hawkinson, stayed for almost fifty.

Life at Work

During the 1930s and 1940s, the home office of Lutheran Brotherhood occupied the twelfth floor (and eventually the eleventh, tenth, and ninth floors) of the Metropolitan Bank Building. The building, which was later renamed the Pillsbury Building, was located at Second Avenue South and Sixth Street in Minneapolis.

The work space was rectangular and open. A few officers had private offices, but most of the employees worked in open areas, their long aisles of desks separated by just a few feet. There were no partitions between desks or between departments, and communication was not difficult. Larry Jost, who worked in the claims department at one end of the long room, often phoned Ethel Ann Johnson, who worked in the premium income division on the other, about some company matter. Jost had a booming voice, and when he got excited, Johnson would simply put the receiver down and listen to Jost without it.

Ceiling fans were located throughout the office, and there was no air conditioning. The humid Minneapolis summers were especially hard to bear, because the men were required to wear shirts and ties, and the women had to wear dresses and hose. Nylon stockings were uncomfortable when it was muggy, and a few daring employees occasionally went to work without them. Those who were caught paid a price. Inga Holm, the no-nonsense assistant of Dr. John R. Petersen, the medical director, once sent a female employee home for not wearing nylons.

Open windows were a necessity in the oppressive heat, and home office employees relied heavily on paperweights. One day, a set of premium cards sitting on a windowsill were blown out the window by a sudden gust. Several employees dashed frantically to the street below, crawling under cars and

The first home office employees to pass a specialized insurance course in 1937 were, from left: Ingolf Lee, Earl Andersen, Chester Hagander, Melvin Hagerness, Kenneth Severud, and Clarence Nelson.

over the tops—anything to retrieve the precious cards. Just as objects occasionally flew out the window, things sometimes flew in, especially birds and bats. Stirred to action by the screams of her fellow employees, Ethel Ann Johnson captured a bat with a wire tray, adeptly scooped the creature into a manilla folder, then escorted it outside.

Employees punched timecards whenever they entered or left the office. Several of the women arrived half an hour early in the mornings so they could play bridge. L. L. Johnson, the shy office manager, often came early, as well, hoping that a fourth player would be needed so that he would be invited to join the game. Bridge was a popular pastime in the women's break room, and devotees made a dash for the bridge table during coffee breaks and at lunchtime.

There were two coffee breaks during the day, ten minutes in the morning and ten minutes in the afternoon. Breaks were strictly enforced; employees who chose to continue working were stopped by their supervisors and forced to quit what they were doing for ten minutes. The breaks had been instituted to take the place of trips to the drugstore, located on the first floor of the Metropolitan Building, where many employees often stopped for a cup of coffee. But the ban was difficult to enforce. Many of the top officers also liked coffee in the drugstore, and they enjoyed talking with any employee who happened to be sitting nearby.

Most workers carried their lunch. During the summer, they often ate on the roof of the Metropolitan Building, receiving a suntan in the process. Others preferred to eat out, despite the stern warnings of Dr. Petersen that too much hot coffee and greasy restaurant food would give them ulcers. One year, during an elevator strike, a few of the men took lunch orders from the rest of the office, picked up takeout food, then brought it back up twelve flights of stairs.

There was no overtime compensation in those days, but when employees worked into the night, which was often, they were allotted seventy-five cents for supper. Mel Sando, a member of the actuarial department, knew of a cafe up the street where one could get a meal for twenty-eight cents. The meal wasn't much, but it was an effective way for young employees to increase their pay by forty-seven cents.

The Officers

The supervisors who directed the home office were a diverse lot. Some were reserved, like L. L. Johnson and Fred Mueller; some were boisterous, like Roy Haugen; some were creative, like Bill Fisher; some were brilliant and eccentric, like Ingolf Lee; some were sticklers for discipline, like Elizabeth Wold. But no matter what their characteristics, they all worked extremely hard and insisted on the same kind of commitment from every home office employee.

As president, Herman Ekern was technically in charge of the home office, but he traveled to Minneapolis just once a week from his office in Chicago. During his absence, the office was supervised by William G. Fisher. Fisher was a stickler about having employees punch timecards, but he devoted most of his time to advertising. A former manager for Ray-O-Vac, Fisher had placed ads in national magazines

Several members of the home office staff displayed their dramatic skills for the field force at an agency meeting in Minneapolis in 1944. No Goods to Buy: or Thomas Says, "Yes," was written by executive vice president Bill Fisher to help counter sales objections. Members of the cast included, from left: Cliff Thompson, Doris Tone, O.R. Jacobson, Mel Sando, Ken Severud, and Betty Morelius.

and knew how to get publicity. Lutheran Brotherhood, at the time, was anything but modern in its approach to promotion, relying primarily on word-of-mouth and *The BOND*. Ekern had always thought that the society's performance and mission were adequate advertising. Preus, however, wanted a new approach to promotion, and had often consulted with Fisher, when he was with Ray-O-Vac, about how the society could apply industrial advertising techniques to fraternalism. Eventually, Preus asked Fisher to join the society.

It was during this period that George Sowers, a leading sales representative from Allentown, Pennsylvania, stood up at a sales conference and asserted that if Lutheran Brotherhood hoped to grow, it needed to follow the merchandising tactics of other insurance companies. During Fisher's tenure, the society began to offer prizes to members who identified relatives or friends who were interested in Lutheran Brotherhood insurance. The society gave away everything from thimbles and kitchen tongs to plates and silverware, and sales grew steadily.

Fisher often worked closely with Carl Teisberg, head of the extension department. A quiet and humble man, Tiesberg worked to establish closer contacts with Lutheran church leaders. At the time, he was National Lutheran Boy Scout Commissioner (and he occasionally wore his formal scouting outfit, hat and all, around the home office). Through his efforts, Lutheran Brotherhood began to sponsor many Lutheran scouting activities during the 1930s, and for many years, the office of the Lutheran Committee of Scouting was based at the home office.

L.L. Johnson served as executive vice president and treasurer, and had long been acknowledged as the leader of the home office. A reserved man with sad eyes, Johnson was thoughtful, kind, and always willing to listen to his employees. He commanded respect by his example, and he inspired discipline among his employees without ever having to say a word about it. When Johnson found it necessary to scold someone, the transgressor inevitably felt so guilty that the infraction never occurred again.

Johnson's career with Lutheran Brotherhood was cut short by a lengthy illness, and during his final years, he was able to work only a few hours per week.

He trembled constantly because of pain, but his kind and gracious demeanor remained intact until his death in 1943. Employees at the home office never forgot that.

If anyone was quieter than Johnson, it was Fred Mueller. The poker-faced secretary of the society in charge of the underwriting and policy departments also supervised the production of *The BOND*. At one time the deputy insurance commissioner of South Dakota, he had signed the certificate that authorized Lutheran Brotherhood to operate in that state. Mueller was extremely precise in his approach to work. He had to be, for his departments were responsible for transforming insurance applications into legal contracts worth thousands of dollars. Each month, Mueller and his workers checked, typed, photocopied, signed, and folded thousands of contract forms and letters.

Ingolf Lee supervised the actuarial and statistical departments. Short and muscular, with a serious Scandinavian face, he was a brilliant man whose ideas were often ahead of their time. It was Lee who suggested that the society begin to use computers, and he laid much of the groundwork for the home office's subsequent entry into the computer age. Self-taught, he became well-known throughout the insurance industry for his actuarial knowledge.

Unfortunately, Lee's ability to sell his ideas did not nearly match his actuarial skills, and his imaginative schemes were often dismissed as eccentric by the board of directors. He worked tirelessly on new ideas for the society, honing them until he felt they were perfect. But by the time he was ready to present his work to the board, certain that every detail was in its proper place, he was unwilling to compromise. Among the directors, Lee was known as a man who exaggerated the potential benefits of his plans; thus, he seldom received the credit that most workers in the home office thought he deserved.

To them, Lee was a gifted teacher, short on ego and long on patience, always willing to share new ideas with the nearest employee. "Do you understand this?" he would ask an unsuspecting subject. If the person said yes, Lee would say, with a twinkle in his eye, "Good. If you can understand it, anyone can." He encouraged his own employees to try their new ideas on him, and gave them a full, attentive hearing. "If you want to understand something better," he was fond of saying, "explain it to someone else."

Roy Haugen, an infantry sergeant during World War I, brought his jovial brand of discipline to the conservation department, whose task it was to remind and convince members not to let their contracts lapse. Haugen had been with the society since 1925, and he knew how things were supposed to be done: his way. During one of Mel Sando's first days at the home office, Haugen noticed him folding letters, and let out a whoop. "What in the world are you doing?" he exclaimed. "Don't you know how to fold a letter? Didn't they teach you that in school?" No, Sando said, they hadn't gotten around to that. "Awright," said Haugen, in his best sergeant's growl. "Here's the way we fold letters around here."

For all his bluster, however, the employees knew that Haugen was a man they could slap on the back, a familiarity that they would never consider with Fisher, Johnson, or Mueller, and they knew they could count on him for a joke when work became too serious. Once, on her way to work, Evelyn Hille was stopped for speeding. Later, at the office, she received an intimidating phone call. "We understand that you have had a brush with the law," the voice said. "Don't you know you could lose your job over this?"

Hille panicked until she recognized the laughter on the other end of the line. It was Haugen. He had been ticketed for speeding that day, too.

Working Women

Although the term *working woman* was not yet in vogue during the 1930s, almost three-quarters of the home office employees were women. For most of them, working was a necessity, and three of them, Betty Wold, Inga Holm, and Lou Madsen, had been with the society since its early years, Holm since 1918.

Wold, who headed the cashier's department and later became director of personnel, was the first woman to head a society department. A demanding supervisor, she was respected more than she was liked. Yet she was always willing to discuss work or personal problems with employees, and many women who worked in other departments turned to her

Each year on September 18, the home office closed for Founders Day, and the staff spent the day relaxing and picnicking. For identification of this 1937 outing, see appendix, page 288.

with problems they felt they could not discuss with their male supervisors.

At the time, there was an unspoken rule that an employee who left Lutheran Brotherhood of his or her own accord generally would not be rehired. One woman had quit to have a baby. Two years later, divorced and with a young child, she needed a job. A male supervisor denied her request to return to the society, but Wold put her foot down. "Look, she needs a job and she's a good worker," she said adamantly. "I think we should take her back." The young mother was rehired.

Wold was not the only woman with clout at the home office. Inga Holm, who assisted Dr. Petersen, the society's medical director, was a member of the underwriting committee. The committee made the

final decision as to whether an applicant of questionable health should be accepted or rejected for insurance. "Doc Pete," as he was known, had a stubborn streak. If he had decided to reject an applicant, it did little good for anyone, especially the district representative who had written the contract, to try to change his mind. Holm was the only one who could handle Doc Pete, and she rescued many applicants from rejection. The field personnel appreciated that.

Lou Madsen was Kelly Neprud's secretary. Neprud was an outgoing man who delegated responsibility for details to his trusted assistant. An exacting, conscientious businesswoman, she made sure the agency department ran smoothly. With Madsen, as with Roy Haugen, there was a right way to do things and a wrong way. She demanded neatness and accuracy, and she insisted that a job be done again until it was done right. If some young employees viewed her as excessively fussy, that was fine. Madsen didn't care

what others thought of her, as long as the job was done correctly.

Madsen once took a trip to Europe. When she returned to the office, she was smoking a cigarette. One young male employee was all agog, for he had never seen a woman smoking in the office. It was true that many of the men smoked, even Doc Pete, but a woman? Madsen, who knew that she was every bit as good a worker as any man, didn't seem to care what he thought. Besides, as the young employee recalled years later, it was the only cigarette he ever saw her smoke.

An Extended Family

Each year on September 18, the home office closed for Founder's Day. Created to honor Ekern, Preus, and the other organizers of the society, it was a day when all the officers and employees relaxed together. Picnics were sometimes held near the Minnesota River, complete with events that included a treasure

hunt and three-legged races, golf, horseback riding, and bicycling, then a picnic. The next day, everyone was stiff from all the activity, but the gatherings usually generated enough funny stories to keep the office in good humor for the next month.

Founder's Day helped to cement many lasting relationships among the young home office employees. They often had fun together, singing, skiing, going to ball games. Romance inevitably bloomed among them. Dave Zetzman, who worked in investments, had his eye on Dorothy Extrom, who worked in the cashier's department. It was almost Christmas, and Zetzman had conveniently picked up a sprig of mistletoe. When Extrom walked down the middle aisle, the alert Zetzman sprang at her with the mistletoe and collected a kiss. That generated some lively office gossip.

Zetzman and Extrom eventually married, as did several other home office couples, such as Kenny Severud and Helen Ingvaldson, Earl Andersen and

Eleanor Bersell, Cliff Thompson and Ann Hagen, Harold Falls and Marian Miller.

These and other home office employees supported each other through good times and bad. After Evelyn Hille gave birth to her first child, she became seriously ill. When doctors decided that she needed extensive surgery and blood transfusions, a call went out to the home office for help. Twelve Lutheran Brotherhood employees went immediately to the hospital to donate blood. Some months later, when the recovered Hille stopped at the home office with her baby, she was met at the elevator by Dave Zetzman, who greeted her and reached for the infant.

He was gone for the next hour, proudly parading the newest member of the home office family.

The President

In his attitude toward money, Herman Ekern, the president of Lutheran Brotherhood, was an extremely cautious man. One night, while he was eating with several home office employees, Ekern suddenly observed that as a young man he had resolved never to co-sign a note for anyone unless he was willing to pay the note himself. "I would advise all of you to pledge to do the same thing," he said soberly. "Never sign something unless you're willing to pay for it."

Ekern's devotion to financial responsibility helped to shape the character of Lutheran Brotherhood in its first thirty years. Although he believed in insurance primarily as a force for social good, Ekern was also committed to fiscal stability, and he viewed the society as one way to encourage that philosophy among Lutherans. As the president of Lutheran Brotherhood from 1929 to 1951, Ekern did not call for new products, nor did he make sweeping decisions that transformed the company's approach to selling insurance. The society's prudent fraternal creed had been firmly established during its first decade, almost solely through Ekern's influence, and he saw little reason to tinker with a good thing.

Although he had great influence on Lutheran Brotherhood, Ekern never kept an office at the society's headquarters in Minneapolis. As president, he visited the home office just once a week, arriving from Chicago by train in the morning and leaving by train at night. Meetings of the society's board of directors were held at his law office in Chicago. Ekern was fully occupied with other business affairs around the country, and always seemed to be rushing to catch the train to Madison, Chicago, or Washington, D.C.

The home office workers viewed Ekern with fond respect. He was always friendly and open (he liked to reminisce about growing up in Wisconsin with fellow Wisconsinite Dave Zetzman), but he was a dignified man, not the sort one joked with or patted on the shoulder. Few employees knew him well because he liked to work alone and usually chose to tackle important projects by himself, spending countless hours perfecting them. Ekern rarely chose to explain his actions to others; the proof of his usually successful efforts was explanation enough.

Preus occasionally visited the home office with Ekern. The contrasts in their personal styles were striking, especially when the two were seen side by side. While the glib Preus was making speeches, Ekern might be talking to the janitor. While Ekern went over a contract change with a young actuary, Preus might be making an important call to New York City or Washington, D.C., with the help of a switchboard operator who nervously hoped that she would not inadvertently disconnect the former governor.

The solid relationship between Ekern and Preus was intriguing, for they could not have been more different. Ekern was small, Preus was large. Ekern was a liberal, Preus a conservative. Ekern was reserved, Preus was outgoing. Ekern immersed himself in detail, Preus was more concerned with the big picture. Ekern was a teetotaler, Preus was not.

While the two appeared to have little in common, they shared an unshakable belief in Lutheran Brotherhood and its mission. In regard to the society and the value of fraternalism, Preus seemed to draw sustenance from Ekern and always backed his ideas, at least publicly. In directing the development

Society Snapshot: 1947

Home office: 608 Second Avenue South, Minneapolis

Number of members: 149,800

Number of employees: 166

Insurance in force: $215,573,110

Assets: $34,819,133

Life insurance death benefits: $260,945

Dividends paid: $712,415

Church loans: $351,906

Society Officers

Chairman of the board: J.A.O. Preus

President: Herman L. Ekern

Executive vice president: William G. Fisher

Secretary: Fred C. Mueller

Investment manager: Harold Ingvaldson

Extension vice president: S. H. Holstad

Medical director: J. R. Petersen, M.D.

Superintendent of agencies: N. Kelly Neprud

Assistant superintendent of agencies: Harold C. Hoel

Actuary: Edward D. Brown, Jr.

Assistant actuary: Ingolf Lee

Comptroller: Lorenz Jost

Cashier: Elizabeth I. Wold

Statistician: Clarence N. Nelson

Registrar: A. Anderson

Announcing
The Leaders for the Year 1947

PERSONAL PRODUCTION
Richard Falck
Northfield, Minnesota
$803,750 Issued and Put-in-Force

AGENCY PRODUCTION
Levi Jesperson
Minneapolis, Minnesota
$2,523,304 Issued and Put-in-Force

The **GO-GETTER** FOR THE INSTRUCTION AND INFORMATION OF OUR FIELDMEN

LUTHERAN BROTHERHOOD *Legal Reserve Life Insurance for Lutherans*

VOL. 21   JANUARY, 1948   NO. 12

Kelly Neprud, Lutheran Brotherhood's director of agencies, started The Go-Getter in 1931 as a way to improve communication between the home office and the field. The monthly publication listed the sales progress of field representatives and discussed new sales techniques. Pictured are the society's top producers for 1947, district representative Richard Falck and general agent Levi Jesperson.

The home office staff is pictured in 1946 at the annual Founders Day picnic. For identification, see appendix, page 289.

of Lutheran Brotherhood, the two men operated in concert, and other directors jokingly accused them of getting together before board meetings to present a united front.

A National Authority

Although Lutheran Brotherhood was one of Ekern's great loves, he was better known around the country for his legal and political work. He was widely recognized as one of the country's top authorities on insurance law, and he placed his personal stamp on a number of insurance and pension innovations.

In 1917, one year after Ekern and Erwin A. Meyers started their law firm in Chicago, America entered World War I. Young, unmarried, and healthy, Meyers appeared to be a good candidate for the military,

and he began to search for insurance that would not be voided if he entered the armed services. He was unsuccessful, and discussed the matter with Ekern. As a result, the two men drafted the first proposal to provide war risk insurance for servicemen and their dependents. The partners went to Washington, D.C., and won support for the plan from several officials, who convinced President Wilson to endorse it. The plan became a bill and was passed into law in October 1917 as the Soldiers and Sailors Act. War risk insurance helped to popularize insurance and greatly increased the number of Americans who bought contracts.

In 1921, an Illinois farmer named George Mecherle started to develop an idea that he could sell automobile insurance to Illinois farmers at the lowest possible cost by using farm mutuals thoughout the state as agencies. Mecherle began a search for "the best insurance attorney in the country" to help him get

A Common Bond

his ideas down on paper. Herman Ekern is your man, he was told, but he's probably too busy to talk to a farmer. At that moment, Mecherle became convinced that no attorney would do except Ekern.

When the two men finally met, Mecherle explained his ideas. They were basically sound, Ekern said, but the plan also contained several flaws. Mecherle was surprised by Ekern's unflattering but honest assessment, and he left Ekern's office "pretty damned mad," as he later told friends. But he eventually came around to Ekern's way of thinking. The resulting plan formed the basis for State Farm Mutual Insurance Company, which became one of Ekern & Meyers' biggest clients.

Ekern did legal work for many other insurance companies, nearly all of them mutuals and fraternals. Because of his advice, most of the companies operated cautiously, investing mainly in municipal bonds and real estate, and, as a result, they weathered

the financial drought of the depression with little difficulty.

Ekern also became recognized as a national authority on pensions. During the 1920s and early 1930s, increasing competition and agricultural failures forced the railroads to cut their work force by half. The railroad unions operated under strict seniority rules, and the youngest workers faced most of the layoffs. To remedy the situation, several young leaders of the Railroad Brotherhoods organized the National Pension Association (NPA). The NPA favored a system that would provide some job security for younger workers, and it clashed with the old guard of the railroad unions, who insisted on seniority rights.

Because of this political battle, the NPA was unsuccessful in finding congressmen who would introduce its pension legislation to Congress, until the organization hired Ekern as its legal counsel. Ekern worked diligently to iron out differences between the NPA and the old union leaders. After a series of protracted negotiations, a bill satisfactory to both parties and palatable to the courts passed Congress in 1935.

Ekern's involvement in the railroad plan and his growing knowledge of pensions led him to offer much valuable counsel to legislators weighing the pros and cons of social security legislation in the mid-1930s. Although many lawyers condemned the idea, Ekern defended Congress's right to enact the Social Security Act, and he was active in lobbying for its passage. It was his belief that social security would help to complement life insurance by guaranteeing "protection for the family and for old age."

During his career, Ekern also authored the insurance codes of Hawaii and Kentucky and wrote several insurance bills that became laws in many states. He also helped to set up the Federal Deposit Insurance Plan, which still insures most of America's banks.

The Political Ekern

Besides his growing involvement with Lutheran Brotherhood and his flourishing law practice, Ekern was still attracted to public service. In 1922, he was elected attorney general of Wisconsin. He was active in negotiations that settled several boundary disputes with Michigan. He made his biggest impact in office by fighting against the Ku Klux Klan, which had become a growing political force in Wisconsin. When the Klan applied for incorporation, Ekern twice turned them down, first on technical grounds and later because of their policy of white supremacy. The Klan eventually was forced to make changes in their bylaws, which allowed them to incorporate, and the group became one of Ekern's most vehement opponents.

Ekern's political mentor, Robert M. LaFollette, died in 1925, one year after finishing a distant third in the presidential race. His death affected Ekern deeply, for the two had always been close. They had never had an argument and were in complete agreement on almost every issue. On several occasions, Ekern had told friends that LaFollette was the greatest statesman of the age, and declared that he would be proud to carry a water bucket for the man.

Ekern carried a symbolic bucket in 1926, running for governor of Wisconsin as the LaFollette Progressive candidate. He was the early favorite, but the race began to turn against him after charges were made that he had profited from illicit gains from his law practice while serving as attorney general. The charges were later proved false, and the man who had made them was censured by the legislature, but the damage had been done. The fact that Ekern was an inveterate teetotaler in a wet state also contributed to his defeat.

A primary reason that he lost, however, was that he was not a good campaigner. A skilled orator in small groups, Ekern lacked the ability to speak to large crowds. He was unable to make complex issues understandable to the general public, and he refused to rely on campaign slogans. He quickly forgot people's names, and declined to endorse products that he did not believe in, merely to gain votes. Ekern once refused to have his picture taken drinking buttermilk—an important political gesture in a dairy state—because he did not like buttermilk.

Ekern refused to compromise his character or beliefs for the sake of popularity, and he paid the price, losing the gubernatorial primary in 1926. Realizing that he lacked the qualities and desires necessary for political success, Ekern did not make another attempt at the governor's seat and settled into the role of elder statesman in the Progressive party. As a favor to LaFollette's son, Philip, who had become governor of Wisconsin, Ekern accepted his appointment as lieutenant governor, then ran for the United States Senate in 1938.

Ekern won the primary, but he was soundly beaten in the general election, as were most other Progressive candidates. It was his last attempt at public office, and, as always, he took the defeat calmly. The morning after the election, he left with Fisher on a Lutheran Brotherhood business trip. During the journey he became so involved in a discussion of insurance that not once did he mention his resounding defeat the day before.

A Belief in Hard Work

Ekern worked faithfully and incessantly, driving himself and those who worked with him. It was common for him to arrive at the office early in the morning, do a full day's work, then return in the evening to do more. He never viewed his labors as a burden, and he jokingly called work his hobby, business trips his vacations, and railroad sleepers and planes his sports. His devotion to activity never interfered with his health, and he was able to boast until late in his life that he had never spent a day sick in bed.

Legal work took him all over the country, and the more renowned he became, the more he traveled. "I made up my mind as a young man never to turn down an opportunity to be at a meeting of importance, to get together with interesting people," he once told Cecil Johnson, one of his law partners. "I think that helps me to become a better man, a more informed man."

Ekern's preferred choice of travel was the train. Associates said that he knew almost every engineer, brakeman, and conductor on the Milwaukee Railroad between Chicago and Madison, and he did not often sleep in a bed that was not rolling. When Ekern was in Minneapolis, he usually worked at the home office until just before the time his train departed. Such was his knowledge of the rails that he rarely had to look up a schedule as he hurried to the station. During political campaigns, Ekern traveled around the Wisconsin countryside by automobile. He did not like to drive, and the role of chauffeur fell to his daughter, Elsie.

At the office, when he wasn't on the road, Ekern was impulsive and disorganized and rarely followed an established work pattern. As his law office grew larger, he established rules of procedure for the office, then became the first to break them. He jumped from one unfinished project to another, immersing himself in detail, constantly tinkering and fixing. "Dad is a stickler for detail," Ekern's son George once told an associate. "He always does things his way. If you turned the Lord's Prayer over to him, he'd rewrite it." Yet Ekern's great mental abilities allowed him to get to the core of a problem almost immediately, and

Herman Ekern speaks from the stump during his campaign for United States Senator from Wisconsin in 1938. Ekern lost the election; it was the last time he ran for political office.

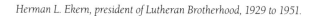

Herman L. Ekern, president of Lutheran Brotherhood, 1929 to 1951.

his eye for detail ensured that he rarely had to correct a mistake in his legal work.

Ekern had decided long ago that the best location for his law practice was in Chicago. His wife did not want to live there, so Ekern lived during the week with Johnson in a Chicago apartment next to the Circuit Court of Appeals, and commuted home to Madison on weekends. The trip became such a habit that Ekern developed a precise method of packing, one from which he never deviated. "You can get a lot of dirty clothes into a small suitcase if you do it right," he told an associate.

Although he enjoyed spending time with his family, he spent most of his waking hours working. Ekern believed that a man's first obligation was to support his family, so he was extremely careful with money. At the height of the depression, a group of Norwegian singers sent him a request for a hundred-dollar donation. He sent them ten dollars, with an acerbic

note attached commenting on their "extravagant idea of my liberality."

As Ekern grew older, he needed glasses. Rather than see an optometrist, he went to a dimestore, selected eyeglasses from a large bin, and tried them on until he found a pair that he could read with, then paid a dollar for it.

However, Ekern was generous with others, and he supported work that he believed in. He often loaned money to friends, relatives, and business associates, made substantial contributions to the Lutheran church and to Lutheran colleges, and contributed liberally to organizations such as the Salvation Army and the YMCA.

And when Lutheran Brotherhood was in financial straits during the depression, Ekern loaned the society several thousand dollars of his own money to keep it afloat.

The Final Years

Throughout the late 1940s, Ekern continued to exert considerable influence in the fiscal and philosophical affairs of Lutheran Brotherhood. Under his leadership, it had grown from a small fraternal society with less than $32 million insurance in force and only $1.7 million in assets to a major insurance group with $366 million insurance in force and $65 million in assets.

However, there was a sense among the younger directors and officers that Ekern, now in his mid-seventies, had become rigid in his thinking. As a result, they felt that Lutheran Brotherhood was not moving as fast as it could. The society must update its marketing methods and its products and push ahead into the modern age; otherwise, it might fall behind the rest of the insurance industry.

Ekern did not see it that way. His primary concern was that Lutheran Brotherhood remain fiscally stable, and he believed that providing reliable products and service to Lutherans was all the marketing plan the company needed. "I hope we never sell more than a billion dollars in insurance," he once told investment department employee Herb Mohr, "because then we'll lose the personal touch." The fragile nature of the society's fraternal tax-exempt status also colored his thinking. "We must not make waves and place our fraternal status in jeopardy," he once said. "Instead, let us be content with steady, natural growth."

The conflict came to a head when a new mortality table was proposed for Lutheran Brotherhood. The *Commissioners' 1941 Standard Ordinary (CSO) Table of Mortality* had become the standard of the insurance industry. The old table, the *American Experience Table*, had served Lutheran Brotherhood well over the years, but national mortality rates had improved dramatically, and almost everyone in the society thought it was time for a change. Only Ekern fought against the use of the new table. So strenuous was his opposition that one day he gave Fisher, his executive vice president, an ultimatum: Either support the old mortality table or resign. Ekern and Fisher postponed making a decision on the matter because the 1951 society convention was approaching. But Fisher, seeing the writing on the wall, lost no time in making arrangements for a new job.

The new table eventually was adopted over Ekern's objection. It was the first indication that the society was slowly slipping from his control. But other signs indicated that the society needed new direction. Because of his advancing age and declining health, which had worsened since his heart attack in 1942, Ekern found it more difficult to travel to Minneapolis and attend to details that he had previously handled with ease. The need for a full-time president who lived in the Twin Cities became increasingly obvious to several directors of the society.

By the opening of the 1951 convention, at which Ekern and Fisher were candidates for the board, it had become apparent to Ekern, as well. He had not campaigned for himself, for he had heard news that there was a movement in the society to elect younger leadership. When he looked out among the convention crowd, he recognized only a few of the delegates. He turned to Fisher. "Billy, who are all these strangers?" he asked. Fisher said he didn't know them.

"Then we're through," said Ekern.

He was right. Preus and Russell Matthias, a member of Ekern's Chicago law firm, were reelected to the board, and Harold Ingvaldson and Kelly Neprud were elected for the first time. Soon after the results of the voting were in, Ekern announced his resignation as president. Carl Granrud, a lawyer from Minneapolis who had served on the board since 1940, was named to replace him.

Ekern took the defeat, as he had taken so many triumphs, with equanimity. "Well," he said to Fisher as he was cleaning out his desk in the home office, "you can't win them all." He was warmed by the fact that Preus, his good friend, had stood by him throughout the convention. He was also consoled by the kind words that followed the convention, for no one ever forgot that the society owed its success, even its existence, to Ekern.

"Lutheran Brotherhood was one of the dreams that Herman Ekern made real," said the August 1951 issue of *The BOND*. "Others have shared with him in the burdens of management and are deserving of high praise also for their contributions, but the chief credit must go to Mr. Ekern. More than any other one man, he personifies Lutheran Brotherhood."

Ekern dreaded the thought of complete retirement, and he continued to offer much valuable advice to the directors and officers. He relinquished his law partnership with Erwin Meyers and entered into a smaller practice with his son, George. He continued to contribute to the Progressive party, even though most of its former members had since become Democrats, but mellowed to the point that he once sported a button supporting Adlai Stevenson, the Democratic candidate, during the 1952 presidential campaign.

As Ekern approached his eightieth birthday, he traveled infrequently, spending most of his time in Madison, where, in his downstairs bedroom, he studied the history of the Norwegian language in America and read the biography of his political hero, Robert M. LaFollette.

There, on December 4, 1954, Ekern died quietly of a stroke.

A Bolder Dream

Led through the darkness by a wandering ray of light, Carl Granrud stepped carefully from the makeshift stairway onto the fourth floor of the new Lutheran Brotherhood building under construction. Granrud, the president of Lutheran Brotherhood, slowly swept the floor with the beam of his flashlight. The open floor, scattered with boards and tools, was surrounded only by steel girders and the flickering lights of downtown Minneapolis. The August night was humid, but a cool breeze curled around the girders.

Granrud's interest in the new structure was compelling. No detail was unimportant to him. Standing in the rubble of construction, one hand clutching the flashlight, the other thrust behind his back, he possessed a Churchillian manner: proud, portly, a man for his time. A broad forehead and short-cropped hair stood out plainly above ruddy cheeks and a gray stamp of a mustache. Nearly sixty years old, Granrud wore his clothes indifferently; his customary gray suit coat and pants were invariably rumpled, and his red tie askew.

The imposing beams and girders that signaled the construction of Lutheran Brotherhood's new home office in 1956 also heralded Carl Granrud's intense desire to expand the society's previously limited horizons.

As he stepped lightly through the debris, Granrud motioned his visitor, T. H. Mikkelson, a general agent from Fergus Falls, Minnesota, over to the edge of the floor. They looked down at the black and silent streets below. "Well," said Granrud optimistically, "what do you think?" Mikkelson took a few steps back. "I think we're going to break our necks." Granrud ignored the comment. "Come over here. I want to show you something," he commanded. "We're putting the actuarial department right here, a row of desks along here, and the offices over there. It's going to be first class." A thin smile crept over his face. "Because you know, Micky, it's important to keep our actuaries happy. They're a nervous bunch. You and I know that two plus two equals four, and they know that two plus two equals four, but they worry about it." Mikkelson shook his head and groaned good-naturedly. The president, despite his executive rank and sophistication, had a weakness for corny jokes.

For the next half hour, Granrud and his flashlight escorted Mikkelson to every floor, every corner of the skeleton structure, explaining what department would go where and why. When they were finished, Granrud turned to his friend. "Well, what do you think of this place?" he asked for the second time. Mikkelson paused. "It's beautiful," he said. "This building is going to do something for the society, Mr. Granrud. People are going to start paying attention to us for a change." Granrud nodded. "You can count on that," he said quietly.

Greeting the Future

By 1951, when the board elected Carl F. Granrud the new president of Lutheran Brotherhood, the society had grown from a regional insurance operation into one of the country's largest fraternal societies. The economy was robust, insurance in force had increased to $366 million, and assets now stood at nearly $65 million. But despite its financial success, the society was not well-known outside Midwestern Lutheran circles, even in downtown Minneapolis. That had been fine with Herman Ekern, whose insistence on fiscal stability had enabled the society to survive and eventually flourish on a modest scale. However, anonymity did not sit well with some other leaders of the society, particularly Carl Granrud. What use was a good business reputation if only a few people knew who you were? At the time, the society was licensed to sell insurance in twenty-nine states; he wanted to sell in all fifty.

The idea of Lutheran Brotherhood having its own home office building was particularly intriguing to Granrud. The society had contentedly occupied a few floors in the Pillsbury Building for two decades. It was a good location, quiet and subdued, an unostentatious office in which a fraternal insurance society could grow steadily and maintain a low profile. That pleased most Lutheran Brotherhood traditionalists. For years, the society had diligently lobbied against legislative attempts to revoke the tax-exempt status of fraternals. In their opinion, if Lutheran Brotherhood became too large, too successful—too flashy—it might be providing opponents with ammunition that could lead to the revocation of that status.

Others disagreed. A new home office, they argued, would aid the society's fraternal mission by giving it a more recognizable identity. The more people knew about Lutheran Brotherhood, the more insurance would be sold, and the more insurance sold, the more fraternal benefits issued to members. The building itself could even be classified as a benefit,

since it belonged to the members of the society and could be used to host a variety of church events and meetings. Besides, a new building was a necessity because the society was growing too fast and the present home office site was becoming too crowded.

In 1952, Lutheran Brotherhood announced plans for a new home office building at the corner of Seventh Street and Second Avenue in downtown Minneapolis. The society had owned the property for several years, thanks to Harold Ingvaldson, the society's investment manager, who had convinced the board to buy it in 1945. The half-block site was occupied by Lee's Broiler, one of the most popular restaurants in the city. It took a lot of nerve to tear down Lee's Broiler, many employees said, because almost everybody ate there. This new building had better be something special.

The original plans called for a two-story structure, costing $1.5 million, that would do more than house the home office staff. "It will be in one sense a monument to the Lutheran pioneers in America," said *The BOND* magazine in June 1952. "The Luther Library, which will be included in the new building, will be a living and working testament to the free spirit of Martin Luther in what is hoped to be the most complete Luther library in the world. Students and pastors from all over will find the library a great asset in their studies."

By 1953, Perkins and Will of Chicago, the building's architects, had decided that the structure should be four stories high, the first floor of stone and the top three of glass. Over the next two years, the optimistic Granrud convinced the board that two more stories should be added to the building. More than anyone else at Lutheran Brotherhood, the president took personal charge of the project. Assisted by his law partner, Gretchen Pracht, whom he had hired to head the society's public relations and advertising department, Granrud decided on the layout of the building, the choice of colors and flooring, even the bathroom fixtures. He often took friends and society workers on tours of the construction site. In Granrud's mind, the new building would become a permanent billboard for Lutheran Brotherhood, a symbol of the society's acceptance as a major presence in the Twin Cities.

The building rose rapidly during 1955 and 1956, as did its price. By the time construction was completed, total building costs amounted to $2.5 million. Granrud kept a close watch on its progress, as he did on those who shared his enthusiasm for the project. Ken Severud, who recently had been named the society's corporate secretary, made regular visits to the building during construction. One day he received a phone call from Granrud. "I see you over at that building every noon when I go over there," the president said. "What do you think of it?" Severud said, "I think it's going to be great." Granrud thought for a moment. "Well, you seem to be the only one interested in it, so you are hereby appointed building manager." Severud gasped. "But I don't know anything about building management," he said. "Nonsense!" Granrud retorted. "You can learn how to manage a building just like you've learned everything else in this job!" And with that, Severud assumed the duties of building manager, a job he held for many years.

Thousands attended an open house at the new structure in May 1956. Two months later, home office employees, district representatives, and officers joined church and community leaders for the dedication of the new Lutheran Brotherhood headquarters. The building's foundation stone was hewn from the rock of the mountain on which stands the ancient Castle of the Wartburg, where Martin Luther lived for a time. The stone was laid by Dr. Gustav M. Bruce, one of the church leaders who had agreed to support the establishment of Lutheran Brotherhood nearly four decades before.

As Granrud and other leaders had envisioned, the new building did much to bring the society into the limelight. Downtown visitors found it hard to miss the striking blue and green glass panels that covered the structure, bringing "the outdoors indoors," as Granrud liked to say. More important to those employees who had suffered through Minnesota's humid summers, recovering documents that had blown through open windows in the old Pillsbury Building, the new home office was air conditioned.

The new building received national acclaim as a notable example of contemporary architecture. *Architectural Record* magazine carried a long article on the new building, and a University of Minnesota architecture professor called it one of the ten best structures in Minneapolis. The building also played an important symbolic role in revitalizing new construction in downtown Minneapolis, for it was the first new major building erected there in a quarter of a century. As such, the green building became a center of community activity. The sixth floor was leased to the Minneapolis Chamber of Commerce, the Downtown Council, and other civic organizations.

The structure also helped Lutheran Brotherhood to serve the church. The Martin Luther Library on the ground floor contained many works by Luther, books written about him, and historic relics from his lifetime and homeland. One wall featured a stained glass window portraying Luther nailing ninety-five theses to the door of the Wittenberg Church, the event that precipitated the Reformation.

The library and the facilities directly below it came to be known as the Lutheran Center, including an auditorium seating nearly three hundred. The facilities became widely used by churches, colleges, and other Lutheran organizations, and played a significant role in the 1957 Lutheran World Federation assembly. Following the assembly, Bishop Hans Lilje, the outgoing president of the Lutheran World Federation, dedicated a symbolic cross made of mosaic tiles set in silver, the tiles expressing Christ's words, "I am the Way, and the Truth, and the Life."

Outside was a sunken garden and terrace. Granrud loved that garden as if it were his own, and he became an expert on the flowers that were planted there each spring. Almost all the flowers were red, Granrud's favorite color. A well-meaning employee once planted white and pink petunias among the red flowers in the garden. Granrud was horrified when he saw them, and he immediately ordered the offending flowers replaced with red ones.

Not averse to an occasional deviation from his orderly world, Granrud did eventually allow peacocks to be placed in the home office garden, which developed into a Minneapolis showpiece and became the site of many ceremonies and civic functions. On one occasion, the archbishop of the Church of Sweden planted a golden locust tree in what, until that point, had been exclusively Norwegian soil. It

A Lasting Foundation

The evolution of the Lutheran Brotherhood home office. Top left: Seventh Street and Second Avenue in downtown Minneapolis in 1954. At center is Lee's Broiler, the popular restaurant that was torn down to make room for the home office. Inset and middle left: Ground was broken for the new home office in 1954. Present at the ceremonies were Directors J. A. Aasgaard, Carl Granrud, and J.A.O. Preus. Bottom left: Workmen lay the foundation of the home office.

Top right: Construction of Lutheran Brotherhood's new headquarters continued through 1955. Middle right: The glass exterior of the six-story home office is added to the frame. Lower right: The majestic new home office, completed in 1956, was the first new major structure erected in downtown Minneapolis in more than two decades. The executive wing is at right.

A Common Bond

As the society grew through the 1950s and 1960s, the green building eventually became so crowded that the board decided to add two floors to the top of the structure. Construction was done in 1969. Inset: The completed eight-story building.

was a major public relations coup for Granrud, who constantly strove to bring together different ethnic branches of the Lutheran church into Lutheran Brotherhood. After the planting ceremony, Granrud let it be known to his employees that under no circumstances was the archbishop's tree to die.

Selling at Home

Besides adding color to Lutheran Brotherhood's image, the green building, as it came to be known in the Twin Cities, aided the society's efforts to gain more members. Granrud, and especially Pracht, understood the importance of image to a fraternal insurance organization. They also knew that it was crucial for the organization to build a lasting identity in the Twin Cities to gain recognition throughout the country. Lutheran Brotherhood couldn't very well build a name among Lutherans in faraway metropolitan centers like Philadelphia or Los Angeles if it was not first appreciated in its home city. By promoting the fraternal organization at home through increased local newspaper, radio, and television coverage, the society began to sell itself more effectively throughout the United States.

Eventually, Lutheran Brotherhood began to advertise in several national secular magazines. The society had always been a regular advertiser in major national Lutheran publications, and that affiliation continued to be strong. But a survey of several thousand Lutheran Brotherhood members by the society's advertising agency, Campbell-Mithun, Inc. of Minneapolis, showed that only about half received Lutheran publications, and even fewer read them. The same survey determined that more of these members subscribed to secular magazines than to Lutheran publications.

On the assumption that these members represented a typical cross-section of all Lutherans, the society decided to accept Campbell-Mithun's recommendation that it begin advertising in *LIFE* and *Reader's Digest*, the most popular secular magazines. The move, Granrud told his representatives, "would help to bring the Lutheran Brotherhood story into Lutheran homes that otherwise might not get to know about it."

Clearly, times had changed since the days when

Lutheran Brotherhood depended on word-of-mouth for its advertising, and when sales representatives were given little more than a rate book and a peptalk. By the early 1960s, the society was furnishing district representatives with a print advertising kit and professionally produced radio commercials. Hundreds of Lutheran Brotherhood billboards were erected at the edges of highways across the country. The society's new attention to advertising did not come cheaply, Granrud often noted, but he thought the investment worthwhile. "Insurance advertisements usually do not attract inquiries in any great volume, because of the nature of the business," he told the society's district representatives in their monthly sales magazine, *The Leader*, "but they do pre-sell the prospect so that when you send him a direct mail letter or ring his doorbell, he will have a pretty good idea of what Lutheran Brotherhood is and does."

The agency department began to develop a growing number of sales aids during the 1950s. Two of the most important were the *Money Plan Book*, which, for the first time, clearly explained to clients what they received when they purchased an insurance contract, and a sales filmstrip that told the fraternal story of Lutheran Brotherhood. Both ideas

originally had been developed by Woody Langhaug, a general agent in Chicago. Langhaug's ideas were refined and updated by the agency department and were put to use throughout the field force. By introducing the filmstrip in 1955, the society became one of the first insurance organizations in the country to produce its own personalized filmstrip.

Two other sales tools played a significant role in the early 1960s: direct mail and the Ana-Tronic computer program. Direct mail, which long had been used by a few top district representatives, allowed the field to reach many more people by mail than it could ever hope to visit in person. The Ana-Tronic program electronically determined how much insurance the prospect needed and illustrated different plans that would fill those needs. The analysis was made by Lutheran Brotherhood's two electronic brains. The IBM computers operated with punch cards and took only a few minutes to process each analysis. The system was extremely advanced for the times, especially since few insurance companies even used computers.

Besides improving sales tools, the society placed a high priority on educating its district representatives. "It is becoming increasingly clear that if anyone is to achieve real success and make a significant

Above: The home office lobby. The mosaic Luther Seal, behind the reception desk, was created by Cyrus Running, art professor at Concordia College, Moorhead, Minnesota.

Below: Paper bags played an important role in the move from the Pillsbury Building to the new home office in 1956. A few of the home office employees involved were: Virginia Johnson, far left; Eleanor Peterson, third from left; Lee Witso, sixth from left; Lenore Anderson, seventh from left; Gen Stivers, ninth from left; Bertilla Wald, tenth from left; Marlys Johnson, sixth from right; Bob Sater, second from right; and Cliff Thompson, far right.

contribution in life—regardless of vocation—he must continue his education throughout his entire career," Granrud told Lutheran Brotherhood's field personnel. "Our business is becoming increasingly complex. More and more members are turning to our field force for assistance on estate planning and tax matters, to list just two subjects. They have every right to expect competent advice. Unless you can provide this advice, they will seek it elsewhere."

To ensure that prospective members did not go elsewhere, Lutheran Brotherhood's agency department began formal education courses. In 1949, the society had appointed Don Lommen, a former high school superintendent and later general agent in Bismarck, North Dakota, as its first director of education. One of the first people to obtain the Chartered Life Underwriter (CLU) degree at Lutheran Brotherhood, Lommen started the society's first school for district representatives in 1955.

After a short time in the field, new district representatives were brought to the home office for a week of intensive schooling. Several years later, Lutheran Brotherhood instituted a management program for general agents. All general agents were to attend the school for one week of classes designed to teach them how to better recruit and train their representatives, keep up agency morale, conduct agency meetings, produce more effective bulletins, and run an efficient office.

In addition to its own education programs, Lutheran Brotherhood began to require field personnel to take as many outside education courses as possible, such as Fraternal Insurance Counselor (FIC), Life Underwriters Training Counsel (LUTC), or Chartered Life Underwriter (CLU). The society's annual sales conventions allowed its representatives to rub shoulders with insurance experts, and field personnel took home ideas from the convention that helped them to improve their own sales techniques.

The results of Lutheran Brotherhood's drive to make its name known (the new home office, increased advertising, effective sales aids, educational courses) were impressive. In 1951, Lutheran Brotherhood had $366 million worth of insurance in force. Eight years later, the society passed the billion dollar mark in insurance in force, joining Northwestern

National Life and Minnesota Mutual as the only Minnesota-based insurance organizations to top that mark. Granrud told the *Minneapolis Sunday Tribune* that he saw no end in sight for the society's growth. "We have about 250,000 members," he said, "and there are about seven million Lutherans in the United States."

Granrud aimed to make every one of them a member of Lutheran Brotherhood.

A Man in Charge

Carl Granrud raised a few eyebrows in 1940 when he was asked to join the board of directors of Lutheran Brotherhood. "I've been on top of this organization from the day it was conceived," he often quipped, and it was true. On June 9, 1917, when thousands of Norwegian Lutherans gathered in the St. Paul Auditorium to organize Luther Union, the St. Olaf College choir had been invited to sing on stage. Sitting in the top row of the choir was a young student named Carl Granrud.

Granrud was used to being on top. His vision and talents merited it; his pride and energy demanded it. He enjoyed the responsibilities of leadership, and he reveled in the many extra hours of work that his position required. Granrud's years as president and, subsequently, as chairman of Lutheran Brotherhood paralleled the society's rise from a regional fraternal society to a national fraternal insurance organization.

Granrud came from a family that valued learning. Both his parents had served on the faculty of St. Olaf College. His father, John, was born in Norway and came to Minnesota when he was two years old. He became a professor of Latin, an expert in the works of Cicero, Horace, and Livy. He was well-known throughout the academic community as a lecturer and writer on Roman architecture, art, and civilization. After leaving St. Olaf, the elder Granrud joined the faculty of Luther College in Decorah, Iowa, and it was there that Carl Fritiof Granrud was born in 1896. Four years later, his father began a long tenure as a professor at the University of Minnesota. The family moved into a house near the university. It was Carl Granrud's home for most of his life.

Carl Granrud graduated from St. Olaf in 1918 and the University of Minnesota College of Law in 1921. For several years, he practiced law with Judge Lars O. LaRue, who was an instructor at the Minnesota College of Law, and served as credit manager and attorney for Thompson Yards, a large lumber supply firm. In 1931, he became general counsel for St. Olaf College and the Evangelical Lutheran Church, which was the beginning of his intimate and occasionally tempestuous associations with several Lutheran church organizations. Nine years later, he was asked to join the board of directors of Lutheran Brotherhood.

By 1951, most leaders of the society recognized the need for younger leadership, and the convention vote validated that opinion. Full of energy and new ideas and only fifty-five years of age, Granrud seemed the logical choice to succeed Herman Ekern as president of Lutheran Brotherhood. Some believed he campaigned for the job, others said he received it by default. In either case, the board elected him to that post following the convention.

As president, Granrud usually could be found in

The expansive Martin Luther Library on the first floor of the new home office. At left is the Reformation Window, a portrayal in stained glass of Luther and his times, by artist Conrad Pickel.

one of two places: at the law offices that he shared with Gretchen Pracht and Arthur Wangaard in the National Building on Second Avenue, or at his more lavish quarters one block south in the new Lutheran Brotherhood home office. In either location, it was clear to the society's employees that he was firmly in command.

Granrud demanded loyalty from his employees and insisted on results. He believed that an alert and anxious employee was a productive employee, and he delighted in keeping them off-balance with a deliberate mix of humor, intimidation, and sarcasm. Like a captain inspecting his ship, he paced through the home office a few times each day, hands clasped behind his back, one or two assistants following at a respectful distance. Granrud was much harder on his officers than on their subordinates, and he enjoyed marching into a department, taking a seat where he easily could be seen by the officers, and

talking for an hour or so with workers in the department. All the while, the officers would sit nervously, wondering what Granrud was saying.

During one tour, Granrud noticed that a few employees were nodding and yawning, and a barbed memo was quickly sent to all the department heads. "It should be unnecessary to point out that the offices have not been built for sleeping quarters," the memo read, "and anyone requiring any rest periods under doctors orders should arrange this matter with the Personnel Department so that proper provision can be made in a manner that is not objectionable."

Granrud was particularly strict about keeping the home office immaculate. Dust was anathema to him, and he carefully inspected for dirt each day during his rounds. Granrud also insisted that all desktops be kept clean. Five of the building's six floors were glass, he reminded his employees, and all of downtown Minneapolis could see inside. To make his point, he occasionally searched the office after 5 P.M. If he found a messy desktop, the entire contents were tossed into the wastebasket. The home office employees quickly learned to keep one desk drawer empty, so that they could place all loose papers into it at closing time.

When Granrud was not wandering about the home office, he was in one of his two offices, leaning back in his swivel chair, feet on the desk and arms resting one on top of the other on his ample belly. Fixing his visitor with a quizzical squint, his eyebrows would arch and the fingers of one hand would begin to tap stiffly, the little finger slightly arched. Then he would hold forth on any of a number of topics, each one individually tailored to the listener. If the visitor were an actuary, Granrud would laughingly suggest that actuaries could not possibly be worth all the money they were paid. If the visitor were a district representative, he would expound on what he always seemed to regard as the desperate state of affairs in the agency department.

Around the home office, when Granrud talked, people listened. It seemed to many employees that Granrud invited workers into his quarters simply to act as an audience for his wry and usually sarcastic commentary. One day he was talking to Don Brostrom, who was then the assistant vice president of the public relations and advertising department, about some business. When they finished their discussion, Brostrom got up from his chair to go back to work. "Sit down!" Granrud roared. "You don't have anything to do." Then he launched into a lengthy monologue about the state of the society.

Granrud's ability to discourse on a variety of topics was matched only by his skill as an interrogator. He insisted on interviewing all prospective male employees, and shrewdly sized up their ability to act under pressure by asking them seemingly pointless questions. Wayne Hellbusch, an underwriter, had prepared himself for what he thought would be a formal interview, but he was taken aback by Granrud's first question: "Do you like to sing?" Singing happened to be one of Hellbusch's favorite hobbies, and he spent the rest of the interview anxiously wondering what else Granrud knew about him.

Apparently innocuous questions also helped Granrud to keep his ear tuned to happenings in the home office. He often called employees into his office merely to ask, "How are things going?" If the response was affirmative, Granrud followed by quizzing the employee about his or her immediate superior. His purpose was less to find out about the superior than it was to ascertain the employee's degree of loyalty. Differing opinions were usually fine with Granrud, but disloyalty was not, and he always maintained an accurate mental file of who supported whom at the home office.

Granrud had other proven methods of obtaining information. Many nights after work, he retired to the Minneapolis Club for a meal and several games of whist with one or more employees. The group began the evening with drinks. Granrud favored scotch and soda, and an extra bottle of soda always sat next to his glass. When his guests ordered another drink, Granrud would fill his glass with more soda. After his guests had loosened up with a few drinks, he would begin his innocent questions: "Well, now, are you having any trouble with the agency department?" If they were, they usually were in the mood to make their opinions known.

The president rarely needed to write down information. He was capable of remembering entire conversations that had taken place several years before, and his ability to remember names, especially those of the wives and children of his employees, ingratiated him with the field force at sales conventions. He worked the crowds there like a master politician, for Granrud understood that the support of the general agents and field force was the key to power within Lutheran Brotherhood.

Granrud's autocratic management style unnerved some employees, yet even those who were somewhat afraid of him respected his abilities and his commitment to the society. They enjoyed his company, his corny jokes, his hearty laugh. Even when he was chewing them out, they felt that he was at least paying close attention to their work. Like a good football coach, Granrud demanded more from his employees than even he felt they could deliver. In the process, he taught his people that they could perform better than they thought they could. He expected excellence, and he took pride in those who achieved it.

Granrud was also an extremely loyal man, and he took care of his employees when they were in trouble. One icy night in Virginia, a general agent was severely injured in an accident and could not work for some time. In those days, few people had medical coverage and disability income, yet Granrud made sure that the agent, who had four young children, continued to receive a regular income and that his medical bills were paid.

If Granrud was sometimes dictatorial with his

President Carl Granrud smiles enthusiastically as he receives over one million dollars in applications written on his birthday. Also pictured are Alice Engstrand, left, and Marilyn Benson.

employees, it was because he loved Lutheran Brotherhood, and he demanded that his employees love it, too. After hiring Mike DeMann, a corporate psychologist, as a society consultant, Granrud sent a district representative to see him. "Mr. Granrud wants you to buy an insurance contract with Lutheran Brotherhood," DeMann was told. "I'm not a Lutheran," DeMann said. "I'm an Episcopalian." The representative said, "That's okay. You work for a Lutheran organization, so the bylaws say it's all right." DeMann explained to the representative that he viewed the request as an infringement on his rights. "You tell Mr. Granrud that I don't respond to that sort of thing," he said.

A few months later, during a meeting with Granrud, the president explained to DeMann why he felt it important that the consultant buy a contract. "I have a son who works with a large corporation," Granrud said. "I would not allow my son to work for that corporation without buying stock in it, because he is then a part of that corporation. I don't care if you buy the smallest contract we have. I just want you to be a part of Lutheran Brotherhood." Finally convinced of Granrud's motives, DeMann bought a contract.

If the home office was sometimes a stressful place to work under Granrud, it was also an interesting place, for he possessed a quick wit that was as entertaining as it was biting. Employees could count on almost one new Granrud story per week, and his humor became the stuff of legend around the watercoolers.

Most comments were directed at his own employees. Russ Smith, a regional agency superintendent, encountered Granrud in the parking lot one day. "I see you're growing a mustache," observed Granrud. "Yes," Smith answered sheepishly. "I'm trying." Granrud quickly inspected Smith's upper lip, then arched one eyebrow. "Well," he said, "I must say that it seems to be adding an air of excitement to an otherwise drab face."

Dick Nelson, then the agency secretary, was once called into Granrud's office after making a minor error. The president's reprimand included a standard line that he quoted to nearly all employees. "You know, Nelson, being president, I get a chance to make a lot more mistakes than you do. Of course, being president, I don't have to live with them if you happen to be one of them."

No employee was immune to Granrud's barbs, not even away from the office. At one sales conference, Granrud made a late-night tour of the hotel nightclub, the dance floor of which was alive with gyrating dancers. One of them was a Lutheran Brotherhood employee. Granrud later took the employee aside and advised him that he did not approve. "I don't think you should be dancing any dance that didn't originate in North Dakota," he counseled.

A Proud Norwegian

Carl Granrud was a complicated leader, for there were two sides to everything about the man. He proudly shepherded the construction of a beautiful home office building, one in which the directors' plumbing fixtures were plated with gold. He instituted sales conventions for his field personnel in exotic locales, yet he was frugal in many other areas. He paid his officers mileage because it was cheaper than furnishing them with company cars, and accepted only a modest salary so that he would be justified in keeping the salaries of the other employees low.

Money was not what drove Granrud. His own rumpled wardrobe attested to that. He wore some of his suits so long that they literally came apart at the seams. Granrud once forgot to take his wallet to a convention because it was still in the pants that were hanging over the back of a chair at his home. "That's the trouble with having more than one pair of pants," he grumbled. "You forget your wallet."

Granrud enjoyed his power and worked hard to ensure his hold on the presidency of the society. Yet he was in no rush to push the company's elder statesmen. He showed only respect, both publicly and privately, for his predecessor, Herman Ekern. He revered the chairman of the board, J. A. O. Preus, for the two were cut from the same cloth. During a tour of the home office, he escorted a district representative through the new chairman's quarters. The representative eyed Preus's chair and said, "Have a seat, Mr. Granrud, just to see how it feels." Granrud was horrified. "I can't sit in that chair," he said. "That's for the chairman. I won't sit in that chair until I'm properly elected."

Much of his respect for Ekern and Preus was based on his own ethnic pride. Granrud grew up in Minneapolis, an area heavily populated with Scandinavians, and he was mindful of how the city seemed to be dominated by the likes of Daytons and Pillsburys—community leaders whose bloodlines ran to the British Isles. "But what these people didn't realize," Granrud was fond of observing, "was that, in time, we Norwegians would outbreed them."

In Granrud's eyes, Lutheran Brotherhood, even when measured by the modest accomplishments of its earliest years, was a testament to Nordic acumen. He and Pracht made sure that the society's successes, and those who were responsible for them, were mentioned in the local paper. He made a habit of introducing his general agents and officers at news conferences and community events. Granrud was a strong advocate for the field, and if

he occasionally grumbled about all the money they made, he was also proud that they were doing so well for the society.

In fact, much of Granrud's life was spent with his employees. Many home office workers and field personnel, regardless of rank, enjoyed dinner or lunch with him at the Minneapolis Athletic Club or the Minneapolis Club. On any afternoon, Lutheran Brotherhood's officers were subject to a call from Granrud. "Can you work tonight?" he would ask, which meant, "Can you have dinner and play whist?" Whist was Granrud's primary release. He played it with employees almost every night, chatting all the while about society and insurance matters. Some of the young officers learned nearly as much about the society's business during games of whist as they did at work.

For all the time they spent with him, for all his belief that the society was a large family, only a few employees knew the private Granrud, because he rarely involved his own family in society affairs. Few employees knew Mrs. Granrud, a quiet, gracious woman who almost never appeared at society functions. An unfortunate employee once invited Mrs. Granrud to a sales convention. She accepted, unbeknown to her husband, who was furious when he discovered that she was packing her bags for the event. He gave the individual a biting rebuke, and Mrs. Granrud continued to be conspicuously absent from society affairs.

One of the few men in Lutheran Brotherhood who knew Granrud well was Harold Hoel, the popular director of agencies. Granrud loved to rib his friend, who was famed for his emotionally charged sales oratories, and he delighted in telling how, at one agency meeting, the sales representatives in the front row were hurriedly taking notes during a fiery Hoel speech. "They weren't taking notes at all," said Granrud. "What they were actually doing was writing down their predictions of how soon Hoel would pass out from the excitement."

Though Hoel was the subject of many of his jokes, Granrud drew sustenance from his friend. He often showed up at the Hoel house late at night, long after the family had gone to bed. The doorbell would ring, Hoel would drag himself out of bed and there, in the doorway, would stand Granrud, smiling and ready to talk. They would make scrambled eggs and toast, play whist, and discuss insurance into the early morning. "Harold, nobody needs more than five hours of sleep a night, anyway," the president often said.

Hoel died in 1961. A few days after his funeral, Granrud was playing whist with general agents at the Minneapolis Athletic Club. Granrud was extremely irritable that night, calling his dinner partners "stupid" or "idiot" with regularity. "Don't get on me, Carl," snapped Walt Cover, a general agent from Appleton, Wisconsin (and one of the few employees who called the president by his first name). Then his voice softened. "I know what your problem is," he said. "It's Harold, isn't it?" Granrud nodded, and tears welled in his eyes.

It was the only time his men had ever seen him cry.

The Civil War

By 1958, the only Lutheran Brotherhood officer whose power rivaled that of Granrud was Kelly Neprud, the vice president of agencies. Neprud, sixty-six, was still a favorite of the general agents and field force, a charismatic leader who massaged their egos, balanced their demands, and lifted their spirits with equal skill. He had assembled and trained the society's first cadre of agents, and had energetically steered the field force on its present successful course. A director since 1951, Neprud also had been a major contributor in the plotting of society strategy for three decades. His exemplary record, plus the fact that he had been with Lutheran Brotherhood longer than any other employee, made the beloved Neprud the logical choice for the title that frequently was bestowed on him at society gatherings: Mr. Lutheran Brotherhood.

However, Neprud had been increasingly absent from work because of illness. In August 1958, Granrud issued a memo to the department heads and members of the agency department. "Due to the prolonged absence and disability of our Director of Agencies, the President will be in charge of the Agency Department," the memo read. "Regular meetings of the agency staff will be called to take care of the department's business." Many employees were privately shocked. To them, Granrud's move seemed a thinly disguised attempt to gain more managerial power. Neprud's sin was not that he missed work, they claimed, but that he was simply too popular with the field to suit the president, who coveted that popularity.

The first major showdown between Granrud and Neprud took place three months later, when several top members of Lutheran Brotherhood's agency in Madison, Wisconsin, including Herb Mullen, the society's leading producer, threatened to quit unless their general agent, Art Koenig, resigned. After a series of talks failed to rectify the situation, Neprud finally decided to ask Koenig to resign and become a writing agent. When Granrud heard about Neprud's decision through Harold Hoel, he was furious. "We can't have our agents telling us who we can hire and who we can't!" he roared. "You get Koenig back on the phone and tell him to stay put. He's still general agent until I say he isn't!" From that time on, Granrud made all the major agency decisions.

The final blow to Neprud came in January 1959, when the board, by a 7 to 5 vote, denied his request for another year as vice president and director of agencies. Neprud had just turned sixty-seven, the majority noted, and his position twice had been extended beyond the society's normal retirement age of sixty-five. It seemed that Neprud was falling into the same trap that so many business leaders, even the humble Ekern (whom Neprud had played a part in retiring) had fallen. He was attempting to hold onto his considerable power by refusing to retire.

Yet even those who conceded that it might be time for Neprud to step down were displeased with the rough manner in which he had been treated. They felt that a man who had given so much to the society deserved better than a brusque farewell, and they began to grumble about Granrud's heavy-handed treatment of Neprud. The opposition made itself known that spring at the Balmoral Hotel in Miami, the site of Lutheran Brotherhood's annual sales conference. Almost immediately upon their arrival, district representatives were pulled aside by Neprud's supporters and given quiet lectures about Granrud's alleged misdeeds, while across the same room, Granrud's boosters were huddled with other sales representatives, giving them their side of the story. In one private meeting of general agents, the atmosphere became so heated with arguments for and against Granrud that one general agent, upset about the apparent lack of brotherly love, dropped to his knees and began praying loudly. At a retirement dinner for Neprud, with Granrud in attendance, several general agents made public their disapproval of Neprud's ouster. "We're supposed to think that Kelly retired on his own," said one. "But we know better and we don't approve of it."

If Granrud had expected a resounding vote of confidence at the Balmoral, he was disappointed. But he at least had learned the identities of those who were criticizing him, one of whom was Herb Johnson, the society's superintendent of agencies. On Monday morning, after returning from the sales convention, Johnson walked into his office and found Granrud waiting for him. "That was a nice show you put on in Miami," Granrud said angrily. "I want your resignation before the day is over." The next day, Granrud also fired Johnson's assistant, Bill Lundquist.

The news of the firings spread like wildfire throughout the home office and the field and inflamed Granrud's critics. How dare Granrud fire two capable employees like Herb Johnson and Bill Lundquist merely because they had criticized him! Did they not have the right to speak their minds without fear of retribution? Was not Lutheran Brotherhood a fraternal society in which free speech was guaranteed and all members were entitled to a voice?

Others, less zealous, saw the situation differently. Yes, they admitted, Granrud could be harsh, but he was the boss. If you publicly criticize the boss or actively campaign against the boss, the result will very likely be the same at any other company, organization, or fraternal society: you will be fired. After all, how can management expect to run an effective insurance operation if its own employees are working against it?

Those essentially were the issues. Critics believed that Granrud was abusing his managerial power by pushing out Neprud, a potential rival, and then arbitrarily firing anyone who disagreed with the move. Granrud's supporters believed that the president was maintaining necessary order. Lutheran Brotherhood ultimately became polarized into two distinct camps, even on the board. Seven directors supported Granrud, and five opposed him. On the pro-Granrud side were Preus, the chairman of the board; Harold A. Smith, Arthur O. Lee, Gordon Bubolz, Dreng Bjornaraa, R. H. Gerberding, and Granrud. On the anti-Granrud side were Randolph E. Haugan, Russell Matthias, J. A. Aasgaard, Thurman G. Overson, and Neprud.

The split between Granrud and Haugan, the influential chief of the Augsburg Publishing House, was big news in Lutheran circles, for the two had long been the best of friends, so close that their families occasionally spent Christmas together. Like Granrud, Haugan was a powerful and strong-willed leader. Some said that from his secluded office tucked away in the recesses of Augsburg, the pipe-smoking Haugan quietly ran the church. True or not, there was little doubt that he was at least influential, because as the manager of Augsburg, he oversaw all the publications of the Evangelical Lutheran Church.

Haugan and Granrud had much in common. They were both protégés of J. A. Aasgaard, the dynamic leader of the old Norwegian Lutheran Church, who, it was said, had built that organization's successor, the Evangelical Lutheran Church, by making Americans out of Norwegians. Granrud and Haugan were among the leaders of their Norwegian-American generation, men who built things that endured. They were enormously interested in the church and in its institutions, and they put in many hours together on the boards of St. Olaf College, Fairview Hospital, and Lutheran Brotherhood. Such was their collective power that they were known as "The Gold Dust Twins," for whenever they focused their efforts on a single goal, it was inevitably achieved. In 1951, when the board of Lutheran Brotherhood had been deciding on a new president, Granrud campaigned for his friend. But Haugan did not want to give up his duties at Augsburg, so he

The directors of Lutheran Brotherhood, front row, from left: Gordon A. Bubolz, J.K. Jensen, Herman L. Ekern, J.A.O. Preus, Carl F. Granrud, Dr. J.A. Aasgaard. Second row: Russell H. Matthias, Dreng Bjornaraa, Arthur O. Lee, N. Kelly Neprud, Randolph E. Haugan, and Harold A. Smith. Photo taken May 1954.

engineered Granrud's election to the post.

The close relationship between Haugan and Granrud continued for a few years at Lutheran Brotherhood, until Granrud began to rely more heavily on the advice of his law partner, Gretchen Pracht. Haugan saw his own influence slipping away, and he increasingly began to question Granrud's judgment on society matters. For example, he privately opposed the construction of the green building, for he thought it too conspicuous and flamboyant for a fraternal organization so closely aligned with the church. Granrud's handling of Neprud, as well as Johnson and Lundquist, confirmed in Haugan's mind the suspicion that Granrud did not want to share power, and gave him the chance to make public his opposition.

Led by Neprud, who had decided not to acquiesce to his forced retirement, the anti-administration group quietly devised its strategy. The 1959 Lutheran Brotherhood convention was scheduled for October, at which time the terms of three opposition directors (Aasgaard, Haugan, and Overson) and one pro-Granrud director (Lee) expired. If the opposition could elect four directors who supported their cause, the board would then be split 6 to 6, and they

might have some chance of controlling Granrud.

The rebels made their first move on April 23 at a meeting of Lutheran Brotherhood's national branch. The national branch was composed of society members across the country who did not belong to a local branch. In the past, national branch meetings had been relatively sedate affairs at which management's nominating committee quietly elected delegates. But that was not to be the case on this night. Several members, most of them pastors, rose to denounce Granrud's allegedly dictatorial managerial practices. Speakers were alternately heckled and applauded, and the chairman, Arthur Wangaard, Granrud's law partner, was constantly interrupted. When he attempted to postpone, table, delay, even adjourn the meeting—anything to prevent the rebel delegates from becoming certified and, therefore, eligible for election—he was shouted down by a resounding chorus. Matthias smoothly took command of the parliamentary proceedings, and by the time the meeting ended, 137 national branch nominees, every one of them dedicated to the ouster of Granrud, had been elected delegates to the quadrennial convention in October.

Granrud was incredulous. He and his supporters had just lost more than 10 percent of the delegates who would be voting at the convention. Who knew how much more support Neprud and Haugan had gained in the field? Granrud became worried. He had already lost enough votes. Now he was losing momentum, and it might be too late to catch up.

Fighting for Votes

By the summer of 1959, many members of Lutheran Brotherhood were talking constantly about the battle for control of the society. Much of the discussion centered around Granrud, and much of it was unfavorable. Stories regularly surfaced about his drinking habits and ruthless managerial methods.

"I am trying to keep a cool and unprejudiced mind in the storm of prejudices that are raging in our Society," the Rev. R. H. Gerberding wrote to one of the dissidents. "As to the slurs about Mr. Granrud, I have seen no evidence and my impression is that outward circumstances have been used by those who would like to discredit him in a grossly unfair manner. In fact, I am convinced that certain people high in the circles of the church have used their easy access to other churchmen to spread that which is mere gossip. Until I am convinced by more direct evidence, I do not wish to discredit him with these 'old wives tales.' Having had thirty years of experience as an executive in church organizations, I know what personal prejudice and gossip can do. Since I realize that Lutheran Brotherhood is essentially a business organization and that its relationship with the Church is simply by the grace of the Church, I feel that as a director it is my responsibility to observe the priority belonging to management, and I propose to stand by those that have been given executive authority. I do not think that is at all out of accord with my position as a minister of the gospel."

Many observers viewed Gerberding's assessment as inordinately beneficent, even taking into account that he was a director of the society. Granrud was

hardly known for his diplomatic abilities, and he had been insulting several church leaders, especially Dr. Fredrick Schiotz, president of the Evangelical Lutheran Church, for years. Most everyone involved with the society, Granrud supporters included, found Grandrud's comments disrespectful, especially considering that Lutheran Brotherhood based its origin and fraternal mission on the very existence of the organized Lutheran church.

Granrud's relationship with the Lutheran clergy was a curious thing, for no group, except his own employees, suffered more of his stinging barbs. "The road to heaven is not necessarily paved with Lutheran pastors," Granrud often said. Perhaps his intimate working relationships with church leaders on such organizations as St. Olaf College, Augsburg Publishing House, Fairview Hospital, and the Evangelical Lutheran Church had exposed him to their human frailties and had made him cynical. From Granrud's perspective, the crux of the present controversy was that some overly pious members of the clergy had decided to interfere in society affairs that were none of their business.

On the other hand, many pastors and lay leaders had seen Granrud's faults close-up, especially his brusque tactics and acerbic tongue. He had become increasingly combative as he had grown older, and had developed a penchant for disparaging those who disagreed with his opinions. These habits might be acceptable elsewhere, perhaps in the courtroom or business world, observers noted, but they seemed inappropriate to religious organizations. Besides, it was revealing that all of the church-sponsored organizations Granrud had once served had begun to sever ties with him.

As the controversy continued to heat up, a number of Lutheran Brotherhood's top general agents decided to cast their lot with Granrud. Their reasoning was this: Management had always supported them, the society was flourishing economically, and so were their agencies. Why change leadership now? When Granrud asked them to help him tell his side of the story, they readily agreed. The group included Woody Langhaug of Chicago; Fred Polzin of Milwaukee, Wisconsin; T. H. Mikkelson of Fergus Falls, Minnesota; Axel Lundring of Los Angeles; and the new superintendent of agencies, John Lienemann, a former general agent from Beatrice, Nebraska. Also on the pro-management traveling team were such general agents as Ole Haroldson from Williston, North Dakota; Merrill Gille from Teaneck, New Jersey; William A. Johnson from Minneapolis; two members of the agency department, Harold Hoel and Don Lommen; and a director, Gordon Bubolz.

Management announced that these agents and officers would be meeting with Lutheran Brotherhood agents and general agents at regional sites across the country for the purpose of informally discussing ideas for improving the agency department and getting acquainted with Lienemann. The dissidents in the field laughed when they received word of the meetings. The pro-management team wasn't coming to get any new ideas, they suspected, but to find out how they felt about Granrud. Most of them decided to play it cool.

At each regional meeting, the scenario was nearly identical. Just after arriving in town, before the meeting, each general agent would be called into a hotel room with several members of the pro-management team. He was then given a peptalk about how well the society was doing, reminded that he owed his loyalty to management, and asked how he felt about the present political situation. "So how are you going to vote at the convention?" Jerry Reinan, a young general agent from Duluth, was asked. "Oh, I don't know," he said innocently, although he was leaning against Granrud. "I guess I wouldn't say if I did know." His questioners pressed him. "Well, when are you going to know?" Reinan shifted in his seat. "Oh, I don't know." And so it went, back and forth, sometimes for two hours or more.

The atmosphere occasionally became tense. When Paul Jacobson, a general agent from Philadelphia, walked into his session at a hotel in Harrisburg, Pennsylvania, he was greeted with two personal letters he had written to Neprud that criticized Granrud. Jacobson was stunned. He said little during the session, then stood and said he had to use the bathroom. Jacobson walked past the bathroom and out the door, then left the hotel. For the next hour, he wandered the streets, mulling the situation over. Finally he found a pay phone, called Neprud, and explained what had happened.

"We found out yesterday that some letters were taken from my office," Neprud answered. "Lou Madsen, my secretary, put your letters in the bottom of a box of carbon paper in her desk. But when she checked the contents of her desk yesterday, she discovered that the letters were gone. I don't know who got them or how they got them, but they're gone. I'm sorry, Paul. I didn't want you to have to get involved in all of this."

Several thoughts raced through Jacobson's mind at once. "So what do I do now?" he asked.

"You don't have to go back to the hotel if you don't want to."

Jacobson relaxed. "That sounds good to me." He hung up and walked to a bus depot, purchased a ticket and went home. A few days later, Jacobson received a letter from Granrud. He had been fired.

As Granrud's supporters continued their travels, visiting district representatives and members, they soon were labeled in unflattering terms for their heavy-handed tactics. Their reputation was puzzling to them, even frustrating. How could it be wrong to solicit support for the people who employ you? But the dissidents held fast. They were at least loyal to the principles on which Lutheran Brotherhood had been founded, they countered, and that was more than could be said for Granrud and his supporters. The way the dissidents saw it, the pro-management team was asking for more than allegiance; they were demanding it, and using veiled threats to accomplish their goals.

Management had been planning a second meeting of the national branch in July to attempt to rescind the earlier election of 137 anti-Granrud delegates. Several general agents were called into meetings and warned not to campaign against management. "We will take a dim view of anyone who brings members to the next national branch meeting," they were told.

"What do you mean by 'dim view'?" one of the agents asked.

"It means that if you appear at the branch meeting or bring members who are not favorable to present management, you will be relieved of your duties." Several members of the field staff, notably

Society Snapshot: 1957

Home office: 701 Second Avenue South, Minneapolis

Number of members: 310,000

Number of employees: 231

Number of field personnel: 683

Insurance in force: $847,517,514

Assets: $137,369,846

Life insurance death benefits: $1,433,194

Dividends paid: $3,103,635

Church loans: $18,883,958

Society officers

Chairman of the board: J.A.O. Preus

President: Carl F. Granrud

Vice Presidents:

Director of agencies: N. Kelly Neprud
Associate director of agencies: Harold C. Hoel
General counsel: Russell H. Matthias
Financial: Harold A. Smith
Church loans: Arthur O. Lee
Underwriting: A. O. Konigson
Chief actuary: Reuben I. Jacobson
Secretary: Kenneth T. Severud
Treasurer: Lorenz Jost
Medical director: H. J. Brekke, M.D.

Assistant vice presidents:

Superintendent of agencies: Herbert A. Johnson
Educational director: Donald E. Lommen
Assistant actuary: Ingolf Lee
Law: Cyrus Rachie
Underwriting: M. E. Andersen
Policyholders service: Clifford L. Thompson
Investments: David R. Zetzman
Alfred Holtan

Lutheran Brotherhood introduced its first filmstrip in 1955. During the next few years, filmstrips became one of the field's most important sales tools. Pictured are several frames from a strip that outlined the definitive sales pitch of the 1950s and 1960s, "You'll Earn a Fortune."

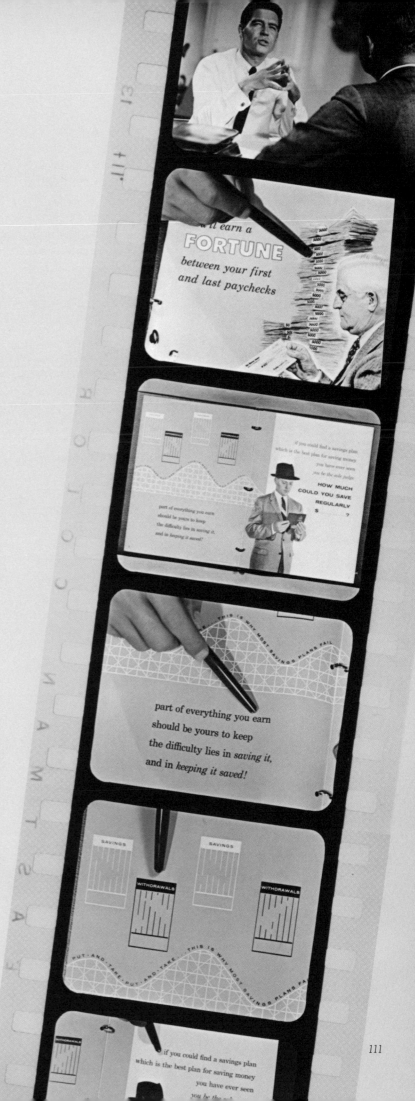

Fred Hoff, general agent at Montevideo, Minnesota, ignored the warning and continued to solicit support for the dissidents. All of them were fired.

What had started as a corporate conflict between two of the most powerful directors of Lutheran Brotherhood had escalated into a battle that engulfed almost everyone in the society. Even those who tried to take shelter were caught in the crossfire. Clair Strommen, a regional superintendent of agencies, had been working closely with Herb Johnson when the battle erupted. He was sympathetic to the dissidents but found it impossible to work in the tense atmosphere, so he took over a new general agency in St. Paul to get away. But the war came to him. One side would call and instruct him to campaign for them, then the other. Strommen began to feel as though he were caught in a vise.

One day, he was called into the home office by Granrud's supporters and led into a room. "The reason we've asked you here is that we want you to campaign for Granrud," they told him.

"I'm not going to campaign for anybody," Strommen insisted. "I'm employed by Lutheran Brotherhood to sell insurance, and that's what I'm going to do."

One of the men suddenly hovered over Strommen. "Do you realize how serious this is?" he asked gravely.

"No, how serious is it?" asked Strommen.

"Well, let me ask you this. Do you love your wife and kids?"

Strommen quickly lifted his six-foot-five-inch frame out of the chair and stared down at the man. His job was being threatened. "Say that again," he snapped.

"Do you love your wife and kids?"

Strommen felt his blood pressure rising. "You people are gutless and spineless," he shouted. "You don't have to worry about me because I'm quitting."

As the battle continued, the casualties mounted.

The Tide Begins to Turn

Amid stories about a train derailment in Wisconsin that injured more than one hundred passengers and attacks on Laos by the North Vietnamese, the battle for Lutheran Brotherhood hit the front page of the *Minneapolis Star* on July 31, 1959. "A long-simmering fight for control of the billion-dollar Lutheran Brotherhood Insurance society broke into the open today," wrote business reporter Harold Chucker, who detailed the results of the second meeting of the society's national branch.

"The meeting last night was called by the management in an attempt to rescind action at a similar meeting last April which elected an anti-administration slate of delegates to the October convention," he wrote. "Pro-management forces charged the April meeting was 'stacked' by their opponents. They lacked a two-thirds majority last night, however, to rescind the April election, and instead elected their own slate of 137 delegates. The result is that two slates of national branch delegates will seek credentials for the convention. Court action may be sought to decide which slate shall be seated."

It was also revealed at the meeting that Russell Matthias, one of the most active of the dissident leaders, had been one of six insurance executives named in a suit alleging that they had bilked a Chicago insurance firm out of more than $2 million. The report dealt a severe blow to the dissident cause, for it raised questions in the minds of many members about the motives of some of the dissident leaders. Granrud played the publicity for all it was worth. "Matthias is moving in on a lot of insurance companies," he told the *Star.* "But our members and people in the field won't stand for it." The story about Matthias also made the anti-management leaders nervous, for they had never been sure where he stood. Matthias was a shrewd politician. It was said that he went where the votes were; at the moment, they were with the dissidents. But if the votes went over to the other side, would Matthias soon follow?

Matthias had learned how to win at an early age. The son of the owner of the old Milwaukee Brewers, then a minor league baseball team, Matthias spent much of his childhood in a ballpark, and he became an outstanding college athlete. He turned his attention to the legal profession, and after graduating from

In an effort to increase the society's name recognition among Lutherans in the 1950s and 1960s, the society began to place advertisements in national magazines. This full-page ad appeared in LIFE magazine on June 19, 1964.

A Bolder Dream

Northwestern University Law School, he joined the law firm of Ekern & Meyers in Chicago. Matthias was bright and so full of energy that he worked day and night. He became known as a fierce competitor, and he quickly developed into a star at the firm of Ekern & Meyers.

Preus often visited Ekern's law office and became impressed with Matthias. With Ekern's blessing, he decided to recommend the thirty-three-year-old Matthias for the board of Lutheran Brotherhood in 1939. Sure, Matthias was young, Preus told Ekern, but the board needed some new blood. Besides, Matthias was of German heritage and a member of the Missouri Synod, and he would add some needed balance to the Scandinavians who dominated the membership of the board.

Following his election, one of the senior directors took Matthias aside and told him, "Now sit down and behave, Matt." The young lawyer took his advice. Matthias kept his mouth shut, listened hard, traveled constantly, and became a member of the executive committee. As legal counsel for the society, he became one of the leading fraternal proponents in the country. Matthias was a skilled practitioner of the "good old boy" method of politics, and he cultivated a roster of legislative contacts that seemed endless. Whenever a bill appeared that threatened the status of fraternals, Matthias hopped on a plane and lobbied his legislative contacts, who then stopped the threat.

Matthias was known for his ability as a lobbyist to read the intentions of other people, but he apparently misjudged Harry Gralnek, the secretary-treasurer of the Highway Insurance Company of Chicago, of which he was president. Gralnek embezzled nearly $1.7 million from the company. After Matthias reorganized the company, he was sued by another former officer, who alleged that Matthias and five others had looted the company of $2 million through stock and real estate deals while appearing to rehabilitate the company. Matthias responded that he had actually saved the company from bankruptcy, and he charged that the suit had been filed out of spite.

The adverse publicity gave Granrud the ammunition he needed to strike another blow at the dissidents. At a special session on August 14, 1959, the board of Lutheran Brotherhood voted 7 to 5 to dismiss Matthias from his position as legal counsel, although he remained a member of the board. In making its decision, the majority stated that his activity on behalf of the anti-management group was "in clear violation of his obligations as legal counsel."

The board also cited a damaging discovery. For years, Matthias had claimed to be a member of St. John's Lutheran Church of Wilmette, Illinois. Early in the battle, however, one of Granrud's men decided to call the pastor of St. John's, and found out that the claim was not true. "Is Russell Matthias a member of your church?" he asked. "Russell who?" said the pastor. Matthias was, at the time, a member of a church, Kenilworth Union, but it was not a Lutheran church. Matthias eventually joined a Lutheran church, but not until July 1959, when, as management put it, "he became uncomfortable as to the position in which he had placed Lutheran Brotherhood in regard to this matter."

The momentum was shifting to management. Embarrassed by the Matthias affair, the dissidents turned their attention to the campaign ahead. They set up headquarters in Minneapolis as the Lutheran Brotherhood Policyholders Committee and began to plan their convention platform. Optimism for the cause was still high, and donations continued to pour in from around the country, including five hundred-dollar checks from a high-ranking Lutheran Brotherhood officer known to the committee only as "Zorro."

In late August, the Policyholders Committee announced its slate of seven board nominees. They included two incumbents, Randolph Haugan and T. G. Overson; Judge Luther Sletten of the Municipal Court in Minneapolis; Paul Onstad, director of a savings and loan in Grand Forks, North Dakota; Dr. Seth Eastvold, president of Pacific Lutheran College and son of C. J. Eastvold, one of the founders of the society; Leonard Gisvold, a banker in Minneapolis; and the Rev. Luthard O. Gjerde, vice president of the Lutheran Free Church.

The committee also announced a platform "aimed at correcting abuses of executive power and strengthening the voice of members." For example, the committee proposed to make the presidency of Lutheran

Brotherhood fully accountable to the board of directors. It charged that Granrud ruled by "fear and favor," as evidenced by the number of employees and field personnel who recently had been fired.

The dissidents campaigned to enlarge the board of directors from twelve to fifteen members. This move would be necessary to gain control of the board and would require a two-thirds majority vote at the convention. They also proposed to make it possible to amend the bylaws by a simple majority vote of the delegates at any convention, or by unanimous vote of the board of directors. The dissidents claimed that this move would ensure greater democracy within the society by strengthening the voice of the delegates (two-thirds of whom were presently required to amend bylaws) and limiting the power of the board (three-quarters of whom could amend bylaws at any regular meeting).

There were other issues. The Policyholders Committee charged that Gretchen Pracht, Granrud's Episcopalian law associate, had become far too powerful within the society. No one said that she was not doing a good job as head of the advertising and public relations department, and her supporters pointed to "the Lutheranism" of her work. Still, asked the committee, was it too much to ask that the officers of a Lutheran fraternal benefit society be Lutheran? However, any claims against Pracht were balanced by the recent discovery of Matthias's own church membership.

Also at issue was the question of synodical representation on the society's board of directors. The society had been created by the Norwegian Lutheran Church of America (which became the Evangelical Lutheran Church [ELC]), and for many years had been managed primarily by directors who were members of that synod. Eight of the twelve current directors were members of the ELC (Granrud included), as were five of the seven reform candidates. Granrud charged that the ELC directors, especially Neprud and Haugan, were simply trying to maintain control of the society. He contended that the

board needed more representatives from other synods, and said that a "good mix" would be one-third from the ELC, one-third from the United Lutheran Church in America (ULCA), and one-third from other synods. The dissidents countered that the ELC deserved majority representation, since more of its members belonged to local branches than any other synod.

As both sides exchanged charges and countercharges, they also matched influential political candidates. In September, the reform slate announced that, if elected, they would name Val Bjornson, Minnesota state treasurer, as president of the society. Bjornson was one of the state's most beloved politicians, and his oratorical skill was such that this descendant of Icelanders seemed capable of transforming even mundane financial reports into spellbinding sagas. Bjornson indicated that he would give up his state post if the dissidents won the convention.

Not to be outdone, management announced that Luther Youngdahl, former governor of Minnesota, was one of its four board nominees. The other members of the slate included Arthur Lee, an incumbent; Harold Hoel, vice president of agencies; and Dr. A. R. Kretzmann, a Chicago pastor and national authority on church art and architecture. Youngdahl was currently a United States district judge for the

A pro-Granrud button worn by members of the field force during the 1959 convention campaign is attached to an informal note outlining suggestions for campaign strategy.

District of Columbia, but back home in Minnesota he was fondly regarded as one of the state's most popular governors. From a large and talented Swedish Lutheran family, Youngdahl was renowned for his abilities as a speaker and his commitment to social causes.

When the slate was announced, Youngdahl said he knew nothing about the dispute within Lutheran Brotherhood. But several days after indicating that he would serve if elected, Youngdahl backed out as a society board candidate, citing a potential conflict of interest with his duties as a public official. He was replaced on the ballot by Bertram Wilde, an investment banker from Philadelphia.

In the meantime, as the convention approached, Granrud and the Policyholders Committee continued to trade frenzied charges and rebuttals. God's name was invoked by both sides, even while they were accusing each other of spying with cameras and tape recorders, and of taking confidential papers from wastebaskets and desks. Only a few zealots were responsible, yet such actions were troubling to the moderates who felt that even political campaigns should be conducted on a higher plane. They agonized over the exodus of talented employees who had left the society or had been fired by Granrud. They believed that all employees, as equal members of the society, had the democratic right to participate in fraternal politics. But they also wondered whether those same freedoms might result in anarchy and create an atmosphere in which it was impossible for the society's leaders to operate Lutheran Brotherhood efficiently.

That observation finally convinced general agent Jerry Reinan of the futility of the fight. Although he had been leaning toward the dissidents, he had been carefully pondering the reasons for the civil war, and he had come to the conclusion that there were none. The closer he examined the situation, the more he saw an arena in which a few powerful leaders grappled for a prize that had little to do with their supporters cheering on the sidelines. Like many others, Reinan did not like Granrud's methods, but for the life of him, he could not see a better alternative on the immediate horizon.

"I'd rather take a licking than have to write this letter but I certainly owe it to both of you," Reinan wrote to two of the dissident leaders. "In any event, after an awful lot of thinking, I can't honestly feel that there is going to be any improvement from upsetting the present administration. . . . This situation has arisen in the past and there is no reason to believe that it won't arise again in the future. So long as we have the form of government that we have, it will be a factor. . . . Obviously, I'm in no position to criticize anyone for being against administration. That is a personal thing. However, in the light of what I've said I can't continue to do so. . . . In my mind, it boils down to one thing—who's to command LB, Granrud, Bubolz, et al. or Haugan, Matthias et al. We all know that no one else has anything to gain from all this. I've decided that I'll take Granrud instead of Haugan and Matthias. . . . I know that my seeming defection will cause hard feelings and still, I'm naive enough to hope that it won't. My best to you both. Sincerely, Jerry."

The Convention

A few months before Lutheran Brotherhood's fifteenth general convention, Ken Severud, secretary of the society, ran into a friend from the Minneapolis Chamber of Commerce in the halls of the home office. "Hey, how come you guys changed your convention date?" the man asked. "We haven't changed our convention," Severud said, puzzled. "You sure have," his friend replied. "I got a letter here from the Leamington Hotel that says you postponed your convention one week." Severud's mouth dropped open when he saw the letter. Sure enough, when he checked with the Leamington Hotel, where the society's convention was scheduled for October 28, he discovered that the owner had booked the hotel to another group on that date.

Severud was frantic. More than thirteen hundred delegates were coming to Minneapolis. They needed a huge hall in which to meet and rooms in which

The 1959 campaign for control of Lutheran Brotherhood attracted enough local attention that the society's general convention was featured on the front page of the Minneapolis Morning Tribune *on October 29, 1959. In the newspaper photo at top right, Granrud checks the convention vote. Reproduced courtesy of the* Star Tribune, *Minneapolis-St. Paul.*

Cloudy
Minneapolis High 42

WEDNESDAY TEMPERATURES
2 a.m. 33 10 a.m. 34 6 p.m. 41
3 a.m. 33 11 a.m. 35 *7 p.m. 41
4 a.m. 33 Noon 35 *Unofficial
5 a.m. 34 1 p.m. 36
6 a.m. 33 2 p.m. 36
7 a.m. 33 3 p.m. 42
8 a.m. 33 4 p.m. 42
9 a.m. 34 5 p.m. 41

Minneapolis Morning Tribune

Vol. XCIII—No. 158 MINNEAPOLIS, MINN., THURSDAY, OCTOBER 29, 1959 FE 3-3111 5c In Twin Cities Area 7c Elsewhere

Lutheran Brotherhood Management Wins Vote

Supreme Court Rejects Speedup of Steel Appeal

India-Red China War Considered Quite Possible

By GRAHAM HOVEY
Minneapolis Tribune European Correspondent

LONDON—Some of the best informed Asian diplomats in London now believe war between India and Communist China is a definite possibility.

They see little chance in present circumstances for effective negotiation of the dispute, arising from several grabs of Indian territory by Red Chinese troops.

They say that to date the Chinese have not shown any interest in genuine negotiations.

And they add that Prime Minister Jawaharlal Nehru of India now is convinced that unless his government takes forceful action it will only invite more territorial "bites" by the Chinese.

Analysis: WHAT THE NEWS MEANS

These diplomats are thoroughly familiar with the latest Indian government thinking on the border dispute. They also have access to whatever information has come via non-Communist diplomatic channels from China.

THEY ARE NOT alarmist; they do not believe China deliberately seeks war or aims to conquer India.

They do believe that an aggressive Red China has decided now to press its claims to some 40,000 square miles of territory long regarded as belonging to India.

By way of giving forceful meaning to these claims, they say the Chinese have moved troops into frontier areas not garrisoned by the Indian army and only lightly patrolled by Indian border police.

These sources doubt that any negotiation can persuade the Peiping regime to withdraw these troops from territory which its own maps now show to be part of China.

BUT NEHRU, they say, cannot tolerate such en-

India
Continued on Page 13

Ace Diplomat Murphy Quits No. 3 Post

WASHINGTON — (AP) — Robert Daniel Murphy, a diplomatic trouble shooter for three presidents, has decided to quit as under-secretary of state to take a job in industry.

The Milwaukee-born Irishman will leave about Jan. 1, ending a colorful 39-year career.

Murphy

Murphy told President Eisenhower of his decision Tuesday. Mr. Eisenhower reluctantly accepted it.

Administration leaders had been hoping Murphy would stay on, either in his present post, the highest a career officer can achieve, or as ambassador to West Germany.

BUT MURPHY, a gangling six-footter with a soft smile, decided that after nearly four decades as a diplomat, the time had come to quit. Friends said the main reason was money.

As the state department's No. 3 man, he earns $22,000 a year, but his job in private business is expected to pay much more. Murphy declined to disclose what his new job will be except to say it will be connected with international affairs.

Wednesday, at the age of 65, Murphy became eligible for full retirement pay. This will be about $15,000 a year.

THERE WERE private reports that Murphy did not agree fully with Secretary Herter and Undersecretary Douglas Dillon on East-West relations, particularly the Berlin crisis.

But state department press officer Lincoln White said he was authorized to state "on

Murphy
Continued on Page Eight

Part of Region Will Warm Up

A general warming trend is predicted for the eastern portion of the Upper Midwest today, but cloudy skies, cool temperatures, occasional light rain and snow are expected to dominate the rest of region.

Predicted highs today include temperatures of 32 to 45 in Minnesota, 30s to 50s in North Dakota, 40s in South Dakota and 40s to 50s in Wisconsin.

—STEEL—

Injunction Stay Stands as Issued

Strike Will Go Into Next Week; Talks to Resume

WASHINGTON — (AP) — The supreme court refused Wednesday to require the Steelworkers union to hurry its appeal from an order that would end the 106-day-old steel strike.

This probably means the strike will drag on at least into next week.

In a brief order giving no reasons, the high court rejected a government request that the back-to-work injunction become effective promptly if the union did not file its appeal by noon today.

BY SO DOING, the court let stand a six-day delay granted the union by an appeals court in Philadelphia, Pa., Tuesday when it upheld the back-to-work order issued earlier by a federal district judge in Pittsburgh, Pa. That delay—intended to give the union time to carry its case to the supreme court—is due to expire Monday.

There was nothing to indicate the high court's action was other than unanimous.

The ruling came a little more than seven hours after the justice department had formally requested the court to lose no time and uphold the back-to-work order "so that the emergency created by the steel strike may not continue longer than absolutely necessary."

THE STEELWORKERS' lawyers opposed the speedup procedure, contending there are serious statutory and constitutional issues involved and that these require unhurried consideration.

Arthur J. Goldberg, union counsel, filed a document questioning the high court's right to take the case at this stage. The union said a delay of a few more days, even a few more weeks, "would not irreparably harm the national interest."

Although the union now has until Monday to file its formal appeal papers, Goldberg indicated he intends to do so on Friday and to follow with a detailed legal brief on Monday.

After the court's denial of the government's speedup bid, Goldberg said "we still intend to proceed as expeditiously as possible. We still hope to negotiate a settlement."

THE GOVERNMENT is opposed to a supreme court re-

Steel
Continued on Page 13

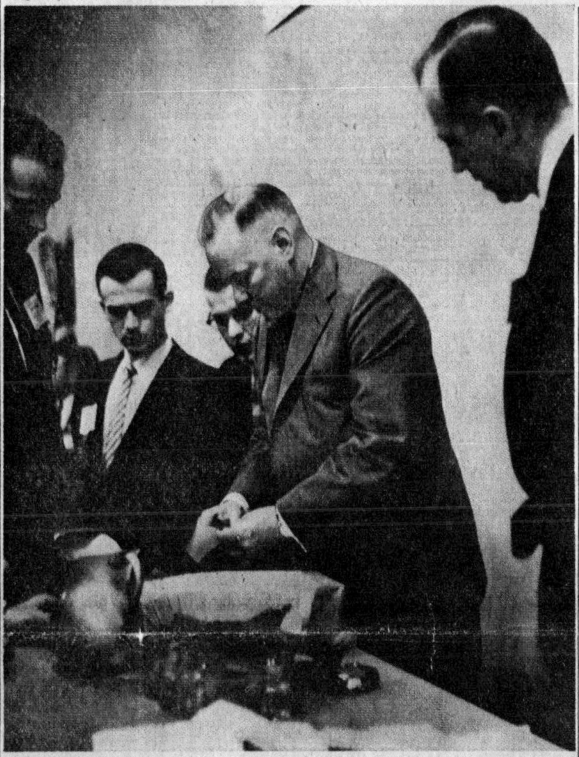

MINNEAPOLIS TRIBUNE PHOTO BY CHARLES BRILL

CARL F. GRANRUD, CENTER, LUTHERAN BROTHERHOOD PRESIDENT, CHECKED DELEGATION VOTE

—BROTHERHOOD—

Ballot on 4 Directors in Doubt

Pro-Management Slate of Delegates Seated, 629 to 551

By DAVID LEE
Minneapolis Tribune Staff Writer

Anti-management forces lost their attempt to take control of Lutheran Brotherhood insurance society Wednesday in a series of three closely-contested votes at the society's quadrennial convention.

But four directors to be elected by the convention to the society's 12-man board were still in doubt late yesterday afternoon.

THE FIRST—and crucial—clash of strength came at noon yesterday when 1,193 delegates from local branches of the Lutheran Brotherhood voted to seat a pro-management slate of delegates from the society's national branch. The secret ballot vote was 629 to 551.

The convention earlier had defeated an amendment to seat the rival anti-management slate by a vote of 622 to 568.

With the pro-management majority vote that was demonstrated in the contest to seat the national delegation plus 97 new votes in the seated national branch, the convention defeated an anti-management proposal to increase size of the society's board of directors from 12 members to 15. The vote was 655 to 611.

THE PROPOSAL needed a two-thirds vote to pass.

The amendment vote spelled an end to hopes of anti-managment forces to take control of the billion-dollar insurance firm.

With only two persons in unexpired terms on the board, the anti-management group needed the larger board and election of more than four of their supporters to gain control.

Anti-management forces in the elections still in doubt last night at best could gain a six-to-six deadlock on the board through election of four of their supporters. This did not appear likely.

THE CONVENTION also defeated a proposed amendment to lower the requirement for amending bylaws from a two-thirds majority to a simple majority.

Yesterday's convention was marked by sharp person-

Brotherhood
Continued on Page Eight

Frederick Mann, Founder of 'U' Architecture School, Dies at 91

Frederick Maynard Mann, who founded and for 23 years was head of the University of Minnesota's school of architecture, is dead.

He died late Tuesday at Healdsburg, Calif. He was 91.

At the time of his retirement in 1936 he had devoted 40 years to the practice and teaching of architecture.

Mr. Mann

He also founded the architecture school at Washington university, St. Louis, Mo., and reorganized the school at the University of Illinois.

Perhaps Mr. Mann's best known design is the University of Minnesota's Memorial stadium, built in the early 1920s.

He also designed the University YMCA building, the Delta Tau Delta fraternity and the Kappa Kappa Gamma sorority houses at the university, many homes in Minneapolis and the Dental building at Rochester, Minn.

IN ADDITION to serving as advisory architect to the university, he was a member of the Minneapolis planning commission from 1927 to 1936 and its president in 1927 and 1931.

Mr. Mann was born in New York City in 1868, but moved with his family to Minneapolis as a boy. He attended high school in Minneapolis and graduated from the university in 1892 with a bachelors degree in civil engineering.

In 1894 and 1895 he earned bachelor and master of science degrees from the Massachusetts Institute of Technology.

AS A STUDENT, Mr. Mann supported himself by doing structural design work for the Northern Pacific railroad.

He was an instructor at the University of Pennsylvania from 1896 to 1901; at Washington university from 1902 to 1910 and at the University of Illinois from 1910 to 1913.

He was called to set up the University of Minnesota's school in 1913.

As far back as 1898, when Mr. Mann was a youthful unknown, he won an award for the design of a memorial church in competition with many of the nation's leading architects.

HE WAS the recipient of the first award for achievement offered by the Minnesota society of the American Institute of Architects (AIA), the first two medals offered by the Beaux Arts Architects, and, in the 1920s, an AIA gold medal in a national competition for the best dwelling in the $75,000 class, the Shaw house at the intersection of S. Morgan Av. and Lake Harriet Blvd.

Other buildings designed by Mr. Mann include the St. Louis Public library and the Masonic Temple in that city, the church of St. John the Evangelist, Philadelphia, Pa., and the University Methodist church, Austin, Texas.

While a student at the University of Minnesota, he played tackle on the 1888 football squad.

Mr. Mann moved to his ranch at Healdsburg, Calif., when he retired.

HE WAS elected a fellow of the AIA and was a member of Tau Beta Pi, Sigma Xi, Psi Upsilon, Alpha Rho Chi, Tau Sigma Delta, the Scarabs club, the American Civil Engineering association, the National Economics league, Minneapolis Engineers club, College Art association and the Skylight and 6 O'Clock clubs.

He was among the dozen founders of the Association of Collegiate Schools of Architecture and also a founder of the Small Home Service bureau, an organization that developed low-cost plans for small homes and exerted considerable influence on domestic architecture in Minneapolis and elsewhere during the 1920s.

Survivors include two daughters, Mrs. Byron J. Olson, Bethesda, Md., and Mrs. Donald Cordry, Cuernavaca, Mexico, and a son, Frederick, Jr., who is advisory architect at the University of Washington at Seattle. Mr. Mann's wife, Grace, died in 1937.

Time has not yet been set for funeral services, which will be at Healdsburg. Burial will be at Cambridge, Mass.

Siamese Kittens Went Fast

All it took to sell a litter of Siamese kittens for Mrs. James W. Balabon, 1612 N. 73rd Av., was a two-line want ad. She got more responses than she had kittens to sell.

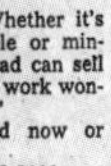

Ima says, "Whether it's animal, vegetable or mineral — a want ad can sell it for you. They work wonders every day!"

Mail your ad now or merely call
FEDERAL 3-3111

Ex-Thye Aid Named to Top Federal Post

By CHARLES W. BAILEY
Minneapolis Tribune Staff Correspondent

WASHINGTON — Robert A. Forsythe of Minneapolis, former administrative assistant to Sen. Edward J. Thye (R., Minn.), Wednesday was appointed assistant secretary of the department of health, education and welfare by President Eisenhower.

Forsythe

Forsythe, 38, will be in charge of the department's legislative program. He has been serving as the agency's congressional liaison officer for the past year.

Active in Minnesota Republican affairs since his return from World War II service in the army, Forsythe came to Washington in May 1953 as chief counsel to the senate small business committee.

HE SERVED in this post under both Republican and

Forsythe
Continued on Page Eight

TURN THE PAGES TO:

Editorials ..4 Theaters ... 4 Peach
Women 15-17
Pictures ..18 Comics 22,23
MARKETS ..24, 25, 3 Peach

Longer Life, 10 Pounds Away —Page 18

Almanac

Fiddling With Punctuation Would Help

Thursday, Oct. 29, 1959
Sunrise 6:47 a.m.; Sunset 5:06 p.m.

Minneapolis visitor to New Ulm, Minn., was startled by an unpunctuated sign on the back of a car. The sign said: "Bob Burns New Ulm." She was more so when she saw the car was that of an insurance company agent.

•

Cloudy with occasional light rain today in the Twin Cities. High today 42, low tonight 30.

•

Minneapolis man had a telephone installed in his bathroom. His 7-year-old daughter was quite impressed and called a friend on the new phone to advise her of the marvel.

The friend was frankly skeptical, so the daughter pulled a handle and let the sound of rushing waters convince her.

Papal Call for Church Council Excites Hope for Christian Unity

(Fifth in a series)
By BARRETT MCGURN
Chief of the New York Herald Tribune Rome Bureau

POPE JOHN'S FIRST YEAR

VATICAN CITY — Last Jan. 25, Pope John, not quite three months in office, summoned a Roman Catholic ecumenical council to foster several objectives and to concern itself with "the whole range of Christian thought."

But the objective that captured the interest of the world was the idea of bringing about a possible unity—or some sort of reunion—of divided Christianity.

This council is expected to be held in Rome, perhaps before the end of 1960, and will be the 21st of its kind in the 20 centuries of Christian history. The last one was held in 1869-70, the council that pronounced the doctrine of papal infallibility in matters of faith and morals.

Last before that was the meeting of the bishops of the Catholic church of 1545 to 1563 at Trent, in northern Italy, to study measures to be taken in the face of the Protestant reformation.

An ecumenical council is a meeting of the bishops of the Catholic church, and, in Catholic belief, has the right to proclaim dogmas which the Roman Catholic faithful are bound to accept as infallible. The pope alone has the right to veto a council's decision.

All 2,500 Roman Catholic bishops, archbishops, and cardinals of the world, including 200 in the United States, will be invited. And presumably they will be asked to sit in judgment on moral problems in the fields of economics, politics and personal conduct which have developed since the last meeting ended in 1870.

Many unforeseen decisions and pronouncements may come from the council. But, now, public discussion centers on the question of how successful this rather extraordinary council will be in bringing any degree of unity among the Christian churches.

The first reactions, even in the pope's own judgment, seem to be that the 400-year-old division between Catholics and Protestants and nine-century-old break between the Catholic and Orthodox churches will not be ended.

But Pope John still cultivates a lively hope that at

Pope
Continued on Page 10

to sleep. He searched throughout Minneapolis for an alternate site, with little luck. Finally he tried the Pick-Nicollet Hotel on Hennepin Avenue and Third Street. "We've got a room big enough for your meeting," the manager there said. "But it's already spoken for by another group." Severud nervously ran his fingers through his hair. "On the other hand," said the manager, "they aren't nearly as big a group as you are. If they'll agree to it, I can put them in another area." They did. Lutheran Brotherhood had a room for its convention.

It was an anxious beginning to what promised to be an anxious meeting. On October 27, delegates checked into hotels scattered throughout downtown, then registered at the home office. Representatives from both the management and reform slates milled throughout the crowded building, passing out campaign literature, eyeing one another closely, trying not to bump into each other. The dissidents were working diligently. Management had refused their request for a list of delegates and alternates from July to late September. Only after Matthias threatened legal action did management release the list, and the Policyholders Committee finally had been able to issue a few campaign bulletins to the delegates in October.

But management was busy, too. That evening, a group of field representatives hosted a testimonial dinner for Granrud, and seven hundred people attended. The show of support lifted spirits among the Granrud forces, for they still were unsure of the outcome. An independent survey of home office employees, sponsored by the Policyholders Committee, had indicated that 90 percent of the home office staff was in agreement with the reforms proposed by the dissidents. Management dismissed that figure as ridiculous. However, there was little doubt that much support for the anti-Granrud forces existed at home and in the field.

Granrud had been stung by reaction to remarks he had made at a meeting of general agents in September. The meeting had been secretly taped by one of the anti-management agents and later made public. During his remarks, Granrud, in his combative style, had taken personal potshots at some of the reform candidates, suggesting that Gjerde was a poor

manager and implying that Gisvold simply wanted the society's money. But his worst mistake had been calling Pastor Maynard Iverson of Bethlehem Lutheran Church of Minneapolis, a congregation to which Neprud belonged, "stupid." There were many pastors among the delegates, and they were angry about the incident. If Granrud hoped to gain their votes, he would have to think of a way to appease them.

The convention was called to order at 10 A.M. at the Pick-Nicollet. The slate of delegates elected at the second meeting of the national branch was seated, while the anti-Granrud group waited in a room across the hall, pending a decision as to which group should be the official national branch representatives. Doormen carefully guarded all entrances to the floor, making sure that only those with delegate's badges were allowed inside. Security was so tight that Orville Freeman, the governor of Minnesota, who was to give the welcoming address, almost didn't get in. When he tried to enter the hall, a husky guard, Clarence Johnson, the society's general agent in Pittsburgh, blocked his way. "You can't go in there without a delegate's badge," Johnson said. "But I'm the governor," Freeman replied. "Makes no difference," the doorman said. "No badge, no admittance." Freeman finally persuaded the man that he was there to speak, and he entered in time to greet the delegates. It was one of the last friendly speeches of the day.

During the next few hours, the delegates heard what they had been hearing for months. Some speakers rose to denounce Granrud as a tyrant who ruled with an iron hand, firing employees who got in his way. Others praised him and turned their attacks on the leaders of the dissidents. Such was the tension in the hall that several pastors stood to plead for a more Christian approach, and the convention parliamentarian delivered a curt reading from *Robert's Rules of Order* on the decorum of debate. It produced little effect. During one exchange, Matthias leaped to his feet to answer an accusation and began yelling at his accusers. Anti-management supporters groaned. Emotional outbursts from trained lawyers were not going to help their cause.

If the rebels expected similar fireworks from Granrud, who was presiding, they were disappointed. He was strangely subdued today. While speakers just a few feet away delivered blistering diatribes against him, he sat calmly, arms crossed in typical fashion, wiggling the little finger of one hand and scratching his face. When one elderly pastor was given the floor, he launched into Granrud with a holy fury. Several pro-Granrud delegates jumped to their feet. "You're out of order!" they shouted. "You're out of order!" Granrud quickly rapped his gavel and grabbed the microphone. "Please, please, this man has something to say," he said, quieting the crowd. "Let him speak."

Then Carl Granrud did something that no one expected him to do. He stepped to the podium and said he was sorry. "I'm sure I've made plenty of mistakes during this entire affair," he said solemnly. "I've said things that I'm sorry for, especially about Pastor Iverson, and I've done things I'm sorry for. I would like to ask for your forgiveness." Many delegates were stunned, especially the Rev. Theodore Heimarck, who had taken the floor to speak against management. Now what could he say? "When one of my brothers begs forgiveness, as a minister of the gospel I cannot do otherwise than to forgive him," Heimarck said. "If he has truly repented, then I do not care which men you elect now to the board of directors."

The tide had turned. At noon, the delegates voted 622 to 568 to seat the slate of 137 national branch delegates pledged to management. The battle, for all practical purposes, was over. The delegates subsequently defeated an amendment, sponsored by anti-management, that would have enlarged the board from twelve to fifteen. They overturned a second anti-management amendment that would have permitted the bylaws to be changed by a majority vote of the delegates. Finally, they elected all four management candidates to the board: Hoel, Kretzmann, Lee, and Wilde. It was a clean sweep for Granrud.

After the convention, a happy Granrud told the *Minneapolis Tribune* that peace had returned to Lutheran Brotherhood. "We've all gone back to work now," he said, "and no one's mad at anyone."

Some of the dissidents weren't so sure. "The agents aren't all happy about this," said one, "and Lutheran Brotherhood sales will not be what they might because of it." He predicted more resignations from the society.

Neprud tried to sound upbeat. "I've given my all

and my best," he said. "I was fighting for friends and a cause, but money licked me and I'm through. But we do feel there is victory in defeat. This has separated the men from the boys, and there just weren't enough men on our side. The real churchmen that stood up against management on this thing should be admired. They had guts and integrity."

Several area pastors said that they would be watching Granrud's performance to determine if his "eleventh-hour conversion," as one dissident described it, had been sincere. "You have a marvelous opportunity to fulfill this mandate of humble responsibility and good stewardship conduct," the Rev. Joseph Simonson, the former U.S. ambassador to Ethiopia, wrote to Granrud. "I genuinely hope and pray that in four years more we can come together in quadrennial convention and applaud you for the way you rose to the occasion, and we shall do so even before that for every evidence of Christian statesmanlike life and conduct, personally and officially. May God lead and direct you!"

The battle for Lutheran Brotherhood was over. All that remained was for the participants to shake hands, but that was easier said than done. Less than a month after the convention, Joseph L. Knutson, president of Concordia College in Moorhead, Minnesota, wrote to Ole Haroldson about some college business. He also expressed his hopes for the society. "I hope the pieces can be picked up and put together again, for Lutheran Brotherhood has meant too much to our people to receive a crippling blow," he wrote. "The thing which grieved me more than anything else about this affair was the break between Carl Granrud and Randolph Haugan. Two men cannot live together the way they did for twenty years morning, noon and night and make the contribution that they did to the church, St. Olaf, Fairview Hospital, and Lutheran Brotherhood, and then break so tragically without hurting themselves and a host of others. They had mutual friends by the hundreds and had they only thought of the embarrassment they were causing their friends, I think they would have gotten together before this fiasco took place."

Mutual friends tried to reunite Granrud and Haugan, but failed.

Selling and Serving

Russ Smith was deep in thought as he maneuvered his car over the sharp ridges of gravel that covered the rural South Dakota road. It was Smith's first solo call as a district representative for Lutheran Brotherhood, and the closer he came to his destination, the more doubts began to nag at him. How should I introduce myself? What if I can't answer all his questions? What if he slams the door in my face? Beads of sweat appeared on Smith's forehead, and he pressed a little harder on the accelerator.

Smith was never nervous when he was in front of his students. He liked teaching, but he was making just a few thousand dollars a year as a high school teacher and coach, and he worried about his ability to support his pregnant wife and their two children. The school board had promised him a raise, but salary negotiations had been more difficult than Smith had liked. He began to think seriously about finding a new occupation.

That occupation would be selling insurance, if Howard Payne had his way. The general agent for Lutheran Brotherhood in Aberdeen, South Dakota,

Lutheran Brotherhood flourished in the small, rural communities where cornfields and Lutherans were plentiful. Among them was Belmond, Iowa, where district representative William R. (Bill) Johnson was a household name.

Payne had been trying for two years to convince Smith to become a district representative for the society. At first, Smith had resisted. He even had swapped cars with a friend for a day so that the persistent Payne would not find him.

Still, Smith had been intrigued with the idea of selling insurance. For an entire year, he vacillated between teaching and insurance. When contract negotiations with the school board stalled, Smith went to Payne and made him an offer. "Look, this is where I'm at," said Smith. "I've got to give myself a test. I want to take the names of ten Lutherans I know in this community and try to sell one or two of them insurance. If I can do that, based on the limited knowledge I have of this business, then I believe that I can be successful. But I've got to do it by myself." Payne agreed.

Now Smith was driving on a lonely country road, alone and apprehensive. His first call was a farmer. When he saw the farm just ahead, his heart began to pound and his mind began to race. He pressed harder on the accelerator. By the time he passed the driveway leading to the farm, Smith was driving seventy miles per hour. Three miles later, he slowed down and pulled the car to the side of the road. He looked at himself in the rearview mirror.

Look, he told himself angrily, you've got to make up your mind. Either you get up enough guts to make that first call, or you're going to honor your teaching commitment.

Smith turned the car around and drove deliberately back to the farm, muttering to himself as he went: Let's go. You can do it. He pulled his car into the driveway, roared into the farmyard in a cloud of dust, and jumped out. He strode purposefully to the farmer's house and pounded on the door. No answer. Smith pounded again. Still no answer. He knocked until his hand began to ache. Finally reality began to sink in: No one was home.

You've Got to Believe

Russ Smith went back to the farm a few days later and made the sale. A few days later he made another. He hadn't conquered all his fears, but anxiety wasn't going to keep him from making any more calls. He was going to succeed as a district representative for Lutheran Brotherhood.

It took a fair amount of confidence to knock on the doors of strangers and try to convince them of the value of insurance. If one couldn't sell oneself, how could one expect to sell anything else? The business of selling life insurance was still extremely challenging, even in the early 1960s. Yes, the arsenal of ammunition available to the Lutheran Brotherhood district representative had grown by leaps and bounds in the last ten years. Despite increasing support from the home office and the general agent, however, the district representative ultimately stood alone. Training, peptalks, new sales materials, none of them would be enough if the representative did not believe in himself or herself and in the product. One couldn't get by solely on technique. One either loved selling or one didn't. As insurance people liked to say, it wasn't the mortality table that was most important; it was the kitchen table. That was where one earned the client's trust.

It was also essential for district representatives to establish a good relationship with the local Lutheran clergy. Pastors who knew about the society or were society members themselves were generally happy to refer representatives to their parishioners, and representatives reciprocated by referring Lutherans who had just moved into the community to pastors of nearby churches. Although some representatives relied heavily on pastors for lists of church members, from which they made random cold calls, others thought that these requests bordered on imposition, and they were content simply to make their services known.

Because most representatives prospected during the day, their first contacts were usually housewives. The representative invariably began with a few words about the mission of Lutheran Brotherhood: "Here are our leaders, Governor Preus and Carl Granrud. Here are the financial figures that prove the stability of our society. Here is what we're doing for the Lutheran church in terms of loans, benevolence payments, and scholarships." The message was obvious: *We are committed to serving the Lutheran church.*

If the housewife seemed remotely interested and if the representative determined that the family qualified for insurance, the representative asked for an interview when the husband would be present, usually that night.

The definitive sales pitch of the 1960s began with what often seemed to the average breadwinner to be a rash statement: "You'll earn a fortune." The sentence seldom failed to pique curiosity, and it begged further explanation: "Mr. Johnson, you will earn a fortune between the ages of twenty-five and sixty-five. I don't know if you've ever thought about that, but if we were to take all the money that you will make during your prime earning years, it would indeed be a fortune. In fact, it could be as much as a quarter of a million dollars."

The intent of this approach was to make the prospect think about the future. That was difficult for young families with more immediate worries, such as house payments and heating bills. For example, most insurance sales during the 1950s had been based solely on single, present needs, such as a new mortgage or a baby. Families added insurance contracts as each new financial obligation surfaced. It seemed far easier to sell prospects in this way, one small contract at a time, than to sell them a comprehensive financial plan for the future.

But that philosophy slowly began to change in the 1960s. Lutheran Brotherhood representatives were taught to determine the entire scope of the prospect's assets, then construct an insurance plan that would cover the gap between those assets and the family's long-term financial goals.

It turned out that the real challenge for the average breadwinner was not so much earning money as saving it, and representatives were taught to quickly zero in on that point. "If you could participate in the best plan for saving money ever invented, Mr. Johnson, how much do you think you could save regularly and systematically? Could you save one hundred dollars a month? Could you save fifty?" The prospect might concede that he could save twenty dollars per month. Having established that figure, the Lutheran Brotherhood representative reviewed the insurance benefits that twenty dollars per month would purchase, whether the prospect lived, died, or quit the policy.

"Live, die, or quit" was a standard sales technique. It covered all the basic alternatives of a contract purchase, and was a more positive approach than the old-time sales pitch in which the threat of death was used as the primary sales motivator. Prospects had learned that there were other advantages to insurance, and that they did not have to draw their last breath to receive them. Most people preferred to think that they would live for many more years. They wanted to know what their insurance would be worth to them when they retired. They preferred to hear about cash values that grew like investments, and they wanted to know about features that allowed them to borrow for their children's education. Protection for life was becoming as important as protection against death.

Having made all the logical monetary arguments for insurance, the Lutheran Brotherhood representative began pushing for the sale. The closer the prospect got to completing the insurance form, however, the more likely the potential for hesitation. The act of signing a check, the dread finality of actually relinquishing money, was enough to rekindle skepticism in most prospects. It was at this point that their decision became emotional, and the representative either answered all their objections satisfactorily or lost the sale. It was as simple as that. Objections were an inescapable fact

of the business. Few prospects, especially young people, wanted to contemplate the fragility of their lives. It wasn't that they would never consider the subject; most simply preferred to postpone the moment until they were much older. That was why insurance agents encountered such resistance. By encouraging the prospect to purchase insurance, they chose the moment.

During the 1950s and 1960s, few representatives quit until they had asked at least five times, in different ways, for the sale. Their persistence was fueled by the industrywide belief that if they didn't make the sale on the first interview, the odds of making it on the second were almost nil. Thus, the difference between success and failure hinged on their ability to close the sale. Faced with that kind of pressure, the society's top producers fought tenaciously for a contract signature.

Some, like Lavern Mausolf, one of Lutheran Brotherhood's leading representatives during the late 1950s and early 1960s, read everything he could find on the art of motivation and persuasion, and applied those principles to his own sales techniques. For example, one source advised the salesman to take the cap off his pen and set it on the table before him, then attempt to tilt the table slightly, just enough to make the pen roll toward the prospect. The object was to get the prospect to pick up the pen, and the goal was to get the prospect to think about signing something, preferably the contract sitting on the table. Pens with no clips were recommended; pens with clips didn't roll.

Mausolf's *pièce de résistance* was a coffin, a tiny model put out by a casket company. "Someday, they are going to raise the lid on one of these for you," he would say. "If that should happen tonight, are your finances in order? Is your family protected?" The use of death as a sales motivator was known as "backing the hearse up to the door." Almost every representative possessed an arsenal of news clippings about breadwinners who had delayed buying insurance and died unexpectedly that same night, leaving their families with no other means of support.

Yet there were more subtle ways to convince prospects of the need for insurance. Smith tried not to let the husband and wife sit together during the

The John Lienemann agency of Beatrice, Nebraska, was Lutheran Brotherhood's leading producer in 1953, 1955, and 1959. Among the members of Lienemann's agency in 1951 were, front row, from left: Bernhard Rosenquist, Lawrence E. Aden, and Robert H. Muehling. Back row: Richard Edmisten, Harold Gloystein, John Lienemann, and Lewis E. Klein.

interview. If they were on the sofa, for example, he would sit between them. Sitting together, they might make a decision based on the opinions of the dominant spouse. Smith wanted them to make up their own minds about insurance. From a central location, it was easier to control the conversation, determine which spouse was more interested in the message, and then focus the pitch on that person.

No matter where the interview took place, the representative was taught to never quit trying to make the sale. If the wife wanted to serve cookies or cake or cinnamon toast, even canned peaches,

it didn't matter, as long as it prolonged the process. Often the husband and wife would tell the representative they needed more time to make a decision. "It looks like a great plan, but we've got to talk this thing over." The implication was clear: Don't call us, we'll call you. Smith occasionally solved that situation by volunteering to go to the store for ice cream. "You guys talk about it while I'm gone," he would say. "Then I'll come back and we'll have ice cream together."

No sales opportunity came too late in the game, even after the seller had conceded defeat. Sometimes body language told the representative that it was too early to quit. Perhaps the prospect had finally relaxed and was slumped in a chair, ready to talk frankly. When that happened, the representative had to be ready: "Tell me honestly, Mrs. Johnson, what was it that prevented us from doing business tonight?"

The response often was simple. Maybe the prospect wanted to pay annually instead of monthly. "Oh gosh, didn't I make that clear? You can pay monthly, quarterly, whatever works for you!" The representative would sometimes pull out the books and start all over again.

But it was also important to be able to read the prospect's feelings, to know when enough was enough. The line between tenacity and temerity was a thin one. In the heat of closing a sale, emotions could sometimes get out of hand. "Just don't get the wife to cry," Howard Payne admonished his representatives. "It's okay to see a little tear in her eye. But don't get her crying, because the husband will get madder than hell. And then you're in trouble."

Lending Support

Lavern Mausolf had been having a terrible week. Sales were down and so were his spirits. He needed a peptalk. Mausolf called his general agent, John Lienemann, and poured out his heart to him. "This business is just too rough," Mausolf complained. "I'm not having any success at all. I don't know if I've got what it takes to make it in this business." Lienemann did his best to reassure Mausolf, then made hurried plans to meet him in a small Kansas town midway between his agency headquarters in Beatrice, Nebraska, and Mausolf's home in Hoisington, Kansas.

When they met over lunch in an old hotel, Mausolf picked up where he had left off on the phone: "I can't sell. They're not buying." Lienemann listened for a few minutes, then launched into an impassioned speech. "Everybody goes through hard times," he exclaimed. "You've got what it takes to make it. I know, or I wouldn't have picked you to join my agency. I believe in you. You've got to believe in yourself. What you need to do is quit complaining, roll up your sleeves, and get to work!"

Just then the phone rang in the lobby. It was for Mausolf. His wife had called to tell him that a prospect had just come by the house and wanted to buy a large contract. "You'd better hurry home," she said. "He seems anxious to get as much insurance as he can."

Mausolf hung up the phone and walked back to the table, grinning broadly. "Who was that?" Lienemann asked. Mausolf told him, sheepishly. "I can't believe it," said Lienemann. "You call me up and complain that things are so hard, and now you've got prospects pounding at your door for insurance." He shook his head and laughed. "What do you need me for?"

Even the best district representatives needed the support of a general agent. The role of the general agent was analogous to that of a football coach. The representatives did the actual playing, but the general agent taught them the fundamentals and helped them practice their skills. He planned the game strategy and called the plays. He kept the players' spirits up and constantly encouraged them to do better. He sometimes balanced conflicting egos and disciplined them when necessary. The winning general agent did not try to compete with representatives. Instead, he concentrated on doing everything possible to create an environment in which they could prosper, for if they prospered, he prospered.

Building loyalty was essential. When his agents complained about losing a contract because of an underwriting decision, Axel Lundring, a general agent in Pasadena, California, immediately called the home office to complain on their behalf, whether he agreed with the decision or not. "If I ever call up and start to get nasty, just tell me to jump in the lake," he always told the underwriters. "Give me a really hard time. Yell at me. And please don't take it personally when I yell back. I just want to show my agents that I'm fighting for them." Lundring even had a speaker phone in his office so his representatives could hear his fiery harangues.

Lundring's representatives occasionally received signed insurance contracts with their names on them as writing agent. "Hey, I've never talked to this prospect," they would exclaim. "Where did this come from?" Lundring knew. He wrote the contracts himself, then distributed them equally among his people. A few general agents still regularly wrote their own business, but Lundring viewed the practice as a sure way to create jealousy among his representatives. To his way of thinking, long-term loyalty was more valuable than short-term profit.

Yet top general agents also knew how to keep their

representatives hungry, for complacency was the kiss of death in the insurance business. Robert Muehling, a member of Lienemann's agency, once asked Ken Severud, the home office secretary, for help in locating Lienemann, who was on the road. "What's the problem?" asked Severud. "I need a $5,000 advance for a down payment on a house, and I need it before the weekend," said Muehling. When Severud checked Muehling's account, he was astounded to find that Muehling had $8,500 in renewals money coming to him. He sent Muehling the money he needed and told him there was enough left over in his account for furniture, too. As it turned out, Lienemann had always instructed his representatives to ignore the renewal notices that came in the mail from the home office. "Just toss those in the wastebasket," he told them. When Lienemann returned from his travels and learned of Muehling's transaction, he was furious. "How do you expect me to keep my people hustling?" he yelled at Severud over the phone. "What are you trying to do to me, ruin my agency?"

Lienemann's ability to motivate his representatives was legendary, and he built a small empire across the flatlands of Nebraska and northern Kansas. Reared on a farm in eastern Nebraska, he was driving a delivery truck for the Swift Company in the early 1940s when his eye caught a small ad in a Lutheran church magazine. The ad pointed out that Lutheran Brotherhood's top agent had made $806 during the previous month. "Nobody can make that much in one month," Lienemann told his wife. "I'll just write to them and see if that ad is true." It was. He signed on with the society shortly thereafter.

Lienemann's only form of transportation at the time was a bicycle. He quickly borrowed $350 from the bank and bought a used car, with which he roared across the back roads of Nebraska. Lienemann was an amiable fellow, the sort of man everyone liked, but he was always in a hurry. Standing in one spot too long made him nervous. After Lutheran Brotherhood appointed him general agent, he bought a new automobile. Lienemann loved that car, for it allowed him to cover even more miles in less time.

Late one night, with not a soul in sight, he neglected to slow down while passing though a tiny town. But the local policeman, who knew Lienemann, spotted him and decided to give him a warning. He honked and took off after him. But the general agent's new car had more horsepower than the lawman's old jalopy, and Lienemann was long gone before he even realized that he was being followed. A few months later, when Lienemann raced through the same town, the policeman was waiting in a brand new squad car. This time he caught up easily with the general agent and pulled him over. "Now, John, when you go through town next time, slow down," he said with a smile. "I've got a new car, see, and you can't run away from me anymore."

Lienemann was a firm believer in monthly agency meetings, even though his agency stretched from the eastern edge of Nebraska to the Colorado border, a distance of several hundred miles. The meetings were important to agency morale. Those representatives who were having good months inevitably helped to fire up those who were not, and they left the meetings saying, "If those guys can do it, so can I." Lienemann's agency was Lutheran Brotherhood's leading producer several times during the 1950s.

When Lienneman moved to the home office to become director of agencies in 1959, his general agency in Beatrice was assigned to one of his representatives, William Thompson. Under Thompson, the agency kept pace as Lutheran Brotherhood's production leader, finishing first in 1961 and 1962. Like his mentor, Thompson believed in the value of spending plenty of time with his representatives in the field. Every Monday morning, with a fresh supply of clothes in his suitcase, he said goodbye to his family for the next four days. Before backing his car down the driveway, he adjusted the seat and made himself comfortable. Comfort was extremely important, because Thompson spent about forty hours per week in his car, driving to meet with his representatives or riding with them as they made calls. Once on the road, Thompson turned on a tape recorder mounted on the floor near the front seat, and began dictating. During the week, he mailed the tapes back to his secretary for transcription. Thompson went through huge stacks of paperwork each week, but it never kept him from spending time in the field.

By spending time with his representatives, the general agent learned how to manage his agency more effectively. Every representative was different. Some had large egos, others did not. Some liked large, open territories, others did not. Some required constant encouragement, others did not. The wise general agent carefully observed the idiosyncrasies of his agency force and tailored his motivational approach to fit each personality. It was the only way to pull together a motley band of insurance representatives, most of whom coveted their independence and open spaces, and put their often disparate talents to work for a common cause. The wise general agent cultivated individuality within the framework of teamwork, within the structure of family.

William A. Johnson understood the value of individuality. His agency, covering sixteen counties west of Minneapolis, was Lutheran Brotherhood's leading general agency in 1963, the first of many achievements. Johnson believed that it was the society's primary task to provide those who sold policies with whatever tools they needed to succeed. He did not believe in conformity for its own sake. He gave his representatives direction when they needed it, but he did not insist that they do things his way. He did not even ask that they work hard for him, but for their clients and for themselves.

Johnson understood that life in the field was radically different from life in the home office. Representatives sometimes got the feeling that home office workers, to whom daily consistency, teamwork, and conformity were most important, viewed them as prima donnas who were used to getting their way and who whined if they did not. But unlike the home office, the field could be a lonely place. The highs were higher there, and the lows lower. The price of loneliness was financial gratification, and all of Johnson's promotional ideas or contests were designed with that in mind. The more immediate the reward, the harder his representatives worked.

The general agent served as the patriarch of his immediate family of representatives. He took time to listen to their troubles and always seemed to be there with a phone call at the right time. He lifted their spirits and took pride in their achievements.

He taught them the skills to make it on their own, yet his door was always open when they needed help. For some, he seemed like a father.

That was the way Russ Smith felt about Howard Payne. He liked being around the general agent, he liked learning from him, he even liked arguing with him. On one occasion, the two were traveling together to a meeting of the South Dakota Fraternal

District representative Lavern Mausolf of Hoisington, Kansas, was Lutheran Brotherhood's leading producer from 1958 through 1960.

Congress, where Payne was the featured speaker. It was a scorching day, over one hundred degrees Fahrenheit, and Payne's car had no air conditioning. During the day, as the hot wind blew in their faces, Smith and Payne vigorously debated a wide variety of topics. The subject was never really important to Payne, for he simply liked to argue. Several hours later, when the two reached the meeting, Payne was hoarse. He stepped to the podium, opened his mouth to speak, and, with all the effort he could muster, managed to produce only a small whisper.

Life on the road with the garrulous Payne was always interesting. When they traveled together,

Newly appointed district representatives put in arduous days at the week-long indoctrination school at the home office during the early 1960s. The program, supervised by Lutheran Brotherhood's educational director, Jerry Reinan, included taping and playback of sales presentations.

Smith and Payne often stayed in an old hotel in Pierre, South Dakota, that had seen its better days around the turn of the century. The bathroom was at the end of a long hallway. A single light bulb hung from the hall ceiling to guide the way back to the room. Occasionally, after Payne entered the bathroom, Smith would sneak into the hall and unscrew the bulb. When Payne turned off the light in the bathroom and stepped back into the hall, he was confronted with total darkness. As he nervously felt his way back to his room, Smith would lunge out of the darkness at him, eliciting a cry of terror. That made up for all of Payne's arguments.

When Smith traveled the outer boundaries of his territory, he often stayed overnight at Payne's home. The general agent's coffeepot was always on, and he always seemed to have a helpful new sales tip, and occasionally, a paycheck. What intrigued the young

Several of Lutheran Brotherhood's top general agents, about 1965. From left, Ole Haroldson, Denver, Colorado; William L. Thompson, Beatrice, Nebraska; Lavern Peters, San Francisco, California; William A. Johnson, Minneapolis, Minnesota; Harry Siemon, Chicago, Illinois; Axel Lundring, Pasadena, California; Walter Beglau, Austin, Texas; and Harry Hendricks, Baltimore, Maryland.

salesman was that the money usually came when he most needed it, not necessarily when he had earned it. That puzzled Smith. He was a good salesman, but his sales weren't that consistent. He never did ask Payne about the checks, but years later, after Payne had died, Smith learned that his friend had done the same thing for others.

Pioneering New Territory

Seldom had Walt Beglau heard so many discouraging words. He was planning to pull up his stakes as a successful district representative in Watertown, South Dakota, and to build a new Lutheran Brotherhood agency in Texas. His task appeared formidable, if not impossible. At the time, in late 1956, there was only one society agency headquartered in Texas.

At the end of the year, the agency ranked fifty-second in total production out of fifty-eight agencies. Beglau alone had accounted for more sales than had the entire Texas agency.

"It can't be done, Walt," said Beglau's friends. "You're a fool for trying. Think about what you're leaving. You're thriving here. How can you leave all this?" But Beglau was adamant. "I need a challenge," he told them. "I know I can do it. I did the job here. Why can't I do it there?" His friends shook their heads. "Texas is not the Midwest," they told him. "They don't know anything about Lutheran Brotherhood down there. Besides, those people think differently than we do."

"Any insurance representative who thinks that way is already whipped before he starts," Beglau snapped. "Those people are just like us. They love their families, and they need protection. They'll buy insurance from me." His friends were still skeptical. "Walt, they've had a drought in Texas for the last seven years," they explained. "It hasn't rained there for a long time. Not many folks have the money to buy insurance." Beglau was becoming angry now. "The day I hit Texas, it's going to rain," he said rashly. "It's going to pour."

Beglau's friends laughed. Once Walt accepted a challenge, there was no changing his mind. But he was used to challenges. During World War II, when Beglau was a sergeant in the United States Army, Allied planes had mistakenly bombed his bunker, killing several of his men and leaving Beglau with a severe concussion. After the war, he and his wife opened a grocery store in Watertown. Beglau liked the business, but he didn't like the long hours, and he began to think seriously about a career in sales. When a buyer for the store finally appeared, Beglau quickly closed the deal. That night, he suffered a stroke that paralyzed one side of his body. He underwent brain surgery and was hospitalized for six months. Some doctors told him he'd never walk again, and they insisted that he not work for at least a year. He was thirty years old.

During his convalescence, Beglau began studying life insurance. When he recovered from his stroke, he joined Lutheran Brotherhood. He was a hard worker, and members appreciated his diligent service. In 1954, Beglau was briefly hospitalized for a heart condition. Shortly after he was released, one of his clients called and asked if Beglau had had an opportunity to make a sale that week. The man knew that Beglau was in the App-A-Week Club and didn't want him to lose his membership. He brought his infant daughter over to the house, and Beglau wrote a life insurance contract for her. It was his only sale that week.

By 1956, Beglau was one of only three district representatives with $1 million or more of annual personal production. When Beglau was offered the opportunity to build his own agency in Texas, he jumped at the chance. Along with a friend, Beglau packed up the family car and began the long drive to Texas to begin preliminary agency work. The farther south the two men drove, the more threatening the sky became. By the time they reached the Red River, between Texas and Oklahoma, large drops of rain began to fall. A few miles later, it was pouring. Beglau sent news clippings of the subsequent flood to all his friends. Within a few years, his agency was one of the society's perennial production leaders.

It took Beglau's kind of faith to build a new agency on the edges of the United States, far from the comfortable lap of the Midwest. Lutherans were few and far between in places like Texas and California in the 1950s and early 1960s, and few of them had ever heard of Lutheran Brotherhood. In the Midwest, or in parts of Pennsylvania, district representatives often had only to mention Lutheran Brotherhood's name to receive a favorable response from their prospects. Agents who depended on that kind of name recognition in Texas or California were likely to elicit little more than a blank stare.

The sheer distance between Lutherans made selling difficult in these new territories. Beglau's territory included nearly 175,000 Lutherans, but they were spread across most of Texas and Oklahoma and all of Louisiana, a vast region that comprised about one-fifth of the geographical area of the continental United States. Most Lutheran churches in Minnesota had more Lutherans than did several counties combined in Texas.

Representatives also discovered a different attitude among some of the Lutherans in these new territories, especially on the West Coast. Once they had passed the Rocky Mountains, it was said, they left everything else behind, including the church. As such, Lutheran Brotherhood representatives often found baptized Lutherans who did not yet belong to a church, or had young children who had not yet been baptized. When they sold these new arrivals fraternal insurance, they passed their phone numbers along to the local pastor. Thus, a mutually beneficial relationship was established between the clergy

and the society. Many representatives on the West Coast viewed themselves almost as missionaries for the Lutheran church, and they took great pride in helping to bring families back into the fold.

Two of Lutheran Brotherhood's most enthusiastic proponents were based on the West Coast. William Schoeler, in Portland, Oregon, and Einar Botten, in Seattle, Washington, constantly preached the society's fraternal message. They were the first to spread Lutheran Brotherhood's story in their area, and they never let their representatives forget the significance of the society's fraternal mission. "We've

M.E. Andersen, assistant vice president in charge of health insurance, and Loren Endorf, claims supervisor, discuss health plans. Along with consultant Ralph Brastad and Phillip Perry, health insurance underwriter, Andersen and Endorf paved the way for Lutheran Brotherhood's entry into the health insurance field in 1962.

got a valuable story to spread among our prospects," Botten told his new representatives. "You're going to learn that story and be able to recite it backwards and forwards."

Botten was the son of a Norwegian immigrant, and he attended school in Norway for several years during his youth. The scenic valley in which he lived

outside of Seattle was heavily populated with Norwegian Lutherans, and Botten sold insurance to nearly every one of them. The remainder of his territory covered most of the Pacific Northwest and parts of southern Canada. Botten was an intensely religious man, and he viewed his insurance career as a direct extension of his faith. The act of selling insurance was not to be taken lightly. He saw it less as a business than as a rite of honor, a transaction in which all parties benefited. Any person who chose to argue the merits of life insurance with Botten might be in for a lengthy debate, for Botton would not deviate from his beliefs.

Bill Schoeler was equally fervent. An ordained minister, he had joined Lutheran Brotherhood while awaiting a church call, and later continued to combine the two careers. During the week he sold insurance and on Sundays he filled in as a preacher at area churches. Because agency funds were

so tight on the West Coast, Schoeler and his representatives rarely ate out when they were on the road. Instead they purchased a loaf of bread, cheese, and a carton of milk, then had lunch under the nearest tree. After Schoeler retired as a general agent, he continued to preach at area churches. After finishing his sermon one Sunday, he sat down behind the pulpit and slumped over as though he were taking a nap. After the service, some parishioners attempted to wake him, to no avail. He had died during the closing prayers.

Fraternal evangelists like Schoeler and Botten helped to demonstrate that Lutheran Brotherhood could succeed in uncharted Lutheran territory, and young general agents like Beglau and Axel Lundring proved it. Like Beglau, Axel Lundring was a native of South Dakota. Because of his severe allergies, doctors had given him just a few years to live in that climate, so he had moved to arid southern California in the

Within the image: LUTHERAN BROTHERHOOD / Health Insurance Convention / French Lick, Indiana / August 4-5-6-7, 1963

The 1963 Lutheran Brotherhood sales convention was held at picturesque French Lick, Indiana.

1930s, and he had joined Lutheran Brotherhood several years later. Within a few years after he was appointed general agent in Pasadena, his agency had become one of the society's annual sales leaders.

Like Lundring, most of his representatives were natives of other states. Perhaps because they felt more isolated among Californians than did their brethren in the Midwest, the Lundring agency had a strong sense of teamwork. Their ability to plan and work together helped them to establish several society records. Lundring was a master at creating new challenges for his representatives. In June 1955, he decided that his agency should write a million dollars in new business in one month. No society agency had ever come close to that mark. Three months later, the Lundring agency reached its goal.

Two years later, Lundring dared his agency to write $1 million of business during July, which perennially was the slowest month of the year. It took some

convincing, but the men finally agreed that they could do it. The representatives maintained their production schedule for the first three weeks of the month. On the last day of July, they met to total up their business for the entire month. Everyone groaned when the final tally was placed on the chalkboard: Only $950,000. Lundring was downcast. Then one representative remembered a contract he hadn't reported. Then another. Lundring began to wave his arms. "Think!" he shouted. "Maybe some of you other guys forgot to report a policy!" Amazingly, several representatives had.

As the total on the chalkboard slowly grew, Lundring, whose face was becoming flushed from the anticipation and excitement, suddenly realized what was happening. "Hold it," he said. "Something fishy is going on here." The room exploded in laughter, and the representatives admitted their complicity: Before the meeting, they had agreed to hold back on enough contracts to keep their total short of $1 million, just so they could see Lundring sweat.

Their real production total had been $1.3 million.

A New Product

By the 1960s, it had become clear that Lutherans could not live by life insurance alone. A complete life insurance plan would help protect a family if its breadwinner died, but such a plan did little good if the breadwinner was injured and unable to work for even a few months. Who would pay for food and clothing? Who would pay the mortgage and other household bills? Who would finance the children's education? The chances of being disabled were far greater than most people thought. According to national statistics, one out of three men who were thirty-five years old would be disabled for longer than three months before reaching age sixty-five.

Lutheran Brotherhood's district representatives had been pushing for health insurance for several years. Granrud listened closely to his field force, and in 1958 he decided to study the idea. He called M. E. Andersen, an assistant vice president in the underwriting department, into his office, and made him a proposal. "Earl, we're thinking of getting into health insurance," Granrud said. "Would you be interested in organizing it?" Andersen was intrigued, but cautious. "Well, it is a brand new field for us," he said. "I'll need more information to get started." Granrud winked. "Don't worry about that," he said. "We'll get it for you."

Much of the expertise the society needed came in the person of Ralph Brastad, a successful health insurance salesman for Massachusetts Indemnity & Life Insurance Company. In 1960, Granrud approached Brastad, a member of his church in south Minneapolis, for his thoughts on how to get started in health insurance.

Brastad told his old acquaintance that the company would have to meet four requirements:

"First," he said, "you'll need a darn good policy. Second, you've got to be careful in your underwriting. Third, you'll need to provide excellent claim

service. Fourth, you'll have to know how to sell it."

He quickly added, "I can help you with all four."

Granrud tried to persuade Brastad to join Lutheran Brotherhood, but Brastad preferred a consultant's role. Over the next two years, he worked closely with Andersen and with Reuben Jacobson, the society's head actuary, and Phil Perry, an underwriter, to help develop what he considered to be a "Cadillac contract." For model plans, they looked at those of Brastad's own company, Massachusetts Indemnity (an insurance plan so well-regarded that it was used as course material at the Wharton School of Finance) and at those sold by several other top health insurance companies.

On January 1, 1962, Lutheran Brotherhood entered the field of health insurance, and Earl Andersen was named to head the program. "Health insurance protects a man's most valuable asset—his earning power," he told *The BOND* magazine. "At present, Lutheran Brotherhood is offering health insurance only to male risks between the ages of twenty-one and sixty. However, this will be expanded to include other types of health insurance protection." Several months later, after numerous requests from Lutheran working women, the society extended its health insurance plan to cover women.

As Brastad had counseled, the society became an extremely careful underwriter. It had to be. Fraternals seldom ventured into the world of health insurance, and the rules were not designed to encourage them to do so. To continue to qualify to sell fraternal health insurance in the state of Illinois, for example, Lutheran Brotherhood had to be making a profit within three years. "You guys are crazy to go into this field with that kind of limitation," several commercial underwriters told Andersen. However, with prudent underwriting and an adequate premium, the society's health insurance program was in the black by its third year.

Andersen was also aided by an assistant who was an expert in health insurance. Loren Endorf was short and stocky, and his puckish face was capped with a flattop haircut. "Stand up, Endorf!" field representatives invariably called out when he took to the podium at sales conventions. The field force was fond of Endorf, and his extensive knowledge of the health insurance business helped to sell the program.

In its second year, Lutheran Brotherhood's health insurance business grew by more than 35 percent over the preceding year. Bolstered by the new product in their portfolio, the field force increased the society's insurance in force to more than $2 billion by 1964.

The Governor

Jacob Aall Otteson Preus, the grand old man of Lutheran Brotherhood, died on May 24, 1961. He was seventy-seven.

If Herman Ekern had served as the brains behind the society's origin and development, Preus had long been its face and its voice. Although the former governor of Minnesota had not served in public office in more than three decades, he was first and foremost a politician, with an outgoing style and a remarkable memory. It was said that you could be introduced to Preus, not see him for twenty years, and he would greet you again by name. Preus brought charisma to an otherwise reserved organization. He was confident and polished, and he gave the society an image of authority.

The venerable Preus was the chairman of the board of Lutheran Brotherhood from 1922 until his death, a period of thirty-nine years. His long reign did not include any specific individual achievements, and it was difficult to characterize his personal management style. Preus defied labeling. He had championed juvenile insurance in the 1920s. He had been closely involved with the society's investment department, and he had continually urged the society to expand its influence. Yet when it came to governing the affairs of the society, Preus had concerned himself more with promoting unity of board opinion than with pursuing his own personal agenda.

Preus had been extremely disheartened by the turmoil of the 1959 convention, but despite the acrimony, he was optimistic about the future of the society. He liked Granrud and placed great trust in his abilities. The two men got on famously, for they had much in common. Each man possessed a caustic wit, a love of conversation, an appreciation of ancient history, and an extraordinary memory. They

also shared an aversion to synodical parochialism.

It was as a politician, not as a churchman or even as an insurance man, that Preus was best known. Two terms as Republican governor of Minnesota, in 1920 and 1922, had ensured his lasting fame. "I wasn't good enough for the ministry," Jake once told a reporter. "So I went into the profession which is the nearest thing to it: politics!" His exceptional ability to remember the names of voters no doubt played at least a small part in his first election. One article claimed that he knew 60 percent of the electorate by their first names. Preus mixed easily with strangers, and his campaign slogan exemplified his familiar, easygoing style: "It's Jake with me."

Preus was elected to the governorship during a bitter struggle over the direction of Minnesota's economic farm policy. The Socialists proposed a program of state ownership to bail out the state's ailing farmers, while the Republicans advocated cooperative marketing. Preus recognized that the farmers needed help, but in his view, cooperative associations were the only effective way to assist them. Cooperation allowed farmers to own their own business, yet allowed them to eliminate unnecessary charges, thus increasing their return. Preus became one of the country's most vocal proponents of cooperatives. During his administration, the legislature enacted several laws to widen cooperative activity, and cooperative sales in Minnesota nearly doubled.

Although Preus was a staunch capitalist, he was also a firm believer in the public good. "The welfare of a state is greater than the ambitions of an individual," he said in his first inaugural address. During Preus's two terms as governor, taxes were raised on the rich mining companies, a rural loan credit bureau was established, a new worker's compensation law was passed, and the forestry department was improved.

In 1923, Preus's political mentor, Knute Nelson, died. Preus decided to enter the contest for Nelson's seat in the U.S. Senate. He lost. Preus later called his first political defeat a blessing, for it convinced him not to spend his life in politics. He completed his second term as governor in 1925 and never again sought public office. He put in a few months as a

Jacob Aall Otteson Preus, chairman of the board of Lutheran Brotherhood, 1922 to 1961.

southeast Minneapolis, near the University of Minnesota. "I'd rather live in a house I can afford than in a mansion that belongs to the state," Preus said. "I don't like being under obligations."

Preus the patriarch was not unlike others of his generation. He was a busy, successful man who attended first to providing for his family, then to spending time with them. Known as "Sire Preus" by the immediate family, he could be gruff and demanding of his children, yet he delighted privately in their accomplishments. "You have no idea what a pleasure it was to see you," he once wrote to son Robert. "Mother and I should be the happiest people in the world if we could raise such fine boys and their father is such a rascal." He was especially fond of his seventeen grandchildren, although he jokingly told friends that it seemed his sons, both of whom became prominent pastors in the Missouri Synod, had taken upon themselves the job of populating the world. And he doted constantly on his beloved wife, Idella.

Although Preus seemed the picture of robust health even into his seventies, he suffered from asthma, hay fever, and other allergies, and occasionally collapsed because he was unable to catch his breath. Because of his condition, Preus usually spent two months each fall breathing clean air at his lakefront cabin in Grand Marais, a port town on Lake Superior in northern Minnesota. Lutheran Brotherhood board meetings were often held at nearby Lutsen during the fall.

Preus kept an office in the green building and spent an increasing amount of time there during his retirement. His presence at the home office was sometimes intimidating, like that of an inspector general. The governor often seemed larger than life to the home office employees, and he did not attempt to downplay his image. He occasionally cashed a hundred dollar check in the home office lobby and

troubleshooter for the Minneapolis Commercial Club, then became a broker for the W. A. Alexander Insurance Company of Chicago. At the time, the firm was the largest insurance company in the Midwest. Preus became one of its most successful salesmen and a vice president.

Preus made a fine living with the company, but like most everyone else who had lived through the depression, he was extremely careful with his money. Although he was always willing to give pocket money to his sons, he tried to teach when he gave. He once sent each of his sons fifty shares of Braniff Airways stock and one of the company's recent financial statements. "I don't want you to just sock these shares away in a drawer," he told them. "I want you to learn to understand and follow the development of this company." Preus was frugal with other people's money, too. During his two terms as governor, the family lived in a large but unpretentious house in

J.A.O. Preus enlisted the help of U.S. Presidential candidate Warren G. Harding during his campaign for governor of Minnesota in 1920. Both Preus and Harding were elected.

"When Good Fellows Get Together"

J. A. O. PREUS
For Governor

WARREN G. HARDING
For President

Their Platform:

SANITY IN PUBLIC OFFICE

Co-operation in Agriculture and Industry

AMERICA ALWAYS

Senator Warren G. Harding, candidate for President of the United States, and J. A. O. Preus,
candidate for Governor of Minnesota, taken at Senator Harding's home at Marion, Ohio.

Prepared and circulated by R. P. Chase, Anoka, Minn., for the candidates.

56

asked for a hundred one-dollar bills in return. Then, like a rich tycoon, he would flamboyantly pull the thick roll from his pocket when he picked up lunch tabs. Preus was also an inspiring orator, and he often regaled employees at coffee breaks with his panoramic views of the world.

Dorothy Zetzman had worked the switchboard during her early days at the home office, and Preus often called her from his office to place calls for him. While Preus talked to his contacts in New York City or Washington, D.C., Zetzman was sweating at the switchboard because she was afraid that she might disconnect him. Years later, she found herself seated next to Preus at a Lutheran Brotherhood dinner. The governor was charming and witty, and he went out of his way to make Zetzman feel at ease. She was pleasantly surprised. This is the man who used to scare me so much? she thought to herself. Why, he's just an old gentleman.

The Battle Begins Anew

In December 1959, just a few months after Granrud's victory over Neprud and the insurgents, the society's board of directors received a letter from a local pastor. "I am writing to you as I send in my premium because I am disturbed about Lutheran Brotherhood Insurance," he wrote. "I see that great advance is being made in selling policies, but there are some things that are being said and have been said about Lutheran Brotherhood that are not good. I realize that some may have been playing fast and loose with the truth, but where there is smoke, there must be a little fire."

Many area pastors and society members agreed. The flames of the 1959 rebellion continued to burn steadily, if less brightly, during the next two years. Granrud was still Granrud, critics privately insisted, and he was not likely to change his dictatorial ways merely because of one well-timed apology. Granrud's supporters shook their heads: When would these people quit interfering with society business? When would they realize that Lutheran Brotherhood must be run like an insurance organization? If the society was only a business, the insurgents rebutted, then why not just take the word *Lutheran* out of the society name?

The anti-Granrud camp had been waiting for any opportunity to renew the fight with management. Their chance came in the summer of 1960, when the board voted to raise the mandatory retirement age of officers and department heads from sixty-five to sixty-eight. The vote allowed four directors who also served as officers, including Granrud, to remain in their jobs. Granrud claimed that the limit had to be raised; otherwise, the society would lose its most experienced leaders. Yet even some of his supporters were irked by the decision, for the 1959 convention delegates had voted to establish sixty-five as the retirement age. The angry insurgents pointed to the decision as another example of Granrud's disregard for the will of the delegates.

Several dismissals of society employees added fuel to the fire. One of the most talked-about incidents occurred shortly after the death of Harold Hoel. Most of the general agents attended the funeral in Minneapolis, then met at the green building. One of them, Einar Botten, suggested that the general agents should play an active role in selecting Hoel's replacement as director of agencies. When word of Botten's statement reached Granrud, the president was furious. The general agent, who had been pushing for an agent's union, was already in his doghouse. Granrud immediately called Botten into his office. "I understand you were getting into our politics," he said. "We don't need your help. You're fired." And with those two words, Botten, who had pioneered the Pacific Northwest for Lutheran Brotherhood, was gone.

That was the last straw for Gordon Bubolz. A Lutheran Brotherhood director since 1942, Bubolz had supported Granrud during the last power struggle, but he had since changed his mind. "Granrud is more interested in his own power than in the fraternal plan of representative government under which the society's delegates are the supreme governing body," he told the *Minneapolis Star*. "He is making a sham and a mockery out of our system, and I didn't want to be party to it."

Bubolz was a prominent attorney in Appleton, Wisconsin, where he was president of the Home Mutuals Group of fire and casualty insurance companies. He had also spent nearly three terms in the Wisconsin legislature, where he was described by reporters as colorless yet earnest, a slow starter who had developed into an influential state senator.

Bubolz joined the insurgents in 1961 and became one of the leaders of a new movement to replace Granrud. The group, which included several local pastors and former society employees who had been fired during the previous battle (including Herb Johnson and Paul Jacobson), named itself The Committee of One Hundred. The committee members planned their strategy throughout the summer. In September 1961, they mailed a booklet entitled *A Call for Reform* to each of the thirteen hundred Lutheran Brotherhood members who had been delegates during the 1959 convention.

The document called for a special convention "to restore effective control of Lutheran Brotherhood to the members and delegates and to prevent a scheming few from establishing a dictatorship in our fraternal organization." It wouldn't do to wait until the next quadrennial convention to clean up the society's affairs, the committee claimed; corrective action was needed as soon as possible.

The issues were essentially the same as they had been two years earlier. The Committee of One Hundred maintained that several directors were beholden to Granrud (who had recently been named chairman of the board after Preus's death), and that he fired employees without just cause. It called for an entirely new board of directors. The committee also charged that too small a portion of Lutheran Brotherhood's fraternal tax savings was passed back to the church, and it advocated an independent group of church leaders to administer the society's benevolences.

The committee asked the delegates to sign two forms. The first was to be sent to Ken Severud, the secretary of Lutheran Brotherhood, requesting a special convention on December 5, 1961, at which these issues could be considered. The second form was to be sent to Peat, Marwick, Mitchell & Co., an accounting firm that would certify the delegate's signature. If more than half of the delegates—645, to be exact—signed the forms, management would be forced to hold the special convention.

News traveled fast in the society, and Granrud had known for some time of the uprising. When he learned of the committee's latest strategy, he hired Robins, Davis & Lyons, a Minneapolis law firm, to examine the special convention forms and to determine what he could do to stop the campaign. A few days later, Julius E. Davis, one of the firm's partners, wrote back to Granrud with good news. Each individual request for a special convention could be legally revoked by the signer at a later date. The delegate simply had to change his or her mind, and say so in writing.

Harold Hoel, vice president in charge of agencies, and John Lienemann, superintendent of agencies, visit with general agent Howard Payne, Aberdeen, South Dakota, in 1960.

Management quickly manufactured revocation forms: "Through a misunderstanding of the issues involved, I signed a written request addressed to you asking that a special meeting of the General Convention be called on December 5, 1961," the form read. "I wish to advise you at this time that I am withdrawing my request and that I am not in favor of the calling of a special meeting of the General Convention on December 5, 1961."

Playing Hardball

A furious struggle ensued for the hearts of the delegates and for their signatures. During one thirty-day period, Granrud and Lienemann, the new director of agencies, flew across the country to thirty cities and presented management's case to the general agents and delegates. Business had never been better, they told their listeners. In the last three years, the total amount of insurance had doubled. In the past ten years, insurance in force had increased to $1.5 billion. Benevolence payments had increased more than tenfold in the last ten years. The society had never been stronger. The field force had never been more united. The employees and agents had never been more loyal.

The same could not be said for the insurgents, whom management described as a small minority who sought to gain power over the society for their own benefit. In one press release, Lienemann pointed out that it was strange that Bubolz should accuse Lutheran Brotherhood's management of dictatorship, while at the same time holding absolute control of his own insurance companies. "The present group of dissidents have told you many things but have given you very few facts," management said in a forty-two-page booklet called *Facts You Should Know.* "They have given you half-truths, false assertions, and spurious charges. They have violently attacked President Granrud to hide behind their true intention of removing all members of the Board of Directors and every officer. They have used high-sounding phrases about benevolence when their purpose appears to

An overhead shot of the 1963 Lutheran Brotherhood Ice Cream Social in the home office garden. The home office garden was the site of many ceremonies and civic functions and occasionally was home to several peacocks.

be one of depriving Lutheran Brotherhood of its advantages as a fraternal insurance organization."

The latter accusation was leveled directly at Arnold Ryden, a Minneapolis businessman, for it was he who supplied most of the insurgent funds. Estimates of his contributions ranged from forty thousand to seventy thousand dollars. Ryden had been approached by the insurgent leaders, sympathized with their cause, and decided to join them. His motivation for doing so became one of management's favorite targets. Granrud characterized Ryden as a common stock promoter who, if given the chance, would transform Lutheran Brotherhood into a mutual, or even worse, a stock insurance company, then pillage its assets.

To some observers, the portrayal did not seem entirely inaccurate. Ryden was a successful but nomadic entrepreneur. He was a financial genius, an honor student at the Harvard Business School, the head of several electronics and investment corporations, and one of the founders of Control Data, a computer corporation whose stock price had multiplied by almost 150 in just three years. Although Ryden often expressed brilliant new ideas, observers noted that he had a hard time working with others. He was impatient and bypassed bureaucratic channels. As a result, he had left almost every company for which he had ever worked, including Control Data, although he exited each job with a hefty compensation package. That was just fine with Ryden. He had always wanted to be his own boss, leaping from venture to venture, and he quickly prospered on his own. It did not seem implausible to Granrud's supporters that the mercurial Ryden might view Lutheran Brotherhood as another opportunity to make a quick profit.

Others painted a very different picture of the man. Ryden had always been a devoted and active churchgoer. He had worked his way through the University of Minnesota, where he served as president of the Lutheran Student Association and graduated with honors. Ryden was a member of the Augustana Lutheran Church Pension and Aid Board, a member of the Board of Regents of Gustavus Adolphus College in St. Peter, Minnesota, and a church trustee. He was extremely generous. When Bubolz

it to the chairman when the insurgents won, as proof that there were no hard feelings.

He never got the chance. Management leveled its meanest blasts at Ryden. After all, he was the outsider; the society's members might fight like cats and dogs with one another, but they would almost certainly band together if a stranger entered their midst. At one point, Granrud and Lienemann released a document, designed to look like a newspaper article, which revealed that Ryden was one of several investors in a Wisconsin hotel complex with four bars. "Arnold J. Ryden Adds Liquor to List of Business Interests," the headline read.

The Committee of One Hundred quickly retorted that among Lutheran Brotherhood's many investments was a five hundred thousand dollar interest in McKesson & Robbins, one of the largest distributors of alcoholic beverages in the country. The society also held investments in several railroads, which had dining cars in which alcoholic beverages were sold. "I am sure that not one of you delegates would say, 'Because of these investments, Lutheran Brotherhood is in the liquor business,'" the committee wrote to the delegates. "Neither is Mr. Ryden, whose investment is only five thousand dollars in a seven hundred thousand dollar motel."

The committee had another question for the delegates. "Since Mr. Granrud has an investment interest (membership) in both the Minneapolis Club and the Minneapolis Athletic Club, and since there are various rooms in these two clubs where liquor may be ordered, would it be fair to state that Mr. Granrud is in the liquor business?"

Charges and countercharges flew during the next few months, during which more than eighty pieces of propaganda were sent by the opposing camps to delegates. The clergy took sides; one pastor would vigorously defend the management, and another would criticize it. Both factions accused the other of spying. Cy Rachie, the society's legal counsel, who was working with the insurgents, claimed that his phone had been tapped. He resigned and joined the Committee of One Hundred. Management intimated that Rachie had been unhappy because

asked Ryden's pastor for background material, the pastor reported that Ryden had made a contribution large enough to pay for a new pipe organ. The local newspapers also reported that he had recently agreed to donate two hundred thousand dollars to Gustavus if a similar amount was raised. Those who knew Ryden well, including several church leaders, dismissed management's accusations against him as preposterous.

Ryden insisted that he had no designs on the society's assets. It was Granrud's management style that bothered him, he said, and that was why he had entered the fray. He wanted to see the society remain a fraternal organization. However, he was intrigued with the investment possibilities of Lutheran Brotherhood, and contemplated the idea of adding mutual funds to its list of products. He even went so far as to print up an imitation stock certificate, called the Granrud Fund, and planned to show

he had not been made general counsel.

The air was thick with intrigue. One rainy night, Severud accepted an invitation to discuss insurgent grievances with Rachie and Ryden. Because Severud preferred not to be seen with them, the committee later claimed, he arranged to drive his car into an open garage, and for the garage to be closed before he got out of the car. The other side had a different story. Rachie had offered to open his garage door so that Severud could easily identify his home, management claimed, and had suggested that he drive into the garage to avoid getting soaked by the rain.

As the news of these and other incidents began to spread among many Lutherans, selling insurance became an increasingly difficult proposition. In several instances, society members dropped their contracts, or prospects declined to purchase insurance because of the turmoil. The general agents' council estimated that the field was $15 million behind its sales goals because of the fight. As a result, most of the general agents signed a document supporting Granrud, and the general agents' council called on Bubolz to resign. "While wealthy individuals, reputed millionaires, play at power politics, we, the agents

The home office services division. Standing in the foreground is Richard Lund, policy services department manager. Note the sign in the background indicating Lutheran Brotherhood's goal of selling $2 billion of insurance by the end of 1964.

NEWS FLASH

WE HAVE WON THE BATTLE!

811 Delegates Indicate They Do Not Want Special Convention

and employees of Lutheran Brotherhood, must pay the price," the council said. "What to them is only a convenient tax deduction is rent and food and clothing for our children."

That did not mean, however, that the field was entirely happy with management. Several district representatives quit rather than state their allegiance to Granrud, and others were fired. Life was especially tense at the home office. One of the few employees who declined to sign a loyalty oath and survived was

On September 27, 1961, a few days after the Committee of One Hundred claimed it had enough delegate signatures to call a special convention that would be likely to unseat Carl Granrud, the chairman countered with a press conference at which he displayed the signatures of what he claimed were a majority of delegates who opposed such a convention. A flyer describing the press conference, reproduced here, was one of more than eighty pieces of propaganda distributed to delegates by both opposing factions.

Cliff Thompson. "I'll be glad to sign a loyalty oath," he told management supporters. "I'm very loyal to Lutheran Brotherhood. But I haven't had such a nice time around here lately. Granrud's been pretty rough on me. If I sign this, am I assured that everything is going to be fine?" "No," he was told. "We can't guarantee you anything."

"Then I'm not interested in signing."

News of the struggle spread quickly to Lutherans throughout the nation. In response to the growing number of inquiries from its members as to the relationship between the church and the society, the American Lutheran Church passed a resolution. It read, in part: "Whereas the Church does not own or control the Lutheran Brotherhood, neither does the Lutheran Brotherhood have any voice in the affairs of the Church, nor has it any unique claim to preferential treatment by the Church."

The Blue Ballot

In September 1961, the Committee of One Hundred wrote to Minnesota Attorney General Walter Mondale and asked him to investigate its claims against the management of Lutheran Brotherhood. Mondale and his staff studied the charges, then turned the matter over to Cyrus Magnusson, the state commissioner of insurance. "I wish to make it quite clear that the Minnesota Insurance Department will not become involved in a controversy between the present management and those who seek to oust this management," Magnusson told the insurgents, noting that "it is the opinion of our department attorney. . .that these charges are of a general nature unsupported by any evidence or not contrary to statute."

Despite the decision, the Committee of One Hundred was confident of victory. On September 27, they told the *Minneapolis Morning Tribune* that in just a few days they would announce that they had at least 645 delegate signatures, enough to force a special convention. But they declined to give the exact number of signatures they had received so far. "It's a question of whether we win by a landslide or not," Ryden said. "We don't want anyone to refrain from sending his signature because he thinks we've got enough."

The insurgents suggested five candidates for the board of directors, including Ryden, Bubolz, and Rachie; the other two were Carl Segerhammar, who was already a society board member and vice president of the Augustana Lutheran Church, and Wendell Lund, a Washington, D.C., attorney. They said they would eventually present at least fourteen candidates for twelve seats, and asked the delegates for additional suggestions. Because management claimed Ryden and Bubolz wanted to take over the society's assets, the insurgents emphasized that "it will be entirely up to you as delegates at the convention whether you wish to have Mr. Ryden or Mr. Bubolz serve as board members."

A few days after the Committee of One Hundred had claimed victory, Granrud told a press conference that Lutheran Brotherhood had received signed statements from 699 delegates indicating that they did not want a special convention. In addition, he said, 142 delegates had informed the society that they did not wish to participate on either side of the controversy. "This means that 811 out of 1,289 delegates have indicated they do not want a special convention this December," Granrud said. "The insurgents cannot obtain the 645 votes they require."

The Committee of One Hundred insisted they had enough signatures, 673 to be exact, to force a special convention. However, almost one hundred of the signers did not want their names revealed. These delegates were employees of Lutheran Brotherhood, the insurgents said, and they feared retribution from Granrud. The Committee thus found itself in an impossible situation. They needed every signature they could get. But how could they deliver all its request forms to the society's secretary, Severud, as required by the bylaws of the society, without Granrud finding out who had signed them?

Rachie came up with the solution. If Severud would pledge under oath that he would not reveal the names of petition signers, the committee would turn the forms over to him. Severud was willing to consider the plan, but Granrud refused, demanding to know the names. We're bound by the society bylaws, he explained, and we're permitted no latitude. That seemed to be strictly a matter of personal interpretation, since the bylaws stated only that the requests must be delivered to the secretary.

Without a guarantee of anonymity, the Committee of One Hundred declined to turn in their ballots, and mulled over their options. What could they do now? The cutoff date for receipt of their request forms had passed. Besides, even if they did succeed in calling a special convention, it appeared they would need two-thirds of the votes at the convention to pass any new amendments to the bylaws. They were not sure they had that much support.

The insurgents decided to simplify matters. They quickly printed a new request form on blue paper, called the Blue Ballot, and mailed it to the delegates. Like the previous form, the Blue Ballot called for a special convention, but with only one item to consider: the election of a new board of directors. It seemed a foolproof plan. The election of new directors would require only a simple majority (645 votes) at the special convention, and the insurgents claimed they had already received that many petitions once. There was no reason to believe that they would not receive that many again.

Now employees who were also delegates could sign the Blue Ballot without the need for secrecy. If the Committee of One Hundred received 645 or more requests, they could legally call for the special convention. If those same petitioners then voted for the new directors at the convention, victory was assured. Thus, even if society employees who signed Blue Ballots were fired by Granrud before the convention, the insurgents explained, they would be reinstated immediately and retroactively after the convention by the new board of directors.

When management learned of the Blue Ballot, they filed suit against the Committee of One Hundred. Enough is enough, they told the court; the insurgents had had their chance and had failed. Management asked the court to invalidate the Blue Ballot and restrain the insurgents from contacting the delegates again. The insurgents promptly filed a countersuit against Granrud and his supporters, charging them with mismanagement.

While the courts considered the opposing claims, Kelly Neprud wrote a letter to the field force. Although he supported the insurgents, he had not participated in any of their activities. The immediate battle was not what concerned him. He was more worried about how the government might view it. Lutheran Brotherhood had come within an eyelash

of being taxed just a few years earlier, and continued infighting was not going to help its fraternal case. "Irrespective of who is right or wrong, irrespective of the validity of the position of the various parties to the current dispute within our society," he wrote, "it should be most apparent to you that we must resolve these disputes, we must put our house in order, before the Legislature does it for us." Neprud, the man who had built the society's sales force from almost nothing, died a few months later.

In the meantime, Blue Ballots streamed into the Committee of One Hundred headquarters. By the end of January 1962, the insurgents claimed to have 626 new requests for a special convention, with many more on the way. They also announced a slate of fifteen candidates for the new board of directors of Lutheran Brotherhood. Ryden was not among the nominees. He had decided that he was too conspicuous a target, and withdrew to assure the delegates of his selfless motivations. Bubolz, Rachie, and Segerhammar were among the nominees, as were several pastors and businessmen from five different synods throughout the country. Also named were two current Lutheran Brotherhood officers, Al Konigson, vice president in charge of underwriting, and Reuben Jacobson, vice president and chief actuary. Neither Konigson nor Jacobson was known as a Granrud supporter, yet both men hurriedly declined the nominations, as did Segerhammar.

It didn't matter. When the insurgents finally delivered 662 requests to Severud on February 5, 1962, they discovered that he had more than one hundred revocations in his possession. The Blue Ballot had failed. "After more than five months of effort and numerous claims by the Committee of One Hundred of enough requests of delegates calling for a special convention," Severud announced, "it is apparent that the majority of our people are not in favor of a special meeting and wish to await the next general convention in May of 1963."

The courts dismissed both the management and insurgent suits, and the Committee of One Hundred eventually disbanded. Ryden lost interest in the struggle, and the other insurgents began to focus their attention on other matters, such as new jobs. The rebels had repeatedly stormed the castle, only to be repelled time and again, and now they had run out of ammunition. Granrud had outlasted the opposition again, and he seemed stronger than ever.

By the time the next general convention rolled around in May 1963, opposition to Granrud had quieted. There were still episodes of grumbling among agents and employees, but they were diffuse and muted. The only organized movement to unseat Granrud came from a small group of pastors led by the Reverend Joseph Simonson of Eden Prairie, Minnesota, and a few former insurgents, including Rachie and Harvey Skaar, a onetime society employee who had served as secretary of the Committee of One Hundred. The group called itself the Movement for Lutheran Brotherhood Reform, and its platform was similar to those of previous opposition groups. However, management easily elected its slate of directors, including Dreng Bjornaraa, Woody Langhaug, A. Herbert Nelson, Russell Matthias, and John Lienemann.

Lienemann had been a Lutheran Brotherhood board member since 1962, when he was named to replace Neprud. More than anyone else, he had worked the hardest for Granrud during the struggle with the Committee of One Hundred, and the chairman had often told the lanky Nebraskan that he was his choice for the next president of the society. Lienemann was well-regarded, even by some of the insurgents against whom he had battled so arduously, for he had a reputation as an honest man.

But Lienemann's honesty eventually got him into hot water with his boss. After the convention, Granrud, who had just turned sixty-seven, began tossing about the idea of raising the mandatory retirement age for officers from sixty-eight to seventy. When he asked Lienemann's opinion of the move, the director of agencies told him flatly: "Nothing doing, Mr. Granrud," he said. "You've been through this once before. You can't afford to get involved in another fight over this. You should have brought this up at the convention. I'm not going along with it."

That fall, the board of directors made its annual appointments of officers. Lienemann was certain that he would be named president, but the board instead elected Harold Smith to the post. Mildly shocked, Lienemann waited to hear that he had at least been reelected as director of agencies. The board read off several more names: "David Zetzman elected financial vice president. Gordon Taft elected superintendent of agencies. Woody Langhaug reelected director of marketing and research. Gretchen Pracht reelected director of public relations-advertising. Ted Feig reelected treasurer." The names continued. When the board finally got around to director of agencies, Lienemann did not hear his own name announced. Instead, he heard Don Lommen's. Later that afternoon, Lienemann phoned Lommen, who was traveling in the field. "You're the new director of agencies," he said abruptly.

"I'm what?" Lommen answered. "What happened to you?"

The line was silent for a moment.

"I've been fired."

Lutheran Brotherhood's powerful chairman, Carl Granrud, clearly stood out from the crowd. With him are members of the society's board of directors in 1966, front row, from left: Dr. Richard H. Gerberding, Russell H. Matthias, Arthur O. Lee, Gordon A. Bubolz, and Dreng Bjornaraa. Back row: Dr. Arthur O. Davidson, A. Herbert Nelson, Bertram M. Wilde, Woodrow P. Langhaug, and Dr. A.R. Kretzmann. Not pictured: Harold A. Smith.

Power and Discord

The telephone rang just once, and Ole Haroldson, a general agent in Denver, Colorado, quickly snatched up the receiver. "Hello," he said, a little anxiously.

"How are you, you old SOB?" said a voice on the other end. Haroldson recognized the voice immediately and relaxed. It was Merrill Gille, a fellow general agent from Teaneck, New Jersey, calling from the home office.

"Man, what a nice greeting that was."

"I thought you would like it," Gille said, laughing.

"Well, I'm used to being treated rough."

For Ole Haroldson, relations with LB's management had become strained. A few days earlier, he and Axel Lundring had been in the home office and happened to visit one of the directors. On this occasion, the two general agents voiced their disapproval of the elections of Gretchen Pracht and Robert Most, both non-Lutherans, as officers. Word of their remarks quickly reached the politically omniscient Granrud, who, almost immediately after Haroldson returned to Denver, gave him a tongue-lashing over the phone, then hung up on him. Haroldson tried to call Granrud back collect, but the chief executive refused to talk to him.

Gille had subsequently called Haroldson, hoping to intercede and reestablish contact between the two longtime friends. It would not be easy; they were both proud, headstrong, and stubborn.

"I've fought for him all my life," Haroldson told Gille, "and I don't know why he should take that attitude and just hang up on an old friend."

Gille reported that Granrud had calmed down now, and he suggested that Haroldson try calling him again. "Time mends all wounds, you know," Gille said. "I talked to him and I said you two better get together. He told me, 'You tell that SOB that he had better call me.'"

"I don't like to be called an SOB, either," Haroldson said, "unless they smile, like you. If you smile when you say it, it's fine."

"Well, you know Carl."

Haroldson and Granrud eventually did begin speaking again, although the nagging feeling persisted that things would never be the same between them. It was 1963, and the memory of two bitter political campaigns was still fresh in Granrud's mind. He was tired of being criticized. It hadn't been easy, trying to build this small fraternal society into a major insurance organization, he thought to himself. Too many people thought they could do the job better. But there could be only one person in charge, and Granrud had been chosen for the job.

Even Granrud's opponents had to admit that he was doing a creditable job. During his years as president and now as chairman of the board, he had helped to build Lutheran Brotherhood from a tiny regional insurance society into a nationwide business operation. Since 1951, the society's insurance-in-force had grown from $366 million to $2 billion, and fraternal payments had increased more than tenfold. And, at a time when many companies were leaving downtown Minneapolis for the suburbs, Granrud had personally overseen the construction of an imposing new building that had revitalized the downtown community. For the first time, people knew who and what Lutheran Brotherhood was.

However, Granrud's accomplishments were rarely as noted as the style in which they were achieved. For all his positive deeds, Granrud's roughshod management style made him politically vulnerable, and he knew it. "People wonder why I keep my old office," he was fond of saying. "I tell them that when I hang my hat up in the morning, I want to be sure it will still be there at night." Even had Granrud not been controversial, the fundamental nature of Lutheran Brotherhood almost guaranteed that he would encounter occasional political opposition. Lutheran Brotherhood was a fraternal society, a representative democracy in which the members and employees possessed a strong sense of ownership. Those who did not agree with management direction or philosophy usually felt free to voice their opposition. Scattered criticism often made it difficult to make tough but necessary managerial decisions. If those voices developed into strong and united opposition, the board members who selected management could be voted out of office. Granrud might publicly call those who opposed him disloyal, but privately he knew that the members ultimately were in charge. He understood that the same political system that had brought him to power might also bring him down. Or did he?

Many of Granrud's longtime supporters, especially general agents such as Haroldson, were beginning to wonder about that. In their views, Granrud, who was approaching seventy, had changed. His mind was still keen and his wit sharp, and he still worked long hours. Yet he also had become increasingly sensitive to any criticism of his actions, intolerant even of minor forms of dissent. The same Carl Granrud who had served as trusted friend and confidant to many church leaders had become increasingly separated from the Lutheran hierarchy, and bitter political fights had turned him inward. On questions of management, it was widely perceived that he had become intransigent, convinced that his way was the only way. No one questioned Granrud's unswerving dedication to the society, no one doubted that he was doing what he thought to be right. But many general agents and employees chafed under what they considered his dictatorial command. They still had great respect for Granrud, even love, for he had been an effective and dynamic leader, but they worried about the future of the society. To their way of thinking, he had fallen into the classic managerial mindset that had caused the downfall so many other leaders: Faced with approaching retirement, he was refusing to relinquish any of his considerable power.

For the past several years, Granrud had become accustomed to almost complete control of Lutheran Brotherhood affairs. He had painstakingly built the society by personally overseeing nearly every facet of its operation, from agency business to bathroom fixtures. He supervised the society directors in much the same way, bending their opinions to conform with his own. When he called for votes at board meetings, he would sometimes say, "All in favor, say aye. All opposed, resign." The board never really knew whether he was kidding. Granrud made it clear that he expected the undivided support of board members and employees alike. Shortly after the green building was constructed, Ken Severud asked Granrud when he was planning to move from his law offices. "Move into the new building?" Granrud said in mock horror. "I should say not. If I do that, people will think I'm working for Lutheran Brotherhood, instead of them working for me."

Granrud's autocratic management style was not markedly different from that of many other leaders of his era. He ruled by force and discipline because that was the way his generation had been taught; one did exactly what the boss said until one became the boss. And his approach had been successful. Yet the society that owed much of its growth to Granrud was, ironically, beginning to outgrow his constrictive style. It was no longer possible for him to maintain complete control of the entire operation, and that frustrated Granrud. The chairman did not suffer imperfection gladly, and he was uncomfortable delegating significant responsibility to anyone other than hand-picked assistants. When he did, and they made mistakes, he often castigated them, sometimes publicly. As a result, some officers retreated into a shell, concerned more about not making mistakes than trying newer, potentially more productive approaches. Creativity took second place to safety.

The best way to be safe was to be loyal. Granrud was an intensely loyal man, and he expected the same of others. When Carl Thomsen was named an assistant vice president, Granrud approached him and shook his hand vigorously. "I want to congratulate you on your promotion," he told the new officer. "Now I hope you know what this means. It means you'll be expected to vote the straight Republican ticket at the next quadrennial convention." Thomsen smiled and nodded. He knew exactly what Granrud was talking about. He was talking about allegiance. There was no middle ground when it came to Granrud: You were either for him or against him, and neutrality would not do.

Granrud was especially loyal to Gretchen Pracht, his longtime law associate, and she to him. Their relationship, which began when he hired her as his secretary, then encouraged her to pursue a law degree, was based on decades of mutual trust. No one in the society could stand between their reciprocal allegiance. Granrud placed absolute faith in her judgment, and in return she gave him unswerving dedication. When it came to business, to know Granrud's mind was to know Pracht's.

Gretchen Pracht had worked hard to succeed in a man's world. A tall, stately, imposing woman, she carried herself with cool deliberation, although she was generally pleasant and gracious to employees. Pracht was also talented, and she quickly took to her new assignment when Granrud named her the society's director of public relations and advertising in 1954. At the time, Lutheran Brotherhood was located unobtrusively in the Pillsbury Building, and

the society's profile was so low that the publisher of *Commercial West*, a regional banking and insurance magazine whose editorial offices were located across the street, did not even know that there was an insurance organization headquartered nearby.

Given free rein by Granrud and aided by the publicity given to the society's new green building, Pracht orchestrated a flurry of promotional activities in the community. She began to place advertisements in national magazines such as *LIFE* and *Reader's Digest*. Dreng Bjornaraa, a society director and a regional head of public relations for U.S. Steel, taught her the finer points of public relations. Pracht quickly became a skilled practitioner of the craft and established close contacts with religion editors across the country. She helped Lutheran Brotherhood establish a regional and national image, and in 1962 she was rewarded for her work by being named the first female vice president in the society's history.

Pracht played an essential role in helping the field spread the word about Lutheran Brotherhood into new territories. When Harry Hendricks was appointed general agent in Baltimore, Maryland, he discovered that few of the Lutherans in the area (most of whom were members of the Missouri Synod) knew anything about the society. He asked Pracht for help, and she suggested putting on an introductory dinner for the local clergy, at which the Rev. A.R. Kretzmann, a director of the society and a well-known Missouri Synod leader, would speak and explain the society's fraternal programs.

Invitations were sent to every Lutheran pastor in the area, but none of the Missouri Synod pastors would come. Hendricks was unclear about his next move, until he consulted with one of his acquaintances, a Missouri Synod hospital chaplain. "We just want to tell these people who we are and what we do," the general agent told his friend. "We're not going to do any selling job on anybody."

"If that's the case, then what you need to do is get these people to come," the chaplain said, naming three influential Missouri Synod leaders in the area. "If they agree, then everybody else will come, too."

When Hendricks explained the purpose of the meeting to the pastors, they agreed to attend, and others followed. About five hundred attended the dinner, which was organized by Pracht. During the next few years, Hendricks brought many members of the Missouri Synod into the society.

Pracht's ability to conceive, then orchestrate, these types of events smoothed the field's pathway, as did her considerable influence within the society. She was a skilled facilitator. Agents who encountered trouble with travel arrangements, for example, were instructed by Granrud to call Pracht for help; she inevitably straightened out any confusion.

Like her mentor, Pracht was proud, decisive, and, when the occasion demanded it, tough. She did not apologize for being a woman, nor did she apologize for not being a Lutheran. This attitude did not endear her to many of the males who occupied the upper tiers of society management. Few of them were used to answering to a woman, and few of them liked it. They were also bothered by the way she seemed to influence Granrud. Too often, it seemed to them, he would approve their ideas, then talk to Pracht and change his mind. That did not sit well with the officers and general agents. The widespread perception that she controlled the aging Granrud perpetuated their fears. It did not appear that he was grooming anyone to take his place, and some feared that he might try to install her as the next president of Lutheran Brotherhood. Whether or not that fear was justified, Gretchen Pracht had become an issue.

On the other hand, perhaps Granrud would rule forever. In 1964, the board raised the mandatory retirement age for directors to seventy-five. The action alarmed the general agents, especially Ole Haroldson. "The field force doesn't trust the board of directors very much," he wrote to A. Herbert Nelson, a recent addition to the board, "and with good reason, because it seems like the bylaws are being made for the benefit of the board of directors . . . But we cannot talk about these things to Carl, because he would blow sky high."

Haroldson was right. A year later, at a sales convention at the swank Four Seasons resort on Lake of the Ozarks in Missouri, Granrud apparently got word of Haroldson's sentiments. As Haroldson was sitting down to eat with friends, Granrud stepped up behind him and rapped him sharply on the back of the head. "You'd better keep your damn mouth shut," he told his old friend. "I heard you've been practicing politics. You'd better watch yourself. I could get rid of you." Haroldson's face turned red, but he managed to maintain his composure. The next day he wrote to Granrud and asked for an apology. "Either you are too stubborn in your old age or are too insecure to accept any criticism," he wrote. "We are not even competing for the same thing. Why should you now all of a sudden distrust me?" Granrud eventually apologized, but Haroldson was still rankled. He began thinking ahead to the 1967 general convention.

Determination and Zeal

The rift between Haroldson and Granrud was surprising, for the two had been close friends for more than twenty years. Haroldson had been one of management's most zealous supporters during the 1959 battle, and, in a fit of fervor, he had even offered to physically whip Granrud's opponents. Few doubted that he could handle the job. Although he was nearly sixty, Haroldson was tall, strapping, and as determined as a man could be. He had encountered the need for resolve at an early age. When he was fifteen, his parents and sister and brother died in a grisly railroad accident, leaving him and five other siblings to fend for themselves. There was no life insurance, because the family belonged to a Lutheran synod that still believed insurance was a sin. The Haroldson farm in western Minnesota was mortgaged, the machinery was old and nearly useless, and farm prices were depressed. Though Haroldson and his older brothers labored vigorously, they eventually lost the farm.

Haroldson found success early in life because he could hurl a baseball with speed and accuracy. He began pitching for money when he was sixteen years old, and supported himself through high school and college with his earnings and an athletic scholarship. After graduating from Concordia College in Moorhead, Minnesota, in 1930, he signed a professional baseball contract with the St. Louis Browns. For the next few summers, he played minor league baseball. In July 1933, while playing for a team in Grand Forks, North Dakota, Haroldson pitched three one-hit

games. But the club was short of pitchers that year, and Haroldson eventually threw his arm out from overuse. His baseball career was finished.

For the next several years, Haroldson taught high school and coached. He was principal, then superintendent of schools in several North Dakota towns. Haroldson began to sell insurance part time for Lutheran Brotherhood in 1939. Two years later, he was recruited by Harold Hoel to become general agent in Fargo and met with the enthusiastic salesman at the Ryan Hotel in Grand Forks. At the time, Hoel's field expense budget was so lean that he asked his prospective general agent whether he minded if they shared the same bed.

Gretchen Pracht, Lutheran Brotherhood's first female vice president and director of public relations-advertising, was named Minnesota's Insurance Woman of the Year in 1964. With her is Cyrus Magnusson, state insurance commissioner.

Haroldson approached his new career with characteristic zeal. He always remembered that his family's farm might have been saved had his father had life insurance, and he became almost fanatical about the need to prepare for the future. "If you don't want to buy insurance from me, at least buy it from somebody," he told prospects. "You absolutely need it." One of his first prospects, a close friend, had been interested in buying insurance but wanted to wait a few weeks to make the decision. Two weeks later,

Luther Forde, standing, and Reuben Jacobson.

On Solid Ground

For more than three decades as the chief actuaries of Lutheran Brotherhood, Reuben Jacobson and Luther Forde played important roles in keeping the society on solid financial ground.

Actuarial science is, in many ways, the foundation of the insurance business. Trained in the science of mathematical probabilities, actuaries calculate and evaluate risk, basically ensuring that an insurance organization takes in the same amount of money (in the form of premiums and investment income) as it is likely to pay out in the future. Because their forecasts form the basis for decisions that will commit the organization to critical, long-term financial obligations, actuaries have been typified as individuals who are intelligent and insightful, trustworthy, deliberate, and conservative. Jacobson and Forde possessed each of those qualities in abundance.

Jacobson's views on financial accountability were mirrored by his work ethic. He ran a tight ship. He was not fond of coffee breaks, and his no-nonsense secretary, Eleanor Miele, used an egg timer to inform employees that it was time to get back to their desks. Waste was as distasteful to Jacobson as inefficiency or laziness. Employees were required to show their old pencil stubs to Miele before they were issued new

ones, and ballpoint pens were soaked in a glass of water to draw out every last drop of ink before they were thrown away.

Simplicity was as important to Jacobson as efficiency. Because actuaries dealt with extremely complex data, they were often regarded by others as the keepers of mysterious and incomprehensible information. But Jacobson understood that actuaries must keep their explanations as simple as possible. "Sometimes actuaries are accused of throwing a fog in front of themselves by saying something like: 'This is actuarially unsound, so forget it,'" he explained. "Maybe it is unsound, but you should be able to explain why. If you can't convince the people around you that you're right, then you might as well be wrong."

When Jacobson retired in 1974, after twenty-one years with the society, he was succeeded by Forde, whose quiet and calm demeanor acted as a valuable countercheck to the volatility of the insurance industry during the next several years.

Forde was elected president and chief operating officer of Lutheran Brotherhood in 1985. Three years later, he was named chief financial officer and the first president of Lutheran Brotherhood Financial Corp.

Haroldson was reading a newspaper in a cafe when he spotted a disturbing headline. His friend had been killed by lightning while doing chores. He was uninsured. Haroldson never again let a prospect get away without making that final pitch.

Many of Haroldson's early prospects were farmers. When he tried to convince them of the need for insurance, they usually pointed to their land and their livestock and their equipment. "That's my insurance," they would say. Haroldson knew it usually wasn't enough. It cost money for a property owner to die. There were medical bills, funeral bills, attorney's fees, taxes due, executive and administrative costs, filing fees, appraisal fees, and inheritance taxes. Haroldson collected copies of actual estates at the local probate court, and used the information to develop Lutheran Brotherhood's first estate planning manual. He became one of the society's leading general agents, and he recruited and trained several district representatives who became top general agents.

As one of the society's pioneers, Haroldson had always been a strong advocate for general agents, and he did not like what he perceived as the connection between Granrud's rising power and the declining influence of the field force. His fears were confirmed in the fall of 1966, when Woody Langhaug, a great favorite of the field force, resigned as vice president of marketing and research. Langhaug cited declining health as the sole reason, but the general agents knew better: The word was that he had gotten on Granrud's bad side and had become increasingly frustrated by what he felt was interference with his department. "The news of Woody resigning has hit the field by now and everyone is wondering with raised eyebrows what the deal is," Haroldson told Nelson. "I have decided to do nothing at the present time but just listen. It wouldn't take much to put them up in arms, I know."

Haroldson had been using Nelson as a confidential sounding board for the past few years, ever since Nelson had been named to the board of directors. Haroldson trusted the jovial Swede, who shared his concerns about the future of the society, and viewed him as someone who might be able to do something about it. After all, Nelson recently had been named

president of Lutheran Brotherhood. In his mid-sixties, with silver hair and silver-rimmed glasses, Nelson had been in the insurance business for more than thirty years. In 1951, he was appointed Minnesota's insurance commissioner by his friend, Governor Luther Youngdahl. He served two years in the post and was later described by the *Minneapolis Star* as "one of the best insurance commissioners in the state's history." Nelson also was known as a devoted family man. A few years after his first wife died, he married Eleanor Peterson, a widow with two children. At age fifty-nine, Nelson, who had three daughters by his first marriage, fathered his first son.

Haroldson's letters to Nelson increasingly broached the subject of Granrud's tight control over the daily activities of the society. In Haroldson's opinion, Granrud, who occasionally was listed in society literature as chief executive officer, was serving illegally in that regard. He was seventy years old, and the society bylaws stated that all officers and department heads must retire from such positions not later than their sixty-eighth birthday. "The only one who can enforce the laws of Lutheran Brotherhood when the board is not in session is the president," Haroldson observed. "Mr. Granrud is chairman of the board and that's all he is." The general agent urged Nelson to bring the matter to the board. "If no one complains, then of course they will get by with it," he added. "I have been waiting to get fired so I could sue. I would win in a walk."

Other general agents were not so sure. When Haroldson asked for Merrill Gille's assessment of his chances against Granrud at the next convention, Gille was frankly pessimistic: "Mr. Granrud is a very clever politician who holds enough power and authority to manipulate the board and staff to get his way. At this time I doubt if anyone in our society can outmaneuver him."

But Haroldson was a headstrong individual, and in April 1967 he decided to confront Granrud. "I have noticed in the past several months, together with many people in Lutheran Brotherhood, that you have been and are under considerable strain as the board chairman and your attempt to perform as the chief executive officer," Haroldson wrote to the chairman. "The heavy added responsibilities which have come

displeasure and annoyance your letter indicated," he wrote.

Granrud subsequently offered to reinstate Haroldson if he would retract his statements and stay away from the convention, but the general agent refused to recant. "The statements which I have made, I believe in my heart to be the truth," he told Granrud. "If you believe them to be wrong and not the truth, then we have an honest difference of opinion, and I only hope our friendship can be recemented. I could never learn to hate you or anyone else in this world. I should be anything but rational if I were to destroy the society which I have helped to build, and I also feel that you have this feeling, too. I think that we both are *overly* dedicated to the success of Lutheran Brotherhood. When that day comes when Carl F. Granrud is to be honored for his many years of dedicated service, I would want to be able to be on that program to show my appreciation, and likewise when Ole B. Haroldson retires, I would like to see your presence to give whatever honors I would be entitled to receive."

In the meantime, Haroldson had plenty of free time on his hands. He decided it was time to organize an underground movement against Granrud. The society's general convention was less than five months away.

An Independent Slate

Haroldson soon learned that he was not alone. Several other society members, most of whom had once been among Granrud's strongest supporters, had become convinced that the chairman would never willingly relinquish managerial control. New, younger leadership that was not beholden to the chairman was desperately needed, they had decided, and an independent campaign would be the only way to ensure that the delegates had a true democratic choice at the upcoming convention. Roald Severtson, a general agent from Seattle, had thought long and hard about an approach that might succeed against Granrud, and was dismayed that Haroldson's letter had alerted the chairman to the possibility of political opposition. "We cannot rely on

your way and the executive workload which you are endeavoring to carry out several years after the normal retirement age of sixty-eight, which is mandatory under Article 9 of our bylaws, has been telling itself on you as well as the entire Lutheran Brotherhood.

"I feel it is my duty as a delegate to inform you and the members of the board of directors of my position in regard to this matter, since I would not like to see each board member possibly being held personally liable for obligations incurred or executive decisions made, which might be held to be illegal and incompatible with the bylaws and the duties and responsiblities of the board of directors of Lutheran Brotherhood."

Haroldson, whose Denver agency at the time ranked seventh in annual sales production, was immediately fired. A few days later, Granrud sent a terse personal note to Haroldson. "I regret the

emotion alone to do this job, Ole, but rather we must rely on cold, calculating logic and facts," he told Haroldson. "In the past everyone who has 'bounced' off Mr. Granrud has acted like a complete amateur, consequently being destroyed in the process. Let this be different. Should this effort fail we must remember that hundreds of field men must continue to serve LB effectively in the field and do so proudly. The 'campaign' must be conducted at a level that will make this possible, with a minimum of or better still, no publicity."

One of the first items on the opposition agenda was the selection of board nominees. Severtson believed that they must meet four qualifications. First, their character must be beyond reproach. If there were any misdeeds in their past, Granrud would surely find them. Second, they must have no previous political background in Lutheran Brotherhood. Any connection with the bitterness of past battles might be turned against them. Third, they must be well-known to most of the general agents. The field would make or break this campaign, and they were entitled to know whom they were supporting. Fourth, the nominees must have the ability to serve effectively. Only if the delegates perceived that new managerial blood was necessary would they have a chance against Granrud's experience; therefore, they must be young enough to serve Lutheran Brotherhood for several years.

Two names came immediately to Haroldson's mind: Jim Krause and Arley Bjella. Tall, slim, and cerebral, Krause was especially well-known among field force members. He joined Lutheran Brotherhood as a special assistant to Granrud in 1961, and later became home office attorney. Krause, thirty-seven, had been a particular favorite of Granrud. His office was next door, and he had spent most of his first year with the society doing management legal work during the battle with the Committee of One Hundred. The memories of that struggle did not rest easily in his mind, and Krause was uncomfortable when he recalled how zealous he had once felt. He had become disillusioned with Granrud's style. He had thought about quitting, but he liked the society and its people, so he took a leave of absence. He won a Bush Foundation fellowship and studied at the Harvard Business School for one year. When Haroldson called him, he was serving an internship with an international insurance company in the Bahamas. Krause decided to leave the warm weather behind that fall. He was going to run.

Bjella was well-known throughout the Upper Midwest as a politician, churchman, and civic leader. At age fifty-one, he was lean and solidly built, and his deeply lined face bore the rugged stamp of his native North Dakota plains. Haroldson had known Bjella for nearly thirty years and had attempted to recruit him as a Lutheran Brotherhood agent when Bjella was a student at the University of North Dakota. Bjella eventually became an accomplished attorney in Williston, North Dakota. Active in state politics, he ran for lieutenant governor in 1950 and served four years as state chairman of the Republican Party. In a recent state poll, he had been named as one of three possible candidates for the governorship. Bjella was intrigued by Haroldson's offer, but he was busy with several other projects and declined to run. However, the persistent Haroldson kept calling him, and Bjella finally accepted. His law office in Williston eventually became the opposition's campaign headquarters.

Bjella and Krause met every one of the independent's qualifications (Krause's political past was deemed insufficient to be a liability), but it was difficult to find other candidates who did. They eventually settled on two businessmen whose only drawback was their anonymity. Herbert Hansen, thirty-seven, a boyish-looking Wisconsin native, was vice president of the Union Bank in Los Angeles, one of the leading financial institutions in the country. Hansen was responsible for coordinating his bank's services to the insurance industry. He was an active church member and Sunday School teacher.

George Wade, thirty-seven, was a prosperous Seattle businessman. Handsome and confident, he had been educated at Yale University and later taught at the University of Washington. An outstanding athlete, he once held the collegiate record for the mile run, and had been on a fast track since entering the business world. Wade was involved with several financial ventures, including a consulting firm, lumberyard, and steel and aluminum fabricating plant.

He had long been an active Lutheran layman and had served as president of two congregations in the Seattle area. He understood that the campaign would be an uphill battle, but he got his first idea of just how long the odds truly were when he told Einar Botten, one of Lutheran Brotherhood's political casualties of 1961, about his candidacy. "I wish you all the best," Botten told Wade, "but you don't have a snowball's chance in hell of winning."

To beat the odds, secrecy was essential. If Granrud found out about the independent campaign, he would surely try to crush it. Only agents and directors known to sympathize completely with the cause were apprised of the underground movement; those on the fence would have to wait. Because of the widely varied political feelings within the society, perhaps the most important addition to the opposition camp was Axel Lundring. Like Ole Haroldson, he enjoyed a sterling reputation among the field force. Lundring had had his share of conflicts with Granrud,

Lutheran Brotherhood's general agents posed during their January meeting at the home office in 1967. With the group are, at far left, front row, Don Lommen, director of agencies, and at far right, front row, Gordon Taft, superintendent of agencies.

but he had not responded by publicly challenging the chairman. Thus, he was not perceived by most as having a personal argument with Granrud, as was Haroldson, who since his firing had been portrayed by the chairman as a malcontent. By joining the opposition, Lundring, who was still working as a general agent, gave instant credibility to the board candidates. Yet even he felt the necessity of secrecy. Haroldson and Lundring both traveled to the group's first meeting under assumed names, Haroldson as Lloyd Wakeford of Osnabrook, North Dakota, and Lundring as Cornelius Sorenson of Yankton, South Dakota. They met quietly at the Thunderbird Hotel in suburban Minneapolis with several others, including Bjella, Krause, Hansen, Severtson, and Langhaug.

The group decided to keep their campaign as

free as possible of animosity. Boisterous charges and personal attacks on Granrud would not help their cause. "This campaign must be conducted in such a manner that we can live with this situation should the effort fail," Severtson said. "Those of us who have been associated with previous elections are weary of the old charges and cliches. We should follow the line that Granrud's administration has done a comparatively good job over the years, but that it is clearly now in the best interest of the society that new leaders be given a chance. No one's job should be threatened. Let's do our best to inform the delegates, then trust in their judgment."

To get on the convention ballot, each of the independent nominees would require thirty delegate signatures. Several general agents, including Haroldson, who had been spreading the story that he might bypass the convention because he was busy working on an invention for irrigating soil, volunteered to begin contacting delegates. Axel Lundring traveled up the coast to visit his son Karsten, then an army lieutenant stationed at Fort Lewis. There, away from the demands of running an agency, Axel waged a telephone campaign for two weeks, calling general agents whom he knew to be sympathetic to a change in leadership. The opposition group had to hurry. The petitions were due at Severud's office by August 25, less than two months away.

While the opposition labored underground, Lutheran Brotherhood was celebrating its fiftieth birthday in grand style, with eighty-one dinners in eighty cities across the United States and Canada on June 13, 1967. More than six hundred employees gathered in Minneapolis, where the society unveiled a new film about its history and held an open house at the green building. Lutheran Brotherhood never had been in better financial condition. It had taken the society forty-two years to reach its first billion dollars of life insurance in force and five years to reach its second billion. Now, just three years later, the society was nearing its third billion. Lutheran Brotherhood had become the seventy-first largest life insurance organization in the United States and the second largest fraternal society in the country.

Occasions such as Lutheran Brotherhood's fiftieth anniversary helped to remind outside observers that service to its members and to the church, not politics, was the foundation of the society. Political confrontations grabbed headlines, but they were rare (which, admittedly, made them all the more noteworthy). Daily service was the true constant. Even during the midst of heated campaigns, when a few leaders with opposing managerial viewpoints had vied for control of Lutheran Brotherhood, business had continued as usual, as nearly one thousand representatives in the field and more than four hundred employees in the home office had continued to write and process insurance contracts for families who needed protection.

Granrud's penchant for controversy also had obscured the fact that during his tenure, Lutheran Brotherhood had contributed more to the church than at any other time in its history. More than $7.5 million had been provided for fraternal activities in the past fifty years, most of it under Granrud, and more than $1 million had been budgeted for fraternal activities in 1967. The money was used by branch members for church construction projects, Sunday School literature, hymnals, and choir robes. It provided Bibles for the newly confirmed and for overseas service personnel, and it financed home and foreign mission projects, welfare institutions, and interdenominational agencies.

Lutheran Brotherhood sponsored many other fraternal activities. The board of directors generally decided which projects to fund on the basis of three considerations: The activity must aid the Lutheran church, be clearly intersynodical, and be operated on a national basis. Projects that met these criteria were given strong support by the society. For example, Lutheran Brotherhood played a leading role in supporting Lutheran Boy Scout groups through its local branches, and for years served as the headquarters for the Lutheran Committee on Scouting.

Dr. Richard Gerberding, a society director, played a leading role in establishing many of the society's early fraternal programs, and education was one of his primary concerns. In 1950, the society instituted an annual program through which it awarded scholarships of three hundred dollars each to juniors at twenty-seven Lutheran colleges. Two years later, Lutheran Brotherhood began to award one thousand-dollar scholarships to Lutheran seminary students. One recipient later informed the society that his scholarship had meant nearly three hundred hours more for study and church activities, instead of washing walls, scrubbing floors, and shoveling snow to pay seminary bills. The society subsequently began scholarship programs for college freshmen, graduate nurses, and social workers and provided faculty fellowships for teachers at Lutheran colleges.

More than 20 million Sunday School teaching aids, including coloring packets and maps of the Holy Land (most of which were Pracht's idea), were distributed free by the society to Lutheran churches across the country. Lutheran Brotherhood subsidized a series of books by Lutheran scholars, helped to finance the promotion of the successful Bible-study program known as the Bethel Bible Series, and sponsored a national series of seminars that brought together pastors from all Lutheran synods for lectures and discussion.

The society also had made a contribution to Lutheran art and music. The Lutheran Center, located in the green building, became frequent host to numerous special events, including worship services, intersynodical forums, and church music seminars. In 1959, led by the Rev. A. R. Kretzmann, a director and nationally renowned religious art expert, the society sponsored its first Fine Arts Festival. The festival included an exhibition of works by Lutheran art students, concerts, dramatic plays, and workshops. The Fine Arts Festival attracted large crowds to the Lutheran Center and became an annual event at the home office.

The society also had loaned nearly $45 million to Lutheran churches for construction during the past five decades, ensuring that Lutheranism would continue to grow throughout the United States and Canada. During the past decade, as Lutheran Brotherhood had become increasingly known among Lutherans, many churches had sought financial assistance from the society for new sanctuaries, educational buildings, and parsonages. Lutheran Brotherhood was not able to meet every request, but met most of those that qualified as sound investments; 15 percent of the society's assets were invested in Lutheran congregations. The loan program also provided a second

benefit for the churches. Because so many society dollars were invested in existing church growth, millions of dollars of church extension funds were released by the various synods for reinvestment in new congregations.

Fraternal programs and church loans were achievements that did not make the front pages of local newspapers, yet they reflected more accurately the daily work of the society than did scattered political battles. Granrud's leadership had undoubtedly been responsible for much of Lutheran Brotherhood's success, and his place atop the society had never seemed so secure. However, it was a political year, with the seventeenth general convention slated for September. Haroldson's letter had alerted Granrud to the possibility of scattered opposition, and he had decided to take nothing for granted. In July he issued a memorandum to the society's department heads. "It has come to my attention that by mistake the words 'Chief Executive Officer' were used in the organization chart of the Society," it read. "As far as I can find out, after a thorough investigation, this title has not appeared anywhere else. In order to clarify matters, I would like to state that I have been elected Chairman of the Board of Directors, and I am not an officer of Lutheran Brotherhood and have not claimed to be."

By late August, the independent campaign had collected almost forty petitions, more than enough to nominate its slate of directors. Haroldson, in a whirlwind of activity during the past several weeks, had collected most of them. The campaign had been quiet and efficient, although a few rumors had drifted into the Granrud camp. Following one insurgent meeting in Chicago, Russell Matthias, the general counsel of the society, who had become a strong Granrud supporter, called Krause and asked if he knew anything about the meeting. Krause refused to answer. "Matt, if Carl Granrud wants to know about some alleged meeting, he can call me himself." Granrud never called.

On August 25, 1967, the independent leaders gathered secretly in Minneapolis. They were sure they had more than enough petitions and had originally planned not to use those signed by general agents, to protect them from possible retaliation.

But they feared that something might go wrong. What if management already had found out that several general agents were supporting independent candidates? What if they had convinced some delegates to revoke their signatures? Krause thought back to the Committee of One Hundred. If enough delegates revoked their petition signatures, the independent nominees would not make it onto the convention ballot, and all their work would be for nothing. That morning, Haroldson called general agent Russ Smith, who had joined the independent movement, at his home. "We're afraid we might be short," he said, "and we'd like to submit your signed petition. When we do that, you'll be completely exposed. In fact, you may be terminated after the convention. We know this must be a tough decision, and we wanted to call and ask your permission." Smith suddenly felt sick to his stomach; he might be signing his employment death warrant. After a few agonizing seconds, he made up his mind. "Go ahead," he said quietly, and hung up the phone.

Lundring must have felt similarly apprehensive, for that afternoon, he marched into the home office with Bjella, Hansen, and Wade, and placed forty-four signed petitions on Severud's desk. His support of outside candidates had become public, as had the the campaign itself. A few minutes later, Bjella and Lundring were called into Granrud's office. The chairman was not pleased by their presence, and he noted sarcastically that Lundring was supposed to be working for him. Yet he was not otherwise uncivil and seemed almost resigned to an independent campaign. Following the meeting, the independent candidates introduced themselves around the home office. Some employees greeted the nominees with open arms, and others quietly shook their hands. Some turned away as they approached. The tension was obvious; any public show of friendliness might prove fatal.

The contest was finally out in the open, and Granrud grudgingly prepared for another political competition. He was becoming tired of these society struggles, but he was not the kind of man to quietly step aside, for although the opposition viewed their campaign as healthy and legitimate competition, Granrud considered it an unauthorized challenge to

his experience and authority. These green young candidates were going to have to beat him. Following the battle with the Committee of One Hundred in 1961, Doug Bronder, an advertising consultant who later joined the society, delighted Granrud at the end of one meeting with a reference to the political threat of 1961: "And as Mr. Ryden might say, 'Thanks for your company, Mr. Granrud.'" The chairman laughed about that comment for years.

Granrud won his political battles because he was willing to outwork the other side. "I don't care where the meeting is or what it's about, always be the last one to go to bed," he told younger supporters. "Sometimes, after almost everyone has gone, something that's important will happen." Granrud was usually the last one to turn out the lights. Yet his usually astute political judgment seemed to be slipping. Several months before the convention, Granrud had written a letter to one of his supporters that ultimately proved to be damaging. "We will have a large Nominating Committee at the next convention," the letter read. "In fact, it probably will be so large that they can do as they did at the last meeting, not only nominate but elect."

The independent campaign was given a copy of the letter and made valuable and extensive use of it. Didn't society bylaws give any member the legal right to run for the board? Wasn't Lutheran Brotherhood supposed to be a representative democracy? Didn't the delegates deserve the chance to make a real choice, not simply rubber-stamp those board delegates chosen by management?

Granrud also had been stung again by the accusation that he was serving illegally as an officer. At the June 28 directors' meeting, the final board session before the convention in September, Granrud had attempted to amend a bylaw that stated that the chief executive officer could fire junior officers. Granrud had already announced that he was not the chief executive officer, and he tried to strike the word "officer" from the bylaw. The minutes of the meeting subsequently stated that the amendment had passed unanimously, as was required when a proposed amendment was brought up at a meeting without prior notice. There was just one problem: Director Gordon Bubolz, who had opposed

Granrud for years, was willing to swear under oath that he had not voted for the measure. Granrud quietly dropped the matter. ("I'm certainly glad this will be your last board meeting," he had told Bubolz, who had decided to retire from the board. Bubolz smiled thinly. It may well be your last meeting, too, Mr. Granrud, he thought.)

On September 1, the society's nominating committee, appointed by the board, named its candidates for the upcoming convention. They included Granrud; Harold Smith, sixty-nine, the society's president emeritus; L. Edwin Wang, forty-seven, executive secretary of the Board of Pensions of the Lutheran Church in America; and Dr. J. A. O. Preus, forty-seven, president of the Concordia Theological Seminary and eldest son of Jake Preus. "We have chosen these names and men with greatest care," said Dr. Adalbert Kretzmann, a society director and chairman of the committee. "This great work

cannot be entrusted to the novice and the untried in this time of the Brotherhood's success."

There was a flurry of activity on both sides in the last weeks before the convention. The independent campaign stayed in close contact with Nelson, who had thus far kept quiet about his support of their cause. Five days before the convention, Nelson decided to reinstate Haroldson, but he also kept this matter to himself, for he had landed in Granrud's doghouse. If all of the independent candidates won, there would be plenty of time after the convention to make the necessary arrangements to bring Haroldson back. If Granrud won, it would probably make no difference; Nelson was certain he would be fired.

About the same time, William A. Johnson, whose general agency in Minneapolis was perennially the society's top producer, was appointed by the General Agents Advisory Council to meet with Pracht. It was not an easy visit. "Unfortunately, there is a lot of sentiment against you right now in the society," Johnson, a strong Granrud supporter, explained. "The council is requesting that you resign from your position as an officer. If you do, they will support Mr. Granrud for reelection." Pracht declined the request. "I already know what people think, Mr. Johnson," she said firmly, "but I'm not going to step aside. I'm a good person and a good officer, and Carl and I have decided to stand together."

If Granrud was nervous about the convention, he did not show it. At one of his last meetings with department heads, he led the group in a stirring rendition of "Bill Grogan's Goat." He had never seemed so confident. A few minutes before he was to leave for Chicago, the site of the convention, Granrud called Gordon Taft, superintendent of agencies, into his office. "Somebody's bringing my suit by from the cleaners before I leave," he said. "I hope you don't mind talking for a bit while I change my clothes." No, Taft answered, that would be just fine. For the next several minutes, while he put on his suit, Granrud expounded on a number of society topics, none of which was related to the convention. As he walked out the door of his office, he spun around suddenly and looked Taft in the eye. "Just remember one thing," he said. "They don't have the votes."

Taft's response was unspoken as he followed Granrud out the door. Mr. Granrud, you're usually right about most things, he thought to himself, but I don't think you're right about this one.

The Last Convention

On September 15, 1967, at the elegant Palmer House in Chicago, the seventeenth general convention of Lutheran Brotherhood convened. The atmosphere was strangely quiet as the 250 delegates registered. The independent candidates were apprehensive, for they wondered if they had enough support. Just a few days before the convention, Krause had talked by phone with Ken Anderson, a lawyer who often did work for the society. "Are you sure Nelson is with you guys?" Anderson asked. "I'll tell you, from talking with him, he's solid for management." That worried Krause. He was sure Nelson was just putting on an act, but at times like this, one could never be sure.

But the management camp was equally tense, for they did not know who was in the opposing camp. If they did not know their adversaries, they would not know whom to court. Granrud's supporters nervously prowled among the delegates, anxiously seeking clues as to their intentions. And yet, for all the intrigue, there were many friendly moments. When Granrud spotted Krause, his former protégé, he stopped briefly to chat. "Gee, I invited you to come down to go fishing with me," said Krause. "I would have, but I was afraid you'd throw me to the sharks," Granrud said.

While the two sides anxiously probed the pulse of the convention, Dr. Lloyd Svendsbye, editor-in-chief of Augsburg Publishing House in Minneapolis, quietly circulated among delegates in the lobby. Svendsbye was not a delegate, but he had long been bothered by what he considered to be the ostentatious manner in which the society made fraternal gifts to the church. Earlier that year, his father had died, and Svendsbye had returned to his native North Dakota for the funeral. During his visit, he consulted an attorney named Arley Bjella about the family estate. Unaware that a petition campaign was already underway, Svendsbye asked Bjella if he had ever considered running for the board of Lutheran Brotherhood. Bjella quietly pulled Svendsbye aside. "I already am," he explained. Svendsbye offered his services to the group and was charged with printing its campaign materials.

Two of those documents, one of them written by Gordon Bubolz, titled *Observations of a Director,* dealt with Granrud's alleged abuses of power. The independent camp had decided to wait until the last possible moment to distribute the literature to the delegates. On the first day of the convention, Svendsbye worked on the materials in a hotel room that was provided for convention participants. He explained to the secretary there that while he was very interested in Lutheran Brotherhood, he was not actually *from* Lutheran Brotherhood. A few hours after Svendsbye had finished his work, Matthias stuck his head into the room. "Has anyone from Lutheran Brotherhood been here?" he asked. "I don't know," the secretary answered. Apparently satisfied that no seditious activity was under way, Matthias returned to the convention.

That night the delegates dined sumptuously in the Grand Ballroom on the fourth floor of the Palmer House. Every one of the known petition delegates and their known supporters was in attendance, and they were watched closely by Granrud's supporters. Ole Haroldson was also there, but nobody was watching him, for management still had no idea that he was working with the independents. After he had finished his dessert, Haroldson slipped out of the room. In his pocket was a copy of the room assignments of the delegates. With the help of several bellhops, to whom he paid a total of seventeen dollars, Haroldson hurriedly slipped campaign materials, including *Observations of a Director,* under the doors of all delegates who might be favorable to the opposition cause. They skipped the doors of delegates who were known to favor Granrud.

The next morning, the delegates were abuzz with questions. Did you find that stuff under your door? What are you going to do? Granrud was furious. At breakfast, one of his supporters denounced the

independent slate as disloyal in a fiery speech to the delegates and accused Wade, an expert in mergers and acquisitions, of planning to plunder the society's assets and move the firm to Seattle. The harangue backfired. Nobody could be that bad, several shocked delegates, still on the fence, thought. They decided to support the independents.

At 10 A.M., the delegates filed into the meeting room of the Palmer House, where they would cast their votes. If Krause had worried about Nelson's allegiance before the convention, his fears were quickly allayed, because Nelson calmly gave the speech of his life. "Like any human activity, it is inevitable that problems arise in Lutheran Brotherhood, problems that need the solution that only a meeting such as this can resolve," he said. "Bear in mind that only you, the delegates, officially chosen to speak for the 600,000 members of this great Brotherhood, can make the determinations. Within

you lies all the power of Lutheran Brotherhood. You speak for all of the members. As you leave here at the final bang of this gavel, it is vital that you will have served them and the Almighty who makes possible all our endeavors, to the best of your ability."

Rather than discuss politics, Nelson chose to direct his opening remarks toward Aid Association for Lutherans (AAL). Headquartered in Appleton, Wisconsin, AAL was the only fraternal benefit society larger than Lutheran Brotherhood. The two societies had coexisted peacefully and noncompetitively for many years, primarily because they served different markets. AAL chose to sell only to members of the Missouri and Wisconsin synods. Lutheran Brotherhood sold contracts to all Lutherans but had made scarcely a dent in the Missouri and Wisconsin synods. Its strength was in the American Lutheran Church and the Lutheran Church in America. However, the powerful AAL recently had decided to

The entire home office staff poses in the garden of the green building in 1967.

open its sales to Lutherans in all synods. The field was wide open now, and the specter of lost contracts loomed ominously in the minds of Lutheran Brotherhood's leaders. "It is with considerable concern that I report to you that a competing society, during the last several years, has pulled away from us in the amount of insurance written by nearly one billion dollars," Nelson told the delegates. "Lutheran Brotherhood is in the position now of having to catch up with its competitors if it is to be the organization its revered founders had in mind fifty years ago. Let us not make determinations here today that will drive Lutheran Brotherhood further behind."

The most effective way to make those determinations, Nelson said, was through a democratic election. "We all are quite aware that there is a contest before us today. This is as it should be in a free Lutheran society in which we fear only the wrath of our creator. I have heard it said that those who become candidates for this high office without the blessings of a small few must be considered disloyal. My friends, to be interested enough in the conduct of our society's affairs to volunteer his service as a director is not a mark of disloyalty. Rather it is a commendable interest in a service that calls for much effort by a director who will think and act as the Lord suggests with pitifully small emoluments."

Before the voting got underway, Granrud was asked to say a few words to the convention. If the independent candidates had been reassured by Nelson's words, they were uneasy as Granrud stepped to the microphone. The chairman was an articulate speaker, comfortable with crowds and quick to put them at ease. He had snatched victory from defeat once before from the podium of a general convention, and he might do it again. Granrud was diplomatic and noncombative today, even as he good-naturedly countered Nelson's comments about AAL. "We aren't doing too badly in our sales," the chairman noted. "The first six months of this year, our sales were $228 million. The sales of this little company that Mr. Nelson referred to, the name of which always escapes me, were $221 million. For the first time, we have surpassed them, and now that we have surpassed them, I think we will keep that up. I think we'd better give our salesmen a hand. They have done a marvelous job."

Granrud was masterful at times like these, personable and witty and warm. This was the Carl Granrud who was loved by his employees. "I'd like to introduce some people who are our sales leaders," he told the delegates. "One of them is Bill Johnson from Belmond, Iowa, our leading district representative. I think I can report him as something like a farmer. He's a man outstanding in his field. Mr. Johnson doesn't actually sell insurance. People come and take it away from him."

"Now I'd like to introduce the people who really do the work in our home office," he said. "For example, over here is Clifford Thompson, who is in charge of life benefits. They tell me he works so fast he pays claims instantly. In fact, he pays claims almost before they are ready. They tell of a man who fell off our building, and as he went past the second floor he was handed a check."

Granrud was rolling now, but like any experienced speaker he knew when to quit. His final words to the delegates were succinct and serious. "When I was elected to head the society some sixteen years ago, I said I would protect the integrity of Lutheran Brotherhood," he said softly. "I have tried to do so."

Although Granrud had relaxed the delegates, the independent supporters, especially those who worked in the home office, had become increasingly anxious by the time the ballots were passed out. The home office delegates were sitting in assigned seats, and the ballots had been printed so that the management slate was listed on one side of the page and the independent slate on the other; thus, it would not be difficult for management supporters to detect on which side the home office delegates had marked their votes. But an unidentified delegate had called the problem to Nelson's attention earlier that day. "The purpose of voting by ballot is to have secrecy," he said. "It is very difficult, I think, for some people to cast their vote if their neighbors are looking over their shoulder. If delegates wish to do so, could they approach the voting table and cast their ballot in secret?"

This observation prompted Nelson to declare at the meeting that delegates could move to any spot in the room to mark their ballots. Freed by Nelson's announcement, several home office employees left their seats and marked their ballots elsewhere. Cliff Thompson cautiously folded his in half, so that it would be nearly impossible to tell which side he had marked. After the vote was completed, the delegates broke for lunch, at which time the ballots were counted by a public accounting firm. Several newspaper reporters waited anxiously for the results. When the delegates returned to the meeting room, the vote was announced.

To be elected, each candidate required a clear majority of the 219 voting delegates in the room. However, the teller committee reported that one ballot had been turned in blank and another was void, dropping the total of legal ballots to 217; thus, each candidate would require 109 votes for election. Krause's name was announced first. He had 139 votes. Bjella was next with 126, and Hansen third with 116. Several opposition delegates crossed their fingers: three candidates elected, one to go. Granrud shook his head, then slumped passively in his chair. Wade took a deep breath and waited to hear his name announced. It was; he had 109 votes. The room erupted with cheers. "You have heard the results of the election," Nelson shouted over the din. "I declare James W. Krause elected to the board, Arley R. Bjella elected to the board, Herbert C. Hansen elected to the board, and George Wade . . ."

Dr. Harold Sponberg, the parliamentarian of the convention, suddenly interrupted Nelson. The two conferred briefly, and Nelson stepped back to the microphone. "The first three men mentioned have been duly elected," he announced anxiously. "But George Wade is one vote shy of majority. We must vote again."

Society Snapshot: 1967**

Home office: 701 Second Avenue South, Minneapolis

Number of members: 591,000

Number of employees: 404

Number of field personnel: 956

Insurance in force: $3,019,890,626

Assets: $421,949,713

Life insurance death benefits*: $5,715,396

Health insurance benefits: $272,494

Dividends paid: $12,677,050

Church loans: $48,070,746

Society officers

Chairman of the board
  and chief executive: Carl F. Granrud

President: A. Herbert Nelson

Chairman, Fraternal Activities: William G. Fisher

Vice presidents:

Health insurance: M. E. Andersen
Administrative assistant: Ralph H. Brastad
Research and development: Irving R. Burling
Chief actuary: Reuben I. Jacobson
Underwriting: A. O. Konigson
Director of agencies: Donald E. Lommen
General counsel: Russell H. Matthias
Administration: Robert E. Most
Public relations-advertising: Gretchen M. Pracht
Superintendent of agencies: Gordon N. Taft
Financial: David R. Zetzman
Treasurer: Theodore Q. Feig
Secretary: Kenneth T. Severud
Medical director: H. J. Brekke, M.D.

* *Combines death benefit proceeds from life insurance contracts and annuities.*

** *Following the September 1967 quadrennial convention, A.O. Lee replaced Carl Granrud as chairman of the board. Two senior vice presidents were named to the top management team: James W. Krause, Administration, and Woodrow P. Langhaug, Marketing.*

50 years young-
$3 billion strong
that's our
"order of business"
in 1967

This is a big year in the history of Lutheran Brotherhood.
  Our fraternal insurance society is celebrating its Golden Anniversary — 50 years of serving the life insurance needs (and more recently, the health insurance needs) of Lutherans of all synods.
  Already in the top 5% of the nation's life insurance organizations, Lutheran Brotherhood expects to join a very select circle by reaching 3 billion dollars of life insurance in force before the end of 1967.
  The quickening pace of Lutheran Brotherhood's growth is emphasized by these facts:
  It took 42 years to reach our first billion, 5 years for the second billion, and now only 3 years for the third billion!
  For outstanding values in life and health insurance, see your Lutheran Brotherhood representative today!

Mail to: Carl F. Granrud, Chairman of the Board
Lutheran Brotherhood Insurance
Minneapolis, Minn. 55402   CW

Please provide information on:
☐ "Retirement Special"   "Executive Special"   "College Special"   "Grandparent Special"

Name
Address
City_____ State_____ Zip_____

Lutheran Brotherhood Insurance
Life and Health Insurance for *all* Lutherans

Lutheran Brotherhood celebrated its fiftieth anniversary with a series of special events and dinners that paid tribute to its long history of service to Lutherans. The society's most important "order of business" for 1967, as described in this national advertisement, was to reach $3 billion of insurance in force by the end of the year.

Assistant vice presidents:

Public relations-advertising: Donald Brostrom
Associate actuary: Luther O. Forde
Agencies: William H. Klausen and Richard J. Nelson
Legal: James W. Krause
Investments: Leona M. Grondahl
               Herbert W. Mohr
               Donald C. Nelson
               John D. Nystul
               Harold A. Ulseth
Church loans: Joanne Rider
Planning and methods: Norman T. Rosholt
Underwriting: Joyce Zniewski
Administration: Arthur R. Zuehlke
Assistant secretary: Richard K. Lund
Assistant treasurers: E. Orion Sward
                        Carl A. Thomsen
                        Stanley C. Townswick

A few delegates began shouting. Both sides were confused. "I must be losing my mind," Granrud told Severud on the stage. "I can count from here all the employees who swore undying loyalty to me. Apparently they aren't voting for me."

Severud shook his head disgustedly. "You heard what the general agents said," he told the incredulous chairman. "People tried to tell you, but you wouldn't listen."

Following a heated discussion on stage, several convention officers determined that the single voided ballot counted as part of the legal voting total, and therefore brought the number of legal ballots to 218. Wade had received 109 votes, half of the legal total, and the voting rules stated that a candidate must receive a clear majority for election; in this case, 110 votes. The officers decided that Wade must run against the entire management slate, none of whom had received more than 102 votes. If no candidate won a majority on the second ballot, then the top two vote-getters would run a third time. The opposition leaders were beginning to sweat. The longer the election dragged on, the better Granrud's chances. Three new directors wouldn't do them any good. If Granrud won, he would continue to control the majority of the directors.

On the second vote, Wade received 106 votes and Granrud 90. He was still four votes short. The three other candidates, Smith, Preus, and Wang, split twenty votes between them and were eliminated from the ballot. The afternoon was passing quickly. A few delegates had planes to catch. Bjella winced as he watched them leave the hall. He had seen political conventions swing suddenly from one side to the other. If the people leaving were independent supporters, the slate might be in trouble. Several general agents and home office employees began thinking about new jobs.

As the convention officials prepared the third ballot, Wade glanced at Granrud. He looked tired, and his eyes betrayed resignation. Wade scanned the crowd of delegates. Some of these people have put their careers on the line for this, he thought. If I lose, it's not going to hurt me; I'll just go home. But they might lose their jobs. He turned to the Rev. John Tietjen, a noted Missouri Synod pastor, who was seated next to him. "I sure wish I had their votes," he said offhandedly, glancing at several Missouri Synod pastors, certain that they would be voting for Granrud. Tietjen turned to Wade and stared at him knowingly. "What makes you think you don't?" On the third ballot, Wade received 116 votes, Granrud 97.

Applause erupted, and scattered cheers drifted throughout the hall. After sixteen years as president and subsequently as chairman, Granrud had

Teller's Report of Votes Cast	
First Ballot	
James W. Krause	139
Arley R. Bjella	126
Herbert C. Hansen	116
George A. Wade	109
Carl F. Granrud	102
J.A.O. Preus	100
L. Edwin Wang	98
Harold A. Smith	77
Second Ballot (217 votes cast)	
George A. Wade	106
Carl F. Granrud	90
J.A.O. Preus	11
L. Edwin Wang	9
Harold A. Smith	1
Third Ballot (213 votes cast)	
George A. Wade	116
Carl F. Granrud	97

been defeated. The hall suddenly became quieter at the mass realization that his reign had ended, and Severud stepped to the microphone. "Ladies and gentlemen, I am sure that we have seen today a fraternal system in operation," he said. "Because of the votes which have been cast here today, we now have two more directors who will not be on the board anymore, and I would like to tell you people that these men have meant an awful lot to Lutheran Brotherhood.

"I don't think it would be at all out of order for us to stand up and give them a rising vote of thanks, Mr. Granrud and Mr. (Harold) Smith, for the years they have given to Lutheran Brotherhood. Now, does anybody disagree with me? If they do, I would like to see them out in the hall."

The crowd laughed, and the applause was long and loud, but among some delegates, the laughter soon turned to tears. Several close friends had put their arms around Granrud. He seemed in shock as he was surrounded by scores of delegates. Russ Smith shook the former chairman's hand, as did all of the newly elected directors, and when he had finished, looked back at the stage where the old warrior was being consoled. Smith felt a deep sense of loss as he remembered the good times. Granrud was such a tremendous leader, he thought to himself. Why did things have to come to this?

The Final Days

That night the victors, including several employees whose jobs had hung in the balance, celebrated in grand style. There was laughing and hugging and kissing and toasts. Lundring and Haroldson and Smith cried. Elsewhere in the Palmer House, Granrud sat stoically in his room, surrounded by close friends. "It's finished," he said tonelessly. "I'm out and somebody else is in." A few of his supporters wouldn't hear of it; they were not yet willing to acquiesce. "I never heard of you quitting," said one. "You've always fought. You're letting them run all over you. You shouldn't let them do that to you." Granrud began to perk up. "Well, I suppose not," he said more optimistically. As the room began to fill with talk of fighting back, Walt Cover, one of Granrud's closest friends, shook his head. Enough was enough, he thought, as he left the room and went to his car. It was a long drive home.

A. Herbert Nelson had scheduled a meeting of the home office staff in Minneapolis for the following Monday morning. As he strode triumphantly into the directors' room, smiling broadly, ready to preside at last, he felt an odd tension in the room. Strange, he thought. A few officers cleared their throats nervously. There at the head of the table sat Granrud. Nelson was momentarily taken aback by this unexpected sight, but he recovered quickly and took a seat at the side of the table near Granrud.

Severud hurriedly took roll call and waited for the inevitable explosion. The room was silent. "What are you doing here, Mr. Granrud?" Nelson asked. "I don't believe you're supposed to be here." The ousted chairman responded with a caustic remark, and Nelson followed with a rejoinder of his own. Severud quietly laid down his pen. No minutes would be taken at this meeting. Don Brostrom, the society's assistant vice president of public relations, squirmed with embarrassment. Like most of his fellow officers, he desperately wanted to leave the room. At the same time, as a former newspaper reporter, he thought he should be taking notes; this story was too good to miss. After a few minutes of verbal sparring with Granrud, Nelson decided that matters had gotten out of hand and abruptly adjourned the meeting.

Years later, several society observers theorized that Granrud might not have decided to fight back but for a newspaper story published after the convention in which Nelson reiterated the familiar charges that Granrud had ruled the society by "fear and favor." Some members of the petition camp, especially Krause, were not pleased when they saw the article, for they had hoped to end the convention on a more conciliatory note. Although Nelson had patiently endured more than his share of unfavorable comments from Granrud during the past several months, they nonetheless viewed the president's remarks as misguided strategy. Granrud was an extremely proud man, and it was not likely that he would let such remarks pass without a fight. By Monday afternoon, the post-convention battle had become public. "You can be sure this thing isn't settled yet," Granrud told the *Minneapolis Tribune* that day. "We don't apologize to anybody for the way this company is run. This is nothing but an attempt to seize control of the company." Granrud claimed that he had been elected chief executive by the board, and insisted that he was still chief executive until removed by the board. That might be a long time. Despite the election of four new directors, the board was still deadlocked 6 to 6 over his right to continue in some executive capacity.

Granrud continued to show up at the home office, issuing orders as if nothing had changed. Unsure who was really in charge, the employees were confused, and little work got done. Nelson finally

Jim Klobuchar

Jim Klobuchar immortalized the quarrel between ousted society chairman Carl Granrud and the new management of Lutheran Brotherhood in his daily column in the Minneapolis Star *on October 7, 1967. Reproduced courtesy of the* Star Tribune, *Minneapolis-St. Paul.*

LOVERS OF INTRAMURAL WARFARE can only admire the ingenuity and fierceness with which the battle was waged this weekend for control of the huge Lutheran Brotherhood insurance society.

It used to be that when Lutherans quarreled the result was a new synod or another picnic at Mount Olivet Lutheran Church.

But the stakes were enormously higher Friday, and the emotions deeper, demanding the last reserves of generalship, stamina and cunning on both sides. And it is with some mingled fondness and regret, therefore, that I must report on the pivotal tactic of the long day's struggle:

Somebody locked the door to the Lutheran Brotherhood Building's gold-plated men's room, the one sanctuary of neutrality where the warring slates of directors could meet on common ground in a spirit of good will and forbearance.

The report is verified by spokesmen for both sides in addition to a neutral janitor who had passed through that portion of the building in a relatively high state of urgency. Its authenticity, accordingly, is beyond dispute.

It's useless to speculate on what set of circumstances, or what degree of bitterness, would drive a man to lock out of the men's room not only his fraternal enemies but his colleagues as well.

The only unchallengeable conclusion is that when the Lutherans fight among themselves, they play rough.

FRATERNAL STRIFE among the Catholics is romper room stuff in comparison. When Catholics have battled, it has been over such trivia as papal abuse of indulgences, the keys to the kingdom, control of medieval armies, should priests marry, the Notre Dame schedule or the Milton Berlesque sermons of Father Fleming at St. Olaf's.

When Jews battled each other, on the other hand, there has always been much uncertainty because they have never stayed in the same place long enough to determine who has the home field advantage. The upshot, therefore, usually has been another clothing store on Hennepin Av.

And so let us briefly reconstruct the angry events leading up to that unorthodox maneuver yesterday. You must be aware that the longtime chief executive, Carl F. Granrud, was rebuffed in his bid for re-election last month. He accused his enemies on the board of "scheming, plotting and conniving."

To which opponent A. Herbert Nelson replied, in the same spirit of Christian moderation that had characterized Granrud's remarks: "(Lutherans) want eradicated forever the tyranny, dictatorship, rule by fear and favor, the wasting of Lutheran Brotherhood earnings on self-glorification, such as went on for the last several years."

Now these are not bad for openers in any Christian dialogue. At the same time they do represent, as one awed bystander observed, a helluva way to get to heaven.

In any event, another facedown meeting between the two forces was scheduled yesterday in the beautiful and lofty Brotherhood Building. This is the green-marbled and excitingly-paned downtown tower which also houses offices of the city's dynamic Chamber of Commerce leaders and therefore is described in some quarters as "The Glass Menagerie."

BY COURT ORDER, Granrud was barred from the building. What the Nelson forces had overlooked, apparently, was that the ousted chief executive was carrying with him not only a good deal of resentment, but also the only readily-accessible key to the gold-trimmed men's room that had been the board's pride for some time.

"Either he's got it," one of Granrud's opponents muttered acidly, "or one of his sympathizers has got it. It's hard to imagine a man being that vengeful."

And yet, without our taking sides in the issue, can the neutralists truly blame the Granrud forces for this resourceful ploy? I mean they DID lock the man out of his own building.

But I know there is enough humanity in our our hearts to sympathize with both parties in this predicament. Philosophically, we can note that in almost every struggle conducted on this scale of ferocity and vindictiveness, it is the innocent who must suffer.

Militarily, I do not know how this maneuver would be classified. Strategically, I suppose, it would come under the broad general heading of a holding action. Ultimately, the Granrud forces lost.

But the battle, if long, at least was suspenseful.

announced over the home office loudspeaker that Lutheran Brotherhood employees were to ignore everything Granrud said or did. When the ousted chairman persisted, Nelson had the locks changed on the home office doors and passed out keys to a few select employees. However, Granrud, who still had many supporters working at the home office, had no trouble entering the building or the executive offices. Nelson ultimately gained a temporary court restraining order that barred Granrud from entering the home office. Tipped off that Nelson was bearing down on him, restraining order in hand, Granrud slipped out of the building just seconds ahead of the irate president, but not before he (or one of his sympathizers) locked the door to the men's restroom in the society boardroom and took the only key. The incident was subsequently immortalized by local newspaper columnist Jim Klobuchar.

For the next week, Granrud's lawyers contended in Hennepin District Court that Granrud was still in charge of the society and was entitled to hold office until a successor was named by the board. Society lawyers countered that the position of chief executive, as Granrud defined it, did not exist. The society bylaws clearly separated the distinct positions of director and officer, and Granrud could not serve as an officer. According to the bylaws, he was too old. The bylaws also specified that the board could elect a chairman only from its current membership. Granrud was no longer on the board, having been defeated at the recent convention; therefore, he could not be in charge. Judge John A. Weeks agreed with the society's attorneys. He ruled against Granrud and upheld the restraining order.

Although the board later rescinded the order, passed a resolution thanking Granrud for his years of service, and voted him an ample annual stipend, Granrud refused to have anything to do with the society for several years. He maintained his law offices in downtown Minneapolis and went to the home office a few times to deliver Christmas presents to old friends, but he never stayed more than a few minutes. He did take advantage of society parking privileges, however, and his shiny Cadillac was seen behind the green building for years. Society employees often saw Granrud and Pracht lunching together, or walking together on the sidewalk outside, and they observed that the home office was not going to be nearly as colorful without the two law partners. Occasionally, when longtime employees ran into Granrud, they urged him to come back for an extended official visit. "Come on now, Mr. Granrud," Dave Zetzman once told his old boss. "You're big enough. You can come back." Granrud steadfastly refused.

But the years softened his anger. In 1976, when a reporter asked Granrud what he thought of the new management of Lutheran Brotherhood, he observed that they seemed to be doing "all right." The diplomatic Bjella eventually convinced the former chairman to join him and several longtime society employees for games of whist at the Minneapolis Club. Through Bjella, with whom he became good friends, Granrud eventually made peace with his beloved society. "I'm too weak to fight and too old to run," he jokingly told friends after suffering a stroke in 1983. "So I've been very, very nice to everybody."

A few months before his death that year, he consented to be a guest at the society's general convention dinner. When he was introduced, several hundred people rose to give him a loud and long standing ovation. Granrud beamed. There would be no politics tonight, only smiles and congratulations and memories of happier days. Carl Granrud, the man who built the green building, the man who, by the force of his own dominant personality, had pushed Lutheran Brotherhood into the modern era, had come home.

The Healing Years

It had been a dark morning in Minneapolis, but the clouds finally had broken, and sunlight was beginning to pour through them. Arley Bjella and George Wade sat in the lobby of the Radisson Hotel, talking quietly. Every few seconds they glanced at the hotel entrance a little anxiously, as though they were waiting for someone. Several minutes later Russell Matthias pushed open one of the heavy glass doors and walked in.

Matthias, the general counsel for Lutheran Brotherhood, was smiling. His eyes were guarded, though, and they carefully searched Bjella and Wade for any clues to their thoughts. But whatever the two men were thinking was not apparent on their faces. The trio shook hands formally. "Good to see you, Mr. Matthias," Bjella said. His voice was firm but cordial. "We're glad to have this chance to talk with you."

The 1970s were a time of healing for Lutheran Brotherhood. During these years, the society became less political, improved its relationship with the Lutheran church, and dramatically increased its support for fraternal programs. One of the society's many successes was its Fire Safety Program, which local branches sponsored in their schools and communities. Pictured on the cover of BOND magazine in April 1975 are, from left, Lutheran Brotherhood chairman Arley R. Bjella, Michael Maijala, Elizabeth Johnson, Lutheran Brotherhood president Woodrow P. Langhaug, Jennifer Kirckoff, and Minneapolis fireman Leroy Salmonson.

Bjella had called the impromptu meeting that morning. It was early October of 1967. The society convention had been over for two weeks, and Carl Granrud's battle to regain control of Lutheran Brotherhood had failed in court. He would not be coming back. It was time for the society to move ahead, yet some residue of bitterness remained, and the board was still deadlocked: six directors dedicated to a new order, six devoted to the ousted leader. The directors had met briefly a few days after the convention, but the atmosphere had been strained, and nothing had been accomplished. If the stalemate persisted, little would ever be accomplished, and the society would suffer for it.

During the past few months, Bjella had come to be considered the leader of the independent candidates. He was relatively new to Lutheran Brotherhood and was not encumbered with the emotional effects of past confrontations and old grudges. An experienced politician, he was known for his ability to negotiate and his desire to compromise. If anyone could unite the directors, it would be Bjella. Yet even he was unsure how to bring about a reconciliation.

Ken Anderson knew how. A Minneapolis attorney who had done extensive work for the society and

produced no results. We can't afford more. If we don't solve our differences, it isn't going to hurt you. It isn't going to hurt me, either. But it is going to hurt this society."

Matthias nodded; Bjella had struck a sensitive nerve. "I agree completely," Matthias said, a little defensively. "But what about Granrud?" Bjella had anticipated that the ousted chairman's name would come up. After the 1959 political debacle, Matthias had worked hard to return to the good graces of Granrud and had become one of his most ardent supporters. He had even quarterbacked Granrud's recent legal campaign for reinstatement.

"Mr. Granrud was not reelected to the board," Wade said firmly. "He is welcome to return to the home office at any time. We'd be honored to have him back and we'd be honored to have his counsel. But Mr. Granrud is not in charge anymore. The delegates say he's not in charge, the bylaws say he's not in charge, and the courts say he's not in charge."

"So who is in charge?"

"The board is in charge now," Bjella said. "All twelve of us. We have all been elected by the convention, we are all legitimate members, and we'd better figure out a way to get along. We can learn from you and you can learn from us. It's our responsibility as directors to set an example for the rest of the society. It's time to start healing old wounds."

Matthias began to say something, stopped, and thought for a moment. "You're right," he said finally. "I'm sure we can work out a satisfactory compromise." He stood and walked to the door. "You know, I've cut hundreds of backroom deals for hundreds of clients," he said. "But I really care what happens to this society."

Bjella and Wade nodded. "I have absolutely no doubt about that," Bjella said quietly. "We'll talk again before the next board meeting."

A Time for Healing

On October 6, 1967, the directors of Lutheran Brotherhood elected Arthur O. Lee the new chairman of the board and Bjella vice chairman. The head

served as parliamentarian at the 1959 convention, Anderson called Bjella after the board's first, unproductive meeting. "I think I understand where you guys are at," he said. "If you want to break this deadlock, the one person you must talk to is Matthias. He's the strongest of the other six, a tough operator, and you would do better to have him as a friend than as an enemy. I think Matthias would probably like to talk, but you're going to have to make the first move. You guys are the new kids on the block." Bjella thought about Anderson's suggestion for a few hours and then called Wade, who agreed that a meeting was a good idea. Bjella next called Matthias; he was willing to talk.

Bjella began the negotiations bluntly. "We can't go on this way," he said. "We've got to work this situation out for the good of Lutheran Brotherhood and get the board members moving in the same direction. We've already had one meeting that

of the society's church loan program, Lee was the obvious compromise choice for chairman. Although he had been a Granrud supporter, he was not the kind of man to wear anyone else's stripes. Husky and broad shouldered, at seventy-two he still looked capable of knocking the opposition to the ground, which he had done regularly as a guard for the St. Olaf College football team. Yet it was difficult to imagine Lee hitting anyone, for he was a gentle and reserved man. His passive manner was belied only

James Krause, left, and Woodrow Langhaug played key roles as senior vice presidents in the home office executive team appointed after the 1967 general convention. The team, headed by president A. Herbert Nelson, was designed to encourage more participatory management by disseminating greater authority among officers and employees.

by his deep, gravelly voice, which he used judiciously. He was most at home in the solitude of his St. Olaf business office, where he had served as manager for many years.

At the October 6 meeting, six directors were elected to the executive committee: Lee, Dreng Bjornaraa, and Harold Lunde on one side; Bjella, A. Herbert Nelson, and Woodrow Langhaug on the other. Nelson continued as president. The terms of the compromise were complete. At the meeting, the board named Granrud as chairman emeritus, adopted a resolution praising him for his twenty-seven years of service to the society, and dismissed the court order barring him from the home office.

A new era of openness had begun at Lutheran Brotherhood. A more participatory management style came into play when a new executive team was elected by the board. Jim Krause and Woody Langhaug were appointed senior vice presidents. Departments involved in marketing functions reported to Langhaug, and those involved in administration reported to Krause. The two men, in turn, reported directly to Nelson, who maintained a supervisory role. The contrast of this regime to Granrud's was startling. Formerly fifteen of seventeen society departments had reported directly to the chairman. While that style had produced a dedicated organization with few excess employees, it also had created some anxiety. Under the direction of the new management team, tensions in the home office began to lessen. Workers slowly began to speak their minds again without fear, and communication between managers and employees improved. The freedom was refreshing. Krause found himself almost grinning at meetings when employees rose to voice dissenting opinions. Either they had forgotten he was there, or they didn't worry about it.

Krause was an innovative thinker, looking to the future, always searching for more effective solutions to old problems. He was a devoted student of management and spent much of his time trying to understand what motivated Lutheran Brotherhood employees. Krause spent several months listening to employees in the home office, and then instituted policies that delegated more responsibility to managers and employees. By distributing authority, he attempted to encourage greater creativity among the rank and file. That was no small accomplishment at the home office, where conformity was generally rewarded. The new freedom produced some errors, but gradually people began to venture out of their shells.

Langhaug devoted much of his time to improving communications between the home office and the field. The general agents had great respect for Langhaug. He had been one of them, and he knew what drove them. He also excelled at public relations, not because he worked hard at it, but because he did not. Langhaug was always himself, a genuinely nice man who had something good to say about everyone. He disliked confrontation, and his genial demeanor sometimes interfered with his ability to maintain discipline, but his kindness, for the most part, was an asset. Langhaug exuded warmth, and warmth was what Lutheran Brotherhood needed right now.

Almost as if to show its excitement about the shift in leadership, the field force made October its greatest sales month ever. That burst of activity enabled Lutheran Brotherhood to reach its golden anniversary goal—$3 billion of insurance in force—by December 14, 1967. Just three more years passed before the society attained $4 billion of insurance in force. The new era of openness was working.

Mutual Funds

During the late 1960s, a new and perplexing challenge confronted the life insurance industry. Inflation had, for the first time, become a significant aspect of American economic life. When insurance agents tried to sell contracts that offered a fixed dollar amount of benefits, prospects repeatedly confronted them with a pointed question: How will this contract help my family if the purchasing power of the dollar continues to decline? The challenge of inflation prompted insurance companies to seriously consider expanding their product portfolios. Should we begin to offer financial products whose value adjusts to the condition of the economy, they wondered, or should we restrict our product line to the guaranteed benefits of life insurance?

The directors of Lutheran Brotherhood spent much of their time debating those questions. A few members, especially Krause, Langhaug, and Bjella, believed that the society should introduce its own mutual fund. By pooling the shares of many investors, mutual funds provided families of modest means with the investing power and safety they would not otherwise be able to afford. Mutual funds were supervised by professional money managers, and the shares were invested across a wide range of stock sources for greater stability. Mutual funds often provided returns higher than certificates of deposit offered by savings institutions, the kind of returns that could help the average American stay ahead of inflation.

To proponents, mutual funds seemed entirely in keeping with Lutheran Brotherhood's purpose. Ours is a fraternal benefit society, they reasoned, and fraternal benefits are not limited to life insurance products. Fraternal benefits include any financial services that help protect the future of our members and their families. When the society determined that its members needed protection from disability, it offered health insurance. It had since become apparent, they concluded, that new investment products such as mutual funds were necessary.

Some board members were nonetheless apprehensive. Some stocks and bonds could be extremely risky, prone to extreme market fluctuations, they observed, and insurance organizations were pledged to do everything in their power to eliminate risk. Lutheran Brotherhood's members placed great trust in the society's historically prudent approach. How, then, could the society, in good conscience, offer its members a product that might fluctuate in value? Besides, a market crash might jeopardize not only the funds of member investors, but the entire reserve that Lutheran Brotherhood had so conscientiously stewarded. There were also concerns that stocks and bonds might endanger the society's tax-exempt fraternal status. Like Lutheran Brotherhood, other large fraternal societies struggled with these questions. Almost all of them decided that, at least for the time being, the potential risks outweighed the benefits, and they declined to add investments to their cache of insurance products.

Lutheran Brotherhood, however, continued cautiously to investigate the possibility of introducing its own mutual fund. The more research the board members did, the more they became convinced of the potential value of the product. Certainly, there were risks involved with investments, but that was true of any financial undertaking. Any mutual fund introduced by Lutheran Brotherhood would be a conservative fund. It would be meticulously managed to avoid large market swings and oriented to the long-term investor; few investors had ever lost money over the long haul. In fact, over a long period of time, a conservatively managed mutual fund would probably perform as well as or better than more perilous stock funds.

The board hired a consulting firm to study alternatives for achieving that goal. The consultants concluded that it was too difficult and expensive for the society to start its own fund. A more suitable option would be to align with an outside investment company. The world of securities was extremely complicated and highly regulated. An outside firm familiar with the legal requirements of the trade would provide the essential organizational and management expertise. However, merely tapping into an already existing fund would not do, either. Lutheran Brotherhood wanted its own mutual fund, a fund that its field force could sell only to investors from within the society's membership. For the next several months, Jim Krause searched for an investment firm that would meet those objectives. He thought he finally had found one, a prominent Wall Street company, when he received a phone call from an old acquaintance.

The friend was Bob Skare, a Minneapolis lawyer who had attended the University of Minnesota Law School with Krause. The two met over lunch, where Skare mentioned that he had heard through the local grapevine that Lutheran Brotherhood was interested in mutual funds. He added that he was doing some work for a private company called Federated Investors of Pittsburgh, Pennsylvania, and thought the firm might work well together with the society. "I've really been impressed with the way they manage their mutual funds," he said. "What's so impressive about them is that they seem to be people of high integrity. During one recent transaction, we had some very difficult negotiations, and Federated could very easily have pulled out or altered their original bargaining position. But their president, Jack Donahue, kept his word on every point that he had started the discussions with. The other side was very impressed."

Krause was somewhat skeptical. "It all sounds very interesting," he told Skare, "but we're just about to put a deal together with another firm. I've been all over the country and I've talked to a lot of people. I'm not sure anyone else has a better solution."

Skare persisted. "I think it would be worth your time to talk to these people," he said. "Federated might be just what you're looking for. They're not looking to do everything themselves; they're just looking for partners. Federated is young and growing. They have the administrative and investment expertise, and they have some funds that are up and running and successful. But they need somebody who has a major marketing system already in place. That's what Lutheran Brotherhood would bring to the venture. I know Federated would be interested in you."

Krause decided to at least talk to the Federated people, Skare arranged a meeting with Donahue, and he and Krause flew to Pittsburgh. Still cool to the possibility of a joint venture, Krause paid his own airfare so that he would not feel obligated. But he warmed to the idea of a relationship with Federated after just one day of meetings with Donahue and his staff. Skare had been right. The staff seemed warm and genuine. More importantly, they knew what they were talking about. That night Krause called Langhaug, who was in New York City on society business. "Woody, you have got to meet these people," Krause said. Langhaug flew into Pittsburgh the next day and joined Krause for a second round of meetings with Federated. He also was impressed with what he heard, and he and

The officers of Lutheran Brotherhood, taken in late 1967. Front row, from left: James Krause, David Zetzman, Gordon Taft, Theodore Feig, and Russell Matthias. Second row, A. Herbert Nelson, Woodrow Langhaug, Kenneth Severud, Don Lommen, Clarence Nelson, M.E. Andersen, Ralph Brastad, Reuben Jacobson, Donald Brostrom, and Irving Burling. Standing: A.O. Lee, William Fisher, Robert Most, Norman Rosholt, Richard Lund, and Harlan Hogsven.

Several men played important roles in the development of Lutheran Brotherhood's first mutual fund offering in 1970. Front row, from left: Clifford Knudten, vice president; James Krause, senior vice president-Administration. Standing: Charles Wallander, executive vice president of Federated Investors, Inc.; Lloyd Ostlund, senior vice president-Law; and Harry Peterson, vice president and director of Agencies.

Krause enthusiastically carried that message back to Minneapolis.

Much of their optimism had to do with Federated's leader, Jack Donahue. A West Point graduate, he had borrowed several thousand dollars from his father-in-law, formed Federated Investors in the 1950s, and built it into an organization that at one time had managed more money than Merrill Lynch. Donahue was Irish Catholic, a devoted family man who sometimes entertained prospective employees at his spacious Pittsburgh home, where he introduced them to his wife and thirteen children. Donahue also encouraged a family atmosphere at work. A generous man, he delighted in sharing his own good fortune with his associates. Because Donahue was so sure of his own managerial abilities, he was not threatened by other strong, confident employees. As a result, he was able to attract a diverse group of individuals with different abilities and temperaments. He carefully assessed their abilities, placed them strategically within the company, and unselfishly nurtured their potential. When his employees clashed, he judiciously settled territorial spats and massaged bruised egos. Like a wise father, he kept his Federated family working toward the same ends.

Donahue was also a persuasive man. Cliff Knudten, a Milwaukee insurance manager, had once been invited to Pittsburgh to interview with Federated. Because he preferred his native Midwest, Knudten was reluctant even to consider a move to Pittsburgh, but he agreed to come. When, over dinner at his club, Donahue offered him an extremely attractive job, Knudten instinctively recited the lines he had rehearsed at home. "I'm very honored by your offer," he said. "But I need to discuss it first with my wife." Donahue nodded. "I understand," he said. "That makes perfect sense. Waiter, please bring us a phone." Within moments a telephone was sitting on the table. "Now you can call your wife." Incredulous, Knudten dialed his home in Milwaukee. "Hi, honey," he said, glancing at Donahue. "Guess where I'm at?" By the time he had finished talking to his wife, Knudten had changed his mind, and had taken the job with Federated.

Donahue's powers of salesmanship did not immediately alleviate the concerns of all the board members about mutual funds. Most of them had accepted the idea, but a few were still nagged by the fear that a mutual fund might compete with and, eventually, dilute the society's ability to protect its members. What if Lutheran Brotherhood's district representatives began to favor mutual funds over life insurance? What if they encouraged members to surrender their life insurance to purchase mutual funds? But Langhaug ultimately affirmed that life insurance would always come first at Lutheran Brotherhood and persuaded the doubters that mutual funds were intended only as a complementary partner in total financial planning.

That the board was convinced that Federated was the perfect partner was evidenced by the speed with which the deal was completed. For almost two years, the board had studied many mutual fund operations, and had finally decided on an investment firm that they were willing to investigate when they learned about Federated in the fall of 1969. Just two months later, on December 19, the directors of Lutheran Brotherhood gave final approval to the Lutheran Brotherhood Fund.

Lutheran Brotherhood thus became the first fraternal insurance society in the United States to sponsor a mutual fund offered through its field force. Some other fraternal organizations, fearing that the rise of investment products would incur the wrath of the federal government and lead to the loss of their tax-exempt status, strongly opposed the move. A fraternal could not do such things, they maintained. Bjella disagreed. The fraternal concept should not constrict the development of new ideas, he argued. It should instead free fraternal societies to better serve their members with inventive financial services.

Starting a Family

Before Lutheran Brotherhood could do that, plenty of work had to be done. The creation of a mutual fund was closely analogous to the creation of a family. Two organizations, Lutheran Brotherhood and Federated Investors, had been introduced and had decided to form a union. These "parents" then created new corporate subsidiaries. Lutheran Brotherhood Securities Corp. (LBSC) was organized to distribute and market the funds through the society's field force. Lutheran Brotherhood Research Corp. (which was owned entirely by the society) was created to manage the investment of the funds.

In early 1970, LBSC set up headquarters in the home office. Over the next several months, two Federated employees, Chuck Wallander and Cliff Knudten, worked furiously to market the fund to the society's members. They had an uphill battle, for few members knew or cared much about mutual funds. When Wallander and Knudten first tried to explain the Lutheran Brotherhood Fund to officers at a home office meeting, they were met with yawns and silence. One vice president was so bored that he turned off his hearing aid.

The reaction of the field force was more favorable, but mixed. As true believers in the value of insurance, some field personnel were not yet psychologically prepared to accept this new product. They did not understand it, nor did they want to. A few even viewed mutual funds as a threat to their livelihood. "We've been in direct competition with mutual funds for years," they cried. "Now all our contract holders will take their money and put it into mutual funds instead of life insurance. You're asking us to cut our own throats."

Langhaug's intercession helped convince the faithful that they were wrong. "We don't want any representative to recommend mutual funds until the prospect is adequately insured," he told them. "Once that is done, the representative who has the fund available will find many more doors open. For example, we'll be able to do more business with older members. And by increasing the income of our members, we'll be able to sell larger contracts and write more permanent insurance."

A few traditionalists steadfastly refused to have anything to do with the funds, but other general agents, such as Walt Beglau, Bill Johnson, and John Falck, began to champion the cause. The acceptance of the field force was crucial to the success of the fund, for they had to pass a detailed broker's examination before they could legally sell it. Several hundred representatives were quickly enrolled in classes, and they spent many hours learning about securities. The society had hoped that three hundred representatives would be eligible in the next two years.

By the end of 1970, about seven hundred Lutheran Brotherhood representatives were licensed to sell mutual funds.

Some were forced to study harder than others. Harry Hendricks, then a general agent in Washington, D.C., passed his broker's examination, only to learn that he was required to pass a much more stringent test in order to be licensed in Virginia. At the time, LBSC was preparing an expensive mail campaign to about 335,000 investment prospects in all fifty states. "If you don't pass the Virginia test in the next week," Hendricks was informed, "we won't be able to sell in that state, and the entire mailing, all forty-seven thousand pounds, will have to be reprinted to reflect the change." LBSC hurriedly arranged to send the nervous Hendricks to a securities expert in Philadelphia. For a solid week, he crammed with his tutor, then took a three-hour examination. He passed.

Following the mailings, in the spring of l970, LBSC announced a charter investment period for several weeks, during which members could purchase shares of the fund with no sales commission charge. Knudten, Wallander, and their tiny LBSC staff put in many long, hectic days during that time. Often, each answered up to one hundred phone calls per day, explaining the concept of mutual funds to fiscally temperate Lutherans whose previous investing experience consisted entirely of bank certificates of deposit. The situation was complicated by the fact that most of the society's representatives were not yet licensed and thus could not legally speak to their clients about mutual funds. That did not sit well with many callers who preferred to deal with their own insurance counsellor. Many of these relationships were of long standing, going back ten years or more.

It was up to Knudten and Wallander to explain why callers could not deal with their own representatives. They also had to explain why the share price of the Lutheran Brotherhood Fund was decreasing.

"The Incredibly Exciting Adventures of Roger, the Lutheran Brotherhood Agent," made its advertising debut in 1969 and was used successfully in magazines and television throughout the early 1970s. By incorporating humor into a sales pitch, the cartoon reflected a loosening of attitudes about how to approach people about life insurance.

During the charter investment period, the stock market went into a minor tailspin. The timing could not have been worse. At the same time LBSC was trying to sell introductory shares for ten dollars apiece, the value of those shares on the stock market had temporarily dropped below ten dollars. The field force was up in arms. Some argued that the society had never before offered an insurance contract that lost money after it was sold. They expressed fear that mutual funds were going to ruin the trust it had taken them years to build. A few days after being persuaded to put several thousand dollars into the fund, one society officer learned that the market price of his shares had dropped. He charged into Knudten's office and demanded an explanation. "You guys are out to rob me!" he shouted.

Most investors were more patient. Shortly after he received his prospectus, one Lutheran Brotherhood member called the LBSC office. "I'd like to purchase

During his seventeen years as chairman of Lutheran Brotherhood, Arley Bjella provided strong leadership, oversaw dramatic changes in the society's fraternal program, and encouraged an atmosphere of communication and reconciliation within the society.

some mutual fund shares," he said. "I prefer to hand over my check in person." He was told to come down to the office. The member drove into the home office parking lot, only to be told he couldn't park there. Undaunted, the investor parked a few blocks away and presented himself at the LBSC office at noon. Sorry, the person you want to see is at lunch, the secretary informed him. The member was directed to the cafeteria "for a free cup of coffee." Once there, he was told he could obtain free coffee only with a special note. So he went across the street to a restaurant. He returned to the home office some time later, made his connection with an LBSC representative, calmly told his story, and cheerfully wrote out a check for two thousand dollars. Wow, the representative thought, as the man left the office, these people must be a rare breed to want to invest after that kind of experience.

They were. During the charter investment offering, a period of just six weeks, more than twelve thousand Lutheran Brotherhood members invested nearly $12 million in the first Lutheran Brotherhood Fund. The society's leaders were amazed. That was almost $2 million more than they had hoped for. What had convinced these fiscally conservative Lutherans to give the fund a chance? Two reasons became apparent. First, there was a need. People realized that economic times were changing. It wasn't necessarily enough to place one's money in a bank and withdraw it thirty years later. The challenge of inflation demanded a different kind of response. Second, although most investors knew little about mutual funds, they knew the society. They invested because they placed great trust in Lutheran Brotherhood. It

was a sobering reminder for the society's leaders.

As enthusiasm for investment products grew among Lutherans during the 1970s, the society began to add more "children" to its family of funds. The Lutheran Brotherhood Income Fund, intended for investors who desired current income, was introduced in 1972. The Lutheran Brotherhood U.S. Government Securities Fund, with bonds guaranteed by the federal government, was introduced two years later. In 1976, Congress passed legislation that, for the first time, allowed Americans to receive tax-free income by investing in municipal bonds. That year, the society introduced its fourth mutual fund, the Lutheran Brotherhood Municipal Bond Fund.

By 1987, Lutheran Brotherhood Securities Corp. had become a major investment subsidiary with a wide array of investment products and a staff of one hundred and a distributor of mutual funds with more than $1.5 billion in assets under management.

The Peacemaker

Art Lee died in 1970, and Arley Bjella was elected chairman and chief executive officer of Lutheran Brotherhood. During his three years on the board, Bjella's leadership abilities had become increasingly evident. Although he had something to learn about the technicalities of insurance, he already knew how to manage people. If Granrud had often wielded power with an iron fist, Bjella exercised power with a velvet glove. He brought a calming influence to a society that had been through years of strife and anxiety. There were many emotional and psychological wounds, especially between the society and the church, and Bjella saw it as the board's task to try to heal them.

An experienced politician, Bjella believed that the office should seek the man, not the other way around. He had never intended to be anything other than a director, for his law practice in Williston was flourishing, but when a search committee had failed to find a Lutheran insurance executive deemed acceptable for the leadership of the society, they turned to Bjella. He agreed to serve on the condition that a new position, chief executive officer, be created for

him. "If I'm going to take the job," he quietly explained, "I need the clout to do it right." The board trusted Bjella's ability to handle the demands of executive power, and accepted his request.

For the next two years, Bjella commuted weekly between Williston and Minneapolis on the Empire Builder. It was a long train ride, yet the open range invigorated him. Invariably, he brightened as the train passed over the gentle hills of western North Dakota. It was the lonely prairie of his youth that had shaped his intense need for privacy, the vast expanse that had taught him to keep in their proper perspective the matters, both large and small, with which he dealt. The constancy of the high plains instilled in Bjella a sense of order and tranquility, and he spent many reflective hours gazing out the window of the train.

Sometimes he thought about his father. In 1889, Asle Bjella emigrated from Norway and eventually settled in the village of Epping, a few miles northwest of Williston. There he opened a blacksmith shop. Fire and anvil were the tools of his trade, and he forged a life for his family in a raw land that was less easily worked than metal. Asle Bjella did not expect that life should be easy. His wife, Clara, died when she was only thirty-six, a victim of the influenza epidemic that swept America in 1918, and he was left to care for their six children. The youngest, Arley, was not yet two years old.

Every year, on the anniversary of Clara's death, the elder Bjella took his children to pray at her grave, and the townspeople of Epping also tried to ease the pain. Many of them helped Asle to raise his children, and they became an extended family to the Bjellas. Arley never forgot their kindness, and he learned at an early age to seek the goodness in people.

The Second World War sorely tested those beliefs. Just out of law school, he joined the United States Army and saw firsthand the death and destruction that was wreaked on Europe. After the conflict, he served as a captain in the Judge Advocate Division in Germany, which was responsible for trying Nazi war criminals. The trials and the stories of horror and inhumanity left an indelible mark on Bjella's psyche.

When he returned from Europe, Bjella married Beverly Heen, his college sweetheart, and formed a law partnership in Williston with Frank Jestrab. Williston was rich with historical significance. It was located at the confluence of the Missouri and Yellowstone rivers and served for years as the last vestige of civilization on the trail to the great Northwest. Nearby were the battlefields of Sitting Bull, the great Sioux chief. And there was oil. When the precious fluid was discovered in the Williston Basin in 1951, the community prospered, as did the fledgling firm of Bjella and Jestrab. The firm eventually influenced much of North Dakota's conservation-minded oil and gas law.

With its sudden infusion of wealth, Williston required strong civic leadership. Along with other local leaders, Bjella played an important role in keeping the various community interests pointed in the same direction, orchestrating projects in a manner that was unobtrusive yet effective. Like his father, who had served as a state representative, Bjella put his energies into community service. He served on the boards of several hospitals and banks, and he

became a prominent member of the state's Republican leadership. He also served for several years on the Board of Social Services of the American Lutheran Church and was a member of the board of regents of Concordia College. He was president of his local congregation and taught the Bethel Bible Series.

Around Williston, Bjella gained a reputation as a peacemaker. He was adept at uniting people of divergent views for a common cause, and his diplomatic manner inspired respect in even his staunchest opponents. It was possible to disagree with Bjella, most of them discovered, and still walk away feeling good about him.

A Time for Healing

There had been much disagreement within Lutheran Brotherhood when Bjella joined its board. During the next several years, as a director and chief executive officer, he encouraged an atmosphere of reconciliation and helped to reconnect a society that had become badly splintered. Bjella gained respect because he gave respect to others. He delegated authority freely and used positive reinforcement as his primary disciplinary tool. His unspoken message to employees was based on simple trust: He assumed that they were competent until they proved that they were not. It was a managerial style profoundly different from that to which many home office employees were accustomed, and Bjella was cognizant of the potential for abuses. But he also believed that Lutheran Brotherhood needed to be healed. Some people had become fearful of making even small mistakes. They needed to reach out.

Bjella was especially determined to depoliticize Lutheran Brotherhood, although he believed that the society's political character was not necessarily a hindrance to its growth, nor a drawback to performance. It was simply the nature of a fraternal society. Bjella believed that corporate democracy was an asset. Under his leadership, the directors passed several amendments to the bylaws that further opened the election process and encouraged more candidates to run for the board. But Bjella also recognized that the society had too long been plagued by factionalism. Passions inevitably outlived the political conflicts they had sparked, and longtime grudges cast

Birth of a Fraternal

Perhaps the supreme tribute to fraternalism is that even friendly competitors can cooperate for the common good.

On May 27, 1970, several officers of Lutheran Brotherhood and Aid Association for Lutherans, which had begun to seek members from the same synodical fields, met to discuss problems created by the recent taxation of fraternals in Canada. Three options seemed open to the societies, which had been serving Canadian Lutherans since the early 1930s: they could (1) continue their current operations; (2) form a Canadian mutual; or (3) combine the Canadian membership of both societies to form a new fraternal. By the time the meeting had ended, the officers had decided to study the third option.

For the next few years, the two largest fraternal benefit societies in America worked together to create a new, independent Canadian fraternal. Reuben Jacobson, Lutheran Brotherhood's senior vice president and chief actuary, coordinated the massive planning effort with Henry Scheig, an actuary who later became the president and chairman of AAL.

On January 2, 1973, Lutheran Life Insurance Society of Canada officially was opened for business. The organization assumed all of the

Lutheran Brotherhood and Aid Association for Lutherans, the two largest fraternal benefit societies in America, combined forces in 1973 to create a new Canadian fraternal, Lutheran Life Insurance Society of Canada. Four representatives of Lutheran Brotherhood and AAL served on the new fraternal's first board of directors, pictured here. Seated, from left: Frederick G. Berlet, Walter L. Rugland of AAL, Edith I. MacIntosh, and Donald W. Axford. Back row: Allan P. Schendel, Norman Nilsen, Arthur Bucholtz, Harold A. Dietrich, E. James Dreyer of AAL, Reuben I. Jacobson of Lutheran Brotherhood, Gregor S. Lund, A.O. Konigson of Lutheran Brotherhood, and Walter A. Schultz.

combined Canadian operations of Lutheran Brotherhood and AAL, including members, assets, obligations, field force, and fraternal activities. Four directors from the two sponsoring fraternal societies, including Jacobson and Al Konigson, LB's head of underwriting, sat on the board of Lutheran Life during a transitional period of several years. During that time, Walter Rugland, chairman of AAL, served as president of Lutheran Life.

Lutheran Life had 26,000 members and life insurance in force of more than $167 million when it was created. By the end of its first year, the new society had sold $19 million of business and had become the twelfth largest fraternal in the United States and Canada.

a pall over relationships that had once been close. There was still a tendency among the employees and representatives of Lutheran Brotherhood to talk about "good guys" and "bad guys." A few officers even consulted lists of political friends and foes when it was time to consider promotions.

Bjella refused to let the practice continue. "I don't want to hear that anymore," he told them. "We're all in the same boat now. I don't care who people voted for at the convention. It doesn't make any difference anymore." Bjella practiced what he preached. He played the leading role in eventually making peace with Granrud, and became his partner at an informal card-playing event that came to be known as the Annual Carl Granrud Whist Night. The two chairmen billed themselves as the leading whist players from Minnesota and North Dakota, and occasionally squashed the competition. Bjella also became good friends with Matthias. The two became

close allies, and they had breakfast together every week for many years at the same table at the Minneapolis Club.

For many years, Lutheran Brotherhood had been strongly influenced by the overwhelming personalities of a few dominant leaders. Because management policies had been based almost solely on their interpretation of the society's mission, disagreements inevitably arose in an organization that considered itself a democracy. To prevent dissension and to keep the society moving in the same direction, Bjella resisted the temptation to enforce his personal views. He instead asked Lutheran Brotherhood to train its collective sights on a higher target: the society's founding articles. Why had the society been founded? What was its purpose? How did that purpose fit into today's world? By focusing attention squarely on that mission, Bjella and the board helped to unite the society's membership. Personality clashes and divergent opinions were unavoidable, but, for the time being, they became secondary to the common cause.

Not that Bjella discouraged differing viewpoints. He possessed a subtle facility for ensuring that the conversation flowed freely at board meetings. Every subject was thoroughly ventilated, and any issue that might affect the future of the society received intense scrutiny from every director. That had not been the case at Lutheran Brotherhood for a number of years. During Granrud's last years as chairman, board meetings typically lasted no more than an hour, for Granrud controlled the agenda and rarely encountered or tolerated opposition. Under Bjella, the board often met for several hours. He decided that the society needed a broader base of board involvement, and he made a concerted effort to seek out the opinion of every director.

From those varied opinions, he sought to build consensus. It was one thing to openly discuss issues, another to resolve them to the satisfaction of everyone involved. Bjella had great faith in the combined wisdom of the board. When the directors were sharply divided on an issue, he attempted to stall any vote until they first hashed out their differences.

This negotiated unanimity was important to Bjella, for he believed that closely split votes might encourage factionalism and threaten the working relationship of the board. In his view it was essential to the psychological health of the society that the directors emerge from closed doors committed to any final decision, fully convinced of the soundness of their consensus judgment. In that regard, Bjella led by example. When decisions went against him, as they did on occasion, he acceded to the will of the majority.

Yet Bjella did not hesitate to assert his considerable power when he felt it was necessary to do so. When one meeting with a group of disgruntled general agents began to turn anarchic, Bjella, who was not presiding, nonetheless decided he had had enough. He angrily pounded his fist on the table and single-handedly regained control of the proceedings.

As chairman, he was also quick to sense the need for coming to a conclusion. A board could talk about some subjects for just so long before the arguments began to lapse into redundancy. When he felt that an issue needed to be decided, he insisted that it be decided. The directors grew to trust his judgment on such matters, for they respected the integrity with which Bjella handled the chairmanship. The key to his power was his willingness to share it.

Bjella also shared his time. Though he rarely roamed the halls of the home office, casually talking with employees as Granrud had done, his door was open. Conversations with Bjella were warm and familiar. There was nothing pretentious about the man; he seemed even to strangers to be honest and genuine, and his attentiveness conveyed the impression that he really cared about what they had to say.

Bjella was not, however, loquacious. His conversational style was governed by a rigid sense of economy, and the knowledge that he must make time each day for many people. He did not care for lengthy conversations, and gently but firmly ended discussions that exceeded what he considered necessary to cover the subject (although he often placed impromptu phone calls or wrote brief notes to friends on the spur of the moment to let them know that he had been thinking about them). Bjella was also serious. He rarely told jokes or anecdotal stories, and

never used off-color language, not because he was prudish, but because it tended to interfere with substantive conversation.

Such discipline drove every aspect of his life. An early riser who required only five or six hours of sleep per night, Bjella was one of the first employees to arrive at the home office each morning, and he usually came equipped with a briefcase filled with materials he had studied at home the previous evening. He was a voracious reader. When he was not working, he read books ranging from the works of Alexander Solzhenitsyn to the historical fiction of Antonia Fraser. To keep informed on current affairs, he reviewed four newspapers per day, as well as materials on management subjects. He honed his mind and body by running eight miles every week, a longstanding routine that kept his weight, even into his sixties, within five pounds of what it had been in college.

Despite his material accomplishments, what society employees would remember most about Bjella were his personal qualities: his integrity and humanity, his compassion and concern. They would remember that years before state and federal governments mandated that businesses open more doors to the handicapped, he had already made that commitment at Lutheran Brotherhood. Bjella knew firsthand the problems and prejudices that faced those who were physically and mentally handicapped, for his oldest son, Lance, was developmentally disabled. He knew the satisfaction his son derived from working in downtown Minneapolis, and he understood that being productive was as important for his son as it was for everyone else. Bjella did not appraise persons for their limitations, but for their abilities, and he sought every opportunity to provide them the chance to contribute.

One such opportunity came on a cool, autumn day. Bjella was walking the family dog through a suburban Minneapolis neighborhood, taking in the beautiful fall colors, when he encountered a young woman who greeted him and smiled pleasantly. "What's your dog's name?" she asked suddenly.

"Her name is Lady," said Bjella.

"Our dog's name is Liza. We brought her with us when we went to England."

Bjella was intrigued with this young person's childlike candor, and he talked with her for a few minutes, during which time she volunteered her family's name. Bjella quickly recognized the name of her father, whom he knew casually through downtown business circles. A few weeks later, he asked the father to lunch, and inquired about his daughter. "Your daughter is different, isn't she?" asked Bjella. "And before you answer that, let me tell you about my son."

When he had finished, the father explained that his daughter did indeed have a learning disability, and was currently undergoing job skills training at a local rehabilitation center. "But she has quite a memory, and speaks another language quite well," her father said proudly. "It won't be long before she'll be looking for a job."

"Well, keep me posted," Bjella said. "Here's the name of our personnel director. If your daughter doesn't find anything down the road, give us a call."

It turned out that the young woman did have some difficulty finding employment, and she was ultimately hired by Lutheran Brotherhood. She became one of its most faithful employees.

Through his own example, Arley Bjella encouraged faithfulness. He quietly brought sensible leadership and discerning judgment to the society. He oversaw financial progress and encouraged fraternal change. He mediated old disputes and inspired new directions. He was a faithful steward.

Fraternal Activity

When Bjella was named chief executive officer, he spent the next several months studying the structure of Lutheran Brotherhood. He met with all of the officers and as many members of the field force as possible. With their input, Bjella determined an agenda of three interrelated priorities. First, he concluded that it was essential to repair the society's bond with the Lutheran church. The political acrimony of the past several years had taken a severe toll on that relationship, both among pastors who had been active participants in one or more of the struggles and among church leaders who, although they publicly maintained a neutral stance, viewed the battles as a blemish on the reputation of the church.

Bjella took a major step toward restoration of trust by depoliticizing Lutheran Brotherhood. He sought out church leaders for advice on how the society could better serve the Lutheran church. "We're not just interested in giving away fraternal dollars," he told them. "We want to know what you think we should do to help you more effectively fulfill your mission." The society subsequently discovered that it was in a unique position, as an organization technically outside the church yet firmly committed to its welfare, to fund projects and forums that encouraged dialogue between the various Lutheran synods.

Bjella was also determined that the society be a responsible corporate citizen. Granrud had made a good start toward that goal, and the green building had helped to revitalize the downtown community. Yet the society had become increasingly withdrawn and insulated during the political years. Some Minneapolis business people were aware of Lutheran Brotherhood's sporadic political campaigns, but knew little about the more substantial fraternal work of the society. Bjella believed that it was important for all corporations, fraternals included, to take a leading role in the communities in which they were located. The very nature of the society's fraternal purpose decreed that it be a good neighbor. Under Bjella's leadership, the society took an active role in many community projects.

The most critical item on Bjella's agenda was fraternalism. In his view, Lutheran Brotherhood had not fulfilled its potential as a fraternal society. Yes, the society met all legal requirements, channeled substantial fraternal payments to its branches and Lutheran church bodies (a total of $1.6 million in 1969), and provided millions of dollars in loans to Lutheran churches. But Bjella thought that Lutheran Brotherhood could do much more. "We have many resources," he told the board, "and yet we're just scratching the surface. Either we make the commitment to be the best fraternal benefit society that we can be, or we might as well become a mutual company."

A few officers, weary of political fights and elections and tired of repeatedly having to justify the society's fraternal status, did not view his pronouncement as particularly threatening. They believed Lutheran Brotherhood simply should become a mutual insurance company and eliminate the confusion. But the vast majority of the society's officers and directors, especially Bjella, were emphatically committed to fraternalism. They viewed themselves as the guardians of a venerated tradition of service, and were not about to see that tradition imperiled. Bjella's challenge galvanized the entire society into action and caused its members to examine, more carefully than they ever had, the true meaning and significance of Lutheran Brotherhood's fraternal mission and history.

Branching Out

Herman Ekern and Jake Preus were strong believers in fraternalism and in the legal reserve system, and it made sense that they should choose to combine these methods when they introduced their insurance plan to the Norwegian Lutheran Church convention in 1917. They recognized that they could not convince unprotected Lutherans of the need for insurance without the support of the church, and they knew that many pastors still opposed the basic concept of insurance. To have actually used the word *insurance* in their proposal undoubtedly would have jeopardized the entire venture. The obvious answer was to propose a fraternal benefit society in which the primary benefit was insurance. Thus, Luther Union was born as a *fraternal benefit society.*

Fraternal benefit societies were required by law to operate for the benefit of members through a network of local lodges, or branches, where members met for fellowship and planning of fraternal activities. (Lutheran Brotherhood always had referred to its lodges as branches in deference to the anti-lodge sentiment of some church leaders.) When it was founded, Luther Union assembled a list of several local branches, enough to meet state licensing requirements, but spent most of its early years simply trying to survive.

The need for a strong network of branches became apparent as the society drifted away from the Norwegian Lutheran Church. Luther Union had little money, and, therefore, was able to support few fraternal activities apart from insurance. The tiny society had high hopes that its affiliation with the Lutheran Brotherhood of America (LBA) would yield not only insurance prospects, but an established organization of local branches through which to extend the benevolent function of the society. Thore Eggen, the president of the society, urged LBA branch leaders to sign up their members for insurance in exchange for a share of the commissions, but his plan generated little interest. By the time the LBA folded, the society had gained a new name but few additional branches.

The first substantial push to organize branches began in the 1930s, when Lutheran Brotherhood established an extension department and appointed C. O. Teisberg as its supervisor. During the next several years, Teisberg wrote letters to congregations across the country detailing the society's new fraternal proposal. "We are in small measure trying to be of greater service to the church," he informed pastors, "and have recently adopted a plan whereby we can be of some material benefit to a local organization within a Lutheran congregation."

The system provided that any congregational organization, such as men's and women's groups, choirs or Sunday Schools, even church councils, could become local branches of Lutheran Brotherhood by adopting the appropriate amendments to their bylaws. Each branch was required to send an annual list of its members to the society, which would pay the local branch one dollar per year for each adult member who held Lutheran Brotherhood insurance. Teisberg's proposal generated immediate interest. Nearly five hundred dollars in fraternal payments were made in 1933.

Over the next three decades, the number of Lutheran Brotherhood branches grew to more than three thousand, and payments to branches increased to almost two hundred thousand dollars per year. The funds were used by local branch members for church construction projects, church supplies, new

Bibles, and contributions to home and foreign mission programs and welfare institutions. Lutheran Brotherhood also contributed several million dollars during that period to church programs that it determined to be intersynodical and national in scope. For example, the society sponsored several scholarship programs for Lutheran college students, seminary students, graduate nurses, social workers, and teachers. The society provided several million teaching aids for pastors, teachers, and students, funded church conferences and seminars on such subjects as family life, international relations, theological trends, and Martin Luther, and subsidized several books written by Lutheran scholars.

Most of these and other fraternal programs were initiated during Granrud's tenure by several directors and employees, including Dr. Richard Gerberding and Dr. A.R. Kretzmann. However, the society had no established department to coordinate its fraternal outreach.

In 1960, Granrud asked Bill Fisher to return to Lutheran Brotherhood as its first director of fraternal activities. Executive vice president of the society during Ekern's presidency, Fisher was an experienced hand at fraternal activities. While serving with the Army Air Corps during World War I, he had come into contact with an organization called the Lutheran Brotherhood of America. It would be three years before the LBA affiliated with a fledgling insurance society called Luther Union, yet Fisher had vivid memories of the LBA. He particularly remembered the young army chaplain who literally threw a rowdy soldier down a flight of stairs for swearing and smoking, because he considered that conduct unbecoming to a Lutheran serviceman. Fisher also remembered the pocket New Testaments the LBA had distributed to soldiers, one of which he still possessed. Fisher resolved to continue that practice at Lutheran Brotherhood. During the 1960s, through the chaplain service, he helped to distribute sixty thousand New Testaments to soldiers in Vietnam.

Fisher, then sixty-five, brought the same flair to fraternal promotion that he had once given to the society's advertising campaigns. He was an unabashed supporter of the fraternal system, and he often traveled the country as an ambassador for the society. In 1962, Lutheran Brotherhood sent out two mobile units, one manned by Fisher, to bring the society into more personal contact with its local branches. The units were stocked with art displays, information about the society's activities, and a promotional movie about the society. During eleven months on the road, the units stopped at nearly two hundred locations, mostly churches, and were visited by an estimated twenty thousand people.

Under Fisher, who had been a national scouting leader for many years, the society also stepped up its already widespread support for scouting. Along with Teisberg, Fisher had first developed the society's program of support for the Boy Scouts during the 1930s. More than $1 million was subsequently channeled into Lutheran scouting activities through local branches. Lutheran Brotherhood also funded training courses for volunteer leaders and pastors and sponsored a national scouting prize, the *Pro Deo et Patria* International Award.

When he was not on the road, Fisher and his wife, Elsie, maintained a policy of fraternal goodwill at their home, a farm of nearly five hundred acres on the shore of Prior Lake, near Minneapolis. Known as Farm Alverne, after the home of Elsie's ancestors in Norway, the property became the site of many fraternal and home office activities. Fisher first became aware of the farm when his car stalled near there in the great Armistice Day snowstorm of 1940, during which nearly sixty hunters froze to death. Fisher was rescued by a truck driver, who towed his car to the nearest town. When the storm finally subsided three days later, Fisher mentioned the farm to Ekern, his boss and father-in-law. The society had long been searching for property on which to sponsor local fraternal activities, and Ekern purchased the farm and deeded it to the Fishers.

Thousands of scouts, Sunday School students, and children with learning impairments were introduced to the sights and sounds of nature at Farm Alverne. A miniature zoological garden, the farm was home to horses, goats, lambs, chickens, ducks, rabbits, wild turkeys, a skunk, a fox, and even a brush wolf. The wolf became renowned among the local population for her apparent ability to tell time. Every morning, just before the village church bell rang at seven o'clock, the wolf let out a series of haunting howls. An inquistive engineer finally discovered that when the church sexton tugged on the long rope leading to the belfry, the bell mechanism made a high-pitched noise before the clapper struck the bell. It was to this almost inaudible tolling that the wolf howled each morning.

Farm Alverne was also populated with peacocks, some of which spent summers in the courtyard garden of Lutheran Brotherhood's green building in downtown Minneapolis. In addition, there were several donkeys, one of them imported from Syria. Fisher often used the donkey to tell his young visitors about Jesus' triumphant ride into Jerusalem on Palm Sunday. One day he received a call at the home office from the irate father of one of the children. "Just what did you mean," the man wanted to know, "when you told my boy you have the donkey that Jesus rode?" On all tours thereafter, whenever Fisher spotted the Syrian donkey, he was careful to say, "This is the *kind* of donkey that Jesus rode."

Fraternal Expansion

Despite all the good it had done, the society's fraternal system had provoked periodic complaints among church leaders during the political years. Some observers attributed the real source of their unhappiness to partisan politics. Others believed their complaints were justified. As a result, during the late 1960s, the new management of Lutheran Brotherhood took a hard look at its fraternal status. While the directors found much that was good about the system, they also discovered elements that disturbed them.

The most persistent charges were aimed at Lutheran Brotherhood's ineffective branch system. Since the early 1930s, when the system was introduced, the society's bylaws had provided that any congregational organization could become a local branch

of Luthern Brotherhood by adopting certain amendments to its bylaws. The only requirement for membership was that the congregation in which the organization existed have at least twenty-five members who owned Lutheran Brotherhood insurance. All other branch members who were not current contract holders were considered social members of the society.

The founders of Lutheran Brotherhood had chosen

William G. Fisher, Lutheran Brotherhood's fraternal pioneer, served the society in a variety of posts between 1935 and 1971, including executive vice president, director, and chairman of fraternal activities. Fisher created a number of inventive programs designed to promote fraternalism; one of his creations was this wagon wheel inscribed with the names of the society's founders. This photo was taken at the Fishers' Farm Alverne, which hosted many fraternal events.

To Please and to Inspire

The Lutheran Brotherhood Collection of Religious Art

Religious art is meant to please and to inspire those who worship God, and it always has been honored at Lutheran Brotherhood. The society sponsored exhibitions of works by Lutheran artists for many years, and, in the 1970s and 1980s, began to place special emphasis on collecting religious art. The current collection of more than two hundred fifty works is composed primarily of prints and drawings and includes works by Rembrandt, Durer, Cranach, Tiepolo, and Ingres.

The print shown opposite, titled, "Knight,

Death, and the Devil," is representative of the quality of the collection. The engraving was done in 1513 by Albrecht Durer and is considered by experts to be one of the German artist's greatest works. The plate presents a Christian knight who, having shielded himself with the armor of God, rides forth despite the threat of death and the devil. A contemporary of Martin Luther, Durer, who was a Roman Catholic, revered the man who started the Reformation.

In addition to its collection of prints and drawings Lutheran Brotherhood owns several religious paintings by prominent artists. Among them is *The Crucifixion*, by twentieth century artist George Bellows. Other artworks are displayed throughout the home office. A series of fifteen walnut panels, hand-carved by Arnold Flaten, former professor of art at St. Olaf College in Northfield, Minnesota, covers the north wall of the dining room on the executive floor. The Reformation Window, a portrayal in stained glass of Luther and his times, which had been located in the Martin Luther Library in the green building, was moved to the new home office along with a Luther medals collection. It is on display in the lobby area. A number of rare Bibles dating back to the sixteenth century, written in several languages, including Icelandic, Swedish, and Norwegian, are periodically on display inside the entrance to the library. Among the most popular of Lutheran Brotherhood's collections are complete sets of Danish Christmas plates crafted by two companies, Bing & Grondal and Royal Copenhagen. It is believed to be the only complete collection of both series of plates in the world.

One of the most famous prints in Lutheran Brotherhood's collection of religious art is titled, "Knight, Death, and the Devil." Pictured at right, it was engraved by German artist Albrecht Durer in 1513. At left are two plates from the society's double collection of rare Danish Christmas plates. It is believed to be the only complete collection of both series of plates in the world.

the congregational branch system because they thought it would afford the tiny society an established channel through which to serve the church. Why spend precious time establishing another fraternal method that might take years to become effective, they reasoned, when a legitimate conduit that would serve the same purpose already existed? The system quickly caught on in churches in which Lutheran Brotherhood contract holders dominated the membership of the auxiliary organization that doubled as the local branch. But in many congregations, only a minority of the auxiliary members actually owned society contracts. Those branches inevitably had little identity with the society.

The problem was that too few people actually knew that they were branch members. If the church choir served as the local branch, for example, it was entirely possible, under the society's fraternal design, that none of the choir members owned Lutheran Brotherhood insurance. That scenario was acceptable in theory. The idealistic Ekern, who had dreamed of uniting the disparate factions of the church, considered every Lutheran in the country a social member of Lutheran Brotherhood. But the concept of social members was considerably less effective in practice than in theory.

It soon became clear to the new directors, especially Herbert Hansen, a new member of the fraternal activities committee, that the congregational branch system was an ineffective method by which to build the kind of grass roots support that fraternals were supposed to encourage. Hansen also believed that Lutheran Brotherhood must increase its basic level of fraternal funding dramatically. The board wholeheartedly agreed, and it charged Charles De Vries, the new director of fraternal activities, with reforming and strengthening the society's fraternal system.

A native of northeastern Iowa, De Vries had first come into contact with Lutheran Brotherhood in 1957. At that time, his pastor used *The BOND* as a reference in a discussion just before De Vries joined the National Lutheran Council in Washington, D.C. Like many employees of the National Lutheran Council staff, De Vries was enrolled in a Lutheran Brotherhood pension program by Eskild Hauglund, a general

agent based in New York City. Short and aristocratic, with a pencil-thin mustache and a dapper wardrobe, Haugland spoke with the thick accent of his native Denmark, smiling constantly throughout his rapid-fire sales delivery. Whatever De Vries said in response, the talkative agent took it to mean that the young man wanted exactly what he was selling. By the time the interview was over, De Vries was still unsure what Haugland had said, but it had sounded good, and the experience had somehow been so captivating that he had decided to join. He had become a Lutheran Brotherhood member.

A few years later, Bill Fisher paraded into De Vries's office. "I am with Lutheran Brotherhood," Fisher flamboyantly explained, "and we want to put on a dinner for the five hundred most influential Lutherans in the city of Washington. I asked Mr. Granrud and Mrs. Pracht who would know who those Lutherans are, and they said that you would know." De Vries said he considered that a vast overstatement, but added that he would do what he could to help. The subsequent dinner, featuring as its speaker the recently appointed secretary of agriculture, Orville Freeman, a Lutheran Brotherhood member, was a resounding success. Several years later, when Pracht began to search for an assistant director of public relations, she thought of De Vries. He went to work for Lutheran Brotherhood in 1966, and was named director of fraternal activities three years later.

When he began his investigation of the society's fraternal structure, De Vries discovered that although many branches were active and much fraternal work was being accomplished, there was a widespread lack of knowledge about the benefits of fraternal membership. During the previous decade, some society leaders had slipped into the habit of referring to members as policyholders, unintentionally creating the impression among some members that their insurance contracts were their only fraternal benefits. But there were several other benefits to membership, including voting privileges, *BOND* magazine, an orphan benefit for children of deceased members, and branch membership, through which volunteer members worked together to help their churches and communities through projects funded by Lutheran Brotherhood. De Vries was determined to build greater awareness of fraternal membership, and began the practice of providing member tours to overseas locations, the first including a visit to the Passion Play in Oberammergau, West Germany, in 1970.

De Vries had just started to study other possible fraternal changes when the Internal Revenue Service knocked on Lutheran Brotherhood's door. In 1970, the local IRS examiners' audit of the society concluded that its enigmatic congregational branch system did not meet the standard set forth in the federal fraternal statute. They recommended that Lutheran Brotherhood's tax-exempt status be rescinded. The announcement sent shock waves through the society. Bjella was particularly disquieted. Little more than a month had passed since he had been elected chairman and chief executive officer. Like the other new directors, he had based much of his directorial campaign on fraternal reform, and now the rug was being pulled out from under him before he had the chance to begin.

Although the national IRS office ruled one year later that Lutheran Brotherhood's congregational branches were adequate, and maintained its tax exemption, the experience added fuel to the society's reform fervor. Lutheran Brotherhood had nearly lost the fraternal status on which the society had been founded. It was time to change and improve the branch system, to ensure that Lutheran Brotherhood become the most effective fraternal benefit society possible, Bjella insisted, not only in the legal sense, but in the literal sense.

The key was to increase voluntarism at the grass roots level. Nearly a decade before, Fisher had realized that the society must do even more to encourage activity among the local branches. "Fraternal programs must be self-administered," he said. "The fact that the Rockefeller Foundation does so much for humanity doesn't make Standard Oil a fraternal because of the money it gives to the public. The Ford Company is not a fraternal because of the Ford Foundation. A fraternal society is fraternal precisely because its members are involved in performing good works, not because the board chooses to bequeath a few grants here and there. A fraternal must validate its claim to that status by virtue of traceable activity at the local branch level."

De Vries agreed. If Lutheran Brotherhood expected its members to actively perform good works, he reasoned, then the society must do a better job of enabling and encouraging its members to perform those works at the branch level. Following a series of meetings with representatives of each of the major Lutheran synods, the fraternal department decided that the most effective method for promoting local branch activity was matching funds.

Matching funds played an essential role in transferring responsibility for fraternal activities from the home office to the branches. In past years, the distribution of most fraternal dollars had been decided by the directors. They had always tried to disburse the funds equitably among various church bodies, but the practice was subject to the perception that the board occasionally granted special favors to friends. However, matching funds gave members the controlling vote in deciding the real direction of the society's fraternal mission. It allowed them to decide, with their own pocketbooks, how the society would spend its fraternal dollars.

Matching funds ultimately became the guiding principle of Lutheran Brotherhood's fraternal program. Through the Branch Challenge Fund, for example, the society provided matching dollars to local branches that carried out fundraising projects of their own choosing, from organizing choir concerts to painting houses. Lutheran Brotherhood matched the money raised by branches up to a specified amount. The society eventually applied matching funds to several types of local branch programs, from community service projects to disaster relief, and continued its strong support of education by matching financial contributions from members to Lutheran schools, colleges, and seminaries.

The society further strengthened local volunteer involvement by developing fire, bicycle, water, and pedestrian safety materials for local branches, which then sponsored these programs in their local schools and communities. Lutheran Brotherhood also provided special training for branch leaders through Life Skills seminars, at which thousands of branch officers learned new leadership techniques and kept up on available fraternal funds and resources.

Bolstered by these developments (and by branch

Aiding the Church

Bjella took seriously and personally that portion of the bylaws that pledged Lutheran Brotherhood to serve the church. The relationship had become somewhat strained during the political years, and Bjella, having already worked hard to depoliticize the society itself, was determined that Lutheran Brotherhood restore that bond.

It was not easy. Some pastors long had been irritated by the manner in which Lutheran Brotherhood dispensed gifts to the church. For years, whenever the society awarded a scholarship or grant, a director or officer had traveled to the presentation. Sometimes the presentation cost more than the award itself. The practice struck the clergy as ostentatious and smacked of charity for the sake of publicity. A few organizations were sufficiently bothered by the practice that for years they declined to apply for grants from Lutheran Brotherhood.

Bjella believed that giving should be its own reward. Determined that the society should strive for less visibility in its gifts to the church, he halted the practice. This move played well with the majority of the directors and with church leaders who had welcomed the financial support of Lutheran Brotherhood, but had felt that the society dictated too heavily the terms of that support. Bjella did not prescribe; he asked. He sought the ideas of church leaders on how the society could better serve the Lutheran church. "Lutheran Brotherhood was not only interested in giving away fraternal dollars," he explained. "It wanted to know what it could do to help them." The churches greatly appreciated his accommodating attitude.

They were also pleased when Lutheran Brotherhood had completed disbanding its congregational branch system and organized its members solely in geographical branches. Many pastors had felt uneasy about the congregational system, because it obscured the lines between Lutheran Brotherhood and individual congregations and tended to create the mistaken impression that the groups were interrelated. Geographical branches dramatically strengthened

funding from Lutheran Brotherhood, which increased to almost $1.4 million annually by 1979), activity exploded at the local branch level during the next several years. In Fort Worth, Texas, branch members helped cater a major convention and donated the profits to a home for the elderly. In Northridge, California, branch members fasted for a day, collected donations from sponsors for the meals they missed, then donated the money to hunger relief programs. In Columbia, South Carolina, branch members sponsored a series of basketball, volleyball, dancing, and billiards marathons to raise funds for a young boy fighting against leukemia. In Shrewsbury, Massachusetts, branch members promoted what unexpectedly grew into a statewide campaign to promote bicycle safety.

Across the country, thousands of Lutheran Brotherhood branches raised millions of dollars for community and church projects. It was a volunteer effort with which members could identify.

member identification; moreover, by voluntarily backing away from congregational auxiliaries, the society also improved the level of trust with the Lutheran church.

The process of changing the branch system had been long and laborious. When the fraternal department was asked to compile a list of which members belonged to what branches, the staff discovered that its computerized branch numbers had been erased from the master computer file. The programmers had wanted to add a new digit to the numbers that identified general agencies, but no space remained on the computer tape, so they had searched for nonessential information that could be eliminated to make room for the new digit. Local branch records had not been considered a major priority, so the numbers identifying them were erased. The result was that the fraternal department had to compile the membership list by hand. Throughout the spring and summer of 1971, most members of the fraternal staff was on their hands and knees, surrounded by huge piles of membership cards, sorting and stacking.

At the same time that the society began to substantially increase its level of fraternal payments to branches and members, it increased grants to the church. Between 1971 and 1980, the society's annual allocation to fraternal activities rose from almost $2 million to nearly $14 million. As word of the society's rising commitment spread, life on the fraternal activities committee became busier. Although Lutheran Brotherhood's financial resources were not infinite, it sometimes appeared that way, and the society annually received hundreds of requests for help from Lutheran organizations. Deciding which requests were most worthy of assistance was particularly difficult; De Vries estimated that for every twenty requests received by Lutheran Brotherhood, one could be granted.

Because its fraternal resources were far outweighed by legitimate demand, Lutheran Brotherhood established new criteria for funding church organizations, guidelines that would help the society respond as effectively as possible to the needs of the Lutheran church. For example, Lutheran Brotherhood decided that it could play an important stopgap role in helping churches through periodic fiscal emergencies.

In 1973, the Nixon administration devalued the dollar by 10 percent, the second time it had done so in fourteen months. The devaluation was considered necessary to counteract the country's burgeoning foreign trade deficit and make American businesses more competitive throughout the world. Although the move helped create jobs in businesses that produced goods for export, it raised the prices that Americans paid for foreign goods. The devaluation also created an overnight deficit of hundreds of thousands of dollars in the budgets of Lutheran overseas missionary organizations.

Lutheran Brotherhood responded quickly to the sudden foreign exchange losses by approving three grants of $125,000 each to mission divisions of the American Lutheran Church, the Lutheran Church in America, and the Lutheran Church-Missouri Synod. The emergency grants helped the churches to continue the same level of support for important missionary work abroad.

The society also helped national church bodies to establish and sustain mission congregations in America. Since the days of Harold Ingvaldson, the society had provided millions of dollars in loans to Lutheran churches. Because Lutheran Brotherhood had pledged to aid the church, some fraternal advocates felt that the society's investment department should subsidize the loans. Yet it was also the department's legal responsibility to earn as much income as possible from each dollar invested; to do less would be unfair to the society's members, to whom the money belonged. The fraternal division ultimately decided that it was a legitimate use of the fraternal budget to subsidize church loans. The Church Extension program annually made $2 million in interest subsidies for mortgage loans at current market rates to new congregations. The net effect of the program was that mission churches received a loan below prevailing interest rates.

Lutheran Brotherhood decided that it could also apply its fraternal resources to selected pilot projects that might ultimately play an important role in the development of the Lutheran church. During the 1970s, for example, there was great concern about the future of the church. Student unrest, the Vietnam War, changing moral and sexual values, and the rapid decline of established social structures led many to wonder whether the church would eventually fade from viable existence. These issues intrigued Lutheran Brotherhood, and in 1978 De Vries began planning an event that would bring together ten leading international futurists for lectures and discussions with hundreds of Lutheran clergy and lay leaders.

During the planning process for this event, the society discovered that it was in a unique position to encourage dialogue among the various Lutheran synods, and that was, in itself, significant. Several of the synods had long been at theological odds and did not worship together. Their doctrinal differences were pronounced enough that Lutheran Brotherhood's branches did not have an official prayer, to avoid offending any of the different factions from which they drew their membership. Yet because the society voluntarily had backed away from its congregational branch structure while increasing its level of fraternal funding for the church, it had earned the growing trust of the various Lutheran bodies. The churches appreciated that Lutheran Brotherhood had taken measures not to portray itself as part of the organized church, yet was still committed to the welfare of the church. Thus, when confronted with critical issues that transcended doctrinal differences, such as the role of the church in future society, the churches were willing to gather together at meetings sponsored by Lutheran Brotherhood.

In 1979, 250 Lutheran leaders from ten different synodical bodies gathered in Houston, Texas, at Lutheran Brotherhood's Colloquium on the Church in Future Society. For five days, these leaders rubbed elbows with renowned futurists like Alvin Toffler and Harlan Cleveland, explored the nature of change, and discussed how the collective Lutheran church could best prepare for and influence the future. It was an optimistic and significant week, and it raised hopes for the decades and centuries ahead. Reconciled to God through Jesus Christ, the participants were free to address themselves to the problems of the world together.

Coming Together

The decade of the 1970s was a watershed in the history of Lutheran Brotherhood, a decade in which the society completely overhauled its branch system, dramatically increased its level of funding for fraternal activities, greatly improved the strength of its volunteer network, and made a concerted effort to effectively serve the church. It was an exhilarating time for fraternal activists at Lutheran Brotherhood. However, the massive buildup came at a time when other Lutheran Brotherhood departments were tightening their belts, so jealousies inevitably developed. The chasm between the society's fraternal and marketing departments became especially wide. Their split had deep historical roots, for there had long been a very fine line between good works and good business.

Most general agents and district representatives believed strongly in the society's fraternal mission, yet viewed themselves as somewhat apart from actual fraternal activities. They rebelled when the suddenly muscular fraternal department attempted to involve them in new programs. To their way of thinking, time spent on fraternal projects was time not spent selling. The field considered that its job was to make money for the society, and that the fraternal department's task was to pass it out to members. The fraternal and marketing departments rarely communicated or cooperated, except when the fraternal department developed projects that were judged to be beneficial to potential sales. Some employees even began to think of Lutheran Brotherhood as two separate companies: marketing and fraternal.

That perception distressed the members of the board, particularly Dr. Lloyd Svendsbye. A director since 1970, Svendsbye had analyzed Lutheran Brotherhood's articles of incorporation and affirmed that everything that the society did was linked to fraternalism. The insurance contract was an important fraternal benefit, as were branch membership and voting rights. Even BOND magazine was a fraternal benefit. Svendsbye observed that the society's founders had pledged both to aid the church and to protect the society's members. In his opinion, the entire society was bound conceptually and historically to cooperate.

Through a project called Operation Integration, the

In 1979, Lutheran Brotherhood sponsored an event that brought together ten different Lutheran church bodies, some of which were at theological odds, for discussions about the nature of societal change and their evolving roles in the future. At the Colloquium on the Church in Future Society, held in Houston, hundreds of Lutheran leaders rubbed elbows with such renowned futurists as Alvin Toffler and discussed how the collective Lutheran church might best prepare for and influence the future. One of the outcomes of the Colloquium was a book, "Here Comes the Future," jointly produced by the ALC's Augsburg Publishing House and the LCA's Fortress Press.

Among the members of the Ad Hoc Planning Committee for the event were:

1. Steven Quist, Evangelical Lutheran Synod.
2. Francis W. Monseth, Association of Free Lutheran Congregations.
3. George S. Schultz, American Lutheran Church.
4. Everald H. Strom, Church of the Lutheran Brethren.
5. W. Kent Gilbert, Lutheran Church in America.
6. Wilhelm W. Petersen, Evangelical Lutheran Synod.
7. Albert L. Haversat, Lutheran Church in America.
8. Thomas E. Herbranson, Lutheran Brotherhood.
9. Robert J. Marshall, Lutheran Church in America.
10. Charles De Vries, Lutheran Brotherhood.

11. Elwyn E. Ewald, Association of Evangelical Lutheran Churches.
12. Robert Overgaard, Church of the Lutheran Brethren.
13. John Schuelke, Lutheran Church-Missouri Synod.
14. Janis Robins, Latvian Evangelical Lutheran Church in America.
15. Robert S. Hoyt, American Lutheran Church.
16. David W. Preus, American Lutheran Church.
17. John P. Strand, Association of Free Lutheran Congregations.
18. Karl Raudsepp, Estonian Evangelical Lutheran Church.
19. Nancy J. Haggmark, Lutheran Brotherhood.
20. Norman D. Sell, Lutheran Church-Missouri Synod.
21. Guido Merkens, Lutheran Church-Missouri Synod.
22. Roland L. Schwandt, Lutheran Brotherhood.
23. Donald O. Imsland, consultant to the colloquium, Human Design, Inc.

society attempted to convey to every field and home office employee the concept that every single function of the society was fraternal and, therefore, interconnected. Svendsbye campaigned aggressively for a name change for the fraternal division, because he thought that its name simply perpetuated the impression of disunion. Svendsbye lost that battle but won the war, for the marketing and fraternal divisions eventually developed a cooperative relationship. The field began to see that benevolent activities laid a strong foundation of goodwill toward the society and, therefore, were beneficial to its marketing efforts. Surveys showed that more than one-third of those who purchased insurance from Lutheran Brotherhood did so because it was a fraternal benefit society, and those who were most heavily involved in church activities were more likely to become members of the society.

One important turning point in the increasingly integrated relationship between the marketing and fraternal departments came when Lutheran Brotherhood introduced the concept of fraternal communicators. Although the geographic branch system was obviously the most effective method for developing strong member identification and grass roots branch activities, the fraternal department worried that the new structure might not allow Lutheran Brotherhood to maintain intimate contact with congregational life. The stated mission of the society was to assist the Lutheran church. Besides, many small congregations had come to depend on the fraternal funds they had once received through their auxiliary branches.

At the same time, the fraternal department was trying to improve communications with legislators who took adversarial positions against fraternal benefit societies. Roland Schwandt, a member of the fraternal staff, observed that Wisconsin school districts were represented by educational advocates who lobbied the state legislature on their behalf. The staff was intrigued by his idea: Why not establish a network of Lutheran Brotherhood branch members to serve as fraternal advocates?

These volunteers became known as fraternal communicators, and they served as essential links between Lutheran Brotherhood branches and their communities and congregations. Fraternal communicators were enrolled in the program by district representatives in their area, who then worked closely with the volunteers to keep them informed about fraternal programs that might help their congregations. It was the communicators' job to pass that information on to their congregations and community. Each congregation in which a fraternal communicator was based also received an annual contribution from the society.

Fraternal communicators brought Lutheran Brotherhood into more intimate contact with congregational life than it had ever been. The program built cooperative ties between the district representatives and geographical branches, and built a powerful and widespread network of voluntarism throughout local churches. About twenty-three thousand fraternal communicators eventually were enrolled in more than two-thirds of the almost eighteen thousand Lutheran congregations in the United States, and the concept became an influential model for many other fraternal benefit societies throughout the country.

Good works and good business, it had turned out, were indeed compatible.

The Importance of Listening

The leadership of Lutheran Brotherhood during the early 1970s had been sensible and sagacious, open and participatory, caring and humane. Bjella, the board of directors, and the managing officers had established a more relaxed and democratic working culture within the society and had strengthened the once tenuous relationship with the Lutheran church.

They had improved the society's fundamental fraternal structure and had begun to build a powerful network of involved branches and fraternal communicators. They had introduced mutual funds, innovative financial products that would dramatically increase the fraternal assets under society management. It had been a peaceful yet productive era.

By the late 1970s, however, many observers had become convinced that things were too calm. After the anxiety and turbulence of the Granrud years, it initially had been necessary to encourage an atmosphere of peace and tranquility. The governmental challenge to Lutheran Brotherhood's tax-exempt status also had convinced the society that it must, first and foremost, sustain its mission. "We are going to maintain Lutheran Brotherhood as a fraternal benefit society," Bjella regularly told home office employees. Preservation, protection, and maintenance became three primary tenets of management philosophy. Faced with perceived threats to its existence, preservation was an appropriate, even aggressive, response. New business growth was steady, if not spectacular, and Lutheran Brotherhood continued to ably serve its members.

However, there were signs that the society had become lulled by caution, and might be missing critical opportunities for growth. The insurance marketplace was rapidly changing; inflation was rising and competition was increasing. Commercial insurance companies were beginning to do a booming replacement business, enticing Lutheran Brotherhood members to give up their existing coverage for new contracts that appeared, at least in the short term, to be financially superior. The society's field force found it increasingly difficult to compete, and were frustrated by what they believed to be an inadequate amount of concern at the home office. The field complained most persistently about the lack of new insurance products. They were told that the computer system could not handle the new products, but it seemed to them that the home office had simply become content to maintain the status quo. Although sales were holding steady for the moment, they worried that the absence of new products would weaken the society in the future. Eventually, worry gave way to impatience, and the field demanded changes from the home office.

Bjella also had become impatient, for he recognized that the society had settled into an excessively methodical, complacent mode. He began to push for several changes, particularly in the way that the society marketed its products, and in 1975 he asked Jerry Reinan, the society's general agent in Fergus

Falls, Minnesota, to return to the home office as director of marketing. A North Dakota native, Reinan had been one of the society's stars, successful in every endeavor to which he had been assigned, from district representative to director of education at the home office. For the past eleven years, his Fergus Falls agency had been one of the society's top producers. He was intelligent, innovative, creative, perceptive, and resourceful. Respected by the field and the home office staffs, he seemed the logical candidate to turn around Lutheran Brotherhood's marketing fortunes.

Reinan had become something of a maverick in recent years, so his return to the home office was a subject of great interest there. Unlike most male employees, who conformed to the unstated yet accepted wardrobe of conservative suits and ties, Reinan favored turtlenecks and plaid bell-bottoms. His straight, black hair hung below his ears, and he sported a mustache. He wore cowboy boots because he liked warm ankles during the winter, and he drove a pickup truck to work. Employees often observed that he resembled a farmer heading for the "north forty" instead of the senior vice president of marketing. Reinan eschewed the standard office accoutrements of his fellow managers. His quarters were instantly recognizable from the windows of neighboring structures; most other offices had gold carpeting, but Reinan's was red. He also equipped his office with an antique swivel rocker, a vintage rolltop desk, and an old Victrola. A sign on his window aptly read, "Office Interior by Goodwill Industries."

Reinan had been hesitant to take the marketing job. He enjoyed his general agency and was reluctant to give up the freedom of the field. Having served in the home office, he had also observed the adversarial relationship that historically had existed between the marketing department and the field, and wondered whether the field's still potent political power might make it difficult to implement unpopular but necessary changes. However, he quickly improved the society's training and education programs, developing more explicit guidelines of expectations for the field. He also organized a program for training future general agents. In Reinan's view, the success of Lutheran Brotherhood depended on its field force, and the field force depended on the support of the general agents. The society always had had some difficulty maintaining an adequate reservoir of competent field managers, and Reinan's program was the first to attempt to build an available reserve.

Despite Reinan's accomplishments, his tenure was marked by stormy relations between the field force and marketing department. Some of the contentiousness in the field stemmed from insecurity. Insurance industry experts had begun to argue that the general agency system was expensive, and many commercial companies and mutuals were moving to alternative sales distribution systems. That worried Lutheran Brotherhood's general agents, who feared that the

home office might decide to phase them out. The society had no such plan in mind, but many general agents had their private doubts, and the home office's attempt to lower what many thought were excessive field expenses compounded their fears and further strained relations.

But their greatest source of discontent was the lack of new insurance products. All this new training was beneficial, the field told the home office, but all the

Jerry Reinan, a successful general agent who became Lutheran Brotherhood's director of marketing in 1975, brought a unique, relaxed style to the home office. He wore cowboy boots, drove a pickup truck to work, and equipped his office with an antique, swivel rocker and a vintage, roll-top desk.

One Enduring Symbol

An organization projects its image through many symbols, one of the most visible and important of which is its corporate trademark.

A trademark becomes significant and successful by its repeated use. During the mid-1970s, Lutheran Brotherhood lacked any consistently used symbol. Instead, the society used a variety of identifiers, including home office building designs, an adaptation of the Martin Luther seal, a road sign shield, a laurel leaf, and several stylized renderings of the Lutheran Brotherhood name.

In 1976, a committee appointed to study the problem selected InterDesign, a Minneapolis-based firm, to create a new, unifying symbol and logotype for Lutheran Brotherhood. Some one hundred possibilities eventually were narrowed to three strong contenders, and the final selection was made after a survey of almost two thousand members, field representatives, and Lutheran clergy.

Once adopted, the new corporate identifier was phased in over a period of a year, its correct usage guided by a style manual and stringent internal controls.

The symbol, known as a "word mark" because it incorporates two prominent letters in the society name, is shaped like a heart to reflect Lutheran Brotherhood's strength and stability and its concern for its members.

Lutheran Brotherhood's new corporate trademark, pictured below, was created to provide the society with a single graphic identity. Shaped like a heart, the trademark replaced a variety of symbols and logotypes, pictured above, that had been used over the years.

training in the world would not be sufficient if Lutheran Brotherhood's salespeople lacked the fundamental ammunition to compete favorably in the marketplace. Increasingly forced to defend the society's static portfolio against updated commercial products, the field force found itself backed against a competitive wall. The inability of the home office to deliver the new products the field force so desperately wanted simply exacerbated their frustrations.

Faced with the prospect of losing both new and old business, field personnel became particularly angry when Reinan suggested that some general agents had settled into a pattern of complacency. It was not a popular analysis, but most observers thought it was plausible. Several general agents, many of them society sales leaders at one time, were nearing retirement, their agency's sales performances had leveled off, and they were not hiring new district representatives to replace those who left or retired. Most directors concurred with the assessment that a malaise had settled on the field. But in their view, it was Reinan's responsibility to reverse the situation. The board was tired of hearing about problems. They wanted to hear solutions.

As the relationship between the marketing department and the field became increasingly tempestuous, Reinan became frustrated, then discouraged. He could see the problems clearly, but was unable to fix them. He had done his best to inspire the field. He had done his best to develop new products. But for a variety of reasons, many of them beyond his control, the field had become dissatisfied with the marketing department. Some observers believed that Reinan had been stifled by the increasingly strident complaints from the field, and they perceived that some members of management, bowing to these political considerations, had not given the marketing director the support that he needed. Others believed that Reinan's loose, individualistic management style, which had once seemed colorful and endearing, had contributed to the discord. Whatever the case, Reinan decided in 1979 that he had finally had enough. He resigned as director of marketing that fall and was assigned the general agency in Denver.

The marketing department controversy brought into sharper focus what many believed to be Lutheran Brotherhood's Achilles heel: the society's inability to adapt quickly to change. Constancy, competence, and trustworthiness had symbolized the society for several decades, and those qualities alone had always been sufficient to guarantee success. But now flexibility and readiness were being added to the list of requirements for survival in the modern marketplace. The belief among field personnel that the marketing department was incapable of developing new and necessary products shook Lutheran Brotherhood loose from any false sense of security it may have possessed, and galvanized the society's leadership. The need for change had become imperative.

With change on its mind, management first turned its attention to the society's computer system. The system and the division that tended it, Management Information Services (MIS), had contributed much to Lutheran Brotherhood's marketing woes. When the research and development department had developed plans for updated products, more often than not, it had been informed by MIS that the computer system simply could not accommodate the changes required. The standard line was, "Sorry. We'd like to help, but we can't change the computer." Those product alterations that were successful took far longer than was judged to be reasonable; it took two years to fit a simple term insurance product into the system. By 1978, the situation had become untenable, and both the field and the home office were completely frustrated. The phrase "MIS can't do it" became the primary verbal symbol of their discontent, a sarcastic reminder that the society could not, or would not, change its monolithic ways.

The inadequacies of the computer sytem were ironic, for Lutheran Brotherhood had prospered precisely because of its electronic capabilities. Computers had become an indispensable tool of the insurance industry during the past two decades. An insurance organization depended on its ability to process millions of numbers every day. There were policies to underwrite, investments to monitor, actuarial statistics to be compiled, and claims to be paid. Without a reliable computer system, no modern insurance organization was capable of adequately serving its contract holders.

But computers, like all forms of machinery, become

obsolete. That was happening to the Consolidated Functions Ordinary (CFO) system, the computer system by which the society had operated since 1964. CFO had performed admirably for many years, sustained by several patchwork auxiliary systems, but the marketplace was changing. Customers demanded products that would enable them to stay ahead of inflation, and insurance companies needed computer systems that would adapt quickly to those needs. Like a classic automobile, CFO had been a consistent performer in its day. Unfortunately, the frenetic insurance industry had come to resemble the Indianapolis 500, and the system was no longer capable of keeping up.

The board recognized that it must replace CFO,

An implementation team, composed of about thirty employees, functioned as a miniature version of the home office for more than two years to smoothly phase in Lutheran Brotherhood's new computer system, LifeComm III. Leading the team was Robert Gandrud, front row, center, later to become president.

but quickly learned that shopping for a new computer system was not an easy task. Few systems on the market were solely capable of meeting the many demands of a large insurance organization. There also were many product features to consider, including software, hardware, and price. The most important consideration of all was the future. A computer system that would perform well immediately or for the next few years was not necessarily a good buy. The computer had to perform effectively for many years. And it had to be able to adapt quickly to new insurance products, for the industry had to meet the demands of rapid change in the market.

The first new computer system selected by Lutheran Brotherhood fell short of meeting those criteria. The system was more flexible than its predecessor in some procedures, but it was just as rigid, if not more so, in most others. The board of directors, which had approved the purchase, felt betrayed. It had been promised flexibility, but the new system had delivered merely another form of rigidity. At its wit's end with MIS, the board decided to reorganize the division.

One of the first changes occurred in 1978, when a new MIS manager was appointed. Bob Gandrud, thirty-four, the most recent head of research and development, had been one of the division's most vocal critics. Time after time, his efforts to develop new insurance products had been stymied by the deficiences of the computer system. Now he was getting a chance to solve the problem, but it would require months of diligent work.

Gandrud thrived on hard work. A large, energetic man who moved from appointment to appointment with long, purposeful strides, he had learned the value of labor on the family farm near Glenwood, Minnesota. He earned a college degree in mathematics and joined Lutheran Brotherhood as an actuary in 1965. Gandrud's self-discipline was complemented by his ability to think clearly under pressure. During his first interview at the home office, he found himself sitting across from the imposing figure of Carl Granrud, who on this day was feeling irritable. "What are you here for?" Granrud inquired gruffly. "I'm here to apply for a job as an actuary," the young man replied. Granrud scowled. "Damned actuaries make too much money," he replied. "That's why I want to apply," Gandrud said with just a hint of a mischievous smile. He landed the job.

The fact that Gandrud played the trombone also endeared him to Granrud; at the time, the Lutheran Brotherhood band was in desperate need of a trombonist. But that was not the sole reason Gandrud was hired. For all his complaints about actuaries, Granrud had great respect for the work they did. They provided some measure of constancy in a turbulent business. The nature of their work demanded that they be industrious and trustworthy, extremely cautious, and unswervingly devoted to solvency. "When I hired Reuben Jacobson to head the actuarial department, I began sleeping well at night," Granrud once observed. "When I hired Luther Forde to assist him, I was able to take a nap during the afternoon, too." It seemed to the chairman that Gandrud was the same type of man.

The life of a young Lutheran Brotherhood actuary included an exacting study regimen. Every actuarial employee was encouraged to work toward membership as a fellow in the Society of Actuaries. The F.S.A. designation, essential for career advancement, could be achieved only by passing ten rigorous actuarial examinations. The program was considered at least as difficult as attaining an advanced degree in mathematics, and it took most employees a minimum of ten years to complete it. The conscientious actuarial student was expected to study about five hundred hours per exam, and Gandrud, who struggled through the exams, put in that much time and more. Every evening he went to bed at the same time as his three young daughters so that he could get up at 3 A.M. to study.

As an actuary, Gandrud brought both discipline and a thorough understanding of product development to his new position at MIS. He was familiar with computers and had experience as a programmer. He also knew the strengths and weaknesses of CFO. He joined the society when the system was being installed, and, through the years, had placed many new products and dividend changes into the system. Gandrud was not a technical analyst, but he understood the concepts of the computer system: how it worked, why it worked, and what would make it perform more efficiently.

Soon after he took the reins at MIS, Gandrud discovered that the computer system was not solely responsible for the delays in product development; the culture in which the division operated also was at fault. The staff was talented and loyal and ready for new ideas. But management methodology had always dictated that no product could be approved and released to the field until it had been tested and retested several times. The allowance for mistakes—even minor errors that could be easily

Society Snapshot: 1977

Home office: 701 Second Avenue South, Minneapolis

Number of members: 881,000

Number of employees: 580

Number of field personnel: 1,132

Insurance in force: $7,724,023,719

Assets: $1,229,971,937

Life insurance death benefits*: $13,723,122

Health insurance benefits: $2,313,548

Dividends paid: $43,450,134

Church loans: $43,606,914

Society officers

Chairman of the board and
   chief executive officer: Arley R. Bjella

President: Woodrow P. Langhaug

Senior vice presidents:

Theodore Q. Feig   Jerome M. Reinan
Luther O. Forde   David R. Zetzman
Lloyd J. Ostlund

** Combines death benefit proceeds from life insurance contracts
and annuities.*

Vice presidents:

Donald Brostrom   Donald C. Nelson
Charles De Vries   Richard J. Nelson
Herman Egeberg   Karl W. Pleissner, M.D.
Robert P. Gandrud   Robert E. Reuter
Harry L. Hendricks   Gordon N. Taft
Harlan J. Hogsven   Clifford L. Thompson
Clifford A. Knudten   Carl A. Thomsen
Alvar O. Konigson   Stanley C. Townswick
Richard K. Lund

Assistant vice presidents:

Raymond J. Bodin   David J. Larson
Earl H. Bonde   Monroe A. Lee
J. Keith Both   Richard C. Lundell
Roger A. Christianson   Lowell M. Mason
Leona M. Grondahl   Eugene A. Moe
Robert M. Hanson   John D. Nystul
Wayne A. Hellbusch   Phillip L. Perry
Otis F. Hilbert   Norman L. Rosholt
Beverly J. Johnson   James M. Walline
Richard J. Johnson   Donald A. Winter
Kenneth A. Kistler

*Lutheran Brotherhood's local branch in Des Moines, Iowa, helped
to build a housing complex for the elderly in Des Moines by sponsoring an ice cream social in 1977. The event and other branch efforts
raised more than $1,500, and the receipts were then doubled with
matching dollars from Lutheran Brotherhood's Branch Challenge
Fund. Below, ground is broken for the new housing complex with
a plow pulled by a team of local volunteers.*

rectified—was nil. Mistakes were unforgivable to MIS managers and those who labored under them. The process of debugging a program became increasingly protracted, and the final 5 percent of a project took longer to complete than had the first 95 percent. The frustrating milieu that this problem created threatened to suffocate employee creativity and growth.

Reinan was well-acquainted with the obstacles of the lumbering system. For years he had fought unsuccessfully for split commissions. Split commissions allowed district representatives who specialized in specific product lines to assist less experienced representatives who wanted help in selling those products. If the sale was successful, the two representatives would share the commission. Reinan viewed split commissions as a necessity in an industry that had become more and more specialized. "It's simply a matter of economics," he once told the field representatives. "Fifty percent of a sale is better than one hundred percent of no sale." Nonetheless, Reinan's attempts to introduce split commissions to Lutheran Brotherhood had always stalled at the door of MIS.

Gandrud prompted MIS to quicken its pace by bringing in several experienced new managers. Because they were unencumbered by a history of failures with the company, it did not occur to them that they should not perform certain system tasks that had frightened former managers. They simply ordered unique approaches that led to change. Within several months, the same people who had plodded through earlier attempts to install split commissions successfully fit the program into the same computer system that supposedly could not adapt to new products. The image of MIS began to change. The division began to deliver its work on time. More important, the division learned to believe in itself. MIS could achieve goals it had once dismissed as impossible.

Future goals would require a different computer software system, however. That fact was inescapable. CFO was not nearly as inadequate as most people in the home office believed, but neither was it equipped for the demands of a rapidly changing marketplace. A few MIS employees believed that Lutheran Brotherhood should build its own system from scratch, but most managers, including Gandrud,

disagreed. The society had been patching systems onto CFO for years, and this approach would not work forever. What Lutheran Brotherhood needed most was a new software system, a system with the flexibility to quickly assimilate novel insurance products.

After several months of study, they were fairly certain that what they wanted was a software package called CFO II, a more flexible version of the society's original system. The idea was to maintain the old CFO system for all old business, then write all new business on CFO II, until Lutheran Brotherhood converted all its business from the original computer system to the new system over a period of several years. The plan seemed to make perfect sense. Employees needed time to adjust smoothly to the newer system, and the home office could not shut down to install it. Hundreds of insurance contracts were written every day, and production in the field had to continue. An abrupt computer conversion in the home office would disrupt the entire operation.

However, a few employees had doubts about the plan, foremost among them two MIS veterans, Earl Bonde and Phil Olson. Unlike management, they were not convinced that CFO II was the complete answer to the society's problems, and they began to question the utility of the proposed system. "Just look at our implementation plan," Bonde observed. "We will have two CFO computer systems operating simultaneously, each one spewing out nearly identical accounting entries. Say we need to make a change in the program function: We'll have to alter two computer systems instead of one. If we purchase CFO II, we'll be doubling our maintenance time and costs. The main drawback of this plan is that it will interfere with the flexibility we're seeking."

Bonde and Olson favored a computer system called LifeComm III. To them, it appeared to be a far better solution, for it would serve as a single, complete business system. They approached Gandrud to try to convince him to look at it. He listened to them, but skeptically, arguing that they had already studied the situation carefully and had agreed on the best solution. The hard-driving Gandrud balked at going back to the drawing board. He was anxious to keep moving forward.

But Bonde and Olson persisted. Gandrud, who had become frustrated with their complaints, finally told them, "Okay, put your ideas down in black and white and give me a formal presentation." In just a few days, Olson marched confidently into Gandrud's office, carrying two charts that Bonde had meticulously drawn. One diagram showed what Lutheran Brotherhood's work environment would be like if it installed CFO II; the other illustrated the society's work environment if it chose LifeComm. The difference was striking, and Gandrud quickly found himself in agreement with Bonde and Olson.

Gandrud was not often wrong, and he did not particularly enjoy the feeling. But the facts seemed clear. It was his duty as a manager, he told himself, to listen to the people who knew more about the technical side of the project than he did. Gandrud resolved to take a closer look at LifeComm. An MIS team (including Gandrud, Bonde, and Olson) was quickly dispatched to Dallas to study a system already in place, and they returned with a consensus opinion: LifeComm is the way to go.

To implement the new system required the participation of many employees in the home office, for the people who could best determine its strengths and weaknesses were those who used it daily. A new system could not be forced on them; they had to help prove that it was the right system. They had to prove that it was *their* system.

However, the entire home office could not halt its daily activities to install a computer system, nor could the field afford to sit idly for even a few weeks. People needed insurance, and the field needed to make a living. The solution was to organize a test office comprised of employees from each division of the home office. First, Gandrud and Ken Kistler, director of the implementation project, took an aggressive request to the head of each division. "We need some of your best employees," they said, "employees you absolutely cannot do without. And we're going to need them for a long time."

A single-mindedness came to dominate Lutheran Brotherhood during this period. As in every other corporate setting, the home office was prone to occasional turf wars. Individual divisions often jealously guarded their own people, assets, and responsibilities.

But the implementation of LifeComm was different. Each department laid aside its territorial bias in favor of the big picture, sacrificing for a common goal. Each division contributed its top employees to the model test office and supported the process when asked for additional employees and resources. Ted Strong, a computer consultant, played a major role in the installation of the system.

For the next two years, these employees functioned as a miniature version of the home office. They ran hundreds of sample contracts through the new computer system. They intentionally threw wrenches into the system—wrong numbers, faulty procedures—to determine how the system handled mistakes. They learned and tested and experimented. And they continually asked questions: How can we adapt LifeComm to the way we do things? Is it possible to change our procedures to better adapt to the system?

The model office was the first of two LifeComm system tests that ran simultaneously during the implementation project. Individual system components had to pass certain stringent MIS tests before progressing to the model test office, where they underwent repeated user tests. If the system component passed both phases, it was then installed in the actual operating system of the home office. By 1980, the entire LifeComm system was successfully up and running, on time and under budget.

In the meantime, Gandrud was asked to head the marketing division. He plunged enthusiastically into his new assignment, but he often mused on the lessons he had learned during the past two years. A manager had to rely on people, he told himself, and Lutheran Brotherhood was full of good people. All they had needed to succeed was a commitment to a common goal, and LifeComm had supplied them with that opportunity. The employees who had once borne the brunt of persistent criticism were the same people most responsible for making the process work.

Gandrud always smiled whenever he thought about that.

Ready for Change

The coffee had been cold for an hour, the doughnuts were getting stale, and the visitors were becoming anxious. They had been sitting for nearly three hours outside the Lutheran Brotherhood boardroom on the second floor of the green building, waiting for the directors to emerge and announce what most observers viewed as a foregone conclusion, that the society would take up new quarters in a major office development project in downtown Minneapolis.

Lutheran Brotherhood's building committee, composed of officers Luther Forde, Stan Townswick, and Ted Feig, had been searching during the past few years for an acceptable solution to the pressing shortage of space in the green building. The board already had decided against constructing a building of its own. The directors also had rejected an invitation to occupy an office tower in the downtown City Center project. But now the building committee had recommended what finally seemed to be the answer: an immense office development costing in excess of $60 million, sponsored by the First National Bank of Minneapolis, that would house both Lutheran

Lutheran Brotherhood's distinctive new home office, which opened in 1981, heralded a new era in which the society maintained its historic commitment to members by making sweeping changes in the ways it developed, marketed, and sold its products.

Brotherhood and the Pillsbury Company.

The society's directors had indicated overwhelming support for the proposal. Several months earlier, they had voted 11 to 1 to deal exclusively with the developers of the project. Only Russell Matthias, the senior member of the board, had openly voiced any opposition. The developers, Gerald D. Hines Interests of Houston, Texas, were so confident that the directors would grant final approval to the project that they had reserved the Minnesota Press Club for a news conference after the board adjourned. Hines had prepared artists' sketches that depicted an office tower about twenty to thirty stories high for Lutheran Brotherhood.

And so they waited for the board to put its rubber stamp on the project. The small anteroom was crowded. Hines had sent a vice president and a public relations representative. They were discussing how to handle the press releases following the approval. A reporter from the *Minneapolis Tribune* had stopped by. Townswick and Forde were present, as were two others who had worked closely with the committee: Otis Hilbert, one of the society's attorneys, and Dave Zetzman, head of the investment department. Feig, who served as board treasurer, was inside the boardroom. Several other officers interested in the project drifted in and out of the anteroom.

The decision had been expected at noon that day, June 10, 1977. As the clock crept toward one, several of the officers shrugged. Nothing to worry about, they assured themselves. Chairman Arley Bjella, who believed in giving full hearing to every important subject, was known to conduct long board meetings. But when the minutes continued to pass, and still no decision had been reached, doubt began to creep into their minds. A few people started pacing.

At two o'clock, more than five hours after the meeting had begun, the directors drifted out of the boardroom. Only a few looked pleased, and several were obviously unhappy. Everyone in the anteroom stood as Bjella walked toward them. "I'd like to make a brief statement," he announced. "The board of Lutheran Brotherhood has decided not to enter the Hines/First Bank project. The board has concluded that it is not in the best long-term interests of the society to enter the project. The board has reaffirmed its decision to maintain the society's national headquarters in downtown Minneapolis and will continue to study further alternatives."

Most of the directors had already left the room, as had the stunned Feig. When he had heard the vote, he had rushed out of the building, fearing he might say something that he would later regret. The Hines people hurriedly packed up their sketches and left. The reporter rushed off to file a story that would appear on the front page of the *Tribune* the next day. The First National Bank project would continue, he wrote, but the developers conceded that it would involve substantially smaller buildings.

Meanwhile, Lutheran Brotherhood was still without a new home. Townswick was crestfallen; moreover, he was confused. The building committee had offered the board a freestanding building, and they had rejected that. Now they had offered what had appeared to be an attractive alternative, and they had not wanted that, either. As he drove home, he wondered, just what did the board want?

Exploring Space

The space problem in the home office first had become evident in 1968. The green building was in excellent shape, but in the fourteen years since it had been constructed, Lutheran Brotherhood had grown almost sixfold. The home office, which for years had occupied the first five floors of the six-story building, had been forced to expand, just the year before, into the top floor. At its present rate of growth, the society would quickly run out of room.

In February 1968, the board decided to construct two more floors atop the green building, adding eighteen thousand square feet to the home office. The addition temporarily solved the society's space problems, but exhausted the structural capacity of the green building; no new floors could be safely stacked above it.

Over the next several years, Lutheran Brotherhood rented space in five downtown locations, including the old Downtowner Motel. The motel, with its basement nightclub in which such jazz greats as Dizzy Gillespie once played, was converted into offices (each complete with bath and shower). Located two blocks east of the green building, the Downtowner was nicknamed "LB East," and housed members of the communications, investment, graphic services, and fraternal departments for several years. Despite the new tenants, the structure apparently retained its reputation as a popular motel. Lutheran Brotherhood employees were often asked by travelers if any rooms were available, and a group of travelers once arrived by bus from the airport and claimed they had reservations.

Because the Downtowner was considered a stopgap measure, the building committee had continued to study more long-lasting solutions, some of which included moving the home office from downtown Minneapolis. Many inner cities had deteriorated during the 1960s, and much of the new business growth was occurring on the outer edges of metropolitan areas. Although Lutheran Brotherhood had always been content in downtown Minneapolis, the committee thought it appropriate to at least ask the question: Would it be advantageous for the home office to move elsewhere?

The society explored several possibilities, from small towns such as Northfield, Minnesota (bastion of Norwegian Lutheranism, near the Twin Cities) to major cities such as San Diego (growing Sunbelt metropolis; no need for skyways or winter coats).

The committee also studied a site in south Edina, a Minneapolis suburb, and even received solicitations from South Dakota and other states.

Ultimately, these surveys confirmed the society's loyalty to downtown Minneapolis. When asked where they would like to move, the majority of Lutheran Brotherhood employees said they preferred to remain downtown. Bjella was especially committed to Minneapolis. "It is my firm conviction that, in the cities of the United States today, the corporations have to be part of the solution and not the problem," he once said, "and I think for us to have vacated the downtown area of Minneapolis would have been a dereliction of our responsibilities to the greater community which we serve. It is impossible to run away from our problems anymore. We live in diverse communities with different people, different needs. We all have to work together and understand and be sympathetic with these problems in order for it all to work out. To live in isolation is not the answer in this day and age, and that is an additional reason why we want to and will stay in downtown Minneapolis."

Having confirmed that decision, the committee tried to decide on the best way to implement it. Perhaps the home office should maintain one central headquarters and continue to add satellite offices throughout downtown; perhaps the society should lease office space. The most viable option seemed to be new construction, and when word got out that Lutheran Brotherhood was running out of room, several developers approached the committee. After some initial space studies, the committee proposed to the board that the society construct a freestanding building with about three hundred thousand square feet of space.

But the board rejected the idea, primarily because of the objections of director Russell Matthias, legal counsel of the society. A new building would mean much more exposure, Matthias said, and too much exposure could prompt legislative regulatory authorities to look unfavorably at the society.

That Matthias, who carried considerable weight with the rest of the board, would not be swayed by the argument that the home office badly needed more space became clear when Luther Forde presented

to the board the projections on which the building's square footage had been based. Head of the actuarial department, Forde possessed as much credibility as anyone in the organization. Conservative, trustworthy, faithful, cautious, deliberate; Forde was all of these. Yet, when he explained that several factors, including business growth and the average number of new employees in each department, had been carefully computed to arrive at the final figure (and the committee believed that three hundred thousand square feet was a conservative calculation), Matthias dismissed the numbers as overblown.

He was particularly upset with the projection that Lutheran Brotherhood eventually would need to expand its legal staff. "Do you mean to tell me, Lute, that you people think we are going to need more attorneys?" asked Matthias, who had once been the society's only lawyer. "Why, I know of a firm in Chicago with $4 billion in assets, and they have only one attorney." It was at this point that the building committee members knew that they would have to develop another plan. If Forde, so careful with numbers, so cautious, so trusted, could not convince Matthias, then nobody could.

The board suggested that the committee investigate what was to become known as the wraparound concept: expanding the green building horizontally by constructing an adjacent tower where the outer garden and parking lot were now located. But it soon became clear that the new tower could not easily be integrated into the original structure; two separate mechanical systems would be needed, and two elevator systems, and all that would be much too costly to maintain.

Thus, the committee had come to an impasse. There had been no board consensus for any of their proposals, and Matthias had been opposed to most of them. The committee knew what the senior director was against, but they were having trouble figuring out what he was for. Besides, the board was then concerned with more immediate matters, especially the building of fraternal programs. For the next few years, the construction issue lay dormant, the reports of the building committee reduced to perfunctory status.

Then, in 1977, shortly after Bjella had told the

committee to renew its efforts, the Hines project had materialized. It had then seemed the most acceptable solution for Lutheran Brotherhood: A partnership with two other highly regarded corporations, Pillsbury and the First National Bank of Minneapolis, a joint venture in which the society could quietly go about its business without attracting too much attention. The financial terms of the deal were extremely attractive, for the developers desperately wanted to attract Lutheran Brotherhood, whom they

considered a reliable tenant that would pay its bills on time. In return, the developers had put a significant amount of cash into the deal and had offered a lease agreement that would allow the society to move whenever it wished and rent the space to other tenants. All that and a prime downtown location only a few blocks from the green building seemed too inviting to ignore.

Although the majority of the board had seen it that way, Matthias had not. When the rest of the

Although the addition of two floors to the green building in 1968 temporarily solved Lutheran Brotherhood's acute space problems, the society's leaders immediately began searching for a more permanent solution. Senior vice president James Krause and Stan Townswick, assistant vice president of corporate planning and administrative services, look south over downtown Minneapolis from the top floor of the green building in 1970. The Minneapolis City Hall is in the background. The Hennepin County Government Center was later erected on the adjacent parking lot south of the city hall. The new home office was erected on the block bordered by Sixth and Seventh Streets and Fourth and Fifth Avenues; a small portion of the block is visible at extreme right and center.

reasons why he believed that the society should not enter the Hines development.

His rationale was this: A fraternal benefit society should not enter into partnerships with other corporations. "It will be the worst of both worlds for us," he said, pausing just long enough after each detailed argument to allow his lunch partner to speak perhaps ten words the entire afternoon. "Not only will we be subject to a huge amount of publicity, being tied up with these people, but we will also not have the strong home office image that we need. No, I think we need our own home office building now. This Hines deal just should not come to pass, and I'm going to do something about it."

A few months later, at the board meeting in Minneapolis, while the building committee stood outside with the confident Hines representatives, anticipating and hoping for final approval, Matthias repeated his arguments to the other directors. For nearly an hour during the executive session, he delivered an impassioned plea not to approve the project. Some directors would remember that it had been his finest speech, and whether or not he actually influenced them, several board members had begun to question the wisdom of the Hines development. In their view, Lutheran Brotherhood was too large to be a mere tenant. Its members would never accept that.

The directors also pointed to a survey that showed that among the largest insurance organizations in the country, only a handful were not headquartered in their own building. Besides, the fear of government intervention was waning. Lutheran Brotherhood had drastically overhauled its fraternal structure, and the government seemed to be satisfied with the changes. Now that they had explored

directors voted to deal exclusively with the Hines project at a meeting in Phoenix, he cast the sole dissenting vote. After the meeting, frustrated that he had not had what he considered enough time to fully state his case because the directors were on a tight schedule, he cornered a young society officer, took him into a nearby restaurant, and bought him lunch. For the next several hours, as storm clouds appeared on the horizon and rain poured down on the desert, Matthias expounded on the

Russell H. Matthias was a director of Lutheran Brotherhood for forty-two years, longer than anyone in the society's history except J.A.O. Preus. He served as general counsel for more than two decades.

hood would not participate in the Hines project.

Although the decision surprised many observers, it turned out that the decision against the Hines project essentially had been a vote for Lutheran Brotherhood's own home office headquarters. Within a few weeks, spurred by Bjella, the board directed the building committee to update its original plans for a freestanding building.

On July 19, 1977, the committee presented its new recommendations. The society should build its own headquarters on land completely owned by Lutheran Brotherhood, they reported, preferably one full block in a stable, downtown environment. The building should contain approximately four hundred thousand square feet of space and should be sufficiently flexible to attract prospective tenants and to accommodate further expansion. The committee estimated that the building would cost about $31 million.

The board quickly accepted the recommendations. Matthias was especially enthusiastic about the project. He was now ready to support the building committee, a position he had made clear just a few days after the Hines vote, when he called Stan Townswick, one of the members of the building committee, into his office.

"Stan, let me tell you how we beat you boys," Matthias said bluntly.

Townswick listened carefully, for it seemed to him that this was the director's way of extending the olive branch, the experienced politician passing on his political wisdom to the next generation.

"I didn't say much during your initial presentation, but I didn't think it was balanced," Matthias explained. "So I took notes and when we went into the executive session, I just ticked off these points on my yellow pad, kind of like convincing the jury. And that's how we beat you boys."

Townswick considered his next words carefully. Matthias had been a persistent thorn in the committee's side, occasionally questioning their credibility and their motives, and Townswick had been

all the other alternatives, including the Hines development, several directors had finally become convinced that the society should build its own headquarters.

By the time the question of approval of the Hines project finally came to a vote, the board had become evenly divided on the issue. They cast secret ballots on slips of paper, and when Bjella counted them, he discovered that there was a tie: Five directors had voted for the Hines project, five had voted against it, and one had abstained. It was his decision now. Although he supported the project, Bjella hesitated to cast an affirmative vote. He was a believer in the collective wisdom of the board, and the board had become fragmented. A building project was an extremely important decision, and an emotional one. Such a decision demanded consensus. Bjella was not about to allow bricks and mortar to become a potential source of division among the directors, so the chairman declined to break the tie. Lutheran Brother-

upset with him just a few days before. But he respected Matthias as a director, and knew that this was no time to question a director. He quickly searched for words that would demonstrate that he was willing to accept the olive branch, and yet still be truthful.

"Mr. Matthias, the one thing I really appreciate is that from day one we knew where you stood on the issues," Townswick finally said. "As soon as you announced you were against it, you maintained that position. Although we disagreed, I do honestly appreciate your consistency."

Matthias smiled broadly; perhaps he had not expected this diplomatic response. "Well, Stan, the important thing is that we agree now," he said. "Now we can work together, and we will work together."

Townswick left the meeting, shaking his head and chuckling at the same time. Matthias had been a formidable opponent; now he would be a formidable ally.

Time and Energy

Russell Matthias was indeed a formidable ally. Then almost seventy-one years old, he had been a member of the board of Lutheran Brotherhood for almost forty years and legal counsel for more than twenty. Matthias was powerful, knowledgeable, shrewd, stubborn, tenacious, intimidating, and tireless. And he was loyal. If participants in the society's political fights had not always been sure which side Matthias was for, they could at least be sure that he would give his absolute allegiance to the one he finally chose.

His strongest allegiance was to Lutheran Brotherhood. It was no secret that Matthias was a wealthy and influential man. During his long legal career, he counseled such insurance giants as State Farm Mutual, and developed insurance codes for the states of Louisiana and Illlinois. He had a successful Chicago practice (having become a partner with Erwin Meyers after Herman Ekern's retirement) with many prestigious clients, and served on the boards of many financial institutions and insurance companies. He was not dependent on his work for Lutheran Brotherhood as a significant source of income; in fact, most insiders believed that he put many

more hours into the society than he was paid for.

He did so because Lutheran Brotherhood was, by Matthias's own admission, his first love. There was something about the society that compelled him; perhaps it was a sense of fraternal mission that drew him to Lutheran Brotherhood, for he believed strongly in fraternalism. Some claimed that the society could not be run without him. Others believed that he had done more to preserve the fraternal system than anyone else in America.

When legislative threats to fraternalism arose around the country, the call would go out from Lutheran Brotherhood for Matthias, who would immediately drop whatever he was doing and take the next plane from Chicago to the site of the challenge; he would remain there until the threat had passed. He galvanized other fraternal lobbyists by his mere presence, and he possessed a keen knowledge of legislative strategy. But his greatest asset was his energy. Matthias understood that the key to lobbying was to contact enough legislators, many of whom knew little about fraternals, and make his position clearly known. Once Matthias had explained the difference between fraternals and commercial companies, opposing legislators often changed their minds, and those who had been sitting on the fence usually cast their votes for fraternals.

It did not hurt that Matthias already knew many of the officials he lobbied. Few insurance lawyers in the country knew more commissioners and legislators, and few had as much influence. Once, during the late 1970s, unbeknown to Lutheran Brotherhood, which diligently monitored such activities, a bill revoking the tax-exempt status of fraternals was passed in both the South Dakota House and Senate. Matthias was quickly dispatched to Pierre. Shortly thereafter, the governor vetoed the measure.

Matthias loved to lobby. He had been trained as a lawyer during the 1930s, when power and influence depended primarily on whom one knew, and he was entirely comfortable in the proverbial smoke-filled rooms in which most political deals were cut. Matthias was an inveterate maneuverer, a student of the old Chicago political school, who gladly performed favors for friends and allies, and expected the same from them. His memory for names was extraordinary (although he sometimes forgot those of the legal staff at Lutheran Brotherhood). It had to be, for he made new acquaintances with every trip, and he always seemed to be on the road.

He had enormous stamina. Even into his seventies, he spent much of his time on planes, and he generally was more energetic the next morning than the younger attorneys who traveled with him. (Perhaps the key to his high energy level was his ability to catnap; he usually was asleep five minutes after boarding a plane.) At times, he would fly back to Chicago, meet his wife, Helene, who would bring him a change of clothes, then immediately catch another plane out. Even when he arrived back in Chicago after midnight, Matthias usually would be at his desk at the office before his secretary arrived in the morning.

His mind was as active as his body. After board meetings at Lutheran Brotherhood, he would make a beeline for the office of Lloyd Ostlund, the society's vice president of law, where for the next three hours he would discuss in great detail what the board had just done. Sometimes young lawyers would filter in after Matthias, hoping to gain some wisdom from the master. After a few hours, they would inevitably begin to yawn or feel the need to visit the bathroom. Only Matthias remained unfazed, alternately twirling and puffing on his ever-present cigar, the air thick with smoke, recounting, dissecting, analyzing, forecasting, pondering. The man did not even stop for a cup of coffee, for he needed no stimulants. Lutheran Brotherhood was his stimulant.

Because Matthias took such keen interest in the affairs of Lutheran Brotherhood, he demanded to be constantly kept informed. He did not like surprises. Savvy officers charged with shepherding crucial projects through the board never failed to check signals with him before board meetings, just to get his input. Those who kept him apprised could usually count on his support, and his support was nearly always essential to success. Unfortunate souls who surprised Matthias with eleventh-hour developments risked failure. His mind could change as quickly as the weather, and he might torpedo the entire venture simply because he had not been consulted prior to the meeting.

While his door was always open to anyone with pertinent information, it was also open to anyone with a problem. Matthias was generally liked and respected by the society's employees, for he took the time to listen to people (though some suspected that he was lobbying them). He asked them about their families, he expressed concern, he sent cards and called when they were ill. His willingness to carry personal causes or complaints to the board was frustrating to the managers whose heads he went over, but it endeared him to many employees.

And if his fellow directors were divided over his heavy-handed political style, Matthias ultimately won their respect for his untiring commitment to Lutheran Brotherhood and to fraternalism. When others wondered whether the fraternal system would last, Matthias held his ground, insisting that the only real threat to fraternalism was if fraternalists themselves stopped believing in it. He never did.

The Anatomy of a Building

With Matthias and the board pushing the concept of a freestanding structure, the building committee moved ahead. The committee had gained two new members since the Hines decision; Luther Forde and Ted Feig had been increasingly involved with other duties (though they continued to consult periodically with the committee), and gave way to Dave Zetzman and Otis Hilbert. Over the next four years, they learned more about buildings and construction details than they had ever dreamed possible, for the project almost completely dominated their lives. They became so attuned to one another that they often woke up in the middle of the night, worried about the same details.

Although the committee eventually interviewed nineteen architects, the choice was easily made. The San Francisco office of Skidmore, Owings & Merrill, designers of the famed Bank of America Building, the tallest building on the West Coast, impressed everyone with their thorough preparation. Throughout the selection process, the committee had thought that some architects had not bothered to get to know the society before making their presentations. But the Skidmore representative, Charles

Bassett, had done his homework. He came to Minneapolis days before his presentation, so he could get a feel for the city. He stood on top of several buildings, taking pictures of the skyline and analyzing the Lutheran Brotherhood site (on the full block bounded by Sixth and Seventh Streets and Fourth and Fifth Avenues). Though he brought no specific design concepts to his first presentation, his ideas about the site closely resembled those of the Lutheran Brotherhood building committee.

For example, the Hennepin County Government Center, a massive vertical structure that extended across two city blocks, was located just opposite the society's new site. Bassett believed that such a dominant building, the seat of government power and authority, had to be respected. Lutheran Brotherhood could, he said, complement the towering structure by attempting to replicate it or by doing just the opposite. The society decided not to try to compete on the Minneapolis skyline and chose the opposite approach, a design that was predominantly horizontal, with a sloping facade that backed away in deference to the government center. The sloping facade also preserved the openness of the government plaza across the street from the Lutheran Brotherhood site. Thus, the society ended up with a building that mirrored its image, distinctive yet conservative.

With the design chosen, only one major obstacle to the project remained: the Treasure Master building. Throughout the years, the society's investment department had purchased several parcels of property on what was to become the building site including the Downtowner Motel on the corner of Seventh Street and Fourth Avenue. By the late 1970s, Lutheran Brotherhood owned almost the entire block. The only parcel it had not acquired was the Treasure Master, a building located on the northwest corner. The society had had opportunities to purchase the property, but had considered the price too high. When the government center project became known, the price of the nearby building escalated with the rising demand.

By the time Lutheran Brotherhood knew that it wanted the entire block and purchased the Treasure Master in 1978, the price had not only sky-

The attractive home office dining center is located inside the cylindrical tube attached to the northwest corner of the building. The unique barrel vault was added to contrast with the gently sloping plane of the building.

rocketed, but several tenants had just signed leases of ten years or more. Most were willing to sell their lease rights to the society, but a few resisted. One tenant, an attorney who leased the penthouse, asked for compensation that was considered exorbitant by Lutheran Brotherhood. As a result, the society decided to erect the new home office around the Treasure Master, so that when the lawyer's lease expired, the old building could be demolished and the design of the new structure completed.

When the lawyer learned that part of the new construction would hang over the Treasure Master penthouse, he filed suit against Lutheran Brotherhood. He used his roof garden for social events and other activities, he told the court, and he had always considered the sunlight and the view part of his lease. The lease made no mention of such amenities, countered the society's lawyers, and the two sides went to trial. (During this episode, Matthias had been consulting with the building committee, thinking of legal strategies, when he jokingly came upon the solution. "What we need are some big brown rats from Chicago," he said slyly, his cigar glowing red hot. "That'll get him out.") Shortly before the judge was about to announce his decision, the attorney suddenly decided to settle out of court; he had apparently decided that he did not have a solid case. Lutheran Brotherhood, which was not completely sure of its own case, quickly agreed.

And so the Treasure Master was finally demolished. A few months later, in the summer of 1978, Townswick was approached by the Minnesota Gas Company, better known locally as Minnesgasco. The company wondered whether the old green building would be open to tenants. The timing could not have been better for Lutheran Brotherhood, which had been considering selling or leasing the building once the new home office was completed. Nor could the prospective tenant have been better, for Minnegasco wanted to occupy the entire building. The society had been hoping for a single tenant, because to have two or more tenants would require extensive remodeling: partitions, more elevators, an additional sprinkler system. Thus, Lutheran Brotherhood conveniently stepped out of the building without having to change anything. Minnegasco even bought much of the old home office furniture. The gas company signed a long-term lease with Lutheran Brotherhood in September 1978, and moved into the green building a few years later.

In the meantime, construction continued on the new home office. There were always minor problems and delays to contend with, and a few major delays, but the situation that attracted the most attention, ironically, was not much of a problem at all. One night Townswick received a call from a Minneapolis reporter. "I have information that more than twelve thousand windows of the wrong size were shipped to the Lutheran Brotherhood construction site," he said. "Is that true?"

Townswick did not have the slightest idea what the reporter was talking about, but he did know that the entire building did not have that many windows. "You'd better check back with your sources," he said. "I'm not aware that that is the case."

"I can't do that now," the reporter answered. "The story has already gone to press."

The story came out the next morning in the local paper, and it was quickly picked up by the wire services. Within a few days, Lutheran Brotherhood had been featured on several radio shows and had received calls from dozens of people across the country interested in buying the windows. A Lutheran missionary in Africa wondered if he could use the windows for solar cookers. An engineer from Detroit said he knew how to easily cut the panels to the right size with a laser beam. One man wanted to buy the glass for secret experiments he was conducting. "You know, I invented perpetual motion," he explained to Townswick, "but the government took my patent away."

It turned out, after all the fuss, that the number of wrong-sized panels actually numbered 1,278. The panels had been cut three inches longer than their frames. The mistake was attributed to computer error, and two replacement shipments arrived from the glass company a short time later. Despite all the hullabaloo, the false report may have done Lutheran Brotherhood a service, for it had focused nationwide attention on the society. "You couldn't get that much publicity if you paid for it," Chuck De Vries, head of the communications department, told the building committee.

The new headquarters was not quite finished when home office employees moved in a few days before Thanksgiving 1981, the day after the worst Minnesota ice storm in almost twenty years had halted nearly all traffic in the state. The building was dedicated several months later. A former president of the society had suggested during the planning stages that the building model be tossed into the ocean, so much did he dislike its design. But almost everyone else loved it, and it was hailed by many local admirers as a striking and adventurous structure, an important addition to downtown Minneapolis.

Two hundred and fifty feet high, with seventeen

stories, the Lutheran Brotherhood building contained 535,000 square feet of space. Copper-colored glass, warm and reflective, covered three sides of the structure; unpolished granite covered the fourth. The west wall was composed of three sloping planes, which caused the structure to taper gently into the sky; because of its grade, the sixteenth floor contained about half the square footage of the first.

A large, cylindrical tube, which attached to the northwest corner of the building, framed the cafeteria on the second floor. It was a curious sight, this barrel-shaped vault, located precisely where the Treasure Master had once stood while the rest of the structure was erected. But the unique addition had been planned long before the society had any troubles with the Treasure Master. Architect Chuck Bassett affectionately called it "a perverse little anachronism," and that was all it was, a gimmick to break up the visual plane of the building.

Russell Matthias lived barely long enough to see the new Lutheran Brotherhood building completed. He had suffered a heart attack while in Africa (one of the few extensive vacations he had ever taken), spent several weeks in a Nairobi hospital, then suffered a second, fatal heart attack in Florida, on March 6, 1982. He had retired from the board of directors a few months earlier, after having served

forty-two years, one of the longest terms in the history of the society. He was seventy-five.

During the early phases of the construction process, Matthias had consulted regularly with the building committee. No detail was too unimportant for his attentive mind. One day, he decided that the new headquarters should have a plaque with the names of the directors on it. "It doesn't matter to me, Stan," he told Townswick. "But a lot of these other directors have big egos, you know."

The committee, burdened with larger concerns, often forgot about the plaque during the next few years, but the tenacious Matthias never did. Every few months, he brought up the subject, wondering where the plaque should go and what it should say. Eventually, he decided that the names of the building committee should be on the plaque. No, the committee members said, they weren't sure that would be appropriate.

But Matthias persisted, and he finally announced that he had talked to Chairman Bjella, who had concurred with his opinion that if the names of the building committee were not on the plaque, then there was not going to be any plaque.

And so the building was completed, plaque and all. It was not the only thing at Lutheran Brotherhood upon which Russell Matthias left his mark.

A Sense of Urgency

The meeting had just begun, but the talk was already turning stormy when Clair Strommen slipped quietly into the back of the room. He was not surprised. It was customary for the District Representatives Advisory Council (DRAC) to report to Lutheran Brotherhood's top district representatives during the society's annual sales conference, and the discussions were always spirited. That the sessions were generally conducted without the attendance of managers from the home office made little difference to the representatives, for they were accustomed to saying what they felt like saying during these meetings, particularly when the topic involved relations with the home office.

Strommen had known of the field's penchant for

candor when he asked DRAC's leaders if he could observe this session. He had been president of Lutheran Brotherhood for just six weeks, since early January 1980, and he wanted to learn more about their concerns. He had heard plenty of favorable and benign comments during his first few days at the sales conference, but those had been at public functions. Now he would hear what the field really thought. Yet even the unflappable Strommen, who had been a general agent during the explosive political battle of 1959, was unprepared for the bitter charges he was about to hear.

The verbal tempest that followed, in many ways, mirrored the weather in Palm Springs that week. Record rains had flooded out most outdoor activities

This plaque lists the names of the building committee and the board of directors at the time the home office was constructed. It is located on the clock column in the lobby of the home office.

in the normally warm and sunny California resort, and there had been a minor earthquake. The representatives, most of whom lived in colder climates, had been especially looking forward to a week in the sun. It was difficult for them to hide their disappointment.

But the district representatives had more on their minds that day than the weather. They had long been frustrated by what they perceived to be a lack of support from the home office. The younger district representatives were particularly dismayed: Just when they had thought they had figured out the life insurance business and were making progress, the rules of the game suddenly had changed. Now a few companies were offering flexible insurance products that appealed to prospects wary of the currently volatile economy; the adjustable contracts allowed clients to modify their coverage to keep pace with inflation and to reap greater dividends during periods of high interest rates.

Lutheran Brotherhood had no such products. Consequently, district representatives found themselves constantly defending the society's stagnant portfolio. Competing insurance organizations were doing a growing replacement business, enticing many Lutheran Brotherhood members to give up their

existing contracts for their accumulated cash values, then using the cash to purchase new contracts at lower premiums. This tactic was known as *twisting*, and was the insurance industry's equivalent of proselytizing. The practice had long been scorned among insurance agents, but it was becoming accepted.

The popularity of twisting backed Lutheran Brotherhood's field force into a corner. It was difficult enough to compete for new business, let alone lose existing clients. Most district representatives were forced to devote an increasing number of hours to conserving old business, and time spent protecting one's own turf was time lost pioneering new prospect territory. Not surprisingly, several aggravated representatives turned to selling part-time for outside brokerage companies. In their view, the choice was not one of loyalty, but of survival. They were being drowned by competition and believed that the home office was unable, or unwilling, to rescue them. The only safe harbor was an outside brokerage company, and plenty of them were ready to help.

It was in this context that the district representatives loudly vented their feelings at the Palm Springs convention. Leaning against the back wall, unnoticed by most of the crowd, Strommen shook his head in amazement. He knew that the society had acute marketing problems; that was why he had been hired. He had been told there were sometimes misunderstandings between the field and the home office; that was true of every insurance organization. But he had never imagined there was so much resentment in the field.

The clamor increased when the representatives began to complain about the way the home office handled preauthorized checks. The subject had been the source of much consternation in the field recently. The use of preauthorized checks, or PACs, was common among insurance companies. Many people who signed up for Lutheran Brotherhood insurance signed a form authorizing their local banks to deduct premium payments directly from their checking accounts. The home office then issued a draft against their checking accounts for the amount of the premium due; the draft was known as a pre-authorized check. The PAC system eliminated the need for premium payments and was usually more convenient for members.

However, the amount deducted from the member's checking account occasionally did not match the amount the member expected to be withdrawn. Sometimes the underwriting took longer than expected, and two months' worth of premiums, instead of one, were deducted from the client's account. Sometimes additional coverages had been added to the contract, and the amount due was greater than what the member had been told by the representative. Sometimes the member did not have enough funds in his or her checking account to cover the amount of the premium. Whatever the case, the field believed that the home office did not properly inform them when anticipated deductions were altered.

The more the DRAC participants talked about the subject of PAC, the angrier they got. "My customers get plenty mad when Lutheran Brotherhood starts messing with their checkbook," said one district representative. "And then I'm the one who has to smooth things over with them. That's pretty poor public relations, if you ask me."

It was at this moment that Strommen found himself the center of attention, and was being asked to speak to the representatives. He had hoped that he could simply remain behind the scenes this week and get to know a few more people before he leaped into the fray, but it hadn't worked out that way. Arley Bjella, the society's chief executive officer, had been unable to attend the conference because of a medical emergency in his family, and Jerry Reinan, the marketing director, had resigned a few months earlier. That left Strommen alone in the spotlight.

But that was where he belonged. Clair Strommen was not accustomed to standing in the back of any room. He was a leader and looked the part. Tall and lean, he moved with a brisk, athletic gait. His long face exuded both confidence and amiability, and there was something unencumbered about the man. His manner was brisk but not frenetic, and he possessed a rare ability to focus 'strictly on the task at hand. Strommen's powers of concentration were most reflected in his eyes. He fixed speakers and listeners alike in his steady gaze, and he clearly conveyed the message that at that moment, sympathetic or not, he was concerned only with them.

Strommen was characteristically blunt with the district representatives when they asked what he could do to solve their problems. "I've been with this society for six weeks," he explained. "I am doing my level best to get up to speed on all the problems we need to solve. But I have to be straight with you. I don't have the slightest idea what you people are talking about." His honesty was disarming, and the room suddenly became quieter. "It's obvious that you are unhappy. So here is what I'm going to do. Within thirty days, each one of you will receive a personal letter from me. I will outline in that letter what the problems are and the process by which we are going to solve them." With that promise, Strommen stepped from the microphone and left the room.

When the new president arrived back at the home office, he appointed three officers to study the situation: Bob Gandrud, the head of Management Information Services; Ted Feig, the treasurer; and Dick Lund, the head of insurance services. He gave them three weeks to isolate the problem, but the solution didn't take that long. When the task force met with the PAC department, they learned that the staff basically agreed with the field force: The system had several flaws. They knew clearly what the flaws were, but no one had ever asked the department to correct them. "If you will let us make a few simple changes in the communication procedure," a PAC employee told Gandrud, "I think almost all of our problems will go away."

They did. What had been perceived as a major problem by the field was quickly solved with a few minor alterations. Strommen then sent his personal letter explaining the procedural changes. The field was impressed. He had kept his promise. He had not told them that the problem could not be solved; instead, he had seen that it was fixed. Even more importantly, he had paid attention to them. That fact alone provided him with instant credibility. The field force believed that here, at last, was someone who was attuned to their changing needs and who understood the nature of their problems.

It wasn't that the home office staff had not listened to the field, for one of their most important jobs was to provide the general agents and district representatives with tools they needed to succeed. When the field succeeded, the society succeeded. The working relationship between the home office and the field was essentially cooperative, but it was also, by its very nature, adversarial. Some in the home office believed that the field complained excessively. Conversely, the field representatives, who felt pressured to create the sales results the home office expected, believed it their duty to point out problems that stood in the way of increased productivity. Even in the best of economic times, there were sure to be a few problems. In periods of economic crisis, they seemed to multiply exponentially. That was the crux of the uprising in the field. The growing volatility of the insurance industry had made them more militant than usual. They were losing business, and they had come to believe firmly that the home office did not appreciate the severity of their dilemma.

Strommen did not dismiss their fears as paranoia, nor did he become defensive when they complained. As a result, he became someone in whom the field force could believe. He was confident and aggressive. He was ready to be their leader. The field was waiting to be led.

The Chance to Work

It was said of Clair Strommen that his intense desire to succeed was the direct result of heredity. He grew up in a family in which children were expected to put their talents to use; if God had seen fit to provide them with unique gifts, then it was their obligation to use them fully. His parents were Norwegian immigrants with strong roots in the Lutheran Free Church. His father, a pastor, served congregations in North Dakota, Michigan, Washington, and southern Minnesota, where Strommen spent much of his youth. His mother was raised in a family in which three brothers became pastors of the Lutheran Free Church.

Like each of his three older brothers (one of whom, Merton, became well-known for his work on the famous book on Lutheranism, *The Study of Generations*, which had been underwritten by Lutheran Brotherhood), Clair Strommen attended Augsburg College, a Lutheran school in Minneapolis. He was a good student, majoring in history and physical education, and excelled at sports. The six-foot-five-inch Strommen was twice voted an all-conference center in basketball, and he was later named to the Augsburg athletic hall of fame.

His greatest physical talent, however, was pitching a baseball. In 1942, shortly after he graduated from high school, he signed a professional contract with the St. Louis Cardinals. During the same week, the team signed a young catcher named Joe Garagiola. Strommen pitched the next four summers in the Cardinal farm system and played basketball at Augsburg during the winter. The Cardinals had high hopes for the lanky pitcher. In his second professional season, he was promoted to Rochester, New York, in the International League. The following summer, he pitched for Columbus, Ohio, in the American Association. Strommen's next stop appeared to be the major leagues.

But his baseball career came to an abrupt end the following winter. Six months after he graduated from college, Strommen was diagnosed with minimal pulmonary tuberculosis. At the time, the bacterial disease was one of the world's leading killers. Strommen's roommate at Augsburg had died of tuberculosis the previous year, as had several other students at the college. Drugs that would prevent or effectively treat tuberculosis had not yet been discovered, so Strommen was hospitalized in a sanitarium in Glen Lake, Minnesota. He spent the next three years there.

For the first fourteen months at the sanitarium, Strommen lay in bed. He was not allowed to stand or even to dangle his feet over the side of the bed during that time. When the tuberculosis bacteria eventually traveled through his bloodstream and settled in his feet, surgeons removed one-third of his left foot, part of his right big toe, and the knob on his right anklebone. His physical condition was complicated by emotional concerns. He had been married to Gladys Boxrud just six months before discovering he had tuberculosis. For the next few years, she supported the family, and came to visit him every night.

Although Strommen had always considered himself a hard worker, his lengthy stay at Glen Lake forever changed his personal philosophy on the subject. If I ever get out of this place, he told himself over and over, I will never complain about having to work. Years later, whenever he encountered ablebodied people whom he believed did not always put forth their best effort, he found it almost impossible to hide his disapproval.

Strommen had planned to become a teacher and coach after his baseball career, but he decided during his hospitalization to pursue another career path. While he underwent rehabilitation at the sanitarium, he took courses in insurance and contract law. He later studied business at the University of Minnesota, and after his release from Glen Lake, went to work for Augsburg College as its director of public relations.

In 1954, Strommen received a call from Herb Johnson, a member of the Augsburg Board of Regents and the director of agencies for Lutheran Brotherhood. Johnson had been having trouble placing a general agent in the Fargo-Moorhead area. Several established field representatives had been offered the position but turned it down. Finally Johnson turned to Strommen, whose experience with life insurance was limited to a few sales for the society. "If you take this job," Johnson told him, "I'll teach you how to sell and then you can teach others." Strommen leaped at the opportunity.

The young general agent soon found out why nobody else had taken the job. In his view, a strong sense of mediocrity pervaded the agency. The majority of the district representatives were part-timers, and they seemed satisfied with what Strommen viewed as piddling sales results. His early suspicions about their lackadaisical attitude were confirmed when Ray Bodin, whom Strommen had recruited in Minneapolis, arrived to work with the agency. The part-timers harassed Bodin, a full-timer, during his first day on the job. "Why are you here?" they asked sarcastically. "Don't you know this county has all the insurance agents it can stand?" Strommen

During a time of significant change in the insurance industry, Clair Strommen dynamically led Lutheran Brotherhood to new levels of financial achievement and fraternal service.

was watching the informal initiation from his office, and didn't like it. After spending a few days in the field with the part-timers, he decided that their sales proficiency and dedication was so lacking that he terminated all of them. That left him with Bodin and three other full-time agents. The quartet became the nucleus of an agency that within three years was one of Lutheran Brotherhood's top five producers.

In 1958, the society appointed Strommen as its midwest regional superintendent of agencies. Unfortunately, the promotion came at a time when civil war was brewing within Lutheran Brotherhood. Strommen's immediate superior, Herb Johnson, had begun to campaign with several others against Carl Granrud. Although Strommen favored the cause of the insurgents, he was more interested in sales than in politics. After six months at the home office, he asked to head a new general agency in St. Paul, hoping he could distance himself from the controversy.

He did not succeed. Both sides demanded that he actively campaign for their cause, but Strommen refused. Eventually, he found himself in an unenviable position: neither side approved of him. The pressure ultimately became too great. When a Granrud supporter suggested that Strommen might be fired unless he campaigned for the beleaguered leader, Strommen decided to leave.

Strommen paid one last visit to the home office in 1959. He thanked Granrud for the opportunities Lutheran Brotherhood had given him, and told him that he would remember the many good things about his time with the society. Granrud was not cordial. "You won't make it," he told Strommen. "You'll come crawling back on your knees looking for a job." Years later, when Strommen joined a country club to which Granrud belonged, the old chairman was knowledgeable and complimentary about Strommen's achievements, and the two became good friends.

Granrud's challenge to Strommen on his final visit to the home office served as a great motivator during the early days when Strommen was struggling to launch his new business. He joined Central Life of Iowa and settled into his new role as comfortably as he had once hurled baseballs through the strike zone. He loved working with his agents in the field, recruiting and training and inspiring them, then watching them prosper. Many people were adept at selling the product; far fewer possessed the ability to identify, attract, and train others who could sell it. That uncommon skill was the marrow of Strommen's success.

During the next twenty years, Strommen established a reputation as one of the leading general agents in the country. His agency was the top producer for Central Life for twelve consecutive years; in 1979, the fifty-member agency produced approximately $2.25 million in life and disability premiums. From its modest beginnings, Strommen and Associates grew to include four other offices and expanded its scope to offer a wide array of insurance and investment services.

During this period, Strommen paid scant attention to Lutheran Brotherhood. Reminiscing was not an integral part of his nature; he preferred to think ahead. Thus, he was somewhat surprised in the fall of 1979 when Bjella asked if Strommen would be interested in becoming president and chief operating officer of Lutheran Brotherhood. The society's acute marketing deficiencies were recognized as its greatest weakness, and Strommen was recognized for his marketing prowess. It seemed a perfect match.

Strommen was not so sure. He had been offered the head marketing job a few years before, but had turned it down almost immediately. The position did not promise the level of power he reckoned would be necessary to implement substantive changes in Lutheran Brotherhood's marketing philosophy; besides, he had not been ready to relinquish the freedom of being his own boss. That consideration also nagged at him as he thought about the board's current offer. Strommen understood only too well the capacity for political turmoil within the society; he feared he might need to make difficult decisions that could provoke political opposition and impede his agenda. In an interview with the board, Strommen was asked if there was any reason why he would not take the job. "Politics," he answered bluntly. "I left twenty years ago because of politics. If I were to encounter the same kind of political atmosphere that prevailed then, it would just be a matter of time before I'd walk out again."

For all his misgivings about the job, Strommen felt drawn to Lutheran Brotherhood. Like all high achievers, he possessed an ample ego and was flattered by the offer. But there was far more to his attraction than that. Strommen had always viewed the society as a community in which a person could make a good living without compromising his or her Christian beliefs. He knew that he would not be seeking a position with any insurance company other than Lutheran Brotherhood at the time. The most visceral evidence of his respect for the society came at an interview with the board. As he sat answering questions with his fingers curled around a coffee cup, he noticed that his hand was shaking. Strommen blinked in surprise, for he was not the sort of man who became nervous easily. I must really want this job, he thought.

Finally sure of his decision, Clair Strommen strode confidently and aggressively into the presidency of Lutheran Brotherhood. The position demanded those qualities in abundance, for the entire insurance industry in the late 1970s was locked in the grip of a powerful revolution. Widespread and radical changes were being forced on a business that had not altered its fundamental approach for more than a century. Insurance companies had begun to discover, painfully, that the promise of safety and constancy was no longer sufficient to ensure their profitability. They would also have to learn how to rapidly adapt to the demands of an increasingly dynamic market. Only those who did would survive.

For many decades, the strength of the insurance industry had been rooted in its unique ability to ensure long-term financial security to policyholders. The basic insurance contract promised not only a guaranteed benefit to the survivors of contract members who died, but a sizable and guaranteed cash buildup to contract members who lived. Life insurance was more than a financial safeguard against early death; it was also a secure and reliable investment for the future. Many people began buying insurance more for the guaranteed retirement income than for the death benefit.

The only trouble with this idyllic fiscal arrangement was inflation. Throughout the 1970s, inflation had become an important factor of American economic life; in the last months of the decade, as the annual rate of inflation climbed toward 14 percent, it became portentous. Everyone worried about runaway inflation, especially life insurance agents, for their attempts to sell contracts that offered a fixed amount of dollar benefits began to fall on a growing number of deaf ears. The value of the death benefit notwithstanding, how could a contract reserve that grew at the annual rate of 8 percent (then the highest rate) provide a hedge against the future, prospects wanted to know, if the purchasing power of the dollar continued to depreciate at nearly twice that pace? More and more consumers concerned about keeping ahead of inflation decided to put their money in investments other than whole life insurance. Those who did purchase insurance often opted for term contracts, which were less expensive than whole life contracts, then invested the difference.

At the same time that insurance organizations were losing old business, their assets were being depleted by consumers who maintained their contracts. Insurance companies were governed by a provision that allowed policyholders to borrow against the accumulated cash values of their whole life contracts. The loan was given at the interest rate specified in the contract; it remained outstanding for as long as the policyholder wished and was simply subtracted when the policyholder collected the cash value from the contract. Typically, consumers borrowed against their cash values at bargain rates, made a profit by investing the money or depositing it in a bank, then repaid the loans when interest rates came down. With market interest rates then hovering around 17 percent, and many older insurance contract loans available between 5 to 6 percent, more consumers than ever before rushed to borrow against their cash values. Few of them were in any rush to pay back the loans.

As a result, life insurance organizations—Lutheran Brotherhood included—were caught in a classic margin squeeze. The sudden increase in contract loans dramatically depleted their assets and greatly reduced their level of investment income. Without the funds necessary to guarantee their obligations to policyholders, insurance companies were forced to borrow at prohibitively high interest rates to make up the difference, which further cut into surplus assets. The cash flow crunch might have been acceptable for a short period of time had enough new contracts been written to make up the difference. But insurance sales had been slowing in 1979, and most industry analysts predicted that they would flatten or decrease during the next year. Contract lapses were sharply on the rise. At that rate, said observers, at least one-third of the nation's life insurance companies would not survive the next decade. Several were already in serious trouble.

It was an insurance executive's worst nightmare. The only hope for the industry was to imitate its competition. To regain the customers it was losing to traditional investments and to retain the capital being lost to outstanding policy loans, the insurance

going to take us where we want to go."

Strommen challenged employees to set goals they had once believed to be unreachable, and then demanded that they achieve them; he taught people to achieve more than they had thought possible. He refused to be dissuaded by those who clung to obsolete standards, for he knew that the volatile insurance environment would reward only those organizations that moved quickly. When officers confronted with newly vigorous demands shook their heads and said it could not be done, Strommen insisted that it must be done.

His first priority was to introduce new products. Strommen began the process by visiting as many general agencies as possible during his first three months on the job. (By the end of his second year, he had traveled to each of the society's seventy-two agencies.) He listened while field personnel talked about their needs, then reported his findings to the corporate staff in the spring of 1980. "Here's what they're saying in the field, and here's what the marketing team has decided we need to do," Strommen told them. "When can we introduce these changes?"

The staff thought carefully. They were always careful; the home office was used to taking a year or more to introduce new products. A philosophy of precision and deliberation permeated most departments, and for good reason. Products poorly designed and hastily implemented could not be scrapped; they had to be tolerated. "We can be ready by November of next year," the cautious staff told Strommen.

"That's sixteen months away," he said, incredulous. "That's right."

Strommen frowned. "If that's all the faster you can move, then you might as well be prepared to lose approximately half of your field force, and then this society is going to be in really tough shape," he said. "I appreciate the fact that we take great care when we introduce new products. But the situation in the industry is so urgent we do not have that much time. We absolutely have got to get going."

industry would have to develop new products sensitive to changing market interest rates. In other words, the entire industry would have to make fundamental changes in the way it had conducted business for one hundred years.

Under Strommen, change occurred at Lutheran Brotherhood with almost unnerving rapidity. After the anxiety and turbulence of the Granrud years, a necessary aura of peace and tranquility had settled upon the society. But in some areas, especially marketing, the society had become too calm. Strommen brought with him a strong sense of urgency and shook Lutheran Brotherhood from its tranquility. Shortly after the new president was hired, Bjella introduced him to society officers by saying, "We have a thoroughbred on board with us now, and like all thoroughbreds, he has a lot of energy and is difficult to control. But we need to get on and ride with this thoroughbred, because he's the one who's

"How fast do we need to move?" asked Bob Gandrud, the soon-to-be appointed head of marketing. "The new computer system is not quite in place yet, but if we don't get too wild in our product design, we can be ready in a few weeks."

"Okay, my thinking is that we take three weeks to design the new products. Matt (general counsel Russell Matthias) has assured me that he'll help us get them approved by the states in two months."

"You can't get products approved that quickly," several officers said.

"Don't say that," Strommen snapped. "If we can get our products designed by the first of June, Matt says we can get them through the states by the beginning of August. Then we can blitz the field by the middle of August."

The *blitz* concept had long been a staple of Strommen's management philosophy. As a general agent, he had kept enthusiasm high by periodically introducing new sales or recruiting campaigns. The typical energy level during a blitz was intense. By introducing several new products in a short time, Strommen capitalized on the ravenous desire of his agents for effective new sales tools. The predictable result was that representatives who already worked hard became almost fanatical in the weeks following a blitz, and production inevitably went through the ceiling. Strommen had similar hopes for Lutheran Brotherhood.

The Great Blitz of 1980 began on August 14. In just two weeks, teams from the home office visited every general agency at more than forty sites across the country. The program, called "Ready for Change," introduced four new insurance products, including an annual renewable term contract, and several improvements and enhancements to the society's existing portfolio. The field force had been impressed by Strommen's assertive response to the preauthorized check problem, and they were even more enthusiastic about his blitz. First-year commission production had been slow that summer, amounting to little more than $500,000 per month. But in September, following the blitz, production rose to $1.4 million. Lutheran Brotherhood's marketing fortunes had begun to turn.

During the product revolution that followed in the next several years, the society overhauled almost every aspect of its insurance and investment portfolio, introducing new whole life products that paid more competitive interest rates. In 1981, the society became the first fraternal insurance organization in the country to offer a universal life contract. Universal life was designed to counter the popularity of term insurance. Term insurance was less expensive than whole life because it offered protection with no cash value buildup. Because of the disparity between the interest rate offered by traditional whole life contracts and many other investments in the late 1970s, many insurance agents counseled their prospects to purchase term rather than whole life insurance and to invest the difference.

Universal life combined the characteristics of both types of insurance. Like whole life, it was designed as a permanent contract with a cash buildup; as with term, only the administrative costs of the contract were deducted from premiums paid by the member. The remainder of the premiums went into the cash fund and paid interest at significantly higher rates than most traditional whole life contracts. Universal life allowed members to raise or lower coverage as their responsibilities changed over the course of their lifetime. For example, a couple could raise coverage when they had children, and lower coverage after the children grew up and bought insurance on their own—all the while building a cash reserve that was competitive with most investments. Universal life quickly became one of Lutheran Brotherhood's most popular contracts.

The society eventually would expand the concept of universal life by introducing variable universal life in 1987. Based on the concept that there was no single product for everyone, variable universal life was a true investment and insurance hybrid. Like traditional life insurance contracts, it offered members a guaranteed death benefit, but, like mutual funds, it allowed them to direct the accumulated value of their contracts into any or all of three investment portfolios, each with different investment objectives. Because it was an investment product, variable universal life was managed and distributed by the Lutheran Brotherhood Variable Insurance Products Company, one of the society's several subsidiaries.

The rise of complex products such as universal life and variable life demanded improved training programs. Lutheran Brotherhood had come to realize that continuing education for its field force was essential to keep pace with the changing nature of the insurance business and of the economy. During Strommen's tenure, the society began several comprehensive career schools for its district representatives. The program provided a continuing curriculum for the field, and ranged from the simplest sales techniques to the complexities of advanced underwriting.

Lutheran Brotherhood also improved its educational programs for district representatives who hoped to become general agents. It was clear to Strommen, as it had been to the marketing department under Jerry Reinan, that the continuing success of the field depended on its ability to maintain a reservoir of well-trained future managers. It appeared on the surface that such a supply was

readily available among the field force, for all district representatives reached a crossroad at some point in their careers. One road pointed toward continued personal sales, another toward field management. But those were the only choices. If the district representative was selected to become a general agent, the training for the position was minimal, a situation analogous to the old practice of sending new representatives out the door with little more than a ratebook and a handshake. Not unexpectedly, the results were mixed. Some general agents prospered, and some did not. Those who floundered often left Lutheran Brotherhood rather than return to personal sales. When that happened, the society lost not only a potentially successful general agent, but a proven representative.

The Assistant General Agents (AGA) program gave budding general agents the opportunity to learn and practice skills necessary to manage an agency before being thrust into that position. AGA participants were required to complete an intensive training program (which usually took two years), after which two options were available: They could seek appointment as a general agent or return to personal production. AGA candidates were sought from three areas: top producers from the society's own field force, proven agents or managers within the insurance industry, and successful people from occupations outside the industry.

The latter category was dear to Strommen's heart, for he had moved from a college public relations job to head a general agency with minimal sales experience. The philosophy of outside candidates ran counter to conventional field wisdom, which held that one could not prosper as a general agent without first serving at least a few years as a district representative. Strommen did not agree. "I did it," he told critics. "Why can't they?" Among the newcomers who became successful insurance managers was Paul Ramseth. A former school

Driving is a way of life for the district representatives who serve rural areas, where long distances often separate potential clients. The most successful producers, like Michael Diemer, of Oconto Falls, Wisconsin, maximize their time by dictating correspondence as they drive to sales interviews. Diemer led Lutheran Brotherhood in combined sales in 1982, 1983, and 1986. He became the society's general agent in St. Paul in 1988.

administrator, Ramseth joined the society in 1981, worked at the St. Paul agency, and later headed the marketing division.

Through the AGA program, several new general agents also joined Lutheran Brotherhood from outside companies. Though traditionalists worried that the new agents had not been sufficiently grounded in the fraternal culture of the society, others viewed their inexperience as an advantage: Newcomers unfettered by the society's old rule would bring fresh ideas to the organization. The fact that Lutheran Brotherhood could attract successful managers from other companies ultimately became a source of pride among the society's homegrown agents.

As the society increased training opportunities for the field, it also improved the environment in which district representatives learned. The old training facilities in the green building had consisted of a single room that was not much larger than an executive office. The room contained a few tables and several chairs, a chalkboard, and a projection screen. A television set was sometimes wheeled in so that the students could review videotapes of their sales techniques. A reel-to-reel tape recorder occasionally played march music during breaks, the Sousa-like reverberations of which inspired the communications department next door to complain.

There were no such complaints about the new education and training center that opened in 1984. The center was equipped with some of the most sophisticated technology available: overhead and videocassette projection and telephone and computer hookups. The largest of the training rooms was horseshoe-shaped. It was geared toward workshops in which interaction was essential. A second room was an amphitheater, with multilevel seating for lectures and video presentations. The smallest training room was designed specifically for audio teleconferences. It featured a large table with built-in microphones and a large loudspeaker in the middle. The system allowed those in the room to converse clearly with a person connected to the room by telephone.

Advancing technology also helped to make the field force more competitive. In 1983, Lutheran Brotherhood introduced its first computer to its general agencies. The small, handheld computer, called "Fast Freddy," allowed district representatives to produce personalized sales illustrations in just seconds, and often eliminated the need for a second interview. Fast Freddy became a fixture in the field during the next three years, until it was replaced by even more powerful, lap-top computers.

During this revolution of products and training and technology, the energetic Strommen, who was named chief executive officer of Lutheran Brotherhood in 1982, worked tirelessly to maintain the sense of urgency he had thrust upon the society. He pushed and cajoled, he cheered and inspired, he compelled and commanded. When employees achieved his lofty goals, he congratulated and rewarded them, then set higher goals. When the field achieved 10 percent annual growth, he asked for 15; when they reached 15, he asked for 20. In almost every respect, Lutheran Brotherhood responded to his pressing calls for change.

There were exceptions. Several months after Strommen joined Lutheran Brotherhood, the marketing department held regional meetings with all of the general agents. They examined the recent growth patterns of each agency and made comparisons with Aid Association for Lutherans. The sales statistics were not encouraging; Lutheran Brotherhood was falling even farther behind its primary fraternal competitor. The worst news concerned the declining size of Lutheran Brotherhod's field force. In 1970, Lutheran Brotherhood and AAL both had about 800 full-time representatives. Ten years later, AAL had about 1,450 representatives. Lutheran Brotherhood still had only about 800.

Strommen was shocked by the findings, for he came from a world of much higher production standards. He had been a star performer himself, and many of his close business acquaintances were top producers in their companies. But now he encountered a situation in which only a handful of the society's agencies were growing and prospering; and even they were not performing near the level to which he was accustomed. Strommen decided to attack the problem first by introducing new products and training programs, but he kept a wary eye on the progress of the general agencies.

Relating to people and to their specific needs is the foundation of counselor selling, an approach that came into widespread use throughout Lutheran Brotherhood in the early 1980s. Supported by new sales tools, more education, and updated products, the field doubled the society's life insurance in force between 1980 and 1987 to more than $20 billion. One of the society's most successful producers was district representative Richard Unger of Gettysburg, Pennsylvania, who led the society in combination sales in 1979 and 1984.

About a year after its initial evaluation, the marketing department again assessed its general agencies. They carefully analyzed each agency and classified them by one of three categories that described their current status: growth, maintenance, or liquidating. To Strommen's dismay, most of the society's agencies were placed into the maintenance or liquidating category.

As the marketing department studied the individual agency graph charts, a classical pattern emerged. Often the general agent had begun his career two or more decades before. Young and hungry, full of vigor, he had recruited and trained representatives and built a prosperous agency that ranked high in the society's standings. During that time, the line of production was sharply vertical. But as the years passed, the agency's growth line began to flatten. Perhaps the general agent was now managing as many district representatives as he thought he could handle. If a representative quit, he hired a replacement, but no more. The agency had entered the maintenance phase. After several years, his line of production began to decline. Representatives who quit or were fired were not replaced. Perhaps the general agent was nearing retirement. He no longer enjoyed working long hours, being away from his family, driving around his territory, searching for additional representatives. Eventually, what had been a slight decrease in production became significant.

From the standpoint of the home office, the decline was simply not acceptable. Robust general agencies were the very foundation of Lutheran Brotherhood. If they were not productive, the society was not productive. A general agency offered tremendous financial rewards, the price of which was exhausting work, interminable hours, and incessant worry. Maintaining the pace required to continually succeed took enormous stamina. Rare was the general agent who could sustain this effort over two or three decades. The society had replaced several general agents every year, for reasons ranging from retirement to lack of production, as far back as anyone could remember.

But the current situation was troubling because it involved so many general agents. At a time when the insurance industry was undergoing major changes of style and substance, many of them were nearing retirement. Just when the already stringent demands of their positions were intensifying, some were winding down their careers. Many did their best to adapt to the sudden rush of change. Only a few refused to try. The general agents were, almost without exception, loyal and committed and successful. They had for years been the backbone of the society. But they had not been prepared for radical change in the insurance marketplace.

Strommen was sympathetic, but he was frank about his high expectations. Along with members of his marketing team, he met with general agents whose agencies fit into the maintenance or liquidating categories, and attempted to find an effective method for getting them back on the growth track. Maybe the general agent needed some assistance in training new representatives. Perhaps he needed to delegate more responsibilities to others. Maybe the general agent, himself, needed more training. The society initiated a management development program for that purpose.

Whatever the case, Strommen made it clear that the society would no longer tolerate liquidating agencies. Numbers do not lie, he told the field. Lutheran Brotherhood will soon collapse if we just wink at liquidating agencies. Maintenance is understandable for a short period of time, he said, but we do not expect any general agency to be in a maintenance phase for long. Our society must have growth to survive.

Having made plain its requirements, the marketing department presented general agents who headed liquidating agencies with several options. They could choose early retirement. Or they could return to personal sales production, which might actually increase their income; they could also pick up subsidiary income based on their production through the society's training allowance program. Or they could choose to try to turn their agency around. Those general agents who did were given six months to meet specific hiring and production standards. If they succeeded, they would be given another six months in which to continue those results, after which they would be taken off probation.

Most of the general agents opted for some form of early retirement. Many turned to personal production. Some brought their valuable years of experience to positions in other departments of Lutheran Brotherhood. Some chose to try to revitalize their agencies, but few succeeded. Between 1981 and 1985, fifty-one of the society's seventy-two general agencies underwent leadership changes. It was a trying time for the society: a melancholy period between two eras, one esteemed and venerated, the other revolutionary and promising.

The period also marked the termination, at least temporarily, of field politics. For years the general agents had been able to influence some members of the board. It was often difficult for home office managers to enforce difficult decisions without some directors interceding on behalf of their disgruntled field constituency. Strommen had made clear his intolerance for such meddlesome tendencies when he was hired, and the board had agreed to refrain from interfering with management. But the tendency eventually resurfaced. After one general agent who was fired for what the marketing department judged to be inadequate sales performance complained to a director, the director instructed the marketing department to reverse the decision. When Strommen was told of the incident, he went to Bjella. The chairman immediately laid down the law: No more interference by the board in management. With that, the matter was closed.

With the dramatic turnover in the general agency force, Lutheran Brotherhood had, in effect, written a new job description for the position, one that required not only increased training, but commitment to new sales methods. The foundation of these methods was based on counselor selling, an approach Strommen recently had introduced to the society, having successfully applied its tenets to his own agency during the 1970s.

Counselor selling proposed a radical shift in the way insurance salespeople had been doing business for several decades. In the past, representatives basically had been taught to get in, make the sale, and get out. The limitations of the product, not the desire of the prospect, generally drove the interview. Thus, making sales depended primarily on the representatives' abilities to convince their prospects to purchase exactly what they were selling, rather than what the prospects wanted or needed.

Although the net result was that prospects received protection for their families (and old-time representatives often noted that they had never heard a widow complain about her husband's insurance contract), these kinds of sales techniques alienated some clients. Prospects felt as though they had been competing with the salesperson, and had lost. That perception, the feeling that they had somehow been manipulated, was sometimes enough to prevent them from again doing business with the representative.

Counselor selling, on the other hand, was driven by the client's needs. The system recognized that the modern consumer had become much more knowledgeable about insurance products and had more choices than ever before. Most importantly, counselor selling acknowledged that the buyer primarily based decisions about insurance on fact, as well as faith. Given a choice, buyers would purchase insurance from the saleperson who offered them a flexible product that was most appropriate

for their individual needs. Counselor selling taught the district representative to view the buying and selling process from the buyer's viewpoint, and to respond according to the buyer's desires. It was not necessary for salespeople to employ coercive closing tactics; given the proper amount of information, the prospects simply made the decision to fulfill their own needs.

When Strommen introduced counselor selling to Lutheran Brotherhood in the early 1980s, the system was widely hailed by the field force. Some older district representatives were less enthusiastic, however, and perhaps even a little insulted. They had always regarded themselves as insurance counselors, and considered their success to be primarily the result of trust that they had worked hard to develop, not through pressure tactics but consistent service. And it was true: Everyone knew dozens of stories about clients who placed their unequivocal faith in Lutheran Brotherhood, such as the young mother from Embarrass, Minnesota, who informed a commercial agent that, yes, the family did want more insurance. "But we'd like to wait for the Lutheran Brotherhood man to come by first," she said. "We really trust him, and I think we'll buy from him again."

The difference between the traditional Lutheran Brotherhood style and counselor selling was that the new system taught a comprehensive and specific course of sales skills. The representatives who, after being handed a rate book and pushed out the door, had practiced relationship selling had done so because of their own intuition; they were effective but did not necessarily know why. Therefore, established representatives who already unconsciously practiced counselor selling methods were able to recognize the skills they possessed, refine them, and become even better.

It was no surprise that the society's perennial sales leaders (the two prime examples being the two William Johnsons, the general agent from Minneapolis and the district representative from Belmond, Iowa) also flourished in the new age of counselor selling, for they had always known how to adapt to the changing marketplace. Buoyed by their efforts and those of new general agents and

representatives, Lutheran Brotherhood's life insurance in force doubled between 1980 and 1987, to more than $20 billion.

Impatient for Excellence

Clair Strommen was meeting with two of Lutheran Brotherhood's leading district representatives at an annual sales convention in Palm Springs. It was 1980, Strommen had been with the society for six weeks, and the subject was field motivation. "You know, one thing I just can't stand is complacency," said Strommen. "I just don't understand it." His listeners chuckled. "Well," said one of the representatives, looking around the room, "get ready for a good dose of it."

Strommen shook Lutheran Brotherhood from its complacency. He demanded great things from others, and he demanded great things from himself. During a period of significant crisis in the insurance industry, he provided strong, focused leadership. He clearly articulated his expectations, showed the society's employees how to meet those expectations, then motivated them to achieve them. He was a hard driver, a perfectionist, and that was what

The board of directors of Lutheran Brotherhood's family of mutual funds in 1987 included, from left: Albert H. Quie, Arnie D. Rydland, Rolf F. Bjelland, Ruth E. Randall, and Charles A. Arnason.

Lutheran Brotherhood needed at the time.

Strommen drove himself harder than he drove others. He did not like to lose, and his competitiveness was especially evident on the racquetball court. Even when he was away from the office, his mind raced with new ideas, most of which he immediately wanted to share with others. It was said of Strommen that there were usually fewer papers on his desk than chairs in his office, for he favored people over details.

It was inevitable that the mercurial Strommen would occasionally chafe under the corporate bit. Like the thoroughbred to which Bjella had compared him, his natural, preferred style was to run freely and swiftly, unencumbered by bureaucratic constraints, and he was used to changing directions quickly. That was not always possible in a large organization like Lutheran Brotherhood, even for the chief executive officer. Strommen was impatient for excellence, and he often became frustrated when

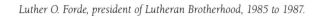

operation. Many officers doubted the wisdom of such a move. In their opinion, the society already had a good thing going with Federated Investors of Pittsburgh. Theirs had been a productive and cooperative partnership since the society introduced mutual funds in 1970: Lutheran Brotherhood Securities Corp. sold the funds through its field force, and Federated, which had become one of the largest and most respected mutual fund organizations in the country, managed them for the society.

Not only would Lutheran Brotherhood be unable to afford the price that Federated would ask for its share of the funds operation, the majority argued, but even if the money were raised, the investment department would not possess the expertise necessary to proficiently manage the funds. The business of managing fund portfolios was a complex endeavor even for experienced investment firms; it was highly regulated by the government and extremely sensitive to market changes that occurred with startling rapidity.

Given the rise of society products that combined the characteristics of insurance and investments, Bjelland believed that it made sense to centralize the funds at the home office, for Lutheran Brotherhood had been gaining investment expertise and could learn more. Strommen agreed. He was also spurred by the fact that some officers had been saying that the transfer could not be done. He did not approve of that kind of negative thinking. In 1983, Strommen got permission from the board to buy Federated's share of the mutual funds operation, and sent Bjelland to negotiate with Jack Donahue, the founder and chairman of Federated.

When Bjelland broached the subject of a buyout, Donahue questioned why Lutheran Brotherhood would even consider taking on that task. "You've got a good thing going with us," he said. "I'm not sure it makes sense for you to add the expense of going it alone."

But Strommen and Bjelland persisted. They arranged for a second meeting in Pittsburgh, and brought with them Lloyd Ostlund, the retired legal counsel of Lutheran Brotherhood, who had a strong

the unwieldy nature of the society slowed his way.

He was especially exasperated by what he perceived as negativism. Strommen was generally perceived by others as gracious, a gentleman. Yet he found it difficult to conceal his anger when he encountered opposition that he thought was based on cynicism. Positive thinking permeated his being, and he demanded no less from others. During one meeting, the mere expression on a person's face upset him, because he interpreted the expression as a negative response to new ideas.

Strommen's emphatic optimism inspired his employees to undertake projects that, at one time, they might have dismissed as impossible. The potent influence of his positive nature was particularly evident when a few officers, notably Rolf Bjelland, the executive vice president in charge of investments, decided that Lutheran Brotherhood would benefit by assuming total control of the mutual funds

background in mutual funds. This time Strommen meticulously went through the reasons why Lutheran Brotherhood wanted to bring the funds back to Minneapolis. "We want to share with you our vision of the future, and how the mutual funds fit into that dream," Strommen told Donahue. "If our reasons for wanting to centralize the funds make as much sense to you as they do to us, great. And if all this doesn't make sense, then we want you to know that we're going to stay with you, and we'll continue to be happy with our relationship."

And then Strommen made his pitch. The insurance industry was changing, he explained, and the society had been changing with it. Lutheran Brotherhood was now in the business of providing total fraternal and financial services to Lutherans, not just separate insurance contracts and mutual funds. Bringing the mutual fund operation to the home

office would make the entire operation more closely connected and more efficient. When Strommen had finished his proposal, Donahue nodded in agreement. "If that's what you're planning, then you really have no choice, do you?"

"That's how we feel about it," Strommen answered.

"Well, then let's talk about the price."

Bjelland, along with Mitch Felchle, Otis Hilbert, and Stan Townswick, developed a purchase strategy, and the contract was signed in May 1985. By 1987, the assets of the five mutual funds totaled $1.5 billion, and Lutheran Brotherhood (through its subsidiaries, including Lutheran Brotherhood Variable Insurance Products Company, Lutheran Brotherhood

Clair Strommen was not the kind of leader who spent most of his time behind a desk, as he proved during Lutheran Brotherhood's "Ready for Change" campaign in 1980.

Real Estate Products Company, Lutheran Brotherhood Research Corp., Lutheran Brotherhood Securities Corp., and Lutheran Brotherhood Family of Mutual Funds) managed $5.8 billion in insurance and mutual fund assets, more than any fraternal benefit society in the country.

Strommen believed that the impossible was possible (for example, bringing the mutual funds to the home office), and he consistently practiced the positive approach that he preached. When he saw or heard about something that an employee had done right, he wrote to the person and thanked him or her. Strommen fostered a strong sense of self-worth within his employees.

That was one of the characteristics he shared with Arley Bjella, the chairman of the board. Strommen and Bjella were, in some significant ways, different leaders for different times, and they occasionally had managerial disagreements. They were like two big ships in a harbor, and when they bumped hulls, it made news around the home office. Yet they respected each other. Strommen admired Bjella for his leadership and integrity; it was Bjella who had supported Strommen and ensured that there was no interference with his management changes. Bjella respected Strommen for

his commitment and drive; it was Strommen who had guided the society to unprecedented success during a time of economic upheaval.

In 1987, two years after undergoing a coronary angioplasty to remove a blockage from one of his arteries, Strommen began to slow his hurried pace. He retired as chief executive officer of Lutheran Brotherhood, and was named chairman of the board, replacing Bjella, who, having turned seventy, had decided to retire from the post he had held for seventeen years.

The mantle of leadership was passed to a man who had worked closely with Strommen to develop and implement new products during the early 1980s. At forty-four years of age, Bob Gandrud, who had served as marketing director and chief operating officer under Strommen, was the youngest president in Lutheran Brotherhood's history. (About a year after he was named president, Gandrud was elected chief executive officer and a board member.) Like his predecessors, Gandrud was strongly committed to the fraternal system. He was a hard worker and a careful listener, and he spent much of his early tenure fostering an atmosphere in which rapid market and technological changes were regarded not as threats, but as opportunities.

A Helping Hand

It had been a sultry Friday, and scattered thunderstorms had been forecast for northeastern Ohio. Youngstown residents looked forward to the rain, and few of them worried much about the possibility of inclement weather, even after the National Weather Service issued a tornado watch at midafternoon. But the skies quickly turned dark and ominous, and when tornado warnings began to shriek throughout the city, Tom Reedy's daughter, Eryn, covered her ears.

"I'm afraid," the ten-year-old told her father.

Reedy, a general agent for Lutheran Brotherhood, pulled his daughter close and gave her a reassuring hug. "Don't worry, honey, they've been sounding warnings for fifty years and we've never been hit with a tornado yet."

This night, however, was different. On May 31, 1985, a series of devastating tornadoes roared through nineteen counties in northeastern Ohio and northwestern Pennsylvania, including the Youngstown area, killing seventy people and injuring hundreds more. Houses and stores and barns in the path of the twisters were reduced to piles of wood and brick. Cars were thrown about like dominoes, some of them with their owners trapped inside. A freight train was ripped from its tracks.

After the storm, the survivors counted their emotional and physical losses. John Goda raced to the Little League baseball field in Wheatland, where his son-in-law had been umpiring, when he heard that a tornado had swept through the area. He searched desperately through the rubble for Dave Kostka, who had married his daughter just one month before, but he could not find him. Only later did he learn that Kostka had died heroically during the storm, alerting players and spectators to the approaching funnel cloud, pushing two panicked children into a low ditch, then throwing his body over them. Kostka was ripped from the ditch by the tornado, but the children survived.

It was a hard night for his family, as it was for all those whose loved ones were killed or injured, and a difficult week for thousands more in Ohio and Pennsylvania. Damage estimates quickly rose into the hundreds of millions of dollars. Houses and business were demolished, families displaced, and plans for the future destroyed. "Where do you start now?" one man asked a local reporter; he had waited out the storm safely in his basement as the twister flattened his house. "To be honest, I think we lost about everything."

As he surveyed the damage around Youngstown, Reedy knew that Lutheran Brotherhood could help. He had worked for the society for more than two decades, mostly in Erie, Pennsylvania, and had seen the good works of the Lutheran Brotherhood branches in that area. The structural fraternal changes implemented during the 1970s—geographical branches, matching funds, and fraternal communicators—had increased the branches' ability to serve the church and community. Reedy had found similarly dedicated volunteers when he returned to Youngstown, his hometown, as general agent in 1984.

Reedy discussed the tornado with several area branch leaders over the weekend, and they called the home office on Monday to determine what they could do for the victims. Bob Engwall, the regional fraternal coordinator responsible for Ohio and Pennsylvania, had been expecting their calls. He had seen several national news stories about the devastation, and, like several others in the fraternal department, had already started thinking about an effective response.

Engwall was well-acquainted with the anguish and upheaval caused by natural disasters. A former Lutheran pastor who had served as a missionary in Tanzania and Peru, he had witnessed the terrible effects of massive earthquakes that killed thousands in Peru. He knew that it was sometimes difficult to believe in the mercy of God at such moments, but it was also God who called upon people to help others who were in need. Engwall had retired from the ministry several years before, but still wanted the chance to serve the church. When a friend told him that there was an opening in the fraternal department at Lutheran Brotherhood, he jumped at the chance.

Engwall knew that the society would use its Disaster Relief program primarily to aid the tornado victims in Ohio and Pennsylvania. Through the program, the society matched on a two-for-one basis funds raised by local branches. For example, if the branch raised a thousand dollars for disaster victims, then Lutheran Brotherhood would add two thousand dollars to that amount, up to a predetermined maximum total. The society had mobilized the relief program successfully on many occasions. Matching disaster funds had aided survivors of the Mount St. Helens volcanic eruption in 1979, and helped residents of Barneveld, Wisconsin, after a tornado destroyed most of their small town in 1984.

But the devastation in Ohio and Pennsylvania was more widespread than anything that the Disaster Relief program had ever tackled. It would be difficult for individual branches, working alone, to make a timely impact on such a massive problem. Besides, the Red Cross and several federal agencies were already helping people throughout the area. It became apparent to Engwall and others in the fraternal department that Lutheran Brotherhood could most effectively help the victims, after the major relief efforts had ended, by combining their efforts into a single coordinated campaign. A few weeks after the tornadoes had struck, the society formed a foundation composed of branch members from around the Youngstown area.

The fraternal division had conceived the foundation concept during the Barneveld relief effort, and it had proven to be a wise method for handling large disasters that involved multiple branches. First, a relief foundation ensured that a representative group of branch members would allocate donations equitably to the needy. Funds raised from Pennsylvania would be distributed to Pennsylvanians, and those from Ohio to Ohioans. Second, 100 percent of all contributions would be used to assist victims. The administrative costs would be borne by the participating branches, out of their fraternal allocations from Lutheran Brotherhood.

As the tornado survivors began the arduous task of putting their lives back together, the society dispatched Engwall and Roald Severtson, a former general agent who now worked for the fraternal department, to Youngstown, where the foundation was to be headquartered. They met with local branch officers and offered advice on how to raise funds. They also assembled several volunteers from area branches for the foundation board. A retired lumberman from Youngstown, Ohio, was named president of the group. The foundation also listed among its eight members a pastor to handle publicity, a certified public accountant to keep track of the finances, and a lawyer to draw up legal papers. Reedy's general agency in Youngstown became the group's mailing headquarters.

The lumberman, Dick Schultz, was representative of the people who belonged to Lutheran Brotherhood branches, for he had long been involved in community activities. An active member of his church, he had served as a trustee, Sunday School teacher, chairman of the parish board, and volunteer purchasing agent for supplies. He had helped to organize the church's food pantry, which provided free lunches monthly to more than a hundred people and distributed food boxes to needy families. Schultz was, at the time, president of his local branch in nearby Warren, and worked closely with community food pantry projects.

During the next several weeks, the foundation volunteers spread the word of their mission through branches in Ohio and Pennsylvania and through local newspapers. They also called fraternal communicators, who passed on information about the project and matching dollars available from Lutheran Brotherhood to their congregations. Due, in great measure, to the efforts of the fraternal communicators, nearly every Lutheran church in the Youngstown area contributed to the foundation.

Lutheran Brotherhood helped the foundation with publicity and maintained close contact with the foundation and area branches through Bill Gordon, a fraternal unit advisor whose territory included the area most devastated by the tornado. Unit advisors were part-time society employees, located throughout the country, who served as liaisons between the home office and the local branches. It was their job to educate branches about new programs and available resources, teach new district representatives about fraternalism, and train fraternal communicators.

Gordon had worked for many years as a chemical engineer for the Lewis Research Center, a National Aeronautics and Space Administration (NASA) laboratory in the Cleveland area. Gordon always had been enthused about his scientific work, but he also had begun to wonder if something was missing. An active churchman, he loved working with his congregation, but his engineering career did not afford him the time to do all that he wanted. His volunteer experience with the Lutheran Marriage Encounter program convinced him that his skills could best be utilized in the church. He took early retirement from NASA, joined his church as director of lay involvement, and became a unit advisor for Lutheran Brotherhood.

New developments such as the unit advisor program encouraged strong lines of communication between the home office and local branches, and communication was critical. Governmental challenges to Lutheran Brotherhood's fraternal status still occurred periodically. It was extremely important that the fraternal department keep accurate records of the number of volunteers who participated in branch projects and the number of hours they spent performing those activities. The only effective method for safeguarding Lutheran Brotherhood's fraternal status was to regularly prove to state and federal legislators that the society's members could administer good works more efficiently than could the government.

While donations poured into the foundation, the board volunteers developed a screening system to determine who would receive the money. The system was based on such criteria as severity of injuries, dwelling and property damages, and disaster relief funds or insurance that victims already had received. Hundreds of applications were sent to families identified by the Red Cross, local governments, and churches. Early in the fundraising process, when they were contacted by the foundation, some Lutheran churches had wanted to raise money for their own members. That was fine, the foundation leaders had responded, but they felt that the community could more effectively help the victims by combining forces. As a result, most churches decided to give to the foundation, and checks were distributed not on the basis of religion, but on the basis of personal need.

By the end of the summer, the Disaster Relief Foundation had collected and distributed more than $200,000 to three hundred families. Forty-two branches in Ohio, Pennsylvania, New York, Michigan, and Maryland joined in the fundraising effort, and Lutheran Brotherhood contributed $128,157 to the total. It was the largest single disaster relief project in the society's history, and attracted much attention in the Steel Belt. Thousands of people contributed to the campaign, many of whom were not Lutherans. When a Catholic priest heard about the relief foundation, he told his congregation, which then raised nearly $5,000 for the foundation.

The campaign was so successful that when local newspapers ran several retrospective stories about the tornado victims around Christmastime, the foundation received a second, unsolicited wave of contributions. The money was distributed to several families over the holidays, and generated many emotional letters from the recipients. "Your name (Brotherhood) has helped restore my faith in brotherhood," one woman wrote.

In the months that followed, during his travels around the country, Engwall encountered many people who were surprised by the success of the tornado relief effort. "I didn't know insurance companies did things like that," they often said. Engwall smiled and thought of all the people who made fraternal projects work, the branch members and leaders such as Dick Schultz, the general agents and district representatives such as Tom Reedy, and the unit advisors such as Bill Gordon. He thought about the thousands of branch volunteers and fraternal communicators and about his fellow fraternal workers back at the home office.

"Lutheran Brotherhood isn't an insurance company," Engwall always answered. "It's a fraternal benefit society."

Telling the Story

Throughout the 1980s, under the leadership of Clair Strommen and Edward Lindell, the new head of fraternal operations, Lutheran Brotherhood enhanced and fine-tuned fraternal programs developed during the previous decade and added new programs, such as unit advisors. In the process, the society dramatically improved what had already been one of the most effective volunteer networks in the country. During 1987, the society allocated $31 million to members, branches, and churches for fraternal activities, and those funds generated millions of dollars more in matching donations from members plus volunteer hours.

Fraternal activities helped keep alive the spirit of community that some social observers feared might be waning in America. One-third of the American people donated their time and skills to help others in 1987, and few organizations harnessed that altruistic desire more effectively than did fraternal benefit societies. Lutheran Brotherhood's branches offered an abundance of volunteer opportunities, and its matching funds gave members the controlling voice in selecting the causes they supported. The society did not simply throw money at social problems, then walk away. Instead, it encouraged its members to get involved and solve the problems themselves.

Through the Friends in Deed program, when at least ten members of a branch volunteered to perform work for families or organizations in their communities, Lutheran Brotherhood paid for the materials to get the job done. Branch members in Toledo, Ohio, used the Friends in Deed program to paint resident cottages at a home for developmentally handicapped adults.

Through the Challenge Fund, branches raised money for projects to buy food, clothing, or other materials for charitable causes, and their funds were matched by Lutheran Brotherhood. When James Fevold, a farmer in Humboldt, Iowa, heard news reports of a drought in Georgia, he decided that he and other area farmers could help, for they had received abundant rainfall and an ample crop that year. Fevold and his Lutheran Brotherhood district representative, Ed Timm, coordinated a campaign among ten area branches to send four semi-truckloads of surplus grain to several Georgia farmers.

Through the Fraternal Communicator program, branch volunteers shared their knowledge of available resources from Lutheran Brotherhood with their congregations. District representatives enrolled almost 1,400 new fraternal communicators in 1987, raising the number of communicators to more than 22,000 and the number of Lutheran congregations served by communicators to nearly 12,000 (about 75 percent of all Lutheran congregations in America). In St. James, Minnesota, fraternal communicator Karen Brennan helped to organize 28 Lutheran congregations in a fundraising effort for the local high school, and the contributions were matched by the society.

Through its extensive scholarship programs, Lutheran Brotherhood supported many Lutheran students, schools, colleges, and seminaries. Mary Margaret Hoy, a student at Newberry College in Newberry, South Carolina, told the society that had she not received a Lutheran Brotherhood scholarship, she might not have been able to attend college.

There were many other fraternal programs, from matching funds for disaster relief to educational resources for Lutheran congregations in both English and Spanish, from interest subsidies for new congregations to matching gifts for member contributions to Lutheran elementary schools, high schools, and colleges. At the home office, specialists were developing and implementing an extensive computer system that would integrate financial and fraternal information about every member. Each file would include the member's personal history and profile, a history of products purchased from Lutheran Brotherhood, and the member's record of involvement with fraternal and branch activities.

An alternative means of distributing fraternal funds, the Lutheran Brotherhood Foundation, was also active. The foundation was created in 1983 to supplement ongoing fraternal programs. Several distinct funding categories, such as integrating single

persons into community and congregational life, were selected each year by the group's board of trustees. The foundation also allowed Lutheran Brotherhood to respond quickly to emergency requests for fraternal funds not covered in the annual fraternal department budget.

The society's fraternal outreach had never been so strong and vibrant. Never had so many of its members contributed so much to their churches and communities. Never had the connection between financial protection and fraternal activities been so closely interrelated. Thus, it struck many society observers as ironic when, in the summer of 1988, Lutheran Brotherhood and several other large fraternal benefit societies prepared for a federal tax study that might modify or even eliminate the tax-exempt status of the American fraternal system as it had existed for more than a century.

Federal tax laws always had contained a specific statutory exemption for fraternals, and every state specifically exempted fraternal benefit societies from paying taxes on insurance premiums. But during studies that eventually led to the 1986 Tax Reform Act, the Treasury Department recommended to President Reagan that the exemption for fraternals be repealed. Large fraternals and commercial insurance companies seemed indistinguishable from one another, the Treasury report charged; thus, the fraternals apparently enjoyed an unfair advantage because of their favored tax status.

To guarantee a level playing field for all competitors, the report concluded, fraternals should be taxed like commercial, stock, and mutual insurance companies. The fraternal tax proposal was eventually eliminated from the final version of the 1986 Tax Reform Act, but the bill also called for the Treasury Department to audit and study fraternals with more than $25 million in annual gross premiums, then make its final recommendation to Congress as to whether they should be taxed.

The Treasury study seemed to signal the possibility of a permanent change in the federal government's perception of fraternal benefit societies. The contention of tax officials that fraternals were no longer appreciably different from commercial or mutual insurance companies was particularly

Society Snapshot: 1987

Home office: 625 Fourth Avenue South, Minneapolis

Number of members: 958,000 (includes fund shareholders)

Number of employees: 936

Number of field personnel: 1,524

Insurance in force: $20,921,932,324

Assets: $4,235,036,877

Life insurance death benefits*: $46,153,813

Health insurance benefits**: $11,127,570

Dividends paid: $124,300,000

Church loans: $134,367,000

Society officers

Chairman of the board: Clair E. Strommen

President: Robert P. Gandrud

Chief financial officer: Luther O. Forde

Executive vice presidents: Rolf F. Bjelland
                           Edward A. Lindell

Senior vice president,
    secretary and general counsel: David J. Larson

Senior vice president
    and treasurer: Stanley C. Townswick

Senior vice presidents:

Mitchell F. Felchle   Donald C. Nelson
Donald D. Hedding   Paul R. Ramseth
Harlan J. Hogsven   William H. Reichwald
Richard K. Lund

Vice presidents:

J. Keith Both   John D. Nystul
David J. Christianson   James R. Olson
Roger A. Christianson   Victoria A.E. Obenshain
Pamela H. Desnick   James R. Olson
Charles H. De Vries   Edwin G. Pfursich
Herman Egeberg   Bruce M. Piltingsrud
Charles E. Heeren   Jerald E. Sourdiff
Otis F. Hilbert   John O. Swanson
Kenneth A. Kistler   James M. Walline

FOR THE FIELD FORCE OF LUTHERAN BROTHERHOOD   November 1987

Welcome Bill Reichwald, LB's new head of Marketing

The Leader *replaced* The Go-Getter *as Lutheran Brotherhood's monthly field publication in 1960. Pictured on the cover of the November 1987 issue is Bill Reichwald, the society's new head of marketing. Reichwald began his career with Lutheran Brotherhood and, at age 27, he became the youngest district representative at that time in the society's history to qualify for lifetime membership in the Million Dollar Round Table. He later served as a successful general agent in St. Paul before being named to the marketing post.*

Assistant vice presidents:

Mary M. Abbey   Lawrence P. Martin, Jr.
William F. Arendt   Eugene A. Moe
Steven J. Bakk   Bruce A. Nokleby
Galen R. Becklin   Philip R. Olson
Randall L. Boushek   Kay J. Owen
James E. Erickson   Linda F. Paulson
Dennis R. Grover   Kevin B. Pedersen
Clifford W. Habeck   Phillip L. Perry
Robert M. Hanson   Dennis K. Peterson
Rosalee E. Hanson   Gregory A. Rogers
Wayne A. Hellbusch   Rolf H. Running
Cathy A. Holmberg   Donn B. Satrom
Beverly J. Johnson   Mark L. Simenstad
Richard J. Johnson   Marie A. Sorenson
Thomas L. Joyal   Lynette C. Stertz
Fred O. Konrath   Joyce A. Tollerud
Karen M. Larson   Donald A. Winter
Paul A. Larson

Combines death benefit proceeds from life insurance contracts and annuities.

**Combines disability income and medical expense benefits.*

worrisome, for fraternals had always successfully countered objections precisely because they had been able to consistently demonstrate that there were differences. Fraternals were grass roots, self-help organizations, they explained, not-for-profit and charitable and benevolent in nature, with a branch system and a representative form of government. Even the types of insurance products provided by fraternals contained distinguishing features and limitations.

Because of these differences, the fraternals emphasized that they did not compete unfairly with commercial insurers. They did not use tax exemptions to undercut premiums. Instead, they priced their products competitively with commercial companies, and used the money that would have been paid in taxes to fund fraternal activities. Moreover, they contended that these valuable activities could be administered less expensively and more efficiently by the fraternals and performed more effectively by their volunteer members than by governmental agencies.

In 1986, for example, the members of twenty-eight fraternal societies in South Dakota had worked 378,000 volunteer hours and returned more than $2 million to the people of the state. By contrast, those same fraternal societies would have returned only $856,000 in premium tax. Without an exemption, the organizations would have been unable to continue to operate effective fraternal programs in South Dakota. Everyone, including the state and its citizens, of whom one in seven were fraternal members, would be losers.

Fraternals had been making these arguments successfully for many years in state legislatures across the country. When legislative challenges to fraternals surfaced, Russell Matthias, Lutheran Brotherhood's general counsel, immediately flew to the scene. An effective lobbyist who cultivated a widespread political network, Matthias knew a large number of politicians and state insurance officers, and he used his contacts to overcome all threats to the fraternal system.

That Matthias was so proficient at his job and so energetic, even into his seventies, was a matter of some amazement among the younger lawyers who worked at Lutheran Brotherhood. One of them,

David Larson, had always told himself, only half-jokingly, that Matthias would probably still be general counsel and give the address at Larson's retirement party. Other society officers felt the same way. Thus, it came as a shock when Matthias, a member of the board for over four decades and general counsel for more than two, died in the spring of 1982.

Larson was named the society's new general counsel. A Minneapolis native, he had attended college and studied law in the East, earning his law degree at New York University. After graduation, Larson had returned to the Twin Cities and joined a private law practice. Thorough and deliberate, the young lawyer became interested in corporate law. He was especially drawn to Lutheran Brotherhood, of which he had been a member for many years. But he steered clear of the society, which was about to settle a major political contest, until the 1967 general convention was over. Impressed with the stability of the new management, Larson joined the society in 1968.

A few years later, Lloyd Ostlund was named vice president of the home office law department, bringing with him valuable experience in mutual funds, a field that the society was then entering. Matthias retained the role of general counsel and continued to manage all fraternal lobbying by himself; like his mentor, Herman Ekern, he always had preferred to work alone. Matthias did meet with Larson and Ostlund once a week, twirling his cigar and sharing in great detail all that he had seen and done that week. In this way, Matthias, who got along especially well with Larson, whose reserved style was so unlike his own, passed on his extensive knowledge of fraternal insurance law and the political process.

Ostlund retired in 1979, so when Matthias died, the mantle of general counsel passed to Larson. He also became a member, as Matthias had been, of the law committee of the National Fraternal Congress of America (NFCA), the national association of fraternal societies of which Lutheran Brotherhood was an active participant.

As he traveled throughout the country responding to legislative challenges, Larson quickly discovered that the power lobbying methods that Matthias had utilized so successfully were no longer as

The Tie That Binds

BOND magazine: *1924-1987*

Lutheran Brotherhood members who received the premier issue of a new publication in May 1924 were greeted with the following message:

"*The BOND* makes its first appearance today, and promises to visit you regularly every month from now on. It aims to be a messenger of good cheer, to spread sunshine and happiness wherever it goes. We bespeak for it a cordial reception in every 'Brotherhood' home. Receive it kindly. It will pay you to cultivate the acquaintance of *The BOND*."

Over the years, *BOND* magazine has attempted to hold to its original course, at least in spirit. It has weathered and been influenced by a number of major changes—in editors, in management, and in Lutheranism. In sixty-three years, it has become something of an institution.

The BOND, as it originally was named, began as a modest, four-page newsletter. Its only embellishment was an ornate nameplate that proclaimed *The BOND* to be "The official publication of the Lutheran Brotherhood."

From the start, the society's goal was clearly not to rival other periodicals of the day, but to build membership and trust in the society. It accomplished this with a mixture of straight-from-the-shoulder facts, clever persuasion, and an occasional tug at the heart.

The BOND's first editor was Thore Eggen. The publication was his idea, and the early issues reflect his dual orientation. As the president of the society, he saw the magazine as a means to make Lutheran Brotherhood a household name among Lutherans. As an ordained pastor, he saw an opportunity to inspire his readers to the practices of faith, thrift, and charity.

In 1924, when the magazine first appeared, the U.S. mail was considered the only reliable medium for communication. Radio was so new that the word *broadcasting* was not yet in dictionaries. So *The BOND* became the society's primary message carrier to the masses of Lutherans.

Luther Forde, now chief financial officer of Lutheran Brotherhood, remembers receiving *The BOND* as a boy growing up during the depression in rural Wisconsin. "*The BOND* was the only magazine I received in the mailbox, and I looked forward to it with great eagerness."

Riddles, games, and other children's fare showed up in 1928, then fell away until the end of 1930, when that section was reintroduced as the Junior Department. A Woman's Page, introduced in 1928, provided recipes, diet tips, and articles with a feminine slant; it was later renamed the Household Page. A health column was added later, then a cartoon page called "The Apple-Sauce Chronicle."

Information on insurance and thrift was emphasized heavily in *The BOND*, along with financial reports on the society's progress, and was complemented with news about Lutheran synods, leaders, and colleges. In the early years, most issues carried one or more photographs of a "One Hundred Percent Brotherhood Family," saluting those families whose every member was insured by the society.

As the magazine has made subtle shifts in editorial direction and style over the years, its constancy has been retained, perhaps because of the long tenures of its various editors. Thore Eggen and Herman Ekern were editors of *The BOND* until their deaths, and associate editor P. O. Bersell contributed regularly to the magazine for thirty-seven years, from 1930 until his death in 1967. Long-standing features provided additional continuity. Departments such as the "Kitchen Korner," "Landmark Churches of Our Faith," and Willmar Thorkelson's "The Year in Lutheranism" ran for decades.

Today, *BOND* magazine is distributed to more than 530,000 member homes. Informative in content, friendly in spirit, the publication continues to serve as the primary communications link between the society and its members.

BOND Editors: 1924-present

Thore Eggen	May 1924-April 1932
Thore Eggen and P.O. Bersell	May 1932-March 1936
Herman Ekern and P.O. Bersell	April 1936
Herman Ekern	May 1936-December 1954
Gretchen Pracht	January 1955-October 1967
Donald Brostrom	February 1968-July 1975
Delores Kanten	August 1975-Winter 1983
Charles De Vries	Spring 1983-present

1924

1925

1932

1933

1940

1941

1942

1943

1944

1945

1952

1953

1954

1955

1956

1957

1964

1965

1966

1967

1968

1969

1976

1977

1978

1979

1980

1981

1926   1927   1928   1929   1930   1931

1934   1935   1936   1937   1938   1939

1946   1947   1948   1949   1950   1951

1958   1959   1960   1961   1962   1963

1970   1971   1972   1973   1974   1975

1982   1983   1984   1985   1986   1987

effective as they had been. Extensive contacts were still important (primarily in order to gain an audience among legislators), and political considerations (such as the millions of Americans who belonged to fraternals) were still influential, but facts and figures were paramount. Fraternal benefit societies had to be prepared to justify, in convincing and detailed fashion, their tax-exempt status. They had to prove, with statistics and practical illustrations, that they could perform those valuable services more effectively than governmental agencies could, and that they would not be able to continue to operate fraternal programs if their exempt status was removed.

The National Fraternal Congress played an aggressive role in telling that story. The association was composed of more than one hundred fraternal benefit societies, from religious societies such as Lutheran Brotherhood and the Knights of Columbus, to ethnic societies such as the Polish National Alliance and Sons of Norway, to general societies such as Modern Woodmen of America and the Degree of Honor Protective Association. These societies accounted for more than $130 billion in fraternal insurance in force and $20 billion in assets, and their total membership numbered more than 10 million through early 1988.

Lutheran Brotherhood was the second largest member of the National Fraternal Congress of America, and had long taken an active leadership role in its affairs. Ken Severud and Arley Bjella, who had played a key role in introducing the fraternal communicator program to the NFCA, had served as presidents of the national association. Several others, including Carl Granrud, had served as officers and on key committees.

There was great camaraderie and cooperation among the members of the National Fraternal Congress, for they realized that if they did not work together, they might lose their fraternal tax status. No individual society was strong enough to defend itself against legislative challenges. If one fraternal society was threatened, they were all at risk. To strengthen the NFCA's own standards for membership, Larson and other members of the law committee began working in the 1980s to implement a model fraternal code in all fifty states. All states had fraternal statutes, but many of them had not been substantially amended for twenty or more years. By introducing a consistent and updated code, the committee hoped to create a standard legal definition that would clarify the many distinguishing features of the fraternals, confirm their tax-exempt status, and modernize the state regulation of their operations. Seventeen states had adopted the new model code by 1988.

In the meantime, periodic challenges continued to arise. The NFCA carefully monitored legislative activity throughout the country, using local lobbyists and informational services. Typically, Larson and other fraternal lobbyists would hear about fraternal tax hearings through this network, and have several days or even weeks to prepare strategy and mobilize fraternal members in the state where tax hearings were scheduled before flying to meet with legislators and testify at hearings. Occasionally, however, legislation to tax fraternals slipped through the cracks, and Larson and his colleagues had to move quickly.

In the spring of 1988, Larson learned from a lawyer contact in Tallahassee that a Florida legislative hearing to consider repealing the tax-exempt status of fraternals had been scheduled for later that day. It was too late to make the hearing, so Larson and other NFCA member lawyers began calling to alert fraternals operating in Florida. The fraternals, in turn, called many of their individual members, who immediately began making phone calls and writing telegrams to their state senators and representatives.

In just a few days, so many fraternal members had responded to the challenge that phones at the state offices were ringing off the hook, and there was far too much mail coming in to even attempt to answer. Fraternal representatives flew to Florida and testified at hearings the following week. After studying figures that quantified the value of fraternal activity in the state, the chairman of the house

The Lutheran Brotherhood board of directors in 1987. Seated, from left: Robert P. Gandrud (ex-officio), Clair E. Strommen, and George A. Wade. Standing: Luther O. Forde (ex-officio), William R. Halling, Lloyd Svendsbye, Herbert D. Ihle, James W. Krause, Judith K. Larsen, Arley R. Bjella, Sigurd D. Medhus, Robert O. Blomquist, Stanford O. Tostengard, and Richard M. Heins.

Robert P. Gandrud, president of Lutheran Brotherhood, 1987 to present; chief executive officer, 1988 to present.

largest fraternals seemed an inviting target. The Treasury Department announced that it was ready to begin its study of the large fraternals, after which it would make its recommendation to Congress as to whether fraternals should be taxed. Experts believed that Congress's ultimate decision would either affirm the tax-exempt status of fraternals for the next several decades, or significantly modify or even eliminate it.

The leadership of Lutheran Brotherhood stressed that the society would always maintain its fraternal commitment, no matter what the final congressional decision, and would attempt to continue its fraternal outreach in some form. However, as President and chief executive officer Gandrud and his team prepared for what would likely be the most significant challenge ever to its fraternal status, Lutheran Brotherhood was confident of the outcome, secure in the knowledge that it was faithfully fulfilling the mission for which it had been created.

Faith and Faithfulness

The passing of time makes great demands on faithfulness, and that is as true of business organizations as of people. External economic forces often determine the ultimate direction of internal corporate policy, and social trends can alter the management style in which policy is carried out. Although change is always necessary for continued success and may be implemented with the greatest care and deliberation, the possibility exists that something of irreplaceable value may be unintentionally discarded in the transition. In many cases, what is lost is the mission for which the organization was created, and the spirit that drives it.

It is due to the foresight of Herman Ekern and Jacob Preus that they founded a fraternal benefit society that was not restricted to a narrow, parochial vision, and therefore was able to maintain its mission and spirit throughout the vicissitudes of the next seventy-one years. By attaching Luther Union to the Norwegian Lutheran Church instead of the Norwegian nationality, Ekern and Preus helped

insurance committee, who had originally proposed that Florida tax fraternals, reversed his position, and successfully brought a motion to take fraternals out of the tax bill.

The Florida challenge resulted in the legislative affirmation of the value of fraternal benefit societies. Once they learned about the work that fraternals were doing in their state and became aware of the numbers of involved volunteers who belonged to fraternals, the majority of legislators responded positively to the fraternal position. In this way, the fraternals have successfully contested every challenge to their tax status.

By the fall of 1988, however, that record stood in jeopardy. The federal deficit had created tremendous pressure to produce additional tax revenue. Congress was looking for billions of new dollars and searching everywhere to find it, including the insurance industry and charitable organizations. The

to promote the idea that religion and insurance were compatible, and subtly encouraged the possibility that the society would eventually become more diverse and thus fulfill their goal of serving Lutherans of all synods and nationalities.

The young society found the diversity it desired by merging with the Lutheran Brotherhood of America and adopting a new name. Lutheran Brotherhood began to build a strong foundation of financial responsibility and member trust during its first decade of existence, a bulwark of stability that enabled the society to survive the upheaval of the depression. It expanded steadily throughout the 1940s, led by dedicated representatives who pioneered new territory, spreading the word about Lutheran Brotherhood and its fraternal philosophy.

The society burst into regional prominence with the construction of the green building in 1956 and, despite political turmoil, continued to grow rapidly through the next decade. The general convention of 1967 was a watershed for Lutheran Brotherhood, bringing to power young leaders who introduced mutual funds to the product portfolio and strengthened fraternal programs and church ties. After struggling to keep pace with radical shifts in the insurance marketplace, the society proved that it could adapt quickly to change. Spurred by energetic management, Lutheran Brotherhood grew at an explosive rate during the 1980s, introducing a variety of flexible insurance and investment products and expanding its already dynamic fraternal program.

The leaders who have overseen these achievements have possessed diverse talents and styles, but at their cores have shared a commonality of mission that

As a fraternal benefit society, Lutheran Brotherhood is governed by its members. Local branches elect delegates to the society's general convention, where the delegates elect directors and decide on amendments to the bylaws.

has not varied appreciably in seven decades. Herman Ekern instilled fiscal discipline in the society, and former governor Jacob Preus provided it with public credibility. Carl Granrud stubbornly built Lutheran Brotherhood's reputation by insisting on excellence. Arley Bjella healed the wounds of past political confrontations with diplomatic skill and led with personal integrity. Clair Strommen energetically pushed the society to new levels of accomplishment.

The policies and directions determined by these leaders and by the board of directors have been dutifully carried out by the officers of the society. Harold Ingvaldson's keen fiscal sense enabled the society to remain solvent during difficult economic times, while at the same time extending valuable loans to churches and farmers. Bill Fisher's promotional skills raised awareness of and enthusiasm for fraternal programs among Lutheran Brotherhood's members, paving the way for the strengthening of fraternal activities during the 1970s. Reuben Jacobson's actuarial acumen kept the organization on sound footing through times both turbulent and tranquil. General counsel Russell Matthias punctuated his dedication to the society every time he flew to the sites of legislative challenges. There were many others. Some officers led quietly, like Art Lee and Luther Forde, and others were more outgoing, like Woody Langhaug and Herb Nelson, but all were effective in their own ways.

There could be no Lutheran Brotherhood without the field force, for insurance operations cannot be managed, fraternalism cannot be promoted, and assets cannot be stewarded unless insurance contracts have first been sold These men and women labored alone, with no guarantees of success and, in the early days, with little training. They succeeded because they believed in the dual value of insurance and fraternalism, and they diligently brought that message to the small towns and farms where the society built its strength. Kelly Neprud and Harold Hoel traveled the back roads, seeking people eager for the opportunity to prosper and willing to make sacrifices for the chance to sell. These recruits, people like Martin Nelson, John Lienemann, and William R. Johnson, became Lutheran Brotherhood in their communities, and pioneers like

Einar Botten, Axel Lundring, Eskild Hauglund, and Walt Beglau developed new territories where Lutherans were few and far between, far from the familiar Midwest.

The home office, where the organizational and administrative work crucial to operational efficiency takes place, has come to symbolize the daily consistency and constancy that characterize Lutheran Brotherhood. Managers like L.L. Johnson and Fred Mueller quietly instilled in their employees the belief that accountability and reliability are virtues. The young people they trained, people like Ken Severud, Al Konigson, Sophie Hawkinson, Cliff Thompson, Dave Zetzman, and Ted Feig, became longtime employees and profoundly shaped the culture of the society during the next four decades by their conscientious example.

That Lutheran Brotherhood has felt deeply about its responsibility to its members has been reciprocated by their enduring trust in the society. The members helped build the society by spreading its message among their neighbors. They responded when it introduced new products, like mutual funds and universal life, and when it adopted innovative financial planning methods, like counselor selling. It is because of their trust that Lutheran Brotherhood is becoming the comprehensive financial resource that Jacob Preus envisioned some seventy years ago, helping its members to protect their families through individually tailored insurance and investment plans.

The society also takes seriously its responsibility to the church. Lutheran Brotherhood was founded for the express purpose of aiding the Lutheran church, and it has responded to its charter by contributing millions of dollars to the institutions and activities of the church. The society is not a part of the church, yet, as an organization that serves Lutherans, it is nonetheless committed to its ministry and welfare. Because the constituency of Lutheran Brotherhood mirrors that of the Lutheran church, the society will change as the church changes, while it continues to search for new and innovative ways to help the church where the church wants help.

Helping others is the basis of fraternalism, and everything about the society, including its people, products, and philosophy, is tied to fraternalism. No other financial organizations can boast of the level of volunteer involvement that fraternals can, or of the democratic form of government that guarantees accountability. At a time when government expenditures are becoming tighter and it seems that Americans are becoming increasingly isolated, fraternals continue to prove that a few people, working together, can still be strong influences for good in their communities. Lutheran Brotherhood's members do not merely purchase insurance contracts. Through their local branches, they also raise money for the victims of hunger and natural disasters. They give of themselves freely, and they give to anyone who needs help, not only Lutherans.

It is this desire to help others, and the fraternal system that makes it possible, that marks Lutheran Brotherhood as an organization that is more than a business. Like almost all organizations, the society is attentive to the bottom line, but it is also guided by a sense of idealism, of shared mission and responsibility, that comes through in even casual conversations. Because of that mission, most members see themselves as a part of something of enduring value.

They share a common bond, and strong bonds endure.

Interview Participants

The following individuals were interviewed for *A Common Bond: The Story of Lutheran Brotherhood*

M. E. Andersen
Albert E. Anderson
Charles Arnason
Charles Austin
Robert Beglau
Walter Beglau
Enfrid Benson
Arley Bjella
Rolf Bjelland
Dreng Bjornaraa (deceased)
Robert Blomquist
Raymond Bodin
Einar Botten
Ralph Brastad
Robert Brinkman
Donald Brostrom
Gordon Bubolz
Martin Carlson
Roger Christianson
Wilbur Claus
Walter Cover
Michael DeMann
Charles De Vries
Michael Diemer
Ruth Downey
Albert Ebbert
Daniel Ebbert
Herman Egeberg
Robert Engwall
Theodore Q. Feig
Mitch Felchle
Eleanor Buck Fisher
Elsie Fisher
William G. Fisher
Luther Forde
Robert Gandrud
Robert Gross
William Halling
Harvey Hamann
Ole Haroldson
Kenneth Hartvigson
Donald Hedding
Richard Heins
Wayne Hellbusch
Harry Hendricks

Don Henninger
Vernon Heslep
Otis Hilbert
Elmer Hjortland
Harlan Hogsven
Welden Ingvaldson
Paul Jacobson
Reuben Jacobson
Frank Jellison
Marietta Johns
Beverly Johnson
Cecil Johnson
Ethel Ann Johnson
Herbert Johnson
Joanne Ryder Johnson
William A. Johnson
William R. Johnson
Kenneth Kistler
Clifford Knudten
Alvar O. Konigson
James Krause
A. R. Kretzmann
Woodrow Langhaug
Judith Larsen
David Larson
John Lienemann
Edward Lindell
Donald Lommen
Norman Lorentzsen
Richard Lund
Richard Lundell
Axel Lundring
Karsten Lundring
Oscar Lyders
Mrs. Russell Matthias
Lavern Mausolf
Sigurd Medhus
Donald Nelson
A. Herbert Nelson
Richard Nelson
Charlotte Nordberg
Glen Nurkka
John Nystul
Philip Olson
Lloyd Ostlund

Donald Padilla
Lavern Peters
Harry Peterson
Bruce Piltingsrud
Gretchen Pracht
Arthur Price
Robert Provost
Cyrus Rachie
Paul Ramseth
Ruth Randall
Robert Rasmussen
William Reichwald
Jerome Reinan
Charles Robison
Norman Rosholt
Walter Rugland
Arnold Ryden
Arnie Rydland
O. M. Sando
Roland and Mildred Schwandt
Rudy Seppala
Roald and Lois Severtson
Kenneth and Helen Severud
Robert Skare
Russel Smith
John Sorbo
James Sparks
Clair Strommen
Lloyd Svendsbye
Gordon Taft
Helen Thal
Carl Thomsen
Clifford Thompson
Willmar Thorkelson
Ralph and Nancy Thorp
Stanley Tollefson (deceased)
Stanford Tostengard
Stanley Townswick
Gilman Tukua
Richard Unger
George Wade
Charles Wallander
Larry Winter
Evelyn Hille Zachman
David Zetzman

Appendix Contents

Articles of Incorporation of Luther Union

We, the undersigned, a majority of whom are adult residents of the State of Minnesota, for the purpose of forming a corporation under and pursuant to Sections 3537 to 3590, inclusive, of Chapter 19 of the General Statutes of Minnesota, and especially Chapter 345 of the Laws of 1907 and Chapter 96 of the Laws of 1915, and any amendments thereto, do hereby associate ourselves as a body corporate, without capital stock, organized and carried on solely for the mutual benefit of its members, and not for profit, and confining its membership to the members of the Norwegian Lutheran Church of America, and we do hereby adopt the following Certificate of Incorporation:

Article 1.

The purpose and object of this corporation shall be to aid the Lutheran Church in extending the Lutheran faith, to foster justice, charity and benevolence, to provide education, instruction, proper entertainments and amusements, to encourage industry, saving, thrift, and development on the part of its members, to give aid in case of poverty, sickness, accident, or other misfortune, and own and operate homes, hospitals and sanatoria, and to furnish protection and relief to its members, their dependents and beneficiaries, through the issue of benefit certificates, and the payment of benefits thereon in case of death, or disability by sickness, accident or old age, and otherwise to promote the spiritual, intellectual and physical welfare of its members.

Article 2.

The name of this corporation shall be the *Luther Union.* The home office shall be in the City of Minneapolis, in the County of Hennepin, in the State of Minnesota.

Article 3.

The supreme legislative or governing body to be known as the Central Union, shall be composed of representatives elected either by the members or by delegates elected by the members through a delegate convention system, as provided in the bylaws, together with such other members as may be prescribed in the bylaws, in accordance with law. The board of directors shall consist of five members to be elected by the Central Union as provided in the bylaws. The officers shall consist of a president,

vice-president and a secretary-treasurer, who shall be elected as provided in the bylaws. The directors and officers shall hold their respective offices until their successors have been elected and have qualified for the discharge of their duties.

Article 4.

The first regular meeting of the Central Council for the election of such officers shall be held on the first Wednesday of June, 1920. The first meeting of the board of directors shall be held at 425 South Fourth Street, Minneapolis, Minnesota, on the sixth day of July, 1917.

Article 5.

The names and places of residence of the persons forming this corporation are:

H.G. Stub of Saint Paul, Minnesota.
T.H. Dahl of Minneapolis, Minnesota.
J.N. Kildahl of Saint Paul, Minnesota.
G.M. Bruce of Red Wing, Minnesota.
S.T. Reque of Saint Paul, Minnesota.
C.J. Eastvold of Dawson, Minnesota.
Th. Eggen and J.A.O. Preus of Minneapolis, Minnesota.
H.L. Ekern of Madison, Wisconsin.

Article 6.

The names and addresses of the members of the first board of directors and first officers are:

Th. Eggen, C.J. Eastvold, S.T. Reque, H.L. Ekern and J.A.O. Preus, as Directors, Th. Eggen as President, C.J. Eastvold as Vice-President and J.A.O. Preus as Secretary-Treasurer

Article 7.

Any person who (has been baptized in the Lutheran faith and) is affiliated with the Norwegian Lutheran Church of America shall be entitled to membership and shall become such by being elected by a local union and accepted in the manner prescribed in the bylaws. Each member shall have one vote.

Article 8.

Assets representing the reserves on all outstanding benefit certificates shall at all times be held in trust for the fulfillment of the payment of the benefits promised in such certificates; and if the regular payments are insufficient to pay all natural death and disability claims in full and provide for such reserves, extra assessments or other payments may be levied upon the members to meet such deficiency.

Article 9.

These articles may be amended by two thirds vote of the members voting thereon at any regular meeting of the Central Union; and unless otherwise provided by law may be amended in like manner at any special meeting of the Central Union, provided notice of the pro-posed amendment has been given with the notice of such meeting.

In Testimony Whereof, we have hereunto set our hands this 13th day of June, 1917.

In the Presence of

L.W. Boe
H.G. Stub
T.H. Dahl
J.N. Kildahl
G.M. Bruce
Th. Eggen
C.J. Eastvold
S.T. Reque
J.A.O. Preus
H.L. Ekern

Bylaws of Luther Union.

Adopted July 7, 1917
Amended August 28, 1917.

1. Plan

The Luther Union is a mutual benefit society, with a representative form of government, with a ritual, not secret, which shall before it is adopted be approved by the president of the Norwegian Lutheran Church of America, and shall contain nothing that has the disapproval of said president or of the church council.

2. Purposes.

The Luther Union is organized for these objects, namely: to aid the Lutheran Church; to foster justice, charity and benevolence; to provide education, instruction, proper entertainments and amusements; to encourage industry, savings, thrift and development on the part of the members; to give aid in case of poverty, sickness, accident or other misfortune; to own and operate homes, hospitals and sanatoria; and to furnish relief and protection to its members, their dependents and beneficiaries, through the payment of benefits in case of death or of disability by sickness, accident, or old age, and generally to promote the welfare of its members.

3. Membership.

Any person who is affiliated with a Lutheran church may be admitted to membership in the Luther Union.

4. Organization.

The Luther Union shall consist of the members organized in the local unions. The supreme governing body shall be the Central Union, composed of delegates elected by the local unions, and of the directors and officers of the Luther Union, provided that the elected delegates shall have not less than two-thirds of the votes nor less than the number of votes necessary to amend the articles or bylaws.

5. Officers.

Each local union shall have five directors and a president, a vice-president and a secretary-treasurer, all to be elected by the union, and to hold office for one year. The Central Union shall at the first meeting elect five directors, one for three years, two for six years, and two for nine years, and thereafter all directors shall be elected for nine years. The directors shall immediately following each regular meeting of the Central Union elect a president, a vice-president, and a secretary-treasurer, who shall each hold office for three years. The directors shall also appoint a manager, who is made an officer of the society and shall be assistant secretary-treasurer. Vacancies in any office shall be filled by the respective boards of directors for the unexpired term. Directors and officers shall hold office until their successors are elected and qualified. Such bonds shall be given as ordered and approved by the respective boards of directors. There shall be a board of sponsors, of which the president of the society shall be president. Such sponsors, not to exceed twenty-five, shall be appointed by the boards of directors and represent the society and advance its interests.

6. *Meetings.*

Regular meetings of the Central Union shall be held every third year, beginning with the year 1920, at such time and place as ordered at the preceding meeting or by the board of directors. Unless otherwise ordered, such meeting shall convene on the first evening of the triennial meeting of The Norwegian Lutheran Church of America. Special meetings shall be held on the call of the board of directors or of one-fourth of the members entitled to participate therein. The secretary shall give at least ten days notice of a special meeting. Regular monthly meetings shall be held by each local union at such time and place as it shall order.

7. *Delegates.*

There shall be one delegate to the Central Union from each local union. Such delegate shall be elected and certified to the secretary of the Luther Union at least thirty days before the regular meeting.

8. *Annual Dues.*

All members shall, on or before the thirty-first day of October, pay annual dues of ten cents per member, which shall be collected by the secretary-treasurer of the Local Unions and remitted to the secretary-treasurer of the Central Union, and placed to the credit of the General Fund to defray the expenses of the society.

9. *Voting and Eligibility to Office.*

Each member, whether social or beneficial, shall have one vote, but shall be entitled to hold office only while a member of The Norwegian Lutheran Church of America.

10. *Insurance.*

No promise of benefits shall be made in any certificate, except upon a sound, adequate and permanent basis, and assets equal to the required reserve shall at all times be held in trust for the payment of the benefits so promised. The funds shall consist of the Benefit Fund, for the payment of insurance benefits and the General Fund, for the payment of expenses in conducting the furthering of the work of the society. The Benefit Fund shall consist of all assessments after deducting the portions herein specifically set aside for the General Fund, and adding interest earnings on all Benefit Funds, with such other sums as may be specifically set over into the Benefit Fund. The General Fund shall consist of the remainder of the assessments upon each certificate for the first certificate year after providing for the cost of insurance, and ten percent of all assessments upon each certificate after the first certificate year, except that on the insurance there shall be annually set into the General Fund an amount equal to that annually set into the General Fund from an ordinary life certificate, issued at the same age, and also all income from other sources than assessments and interest earnings on Benefit Fund.

11. *Amendments.*

These bylaws may be amended by a two-thirds vote of those present and voting thereon at any regular or special meeting of the Central Union, or by unanimous vote of the board of directors when the Central Union is not in session; but no amendment shall take effect or apply in regard to sections 1 and 3 of these bylaws unless adopted by unanimous vote of the board of directors of the Central Union, and after notice given to all members by two-thirds vote of those present and voting thereon at any regular or special meeting of the Central Union.

Articles of Incorporation and Bylaws of Lutheran Brotherhood (Amended)

Restated Articles of Incorporation as amended by the General Convention on May 16, 1987.

We, the undersigned, a majority of whom are adult residents of the State of Minnesota, for the purpose of forming a corporation under and pursuant to Section 3537 to 3590, inclusive, of Chapter 19 of the General Statutes of Minnesota, and especially Chapter 345 of the laws of 1907 and Chapter 96 of the laws of 1915, and any amendments thereto, do hereby associate ourselves as a body corporate, without capital stock, organized and carried on solely for the mutual benefit of its members, and not for profit, and confining its membership as hereinafter provided, and we do hereby adopt the following Certificate of Incorporation:

Article I

The purpose and object of this corporation shall be to serve its membership by aiding the Lutheran church bodies, their institutions and congregations, fostering patriotism, loyalty, justice, charity, and benevolence; providing education and encouragement of the arts; encouraging industry, saving, thrift, and development on the part of its members; giving aid in case of poverty, sickness, accident, or other misfortunes; owning and operating homes, hospitals and sanatoria; furnishing protection and issuing benefit contracts, and making payment of benefits thereon in case of death, or disability by sickness, accident or old age; and otherwise promoting the general welfare of its members.

Article II

The name of this corporation shall be LUTHERAN BROTHERHOOD. The Home Office shall be in the City of Minneapolis in the County of Hennepin, in the State of Minnesota, or in such other location as the Board of Directors may determine.

Article III

The supreme legislative or governing body to be known as the General Convention, shall be composed of delegates elected by local branches, or of delegates elected through a delegate convention system, as provided in the Bylaws, together with such other delegates as may be prescribed in the Bylaws in accordance with law. The Board of Directors shall consist of not less than five nor more than fifteen members. The officers shall consist of a president, one or more vice presidents, a secretary, a treasurer, and such other officers as the Board of Directors may determine, who shall be elected as provided in the Bylaws. The directors and officers shall be selected and hold their respective offices pursuant to the provisions of the Bylaws. No director shall be personally liable to the Society, its General Convention or its members for monetary damages for breach of fiduciary duty as a director, except to the extent such exemption from personal liability or limitation thereof is not permitted by applicable laws.

Article IV

The first regular meeting of the General Convention for the election of such officers shall be held on the first Wednesday of June, 1920. The first meeting of the Board of Directors shall be held at 425 South Fourth Street, Minneapolis, Minnesota, on the sixth day of July, 1917.

Article V

The names and places of residence of the persons forming this corporation are:

H.G. Stub of St. Paul, Minnesota.
T.H. Dahl of Minneapolis, Minnesota.
J.N. Kildahl of St. Paul, Minnesota.
G.M. Bruce of Red Wing, Minnesota.
S.T. Reque of St. Paul, Minnesota.
C.J. Eastvold of Dawson, Minnesota.
Th. Eggen and J.A.O. Preus of Minneapolis, Minnesota.
H.L. Ekern of Madison, Wisconsin.

Article VI

The names of the members of the first board of directors and first officers are:

Th. Eggen, C.J. Eastvold, S.T. Reque, H.L. Ekern, and J.A.O. Preus as directors; Th. Eggen as president, C.J. Eastvold as vice president, and J.A.O. Preus as secretary-treasurer.

Article VII

Any person who: (1) has been baptized in the Christian faith or is affiliated with a Lutheran church organization, and (2) professes to be Lutheran, shall be entitled to membership and shall become a member in the manner referred to in the Bylaws. Each adult benefit contract member shall have one vote for delegates to the General Convention.

Article VIII

Assets representing the reserves on all outstanding benefit contracts shall at all times be held in trust for the fulfillment of the payment of the benefits promised in such contracts; and if the regular payments are insufficient to pay all death and disability claims in full and provide for such reserves, additional payments may be required to meet such deficiency. One or more separate accounts may be established and operated to support contracts issued on a variable basis in accordance with applicable laws, and to the extent the provisions of this Article are inconsistent therewith such provisions shall not apply to the separate accounts or contracts issued on a variable basis.

Article IX

These Articles may be amended by a vote of not less than two-thirds of all delegates voting thereon at any regular meeting of the General Convention; and unless otherwise provided by law may be amended in like manner at any special meeting of the General Convention, provided notice of the proposed amendment has been given with the notice of such meeting.

The above Restated Articles as amended by the General Convention at its meeting held on the 16th day of May, 1987, shall supersede and take the place of the Articles of Incorporation originally adopted on June 13, 1917, and all amendments thereto.

In testimony whereof, we, the present members of the Board of Directors have hereunto set our hands this 24th day of June, 1987.

Arley R. Bjella	Judith K. Larsen
Robert O. Blomquist	Sigurd D. Medhus
William R. Halling	Clair E. Strommen
Richard M. Heins	Lloyd Svendsbye
Herbert D. Ihle	Stanford O. Tostengard
James W. Krause	George A. Wade

Amended *Bylaws* as adopted in part by the Board of Directors on June 24, 1987.

Section 1
ADMISSION TO MEMBERSHIP

Admission to membership and benefit contracts may be obtained upon application and approval by such officers and upon such conditions as the Board of Directors may determine.

Section 2
ORGANIZATION OF BRANCHES

LUTHERAN BROTHERHOOD shall consist of members organized in branches. The members who do not belong to a local branch shall constitute and be members of a separate branch designated as a regional branch. Local branches, regional branches, or any combination thereof shall be established, and governing rules and regulations shall be prescribed in accordance with these Bylaws. A member may elect to belong to a branch of his own choice. In the event a member wishes to transfer from one branch to another, such transfer is effective ninety days following receipt of notification by the Secretary of LUTHERAN BROTHERHOOD. Notice of a meeting of any branch may be published in the Lutheran Brotherhood BOND, the official publication of LUTHERAN BROTHERHOOD, and any such notice shall be deemed sufficient notice to all members of such branch. Branches may admit social members.

Section 3
THE GENERAL CONVENTION

A. The supreme governing body of LUTHERAN BROTHERHOOD shall be the General Convention, composed of delegates as provided in Section 6 of these Bylaws, provided that the elected delegates shall have not less than two-thirds of the votes. The Chairman of the Board of Directors of LUTHERAN BROTHERHOOD shall preside at all meetings of the General Convention. In the event that the Chairman of the Board of Directors is unable to serve, the Vice Chairman of the Board of Directors shall preside. In the event neither is able to serve, another board member or officer designated by the Board of Directors shall preside.

B. Regular meetings of the General Convention shall be held every fourth year from 1975, at such time and place as fixed by the Board of Directors.

C. The Chairman of the Board of Directors shall propose to the Board of Directors a Nominating Committee from the list of certified delegates prior to each regular General Convention to select nominees for the Board of Directors' positions to be filled. The Chairman of the Board of Directors shall report to the Board of Directors the recommendation of a Nominating Committee, at a regular or special meeting, and the Board of Directors shall confirm or, in the alternative, substitute, add to or delete names of those proposed by the Chairman of the Board of Directors and appoint the Nominating Committee. The appointed Nominating Committee shall make its report to the delegates by mail at least forty days prior to the General Convention and to the General Convention. In order to assure the preservation of the representative form of government, guaranteed by the fraternal laws of the State of Minnesota, the only other method of making nominations for directors to the General Convention shall be by filing with the Secretary of LUTHERAN BROTHERHOOD at least twenty days prior to the date of the General Convention a petition containing the name or names of the proposed nominee or nominees, such petition of a nominee or nominees to be signed and subscribed to by not less than ten percent of the certified delegates to the General Convention. Notice of the names of those persons duly petitioned and thereby nominated for director shall be provided to the certified delegates by mail prior to the General Convention.

D. The Chairman of the Board of Directors of LUTHERAN BROTHERHOOD shall also appoint General Convention committees, including a committee to audit the expense accounts of the delegates and alternate delegates, a Credentials Committee, a Resolutions Committee, and such other committees as may be deemed necessary for transacting the business of the General Convention.

E. Special meetings of the General Convention shall consist of the elected delegates certified to the last preceding regular General Convention together with the ex-officio delegates as provided in Section 6 and may be called by not less than two-thirds of the members of the Board of Directors or on written request signed by not less than two-thirds of said delegates in good standing, as defined in Section 6. If one or more of the said delegates ceases to be an adult benefit contract member in good standing, as provided for in Section 6, with respect to the General Convention, such person shall be ineligible to be a delegate and such vacancy or vacancies shall be filled by one alternate or alternates respectively, and if any elected alternates shall fill such vacancies as defined herein, such alternates shall assume all of the obligations and responsibilities of the delegate replaced.

F. Any undertaking by delegates or others to call a special meeting of the General Convention shall be governed by the following rules:

(1) Prior to or at the time of any solicitation of any written requests for a special meeting of the General Convention, the Secretary shall be notified in writing by any delegate or group of delegates of the intention to seek a call of a special meeting of the General Convention. Such notice shall be filed with the Secretary and shall specify the business to be considered at the special meeting of the General Convention.

(2) Any written requests of the delegates shall be filed with the Secretary no sooner than thirty days after the said notice and within sixty days after the notice and shall be dated and signed after the date of the notice.

(3) When any written request is so filed with the Secretary such shall be deemed a final filing and no amendments thereto nor subsequent written requests concerning the same subject matter shall be accepted by the Secretary.

(4) When the Secretary has counted and verified the written signatures, and those revocations filed and bearing a date prior to the filing of the written request, and the number of valid written signatures thereon is insufficient to convene a special meeting of the General Convention, then no further written request shall be circulated or filed involving the same subject matter for one year from the date of filing said request.

If, in the determination of the Secretary, a request is proper and complies with all legal requirements, the Secretary shall certify and file the request with the Board of Directors. Thereupon, the Board of Directors shall set a date and place for such special meeting of the General Convention, which shall be not less than thirty days nor more than ninety days from the date of the receipt of said written request by the Secretary. If a special meeting of the General Convention is called by either the Board of Directors or by action of the delegates as prescribed herein, the Secretary shall give to each delegate twenty days written notice of such special meeting of the General Convention, specifying the business to be considered at such a special meeting of the General Convention.

Section 4
THE BOARD OF DIRECTORS

A. There shall be twelve directors, four of whom shall be elected at each regular quadrennial meeting of the General Convention for a term of twelve years each.

B. No person who is an officer or director of LUTHERAN BROTHERHOOD shall be paid any commission, fee, or other compensation for writing any contract of insurance with LUTHERAN BROTHERHOOD while such person is an officer or director, nor shall any officer or director hold a contract as agent or general agent during the term as an officer or director of LUTHERAN BROTHERHOOD. At least nine members of the Board must be persons other than officers, employees or persons receiving compensation for current active service to the Society, excluding director fees. No officer or employee of LUTHERAN BROTHERHOOD shall receive a Board fee for serving on the Board of LUTHERAN BROTHERHOOD or on the board of any LUTHERAN BROTHERHOOD subsidiary.

C. No person elected as a director at the Eighteenth General Convention in 1971, or thereafter, shall continue to serve as a director after attaining age seventy (70); provided that any director elected prior to the Eighteenth General Convention may continue to serve as a director to the end of the elected term or any successive term without regard to the age limitation herein specified; provided that any such director shall retire upon reaching age seventy-five (75).

D. The Board of Directors, following each regular meeting of the General Convention, and annually thereafter, shall elect a chairman of the Board and a vice chairman from among its members, and shall elect annually the following senior officers: a chief executive, a president, one or more vice presidents, a secretary, and a treasurer. One or more of the above offices may be held by the same person. The Board may, in its discretion, designate one or more of said elected vice presidents as executive vice president or senior vice president, respectively. The senior officers shall hold office at the pleasure of the Board of Directors. The Board of Directors may elect annually such other officers as it may deem prudent, who shall be junior officers and who shall hold office at the pleasure of the Board of Directors or until removed by the Chief Executive. A vacancy in any office may be filled by the Board of Directors. No person shall be discriminated against as an officer, director, employee, general agent or district representative of LUTHERAN BROTHERHOOD because of race, color, national origin, age or sex. Each person who serves as director, officer, general agent or district representative must be an adult benefit contract member of LUTHERAN BROTHERHOOD.

E. The Board of Directors may appoint by a majority vote of the entire Board of Directors a director to fill a vacancy in the Board until the next regular or special meeting of the General Convention, at which time the General Convention shall elect a director to complete the unexpired term, if any. A vacancy may be declared upon the happening of any of the following events: (1) death, (2) resignation, or (3) disability. Disability may involve either physical or mental disability which seriously affects the ability of a director to participate in the meetings of the Board. Such physical or mental disability shall be certified to after examination by one or more physicians selected by majority vote of the remaining directors. A director shall be deemed to be disabled if he or she is unable to attend five (5) consecutive regular meetings of the Board of Directors, because of such disability.

F. The Board of Directors may create committees and define their powers and duties and shall also elect from its membership an Executive Committee of not less than four nor more than six members, a quorum of which shall consist of three members. Such Executive Committee shall have and exercise all the powers of the Board of Directors while the Board is not in session, except the power to amend the Bylaws and matters over which the Board of Directors has retained jurisdiction. The Executive Committee shall also perform such duties as are specifically delegated to it by the Board of Directors.

G. Regular and special meetings of the Board of Directors shall be held as determined by the Board or on call of the Chairman of the Board, or on written request signed by any four directors and filed with the Secretary.

Section 5
INDEMNIFICATION

A. The Society shall indemnify every person who is or was a party or is or was threatened to be made a party to any action, suit, arbitration or proceeding, whether civil, criminal, administrative or investigative, by reason of the fact that such person is or was a director, officer, employee or agent of the Society, or is or was serving at the request of the Society as a director, officer, employee, agent or trustee of another corporation, partnership, joint venture, trust, employee benefit plan, or other enterprise, against expenses (including counsel fees), judgments, claims, liabilities, penalties, forfeitures, fines and amounts paid in settlement actually and reasonably incurred by such person in connection with such action, suit or proceeding, to the full extent permitted by applicable law. The indemnification provided hereby shall continue as to a person who has ceased to be a director, officer, employee, agent or trustee and shall inure to the benefit of the heirs, executors and administrators of such person. Such indemnification shall include advances of expenses in advance of final disposition of such action, suit or proceeding, subject to the provisions of any applicable statute.

B. The Society shall have power to purchase and maintain liability insurance on behalf of any person who is serving in any capacity mentioned in Paragraph A of this Section, whether or not the Society would have the power to indemnify such person as herein provided.

Section 6
DELEGATES TO THE GENERAL CONVENTION

A. The Board of Directors, by a majority vote of the entire Board, shall divide the membership of the Society in Delegate Districts. In so doing, the Board of Directors shall take into consideration geographical boundaries, the number of adult benefit contract members, general agency territories and any other factors that the Board of Directors may consider material, and shall set the boundaries of the Delegate Districts accordingly.

B. Each Delegate District shall be entitled to delegates based on the number of adult benefit contract members in good standing as of the certification date, which shall be a date not more than twelve months preceding the date of the regular meeting of the General Convention. As of the certification date, the Board of Directors shall allot delegates to each Delegate District as follows: each Delegate District shall be entitled to two delegates and an additional delegate or delegates as determined by the Board of Directors on the basis of the number of adult benefit contract members residing in said District. In addition to the allotted delegates to each Delegate District, each Delegate District shall elect two alternates to act as delegate or delegates should one or more of the elected delegates (i) for any reason be unable to serve at the regular meeting of the General Convention, or (ii) be declared by the Board of Directors not to be a delegate in good standing.

C. The Board of Directors shall cause to be published in the Lutheran Brotherhood BOND, in no event less than five months preceding the date of the regular meeting of the General Convention, the official certification of the number of delegates to which each Delegate District is entitled. In the same issue of the Lutheran Brotherhood BOND, the Board of Directors shall direct the Secretary to publish the boundaries and the number assigned to each Delegate District, the time and place for the Delegate District balloting to elect delegates to the regular meeting of the General Convention, the time and place of the General Convention, the name of the Deputy Secretary for each Delegate District and the manner of nominating delegates. The Delegate District balloting shall be held within two months following the publication of notice in the Lutheran Brotherhood BOND. The aforesaid publication in the Lutheran Brotherhood BOND shall be deemed sufficient notice to all members.

D. Delegates and alternates from the Delegate District shall be chosen and qualify in the following manner:

(1) The Board of Directors shall appoint a Deputy Secretary for each Delegate District, who along with any assistants that might be designated, shall carry out the following duties:

(a) The Deputy Secretary shall appoint a District Nominating Committee made up of members residing within the Delegate District to nominate candidates for delegates and alternates.

(b) A register shall be maintained of all members requesting a ballot.

(c) The Deputy Secretary shall transmit to the Secretary the voted ballots and the registration lists.

(2) The District Nominating Committee shall file its report in duplicate, one copy with the Board of Directors and one copy with the Deputy Secretary, not later than twenty-five days prior to the date set for the Delegate District balloting. Nominations for delegates or alternates may also be made by a petition signed by not less than thirty-five adult benefit contract members residing in the Delegate District. Residence shall be determined as the residence of record of the contract member. The petitions or certification of the Branch Secretary of nominations for delegates or alternates shall be filed with the Board of Directors and Deputy Secretary in the same manner required of the District Nominating Committee.

(3) Any candidate for a delegate or alternate or elected delegate or alternate must be an adult benefit contract member residing within the Delegate District and a member in good standing; provided that only one candidate who is a district representative or general agent of LUTHERAN BROTHERHOOD may be elected and vote as a delegate from each Delegate District. In order to be a member in good standing, the candidate or elected delegate or alternate:

(a) Must be an adult benefit contract member.

(b) Must not have business or personal interests which would constitute a conflict of interest in relation to the business operation of LUTHERAN BROTHERHOOD. The Board of Directors or a subcommittee thereof shall determine whether a delegate or a candidate for delegate is or is not in good standing: (i) the Board of Directors shall cause the Secretary to give written notice to said delegate or candidate for delegate of the charges specifying wherein the former apparently fails to comply with Paragraph D (3) of this Section; (ii) the challenged delegate or candidate for delegate shall be afforded the opportunity to appear personally before the Board of Directors, or its subcommittee, or to answer the charges in writing within twenty days; (iii) the decision of the Board of Directors or a subcommittee thereof as to whether or not the delegate or candidate for delegate is in good standing shall be final.

(4) The vote of a member must be cast in person at a designated location in the Delegate District in which he resides, except that the Board of Directors may provide for the return of marked ballots by mail to the Secretary. A member shall be entitled to but one vote regardless of the number of adult benefit contracts issued to the member.

(5) The Secretary shall count the ballots under the supervision of the Board of Directors or committee thereof. The candidates receiving the highest number of votes shall be the duly elected delegates for the respective Delegate District, and shall be equal in number to the number of delegates allotted to a particular Delegate District, and the candidate for alternate receiving the highest number of votes shall be the duly elected first alternate and the candidate receiving the second highest number of votes shall be second alternate for the respective Delegate Districts. In the event of a tie vote as to a delegate or an alternate, the election shall be decided by lot by the candidates involved, under the direction of the Deputy Secretary. The names of the delegates and alternates so elected, together with the names of the ex-officio delegates, shall be certified to by the Secretary and published in the issue of the Lutheran Brotherhood BOND no later than the second month preceding the month in which the regular meeting of the General Convention convenes. Such listing in the Lutheran Brotherhood BOND shall constitute an official certified list of the delegates and alternates for the next regular meeting of the General Convention, and upon the election and the qualification of delegates to the General Convention the term of office of previously elected delegates shall cease. The publication in the Lutheran Brotherhood BOND shall be deemed sufficient notice to all members and delegates.

(6) The expenses of the Deputy Secretaries in connection with the delegate elections, and the expenses of the delegates to any regular or special meeting of the General Convention shall be determined and fixed by order of the Board of Directors.

E. Ex-officio delegate representation at the General Convention shall be determined as follows:

(1) The senior officers, each director, and certain junior officers as provided in subparagraph (2) of this Paragraph, who hold such positions at the time of any regular or special meeting of the General Convention shall be ex-officio delegates to the said General Convention, each entitled to one vote. Any person ceasing to hold one of such positions shall cease to be a delegate.

(2) The Board of Directors shall establish a procedure for the selection by lot of ex-officio delegates from among the junior officers. The number of such additional Home Office ex-officio delegates shall be one-third of the total of directors and senior officers, as of ninety days prior to the General Convention.

Section 7
BENEFIT CONTRACTS, SEPARATE ACCOUNTS, FUNDS AND APPORTIONMENT OF DEFICIENCY

A. The Board of Directors shall provide for benefit contracts to be issued, upon application and acceptance in a manner and upon such conditions as the Board may determine, to persons: (1) baptized in the Christian faith or affiliated with a Lutheran church organization, and (2) who profess to be Lutheran, as provided in the Articles of Incorporation. The Board of Directors may provide for the establishment and operation of one or more separate accounts and issue contracts on a variable basis providing for the dollar amount of benefits or other contractual payments or values thereunder to vary so as to reflect the investment results of such separate accounts.

B. Benefit contracts may be issued on such basis, form, and for such benefits and naming such persons as beneficiaries, as the Board of Directors may direct. The Board of Directors may to the extent it deems necessary adopt special procedures for the conduct of the business and affairs of any separate account.

C. The assets of LUTHERAN BROTHERHOOD shall be kept in one fund or such funds as the Board of Directors shall prescribe or the laws shall require.

D. In the event of the impairment of the solvency of LUTHERAN BROTHERHOOD, an apportionment shall be charged against each outstanding benefit contract on the basis of the member's equitable share of the deficiency as determined by the Board of Directors. The provisions of this subparagraph D shall not apply to contracts issued on a variable basis.

Section 8
PROVISION APPLICABLE TO BENEFIT CONTRACTS

A. The benefit contract of a member shall consist of the application, the benefit contract, any amendments or riders thereto, and the Articles of Incorporation and Bylaws now or hereafter in force, except that a contract on a variable basis shall be subject to the Articles of Incorporation and Bylaws in force on the date of its issue.

B. The benefit contract shall also be governed by the following specific provisions, unless such contract provides otherwise, or unless such provisions are prohibited by state law:

(1) Upon disaffirmance of a benefit contract by a minor, only the cash surrender value of the contract shall be payable, and tender of such sum shall be a complete discharge of all liability on such contract.

(2) Payment of any claim under a benefit contract pursuant to the contract or any assignment thereof without notice to the Society of any alleged conflicting claimant shall be a complete discharge of the obligation for such claim on the contract or assignment.

(3) In case a benefit contract is lost, destroyed or beyond the member's control, such member may, on a form furnished by LUTHERAN BROTHERHOOD, have a substitute contract or other evidence of coverage issued in its place. No requested change from the original contract shall be effective until the date of issue of the substitute contract.

Section 9
ROBERT'S RULES OF ORDER TO GOVERN

Unless otherwise provided in the Articles of Incorporation or the Bylaws of LUTHERAN BROTHERHOOD, the latest edition of Robert's Rules of Order shall govern the proceedings at all meetings. No vote by proxy shall be recognized in any meeting of the General Convention or of the Board of Directors.

Section 10
AMENDMENTS TO BYLAWS

A. These Bylaws may be amended by a vote of not less than two-thirds of all delegates voting thereon at any regular or special meeting of the General Convention, or by a vote of not less than three-fourths of all the members of the Board of Directors at any regular or special meeting of the Board of Directors.

B. In order to be considered by the Convention, any proposed amendment to the Bylaws, other than an amendment submitted by the Board of Directors, must be signed by at least ten percent of the certified delegates to such Convention. Any proposed amendment shall be filed with the Secretary of LUTHERAN BROTHERHOOD at the Home Office at least forty days prior to such meeting. A copy of the proposed amendment shall be forwarded by the Secretary to each delegate at least twenty days prior to such meeting.

C. Any member of the Board of Directors must file a proposed amendment with the Secretary of LUTHERAN BROTHERHOOD at the Home Office twenty days prior to a regular or special meeting of the Board of Directors in order to have the same considered by the Board of Directors.

D. Amendments may also be passed without prior notice by unanimous vote of the General Convention or of the Board of Directors.

E. Any Bylaw provision relating to the retirement age of directors may be amended only by the General Convention in accordance with this Section.

Minutes of Meeting of Board of Directors

Luther Union

July 6th, 1917.

Meeting held at Augsburg Publishing House.
Following members present:

Th. Eggen, President
H. L. Ekern
C. J. Eastvold
S. T. Reque
J. A. O. Preus

The by-laws were unanimously adopted, and thereupon approved by Rev. H. G. Stub, President of the Norwegian Lutheran Church of America. (See note.)

It was moved, seconded and carried that the Secretary-Treasurer furnish a bond to the Society as may be required by the Department of Insurance of the State of Minnesota.

The Board of Directors recessed, during which time they considered the advisability of organizing a fire insurance arrangement whereby the Norwegian Lutheran Church of America might carry its own fire insurance.

Secretary Preus made an informal report to the Board of his investigations of the feasibility of organizing another insurance concern under the laws of the State of Illinois. Motion made and carried that Director Ekern be requested to prepare a plan in conformity with the laws of Illinois to be submitted to the Board of Directors and considered at its next meeting.

The period of recess having expired the Board of Directors adjourned to meet at 10 o'clock A.M., July 7th.

Secretary

Charter Members of Lutheran Brotherhood

Contract
Number

1. Mrs. Emma J. Aaberg
2. Rev. Moses B. Anderson
3. John Andrew Berg
4. Herman L. Ekern
5. Andrew K. Olson
6. Even E. Ellertson
7. Oscar J. Ellertson
8. Carl O. Teisberg
9. Rev. Mons Sotendahl
10. Rev. Peder E. Moen
11. Michael R. Mandt
12. Parnell A. Evanson
13. Sander E. Midboe
14. Rev. Anders H. Thorson
15. Prof. Wilhelm R. Rognlie
16. Rev. Nils J. Njus
17. Edon A. Arnes
18. Gilbert K. Jordet
19. Swen J. Peterson
20. Oliver L. N. Wigdahl
21. Rev. Vigleik E. Boe
22. Rev. Overt Skilbred
23. Jacob G. Rugland
24. Rev. Christopher M. Hallanger
25. Emil H. Gilbertson
26. Selmer C. Hilleboe
27. Rev. Daniel J. Borge
28. Rev. Swen J. Njaa
29. Dr. Gottfried W. Collerstrom
30. Nels S. Nelson
31. Inger Anna Fredricks
32. Jerome Harris Evanson
33. Lydia Marie Skordahl
34. Peter S. Evanson
35. Knut A. Sather
36. Edwin L. Bilden
37. Henry O. Wickney
38. Ole Solum
39. Arthur Oliver Hagen
40. Olaus B. Valtinson
41. Carl S. Gransberg
42. Jorgen D. Runsvold
43. Elvin C. Haga
44. Andrew V. Lane
45. John R. Rasmusson
46. Mrs. O. N. Jordheim
47. O. N. Jordheim
48. Nels Benjamin Hanson
49. Peter G. Vildmo
50. Abel E. Lien
51. Peter O. Sathre
52. Alfred Bertin Mickelson
53. John M. Mason
54. Nels Rudolph T. Braa
55. John K. Sveen
56. Omar Brenne
57. Mrs. Elise J. Rasmusson
58. Carl M. Anderson
59. Wilhelmina G. F. Hammer
60. John Timroth
61. Theodore Kvilhaug
62. Prof. Rasmus Bogstad
63. Mrs. Henrietta L. Holte
64. Halvor Holte
65. Rev. Hartwick C. Smeby
66. Rev. O. N. Nelson
67. Rev. O. C. Myhre
68. Oscar Fredricks
69. Selmer F. Ellertson
70. Rev. Theodore Hokenstad
71. Rev. Sigurd C. B. Knutsen
72. Arthur S. Erickson
73. Ole G. Kolsrud
74. Joseph Tetlie
75. Rev. Thomas J. Knutson
76. Johannes Sangstad
77. Emma Froiland
78. Carl M. Froiland
79. Donald J. Haugen
80. Rev. Geo. O. Lane
81. Sylfest Peder Orwoll
82. Rev. K. O. Kandal
83. Rev. John C. Hjelmervik
84. Rev. John N. Midtlien
85. Wilhelm T. Hexom
86. Rev. Thore Eggen
87. Wilhelm J. E. Madson
88. Olga M. Hjelmervik
89. William B. Ingvoldstad
90. Jens M. Clemson
91. Rev. Olaf Lysnes
92. Leonard Melvin Bilden
93. Arnold Hasle
94. Oliver Ruben Johnson
95. Edward Johnson
96. Mrs. Elsie Alverne Fisher
97. Carl J. Lilleskov
98. Clarence A. Larson
99. Jerry M. Hardy
100. Rev. Halvor H. Knudsvig
101. Price Murray Honeywell
102. Hon. Laurits S. Swenson
103. Harvard Larson, Sr.
104. Alfred L. Larson
105. Rev. Harold Hansen
106. Erik Hetle
107. Constance B. Norby
108. Camuel M. T. Carlson
109. Rev. Johan F. Swenson
110. Rev. Botolf J. Rothnen
111. Mrs. Phoebe Lysnes
112. Rev. Knut O. Lundeberg
113. Joseph Oscar Ensrud
114. Peder Tangjerd
115. Rev. S. Theodore Thompson
116. Rev. Magnus L. Dahle
117. Rev. Christian S. Thorpe
118. Rev. Gustav O. Fjeseth
119. Hans J. Fladmoe
120. Jens Anderson
121. Julian M. Saugstad
122. Carl M. Vevle
123. Alfred Amundson
124. Lars Pedersen Seierstad
125. Rev. Olaf Carlson
126. Nels Larsen Mykkeltvedt
127. Henry Peterson Grimsby
128. Rev. Eberg C. Tollefson
129. Rev. Lauritz S. J. Reque
130. Rev. Geo. O. Lillegard
131. Rev. B. J. Larsen
132. Rev. Lewis Moe
133. Rev. Aksel H. Trygstad
134. Fridtjof B. Anderson
135. Jorgen M. O. Gudal
136. Dr. Jorg G. Vigeland
137. Gustave H. Gilbertson
138. Haldor Andrew Wichman

139. Edwin Odin Stavig	189. Rev. Martin Norstad	239. Herman Roe
140. Albert Ingwald Hagen	190. Rev. John S. Sunde	240. Bennie O. Pederson
141. Louis I. Roe	191. Bendick M. Sletteland	241. Rev. Harold Farseth
142. Rev. John L. Johnson	192. Rev. Henry O. Shurson	242. Ubert M. Millang
143. Ludvig E. Larson	193. Rev. Gustav M. Bruce	243. Mrs. Ida Johnson
144. Magnus Pederson	194. Gilbert A. Olson	244. Leo J. Huseby
145. William C. Benson	195. Rev. Lauritz Larsen	245. Rev. Bergel A. Johnson
146. Rev. Jacob Wilhelm Rosholt	196. Anton E. Anderson	246. Joseph Benjamin Losen
147. Rev. J. J. Ekse	197. Rev. J. H. Preus	247. Olaf H. Nelson
148. Rev. S. A. Stenseth	198. Justin M. Snesrud	248. Rev. J. Torval Norby
149. Rev. Ole Otterson	199. Rev. Ole A. Norem	249. Rev. Thomas Severin Stockdal
150. Rev. Rudolph M. Fjelstad	200. Edward B. Olson	250. Alfred H. Amundson
151. Christian A. Davick	201. Almer Norman Eggen	251. Evelyn I. Hilleboe
152. Martin L. Loven	202. Prof. Ole E. Rolvaag	252. Rev. N. C. A. Garness
153. John T. Bondhus	203. Hanna F. Hanson	253. Sophie H. Stearns
154. Alfred O. Morkre	204. Theodore O. Taraldson	254. Peter Oscar Rosendahl
155. John Kendall Chorlog	205. Arnold M. Morem	255. Gustav B. Wollan
156. Rev. Alfred Bredesen	206. Archie M. Anderson	256. Rev. Andrew Olson Bjerke
157. Clara M. Minne	207. Hallward J. Thornby	257. Carl J. Rice
158. Rev. Halvor Fredrick Huseth	208. Rev. Oscar C. Hellekson	258. Carl L. Johnson
159. Olai A. Lende	209. Gertrude M. Hilleboe	259. Merwin B. Tollefsrud
160. Abraham Vold	210. Prof. F. Melius Christiansen	260. Julius C. Sandbeck
161. Andrew Wm. Ramstad	211. Harold C. Omgolt	261. Elias Rachie
162. Anton Odden	212. Prof. Jacob Tanner	262. Mrs. Else Gustafson
163. Peter G. Erickson	213. Rev. Z. J. Ordal	263. Thormon Ohlgren
164. Louis Ness	214. Prof. Carl A. Mellby	264. Rev. Gustav Hegg
165. Rev. S. J. N. Ylvisaker	215. Ole John Nesheim	265. Rev. Sivert S. Westby
166. Rev. Daniel Halvorsen	216. K. Olaus Finseth	266. Amos O. Hauge
167. Gustav T. Lee	217. Rev. Oscar Peter Stavaas	267. Rev. Johan A. Aasgaard
168. Rev. Elling Ellingson Eidbo	218. Martin Vance	268. Agnes Geline Hilleboe
169. Stephanus G. Reinertson	219. Rev. Nils J. Lohre	269. Oliver Pederson
170. Rev. Einar Rudolph Anderson	220. Sigrid E. Thorgrimsen	270. Sibert E. Siverson
171. Otto A. Ulvin	221. Christopher R. Sylvester	271. Mrs. Agnes E. Tengdin
172. Rev. Paul Koren	222. Rev. Conrad B. Runsvold	272. Jerome Jorgenson
173. Rev. Edward Risty	223. August Alfred Evanson	273. Thenora Sindland
174. Gustav Flaaten	224. Rev. Orlando Ingvolstad	274. Thor A. Larsen
175. Rev. Halvor O. Fjeldstad	225. Newell H. Dahl	275. Tillman Orvenus Morem
176. Joseph Sylvester Strate	226. Rev. Martin Hegland	276. Martin L. Ullensvang
177. Mrs. Anna Stub	227. Rev. Geo. Loftness	277. Ignatius Bjorlee
178. Norman W. Nelson	228. Rev. Carl K. Solberg	278. Carsten Thorvald Woll
179. Anna Mabel Solberg	229. Allan Victor Steen	279. Rev. John Olaus Dahle
180. Kaia S. Dahl	230. Knute O. Berg	280. Thorsteii S. Rovelstad
181. Elmer Jacobson	231. Gustav Staff	281. Hersleb A. Helsem
182. Johan A. Swanson	232. Rev. Alfred Otto Johnson	282. Bessie Mabel Hellekson
183. Edgar N. Nordgaard	233. Mrs. Almo Hilleboe	283. Otto Alfred Johnsen
184. Olaf L. Jensen	234. Herman H. Dahl	284. Oscar Horvei
185. Rev. Ole J. Marken	235. Hugo Otto Walter	285. Rev. Arnt Vaaler
186. Ingomar A. Morkre	236. Johanna Hanson	286. August Herman Andresen
187. Selmer N. Lilleskov	237. Martin M. Wold	287. Rev. Halvor Bjornson
188. John M. Ellingboe	238. Geo. O. Berg	288. Oscar Johan Forton

289. Ole J. Lundly
290. Norval Nelson
291. Rev. Synther Storaas
292. Rev. Edward Martinus Stensrud
293. Elmer H. Helgeson
294. Rev. Helmer Halvorson
295. Anna Marie Sorenson
296. Selmer E. Jacobson
297. Mrs. Rose P. Gould
298. Prof. Michael J. Stolee
299. Henry Langum
300. Gust Thompson
301. Ingvald Messenlien
302. Mary A. Feuerhak
303. James A. Anderson
304. Mrs. Maren Sather
305. Hilda Lund
306. Arnold G. Benson
307. Jacob O. Tweten
308. Clarence A. Knutson
309. Paul Gerhard Schmidt
310. K. Andrew Holstad
311. Odd Gornitzka
312. Rev. Harold Berg Kildahl
313. A. C. Wiprud
314. Miss Delma C. Evenson
315. Dagny Aasen
316. Martin E. Waldeland
317. Rev. Rasmus Malmin
318. Albert J. Skaarsheim
319. Emil H. Erickson
320. Edward I. Bergum
321. Hans L. Waage
322. Gustav L. Vatland
323. Kristine Ulrike Anderson
324. Geo. M. Johnson
325. Geo. T. Morem
326. Adolph George Helgeson
327. Stella Regina Helgeson
328. Melvin S. Helgeson
329. Alma Dahlen
330. Alma Selmina Haugen
331. Theodore G. Rosholt
332. Rev. H. O. Gronlid
333. Rev. Jacob M. Hestener
334. Jennie C. Wick
335. Adolph M. Wick
336. Gudmund Kluxdal
337. Thore L. Rosholt
338. Ole L. Sateren

339. Olav A. Hougen
340. Goodwin J. Hoff
341. Ella Lealah Erickson
342. Oscar H. Reinholt
343. Peter O. Holland
344. Prof. Ditler Restad
345. Clifford A. Engebretson
346. Selma Dahlen
347. Nora Gronlid
348. Stina Joselina Peterson
349. Rev. Conrad Silas Halvorson
350. John Ritland
351. Fremont Rudolph Applen
352. Mrs. Eva Warden
353. Marie M. Feurerhak
354. Lewis M. Skaaren
355. Morris E. Skaaren
356. Jacob N. Jacobson
357. Wm. O. Erickson
358. Signe M. Alfson
359. Oscar Knudson
360. Geo. Haakon Olson
361. Jacob A. O. Preus
362. John Norgaard
363. Oscar C. Martinson
364. Harry Gregerson
365. Walter Ferdinand Erickson
366. Arnold M. Nelson
367. Henry Eidsvold
368. Walter Ernest Peterson
369. Olaf Houkom
370. Dr. Ivar Sivertsen
371. Emil H. Eriksen
372. Geneva E. Horsrud
373. Arthur Reginald Kingsburg
374. Mrs. Idella Haugen Preus
375. Ole Selmer Suftestad
376. Alfred B. Nygaard
377. Roland M. Torgerson
378. Martin Johan Hermanson
379. Alfred Oppegard
380. Anton Ask
381. Clarence Ferdinand Larson
382. Clarence Arnold Larson
383. Oscar F. Johnson
384. Rev. O. Nicolai
385. Conrad Raymond Waldeland
386. Tilden O. Harstad
387. Clarence A. Storhoff
388. Martin O. Sletvold

389. Joseph O. Sorum
390. Ilot B. Sorum
391. Rev. John R. Lavik
392. Andrew P. Lee
393. Richard Mentor Vordale
394. S. Melvin Oas
395. Revel Justin Jacobson
396. Martin L. Jacobson
397. Carl K. Nelson
398. Ada L. Johnson
399. Mrs. Tressie Cornelia Elton
400. Clarence Sikle
401. Miss Taaraand Vik
402. Olav M. Coll
403. I. E. Rosholt
404. Bernt Minsaas
405. William O. Lund
406. Mollester E. Carlson
407. Thomas L. I. Carlson
408. Julius J. Anderson
409. Ole J. Kvale
410. Luella T. Carlson
411. Thomas Ask
412. Cornelius Ask
413. Olaf O. Erling
414. Paul J. Lauritson
415. Oscar S. Hoff
416. Leonard Alfred Larson
417. Olaf J. Rustad
418. Bernie E. Ramsey
419. Selmer Edwin Sethre
420. Aleda Louise Sethre
421. Leila Mildred Moe
422. Alfred L. Vadheim
423. Mrs. Lillian A. Quale
424. Carl C. Quale
425. Rev. Theo. Eben Sweger
426. Roy I. Ricksham
427. Arthur Skrukrud
428. Rev. Henry T. Braa
429. Joseph Humble
430. Gilbert E. Gilbertson
431. Claudia Dahl
432. Albert K. Belverud
433. Rev. Truman Harvey Benson
434. Erik Waldeland
435. Sigurd Henry Holstad
436. Oscar C. Fremo
437. Carl M. Roan
438. John M. Hill

439. Ole Benjamin Hill	471. Clarence Strommen	503. Emma Ekern
440. Herman Thomson	472. Rev. Sander Tollefson	504. Leah O. Gjorvad
441. Anders M. Sundheim	473. Kenneth Nash Julsrud	505. Gerhard E. Strote
442. Rev. C. E. Sybilrud	474. Grace Esther Holstad	506. Andrew J. Anderson
443. Lars W. Boe	475. Mrs. Karen Marie Sperati	507. Hans M. Orfield
444. Henry C. Halverson	476. Rev. Sigvard T. Regue	508. Oscar F. Melby
445. Florence H. Johnson	477. Irvin B. Westby	509. Harry D. Kreiser
446. Gladys L. Koehn	478. Arthur J. Strate	510. Samuel O. Samuelson
447. Theodore G. Williams	479. David Svenungsen	511. Melvin P. Kaatrud
448. John M. Pedersen	480. Olaf Johanne Nash	512. Dr. Odd Eckfelt
449. Walter S. Peterson	481. David S. Walter	513. Rev. Oluf Asker
450. Helma Louis Wright Drake	482. Alexander M. Lunde	514. Rev. Kristofer N. Tvedt
451. Thorsten T. Thompson	483. Rev. John N. Walstead	515. Rev. Carl Wm. Landahl
452. Rev. Christian N. Sandager	484. Gunther A. Westby	516. Rev. Nokolai A. Larson
453. Rev. Lars O. Onerheim	485. Rev. E. I. Strom	517. Else M. Fredricksen
454. Selmer J. Strandjord	486. Gustav L. Winger	518. Albert Anderson
455. Rev. Corelius G. Naeseth	487. Dr. John R. Petersen	519. Arthur S. Olson
456. Henry Sigvard Johnson	488. Rev. Johan Carl Keyser Preus	520. John B. S. Grindvik
457. Rev. Peter J. Nestande	489. Rev. Carl O. B. Ness	521. Rev. Erick Sovik
458. Oscar Henry Kjorlie	490. Samuel T. Throbeck	522. Rev. Arthur Laurence
459. Erick N. Larson	491. Mabel C. Redalen	523. Never issued
460. Rev. Hans C. M. Jahren	492. Anton S. Larson	524. August W. Haugan
461. Rev. Ove J. H. Preus	493. Oliver Gordon	525. Martin A. Christenson
462. Martin Paulson	494. Lila Bragstad	526. Dr. Louis H. Braafladt
463. Adolph Gullickson	495. Olaf G. Malmin	527. Peder T. Konsterlie
464. Olga G. Overland	496. James Leland Larson	528. Edward Sovik
465. Rev. Sigurd M. Moe	497. Ole Hytjan	529. Rev. Geo. Olaf Holm
466. Clara Olina Jensson	498. Mrs. Amanda Sunstad	530. Rev. John M. Rohen
467. Ole R. Jensson	499. Nils N. Ronning	531. Paul N. Aasen
468. John B. Gjerdrum	500. Rev. Martin Ovidius Sumstad	532. Syvert Alsager
469. Norman Strommen	501. Prof. Paul M. Glasoe	533. Berthina S. Horvick
470. Jorgen A. Strommen	502. Rev. Nils Kleven	534. Tonnes L. Ekeland

Model Fraternal Code

For many years, all fifty states have had statutes governing the definitions and activities of fraternal benefit societies. Although the statutes were roughly comparable, they sometimes differed in subtle yet significant ways. In the 1980s, the National Fraternal Congress of America (NFCA) began working to introduce an updated, model fraternal code in all fifty states that would eliminate the statutory distinctions that encouraged legislative challenges, and place more of the burden of compliance on the shoulders of individual fraternals. Seventeen states had adopted the model fraternal code by 1988. Following are excerpts from the model fraternal code approved by the NFCA in 1983.

Section 1.
FRATERNAL BENEFIT SOCIETIES.

Any incorporated society, order or supreme lodge, without capital stock . . .whether incorporated or not, conducted solely for the benefit of its members and their beneficiaries and not for profit, operated on a lodge system with ritualistic form of work, having a representative form of government, and which provides benefits in accordance with this Article, is hereby declared to be a fraternal benefit society.

Section 2.
LODGE SYSTEM.

(a) A society is operating on the lodge system if it has a supreme governing body and subordinate lodges into which members are elected, initiated or admitted in accordance with its laws, rules and ritual.

Section 3.
REPRESENTATIVE FORM OF GOVERNMENT.

A society has a representative form of government when:

(a) it has a supreme governing body consituted in one of the following ways:
   (1) Assembly. The supreme governing body is an assembly composed of delegates elected directly by the members or at intermediate assemblies or conventions of members or their representatives, together with other delegates as may be prescribed in the society's laws.
   (2) Direct Election. The supreme governing body is a board composed of persons elected by the members, either directly or by their representatives in intermediate assemblies. . . .

(d) each voting member shall have one vote; no vote may be cast by proxy.

Section 5.
PURPOSES AND POWERS.

(a) A society shall operate for the benefit of members and their beneficiaries by:
   (1) providing benefits as specified in Section 16; and
   (2) operating for one or more social, intellectual, educational, charitable, benevolent, moral, fraternal, patriotic or religious purposes for the benefit of its members, which may also be extended to others.

Section 12.
INSTITUTIONS.

A society may create, maintain and operate, or may establish organizations to operate, not for profit institutions to further the purposes permitted by Section 5 (a) (2). . . .

Section 16.
BENEFITS.

(a) A society may provide the following contractual benefits in any form:
   (1) death benefits;
   (2) endowment benefits;
   (3) annuity benefits;
   (4) temporary or permanent disability benefits;
   (5) hospital, medical or nursing benefits;
   (6) monument or tombstone benefits to the memory of deceased members; and
   (7) such other benefits as authorized for life insurers and which are not inconsistent with this Article.

Section 24.
TAXATION.

Every society organized or licensed under this Article is hereby declared to be a charitable and benevolent institution, and all of its funds shall be exempt from all and every state, county, district, municipal, and school tax other than taxes on real estate and office equipment.

General Conventions of Lutheran Brotherhood

Number	Date	Place
1st	June 2, 1920	Lutheran Brotherhood office, Minneapolis
2nd	December 9, 1921	Morrison Hotel, Chicago
3rd	November 30, 1923	Curtis Hotel, Minneapolis (continued April 11, 1924 and October 9, 1924 at Lutheran Brotherhood office)
4th	June 5, 1925	West Hotel, Minneapolis
5th	June 24, 1927	Edgewater Beach Hotel, Chicago
6th	October 31, 1929	Palmer House Hotel, Chicago
7th	July 30, 1931	Curtis Hotel, Minneapolis
8th	July 28, 1933	Palmer House Hotel, Chicago
9th	June 28, 1935	Curtis Hotel, Minneapolis
10th	July 28, 1939	Curtis Hotel, Minneapolis
11th	July 31, 1943	Curtis Hotel, Minneapolis
12th	August 1, 1947	Curtis Hotel, Minneapolis
13th	June 21, 1951	Hotel Leamington, Minneapolis
14th	October 12, 1955	Radisson Hotel, Minneapolis
15th	October 28, 1959	Pick-Nicollet Hotel, Minneapolis
16th	May 18, 1963	Conrad Hilton Hotel, Chicago
17th	September 16, 1967	Palmer House Hotel, Chicago
18th	May 8, 1971	Palmer House Hotel, Chicago
19th	May 3, 1975	Palmer House Hotel, Chicago
20th	May 5, 1979	Conrad Hilton Hotel, Chicago
21st	May 7, 1983	Lutheran Brotherhood Building, Minneapolis
22nd	May 16, 1987	Lutheran Brotherhood Building, Minneapolis

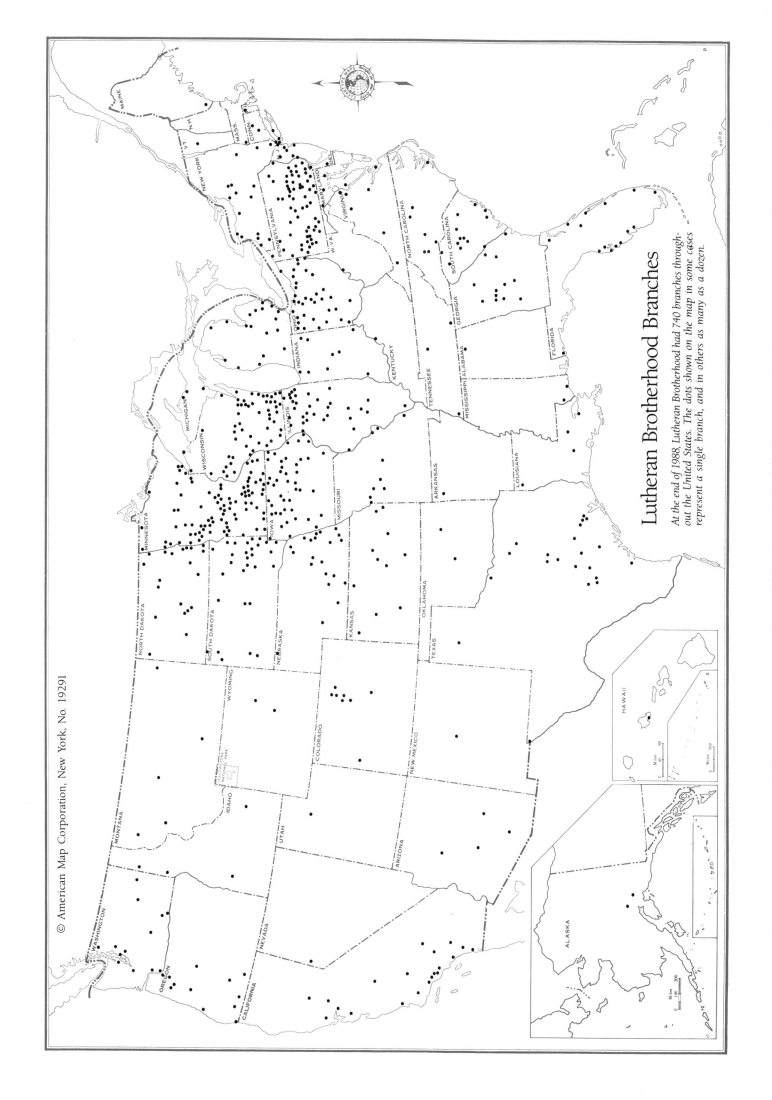

Lutheran Brotherhood Branches

At the end of 1988, Lutheran Brotherhood had 740 branches throughout the United States. The dots shown on the map in some cases represent a single branch, and in others as many as a dozen.

© American Map Corporation, New York, No. 19291

Directors of Lutheran Brotherhood: 1917-1988

Director	Service	Field	Residence
C. J. Eastvold	1917-1929	religion	Dawson, Minnesota
Thore Eggen	1917-1936	religion	Minneapolis, Minnesota
Herman L. Ekern	1917-1951	insurance law	Madison, Wisconsin
J. A. O. Preus	1917-1961	insurance	Chicago, Illinois
S. T. Reque	1917-1920	religion	St. Paul, Minnesota
Paulus List	1920-1925	publishing	Chicago, Illinois
C. M. Roan	1920-1946	medicine	Minneapolis, Minnesota
Charles H. Boyer	1920-1942	insurance	Philadelphia, Pennsylvania
Otto Mees	1920-1947	education	Columbus, Ohio
N. A. Nelson	1920	insurance	Chicago, Illinois
Louis M. Nelson	1920-1942	business	Evanston, Illinois
P. O. Holland	1920-1939	education	Northfield, Minnesota
Alva Davis	1926-1935	insurance	Altoona, Pennsylvania
P. O. Bersell	1927-1943	religion	Rock Island, Illinois
P. S. Peterson	1929-1947	business	Underwood, Iowa
E. Clarence Miller	1935	banking	New York City, New York
J. K. Jensen	1935-1955	business	Janesville, Wisconsin
Luther A. Harr	1937-1950	economics	Philadelphia, Pennsylvania
Russell H. Matthias	1939-1981	law	Chicago, Illinois
Carl F. Granrud	1940-1967	law	Minneapolis, Minnesota
J. A. Aasgaard	1942-1959	religion	Minneapolis, Minnesota
Gordon A. Bubolz	1942-1967	insurance	Appleton, Wisconsin
Harold A. Smith	1943-1967	banking	Elbow Lake, Minnesota
William G. Fisher	1946-1951	insurance	Minneapolis, Minnesota
Arthur O. Lee	1947-1970	insurance	Northfield, Minnesota
Randolph E. Haugan	1947-1959	publishing	Minneapolis, Minnesota
Harold Ingvaldson	1950-1953	insurance	Minneapolis, Minnesota
N. Kelly Neprud	1951-1962	insurance	Minneapolis, Minnesota
Dreng Bjornaraa	1953-1973	public relations	St. Paul, Minnesota
T. G. Overson	1954-1959	church finance	Minneapolis, Minnesota
R. H. Gerberding	1955-1967	religion	Minneapolis, Minnesota
Harold C. Hoel	1959-1961	insurance	Minneapolis, Minnesota
A. R. Kretzmann	1959-1971	religion	Chicago, Illinois
Bertram M. Wilde	1959-1966	finance	Philadelphia, Pennsylvania
A. Herbert Nelson	1961-1973	insurance	Minneapolis, Minnesota
Carl W. Segerhammar	1961-1963	religion	Los Angeles, California
John W. Lienemann	1962-1965	insurance	Minneapolis, Minnesota
Woodrow P. Langhaug	1963-1987	insurance	Minneapolis, Minnesota
Arthur O. Davidson	1965-1971	education	Staten Island, New York
Harold I. Lunde	1966-1975	finance	Minneapolis, Minnesota
Arley R. Bjella*	1967-present	law	Williston, North Dakota
Herbert C. Hansen	1967-1973	banking	Los Angeles, California

Director	Service	Field	Residence
James W. Krause*	1967-present	business	Minneapolis, Minnesota
George A. Wade*	1967-present	business	Seattle, Washington
Lloyd Svendsbye*	1970-present	education	Sioux Falls, South Dakota
Kenneth T. Severud	1971-1982	insurance	Minneapolis, Minnesota
Richard M. Heins	1971-1988	insurance	Madison, Wisconsin
Norman M. Lorentzsen	1973-1986	transportation	St. Paul, Minnesota
Martin E. Carlson	1973-1979	church administration	St. Petersburg, Florida
Stanford O. Tostengard*	1973-present	business	Houston, Texas
Helen M. Thal	1975-1986	education	Clearwater, Florida
Robert O. Blomquist*	1979-present	banking	St. Louis, Missouri
Clair E. Strommen*	1981-present	insurance	St. Paul, Minnesota
Sigurd D. Medhus*	1982-present	business	Stamford, Connecticut
Judith K. Larsen*	1986-present	science	Palo Alto, California
William R. Halling*	1986-present	accounting	Bloomfield Hills, Michigan
Herbert D. Ihle*	1987-present	business	Minneapolis, Minnesota
Mary Ellen Schmider*	1988-present	education	Moorhead, Minnesota
Robert P. Gandrud*	1988-present	insurance	Minneapolis, Minnesota

*1988 Board

Committees of the Board (as of July 1, 1988)

Audit Committee
Richard M. Heins, chairman
Herbert D. Ihle
Lloyd Svendsbye
Stanford O. Tostengard

Executive Committee
Clair E. Strommen, chairman
Arley R. Bjella
Herbert D. Ihle
James W. Krause

Fraternal Activities Committee
Stanford O. Tostengard, chairman
Arley R. Bjella
William R. Halling

Investment/Finance Committee
Robert O. Blomquist, chairman
Richard M. Heins
Herbert D. Ihle
Sigurd D. Medhus

Marketing/Operations Committee
James W. Krause, chairman
Judith K. Larsen
Lloyd Svendsbye
George A. Wade

Mutual Funds/Subsidiaries Committee
George A. Wade, chairman
Arley R. Bjella
William R. Halling

Board Policy and Personnel Committee
Sigurd D. Medhus, chairman
Robert O. Blomquist
James W. Krause
Judith K. Larsen

Top Executives of Lutheran Brotherhood: 1917-1988

Chairmen, chief executive officers, and presidents

Thore Eggen, president, 1917-1929.

J.A.O. Preus, chairman of the board, 1922-1961.

Herman L. Ekern, president, 1929-1951.

Carl F. Granrud, president, 1951-1963; chief executive officer, 1963-1967; chairman of the board, 1961-1967.

Harold A. Smith, president, 1963-1966.

A. Herbert Nelson, president, 1966-1970.

Arthur O. Lee, chairman of the board, 1967-1970.

Arley R. Bjella, chief executive officer, 1970-1982; chairman of the board, 1970-1987.

Woodrow P. Langhaug, president, 1970-1979.

Clair E. Strommen, president, 1980-1985; chief executive officer, 1982-1987; chairman of the board, 1987-present

Luther O. Forde, president, 1985-1987.

Robert P. Gandrud, president, 1987-present; chief executive officer, 1988-present.

Corporate Secretaries

J.A.O. Preus	1920-1923
C.M. Roan	1925-1939
Fred C. Mueller	1939-1955
Kenneth T. Severud	1955-1975
Gordon N. Taft	1975-1984
David J. Larson	1984-present

General Counsels

Herman L. Ekern	1920-1953
Russell H. Matthias	1953-1982
David J. Larson	1982-present

General Agencies of Lutheran Brotherhood

(as of December 31, 1987)

Alaska Agency, Anchorage, Alaska
Fred B. Armold, Lenexa, Kansas
Robert L. Beglau, Austin, Texas
Joseph E. Bjordal, Chippewa Falls, Wisconsin
Stephen R. Bolt, Hendersonville, Tennessee
John F. Bower, Charlotte, North Carolina
Barry L. Bowles, Woodland Hills, California
Robert Brinkman, Maitland, Florida
Richard E. Brown, Sioux Falls, South Dakota
Arlan Burmeister, Austin, Minnesota
Glen R. Bye, Fargo, North Dakota
Columbus Agency, Westerville, Ohio
William E. Davis, Omaha, Nebraska
Rodney W. Densmore, Spokane, Washington
Jerry F. Donahe, Portland, Oregon
Hildred L. Dungan, Allentown, Pennsylvania
Daniel Ebbert, Reading, Pennsylvania
Wil Fahlsing, Lakewood, Colorado
R. John Falck, Northfield, Minnesota
Charles Farrand, Fort Wayne, Indiana
Lawrence F. Green, Centerville, Ohio
Richard E. Grorud, Watertown, South Dakota
Kenneth B. Hartvigson, Jr., Seattle, Washington
Hawaii Agency, Kaaawa, Hawaii
Vernon F. Heinlein, Grand Rapids, Michigan
Kent H. Heise, Rockford, Illinois
Edward G. Hellier, Springfield, Illinois
Lyle R. Hemingson, Duluth, Minnesota
Harry L. Hendricks, New Oxford, Pennsylvania
Rodger P. Hendricks, Williamsport, Pennsylvania
Gus Hendrickson, Saginaw, Michigan
Jean Henrichs, Bloomington, Illinois
Wilfred H. Heuer, Lancaster, Pennsylvania
Ray Holmquist, Cedar Rapids, Iowa
Donald D. Jacobsen, Sioux City, Iowa
Marietta L. Johns, Houston, Texas
Bernard Johnson, Manchester, Connecticut
Donald P. Johnson, Grand Forks, North Dakota
Stephen M. Johnson, Stevens Point, Wisconsin
William A. Johnson, Minneapolis, Minnesota
Neil Kittlesen, Mankato, Minnesota
Mark W. Leissring, Waukesha, Wisconsin

Richard C. Lundell, Gold River, California
L. Karsten Lundring, Woodland Hills, California
Edward J. Miller, Columbia, South Carolina
Dennis C. Muehling, Des Moines, Iowa
Karl W. Mueller, Rochester Hills, Michigan
Alvin J. Neujahr, Billings, Montana
Glen R. Nurkka, Phoenix, Arizona
Steven A. Olson, Annandale, Minnesota
Harlan Pals, St. Charles, Missouri
John Petersen, Elmsford, New York
Frank A. Peterson, Bismarck, North Dakota
Harry Peterson, Fergus Falls, Minnesota
Robert Rasmus, Madison, Wisconsin
Robert Rasmussen, Red Bank, New Jersey
Thomas P. Reedy, Boardman, Ohio
William Reichwald, St. Paul, Minnesota
Richard Reimet, Flourtown, Pennsylvania
John R. Richmond, West Allis, Wisconsin
Kent R. Rolfing, Wichita, Kansas
Timothy A. Romig, Baltimore, Maryland
Joseph Ruisi, Johnstown, Pennsylvania
Warren K. Sauter, Pittsburgh, Pennsylvania
Douglas A. Scholla, Fairport, New York
Karl A. Seim, Bowling Green, Ohio
Rudolph Seppala, Marquette, Michigan
Harry Seimon, Sterling, Illinois
Jeffry Smith, Neenah, Wisconsin
Ronald G. Smith, Westlake, Ohio
Neil Sorum, Mason City, Iowa
Wayne Thaemert, Dale City, Virginia
William L. Thompson, Lincoln, Nebraska
Robert C. Tollefson, Palatine, Illinois
Utah Agency
Dean C. Vilmo, La Crosse, Wisconsin
Jeffrey Wells, Naperville, Illinois

Top General Agents

Annual Production through 1987*

Life Insurance: 1936-1983

A. H. Arneson, Clarkfield, Minnesota, 1936.

Walter C. Beglau, Austin, Texas, 1970, 1978.

A. J. Boehne, St. Louis, Missouri, 1940.

Einar N. Botten, Seattle, Washington, 1949.

M. J. Emerson, Sioux City, Iowa, 1948.

H. D. Foster, Harrisburg, Pennsylvania, 1938, 1941.

Ole B. Haroldson, Williston, North Dakota, 1943.

J. O. Hembre, Montivideo, Minnesota, 1944.

Levi Jesperson, Minneapolis, Minnesota, 1946, 1947.

Sylvert A. Johnson, Minot, North Dakota, 1945.

William A. Johnson, Minneapolis, Minnesota,
1962-1969, 1971-1977, 1979.

Woodrow P. Langhaug, Chicago, Illinois,
1950, 1951, 1955-1957.

John Lienemann, Beatrice, Nebraska,
1953, 1954, 1959.

Axel C. Lundring, Pasadena, California, 1958.

T. H. Mikkelson, Fergus Falls, Minnesota, 1952.

Harry L. Peterson, Fergus Falls, Minnesota, 1980.

H. L. Rothfuss, Williamsport, Pennsylvania, 1937.

Karl Seim, Findlay, Ohio, 1981-1983.

George M. Sowers, Allentown, Pennsylvania,
1939, 1942.

William L. Thompson, Beatrice, Nebraska,
1960, 1961.

Life Insurance: 1984-1987

Division 1

William A. Johnson, Minneapolis, Minnesota, 1987.

Harry L. Peterson, Fergus Falls, Minnesota,
1984-1986.

Division 2

Kenneth B. Hartvigson, Jr., Seattle, Washington, 1987.

Frank A. Peterson, Bismarck, North Dakota,
1984-1986.

Division 3

Kenneth E. Jensen, Hutchinson, Minnesota, 1985.

Mark W. Leissring, Waukesha, Wisconsin,
1984, 1986.

Neil P. Sorum, Mason City, Iowa, 1987.

Division 4

Rodney W. Densmore, Spokane, Washington, 1987.

R. John Falck, Northfield, Minnesota, 1984.

Neil P. Sorum, Mason City, Iowa, 1985, 1986.

Health Insurance: 1961-1983

Walter C. Beglau, Austin, Texas, 1968-1971.

William A. Johnson, Minneapolis, Minnesota,
1963, 1972, 1975-1978, 1980-1982.

Axel C. Lundring, Pasadena, California,
1962, 1964-1967.

L. Karsten Lundring, Woodland Hills, California,
1973, 1974, 1983.

Rudy Seppala, Marquette, Michigan, 1979.

Health Insurance: 1984-1987

Division 1

L. Karsten Lundring, Woodland Hills, California,
1984-1987.

Division 2

Charles Austin, Sioux Falls, South Dakota, 1984.

Kenneth B. Hartvigson, Jr., Seattle, Washington,
1985-1987.

Division 3

Richard Brown, Sioux Falls, South Dakota, 1987.

Arlan Burmeister, Austin, Minnesota, 1984.

Daniel Ebbert, Reading Pennsylvania, 1985.

Glen Nurkka, Scottsdale, Arizona, 1986.

Division 4

Rodney W. Densmore, Spokane, Washington, 1987.

Neil Kittlesen, Mankato, Minnesota, 1984, 1986.

David Pearson, Hershey, Pennsylvania, 1985.

Mutual Funds: 1970-1983

Ray Aden, Littleton, Colorado, 1973.

Robert Behnken, Brookville, Ohio, 1972.

Larry Brazie, Vandalia, Ohio, 1974, 1978.

Robert Brinkman, Maitland, Florida, 1982.

Harvey Hamman, Portland, Oregon, 1971.

William A. Johnson, Minneapolis, Minnesota,
1976, 1977, 1979-1981, 1983.

Edwin Miller, New York City, New York, 1970.

William L. Thompson, Beatrice, Nebraska, 1975.

Investment Products: 1984-1987

Division 1

Robert Brinkman, Maitland, Florida, 1984-1987.

Division 2

Paul Anderson, DeForest, Wisconsin, 1985.

Mark Leissring, Waukesha, Wisconsin, 1987.

Ray Cline and John Bower, Charlotte, North Carolina, 1984.

Jeffry Smith, Neenah, Wisconsin, 1986.

Division 3

Daniel Ebbert, Reading, Pennsylvania, 1985.

Kenneth Jensen, Hutchinson, Minnesota, 1984.

Don Johnson, Grand Forks, North Dakota, 1986, 1987.

Division 4

Rodney W. Densmore, Spokane, Washington, 1985.

Lyle Hemingson, Duluth, Minnesota, 1987.

Neil Kittlesen, Mankato, Minnesota, 1984, 1986.

Combination: 1962-1983

Walter C. Beglau, Austin, Texas, 1970.

William A. Johnson, Minneapolis, Minnesota, 1962-1969, 1971-1983.

Combination: 1984-1987

Division 1

William A. Johnson, Minneapolis, Minnesota, 1985-1987.

Harry L. Peterson, Fergus Falls, Minnesota, 1984.

Division 2

Kenneth B. Hartvigson, Jr., Seattle, Washington, 1986, 1987.

Harry L. Hendricks, New Oxford, Pennsylvania, 1985.

Alvin J. Neujahr, Billings, Montana, 1984.

Division 3

Don Johnson, Grand Forks, North Dakota, 1984-1986.

Neil P. Sorum, Mason City, Iowa, 1987.

Division 4

Rodney W. Densmore, Spokane, Washington, 1985, 1987.

R. John Falck, Northfield, Minnesota, 1984, 1986.

Fraternal: 1982-1983

Ronald G. Smith, Fairview Park, Ohio, 1982.

Ray Holmquist, Cedar Rapids, Iowa, 1983

Fraternal: 1984-1987

Division 1

William A. Johnson, Minneapolis, Minnesota, 1984-1987

Division 2

William E. Davis, Omaha, Nebraska, 1984, 1986, 1987.

Ray Holmquist, Cedar Rapids, Iowa, 1985.

Division 3

Arlan Burmeister, Austin, Minnesota, 1984-1986.

Neil P. Sorum, Mason City, Iowa, 1987.

Division 4

R. John Falck, Northfield, Minnesota, 1985, 1987.

Neil P. Sorum, Mason City, Iowa, 1984, 1986.

Agency of the Year: 1969-1987

David Asp, Austin, Minnesota, 1976.

LeRoy Backberg, Fargo, North Dakota, 1979.

Ray Cline, Concord, North Carolina, 1973.

R. Stacy Gongaware, York, Pennsylvania, 1972.

Harry Hendricks, New Oxford, Pennsylvania, 1985.

Donald Johnson, Grand Forks, North Dakota, 1983.

Glen Johnson, Des Moines, Iowa, 1977, 1978.

Mark Leissring, Waukesha, Wisconsin, 1986.

Lavern Mausolf, Shawnee Mission, Kansas, 1971.

Dennis Muehling, Des Moines, Iowa, 1984.

Karl Mueller, Rochester, Michigan, 1970.

Harry Peterson, Fergus Falls, Minnesota, 1980-1982.

Karl Seim, Findlay, Ohio, 1969.

Harry Siemon, Addison, Illinois, 1975.

Russel Smith, Rapid City, South Dakota, 1974.

Neil Sorum, Mason City, Iowa, 1987.

*Life and health insurance leaders based on volume from 1936-1963; potential first year commission (PFYC) from 1964-1987. Mutual funds leaders based on volume from 1971-1973; PFYC from 1973-1987. Mutual Funds renamed Investment Products in 1984.

Top District Representatives

Annual Production through 1987*

Life Insurance: 1925-1987

A. H. Arneson, Madison, Minnesota, 1933, 1934.

Robert E. Behnken, Brookville, Ohio, 1964, 1965, 1967-1969.

Enfrid C. Benson, San Francisco, California, 1955.

Robert M. Benson, Evanston, Illinois, 1950.

Marvin Calahan, Havre, Montana, 1972.

William H. Campbell, Chicago, Illinois, 1963, 1966, 1971, 1987.

Richard Dicks, Lancaster, Pennsylvania, 1986.

Michael Diemer, Oconto Falls, Wisconsin, 1983.

Mike Engelstad, Fort Collins, Colorado, 1978, 1979.

Alfred Hedegaard, Atlantic, Iowa, 1952.

Richard J. Falck, Northfield, Minnesota, 1947-1949.

J. M. O. Gudal, Minnesota, 1925.

Victor A. Johnson, Osceola, Nebraska, 1929.

William R. Johnson, Belmond, Iowa, 1970, 1973, 1976, 1980-1982.

James Jones, Fort Wayne, Indiana, 1977.

Woodrow P. Langhaug, Minneapolis, Minnesota, 1944.

Melvin Mathison, Fergus Falls, Minnesota, 1951.

Lavern Mausolf, Hoisington, Kansas, 1958-1960.

Herbert Mullen, Stoughton, Wisconsin, 1956, 1957.

Martin Nelson, Northfield, Minnesota, 1935-1941.

S. F. Rarig, Catawissa, Pennsylvania, 1945, 1946.

George M. Sowers, Allentown, Pennsylvania, 1942, 1943, 1953.

Ronald Speckman, Cape Coral, Florida, 1974, 1975.

Herbert F. Steigler, Wilmington, Delaware, 1961, 1962.

Richard Unger, Gettysburg, Pennsylvania, 1984, 1985.

James B. Williams, Baltimore, Maryland, 1954.

Christian Zander, Omaha, Nebraska, 1926-1928, 1930-1932.

Health Insurance: 1962-1987

Rolland Aulich, Chatfield, Minnesota, 1974, 1981.

Robert E. Behnken, Brookville, Ohio, 1967.

William H. Campbell, Chicago, Illinois, 1969.

Michael Diemer, Oconto Falls, Wisconsin, 1972, 1977, 1979, 1980.

Ronald K. Evenson, Harmony, Minnesota, 1970, 1971.

Michael George, York, Pennsylvania, 1985.

Tim Griesse, Hewitt, Texas, 1983.

Walter L. Heidenson, Chicago, Illinois, 1963.

Harold Helwig, Mount Horeb, Wisconsin, 1978.

Robert Hintz, Tustin, California, 1987.

Clifford C. Larson, Scandinavia, Wisconsin, 1965.

Towne Makela, Alexandria, Minnesota, 1973.

Paul G. E. Meyer, Michigan City, Indiana, 1962.

Ed Miller, Jr., Columbia, South Carolina, 1986.

Charles J. Nelson, Elgin, Illinois, 1968.

Gordon Shive, Seven Valleys, Pennsylvania, 1975, 1976, 1984.

Paul Tinker, Lancaster, Ohio, 1982.

James Wang, Sylvania, Ohio, 1964.

Robert Zemcik, Findlay, Ohio, 1966.

Mutual Funds: 1970-1987

Ed Aden, Gothenburg, Nebraska, 1973.

Robert E. Behnken, Brookville, Ohio, 1974, 1977.

Larry Brazie, Middleburg Heights, Ohio, 1972.

David Hamre, Miami, Florida, 1979-1985, 1987.

Don Henninger, Hastings, Nebraska, 1975, 1976, 1986.

William Schuettler, Pottsville, Pennsylvania, 1970.

Robert Schuon, New York City, New York, 1971.

Lavern Talley, Springfield, Ohio, 1978.

Combination: 1962-1987

Robert E. Behnken, Brookville, Ohio, 1964, 1965, 1967-1969, 1974.

Marvin Calahan, Havre, Montana, 1972.

William H. Campbell, Chicago, Illinois, 1963, 1971.

Michael Diemer, Oconto Falls, Wisconsin, 1982, 1983, 1986.

William R. Johnson, Belmond, Iowa, 1966, 1970, 1973, 1975, 1976, 1978, 1980, 1981, 1987.

James Jones, Fort Wayne, Indiana, 1977.

Herbert F. Steigler, Wilmington, Delaware, 1962.

Richard Unger, Gettysburg, Pennsylvania, 1979, 1984.

John Williamson, Davidsville, Pennsylvania, 1985.

Most Valued Producer: 1974-1987

Michael Diemer, Oconto Falls, Wisconsin, 1982, 1983, 1986.

William R. Johnson, Belmond, Iowa, 1974**-1978, 1980, 1981, 1987.

Richard Unger, Gettysburg, Pennsylvania, 1974**, 1976**, 1979, 1984, 1985.

*Life and health insurance leaders based on volume from 1936-1963; potential first year commission (PFYC) from 1964-1987. Mutual funds leaders based on volume from 1971-1973; PFYC from 1973-1987. Mutual Funds renamed Investment Products in 1984.
**MVP double-awarded in 1974 and 1976.

Brotherhood Builders

Employees with fifteen or more years of service (as of December 31, 1987).

Years of Service

48	David Zetzman*	29	Donald Winter	22	Ruth Swanson*	18	Mary Jo Campbell
47	Sophie Hawkinson*		Harlan Hogsven		Sally Weikleenget*		Jeanne Sheehy
45	Al Konigson*		Eleanor Miele				Della Nordstrom
	Clifford Thompson*		Arlys Eidem	21	Diane Lentz		Gregory Rogers
44	Arvid Carlson*		Karen Larson		Patricia Bjork		Dixi Vaux
	Margaret Lepp*	28	Sharon Strand		Lavonne Person		Susan Johnson
43	Margaret Dittes*		Betty Hill		Kenneth Kistler		Leigh Carlson
42	Kenneth Severud*		Margarete Pobig		Charles De Vries		Diane Giese
	Lorraine Keiran*		Rosalee Hanson		Andrea Johnson		Galen Becklin
	Ruth Downey*		Raymond Bodin*		James Hins		Sandra Beck*
41	Leota Swanson		Arthur Thilquist*		Keith Both		Paul Gemilere*
40	Jessie Hurtubise		Theodore Feig*		Carl Brummer	17	Otis Hilbert
	Earl Andersen*	27	Richard Lund		Gwendolyn Steele		Thomas Johnson
	Ethel Johnson*		Sonja Risser		Merlyn Crumpton		Valerie Onstad
	Herbert Mohr*	26	Eugene Moe		Richard Neuman*		Sharon Ehrlichmann
38	Joyce Johnson		Wayne Hellbusch	20	Jane Rosin		Merridee Stueber
	Donald Nelson		Palmer Eidem		Sandra Breed		Mary Wenum
	Astrid Johnson*		Nancy Fodstad		Dennis Grover		Donn Satrom
	Lillian Reine*		Caroline Burley		Dennis Bornes		Mary Hendrix
	Leona Grondahl*		Vernon Suhr		Patricia Biggs		Ilga Dulbe
37	John Nystul		Arthur Zuehlke*		Nancy Pearson		Steven Bakk
	Josephine Mohl*	25	Roger Christianson		Judith Forslin		Mona Eckman
36	Lou Madsen*		Eldora Anderson		James Habeck		Elvera Alseth*
	Kathrine Solstad*		David Williams		Donald Brostrom*		Helen Berg*
	Norman Rosholt*		William Arendt		Reuben Jacobson*		Marjorie Porath*
35	Woodrow Langhaug*		Bruce Nokleby		Monroe Lee*		Darlyne Magnuson*
	Elmer Romundstad*		Stanley Townswick		Richard Nelson*	16	Judy Hudson
	Doris Ripczinski*		Roy Peterson*		Oliver Korte*		Lawrence Martin
	Deloris Seemann*		William Fisher*	19	Joyce Swedean		Dennis Peterson
34	Marles Johnson	24	Arthur Peterson		William Fors		William Reichwald
	Herman Egeberg*		Richard Johnson		Kathryn Smith		Deloris Kanten*
33	Douglas Segelstrom		Vernon Carlson		David Larson		Arley Bjella*
	Joanne Ausing		William Larson		Russell Morris	15	Charles Coles
	Hans Schink		Theodore Stundahl		Janis Aurentz		Carol Kelly
	Martha Johnson*		DeVona Winter		Susan Adix		Thomas Joyal
	Helen Pearson*		Vicky Jacobson		Jane Anderson		Lynette Johnson
	Richard Hoppenrath*		Lowell Mason		Marsha Cameron		Rosemary Richter
32	Shirley Dallmann	23	Ruth Jelinek		Sharon Olson		Mary Abbey
31	Phillip Perry		Emma Ziemke		Ardis Ronnei		Nancy Dahlke
	Vija Brivkalns		Sandra Anderson		Wendy Line		Joycelyn Bradford
	Delores Volkers		Joyce Nevala		James Walline		Betty Currier
	Gordon Taft*		Philip Olson		Virginia Palm		Russell Juvrud
	Carl Thomsen*		Diana Glasser		Cheryl Foye		Marlene Hanson
30	Beverly Johnson		Richard Bistodeau		Ruth Thayer*		Mitchell Felchle
	Erwin Moe		Mildred Wilson*		Betty Young*		Eleanor Pearson*
	Vonna Peterson		Richard Ward*		Joyce Malaske*		Irma Rulikovs*
	Luther Forde	22	Betty Mischke	18	JoAnn Bass		*Retired*
	Donald Lommen*		Robert Hanson		Bruce Piltingsrud		
	Jennie Lorentson*		Bradley English		Vicki Bruns		
			Robert Gandrud		Roxana Ponath		
			Merwin Dreher		Rolf Running		
					Edward Stang		
					Jerald Sourdiff		

Number of Employees: 1917-1987

Full-Time Employees Only

Year	Number	Source	Year	Number	Source	Year	Number	Source
1917	2	payroll register	1937	81	annual statement	1964	352	quarterly report
1918	4	payroll register and annual statement	1938	78	annual statement	1965	363	quarterly report
			1939	108	annual statement	1966	385	quarterly report
1919	5	annual statement	1940	83	annual statement	1967	400	quarterly report
1920	3	annual statement	1941	96	annual statement	1968	419	monthly report
1921	6	annual statement	1942	100	annual statement	1969	439	monthly report
1922	6	annual statement	1943	102	annual statement	1970	482	monthly report
1923	5	annual statement	1944	110	annual statement	1971	502	monthly report
1924	7	annual statement	1945	121	annual statement	1972	502	monthly report
1925	14	annual statement	1946	149	annual statement	1973	517	monthly report
1926	15	annual statement (17-payroll register)	1947	160	annual statement	1974	523	monthly report
			1948	172	annual statement	1975	529	monthly report
1927	23	annual statement (23-payroll register)	1949	175	annual statement	1976	553	staffing
			1950	179	annual statement	1977	578	staffing
1928	28	annual statement (28-payroll register)	1951	210	annual statement	1978	597	staffing
			1952	194	annual statement	1979	624	staffing
1929	36	annual statement (40-payroll register)	1953	198	payroll register	1980	647	staffing
			1954	209	payroll register	1981	658	staffing
1930	48	annual statement (46-payroll register)	1955	215	payroll register	1982	672	staffing
			1956	250	payroll register	1983	720	staffing
1931	50	annual statement	1957	256	payroll register	1984	737	staffing
1932	50	annual statement	1958	248	quarterly report	1985	794	staffing
1933	51	annual statement	1959	256	quarterly report	1986	859	staffing
1934	64	annual statement	1960	278	quarterly report	1987	936	staffing
1935	73	annual statement	1961	290	quarterly report			
1936	67	annual statement (unclear if officers included)	1962	319	quarterly report			
			1963	351	quarterly report			

Number of Field Personnel: 1951-1987*

Includes Part-Time Employees

Year	Number	Year	Number	Year	Number	Year	Number
1951	149	1961	813	1971	1,110	1981	1,098
1952	195	1962	821	1972	1,063	1982	1,128
1953	223	1963	849	1973	1,034	1983	1,247
1954	248	1964	873	1974	1,041	1984	1,334
1955	270	1965	907	1975	1,087	1985	1,391
1956	353	1966	972	1976	1,086	1986	1,466
1957	394	1967	956	1977	1,132	1987	1,574
1958	456	1968	981	1978	1,158		
1959	730	1969	1,004	1979	1,155		
1960	825	1970	1,066	1980	1,132		

*Statistics for years 1917-1950 not available.

Growth of Assets and Insurance in Force: 1918-1987

Year	Assets	Insurance in Force	Year	Assets	Insurance in Force	Year	Assets	Insurance in Force
1918	$ 6,735	$ 676,500	1942	$ 15,434,430	$ 89,812,792	1966	$ 376,301,089	$ 2,689,915,587
1919	19,830	1,115,000	1943	17,878,949	101,115,454	1967	421,949,713	3,019,890,626
1920	47,943	2,193,500	1944	20,877,515	118,500,521	1968	473,554,988	3,339,373,369
1921	96,302	3,123,874	1945	24,448,645	138,755,513	1969	521,802,112	3,679,046,333
1922	162,335	3,676,500	1946	28,894,359	175,820,660	1970	579,169,189	4,033,015,163
1923	237,789	4,112,500	1947	34,819,133	215,573,110	1971	651,289,611	4,434,161,716
1924	319,088	5,310,500	1948	41,489,919	252,984,452	1972	718,902,503	4,798,339,931
1925	431,157	9,390,000	1949	48,830,072	283,878,841	1973	782,409,226	5,283,117,540
1926	640,589	14,898,265	1950	56,585,809	318,627,809	1974	859,687,453	5,800,698,068
1927	907,627	20,551,205	1951	64,717,062	366,433,251	1975	971,195,880	6,330,644,437
1928	1,285,817	26,370,926	1952	73,919,742	415,138,220	1976	1,097,946,603	6,927,330,410
1929	1,781,500	31,782,650	1953	84,329,974	479,548,381	1977	1,229,971,937	7,724,023,719
1930	2,420,549	37,675,188	1954	95,792,253	551,333,330	1978	1,375,212,094	8,475,851,725
1931	3,053,765	40,763,698	1955	108,128,506	633,760,967	1979	1,535,014,619	9,294,875,061
1932	3,669,975	40,977,778	1956	122,027,636	729,909,992	1980	1,706,249,659	10,094,415,626
1933	4,198,808	42,568,441	1957	137,369,846	847,517,514	1981	1,930,701,656	10,899,999,842
1934	4,803,161	45,996,821	1958	156,024,827	969,197,497	1982	2,217,859,969	11,452,516,892
1935	5,559,928	51,028,342	1959	176,668,457	1,137,801,144	1983	2,528,660,864	12,340,970,580
1936	6,497,321	56,190,263	1960	197,859,617	1,307,221,664	1984	2,853,119,561	14,175,926,039
1937	7,523,062	61,097,084	1961	217,105,947	1,476,100,082	1985	3,256,106,327	16,232,374,319
1938	8,737,365	65,334,512	1962	239,380,769	1,646,000,000	1986	3,711,002,394	18,395,408,495
1939	10,043,257	69,713,722	1963	266,603,317	1,883,441,436	1987	4,235,036,877	20,921,932,324
1940	11,457,782	74,888,463	1964	300,736,981	2,088,880,393			
1941	13,415,045	82,385,802	1965	338,614,111	2,307,552,080			

Growth of Mutual Funds: 1970-1987

Year	Assets under Management	Year	Assets under Management	Year	Assets under Management	Year	Assets under Management
1970	$14,348,427	1975	$110,196,000	1980	$385,404,975	1985	$ 969,988,000
1971	$18,587,754	1976	$152,539,706	1981	$756,874,487	1986	$1,318,588,000
1972	$58,148,624	1977	$154,719,000	1982	$829,829,283	1987	$1,530,705,000
1973	$57,528,832	1978	$148,696,000	1983	$704,326,000		
1974	$80,679,000	1979	$265,204,000	1984	$819,646,000		

Group Photo Identification

This picture of the home office staff was taken in September 1937 at the Minneapolis Auto Club. The photo appears in Chapter Three, pages 82-83.

1. Hazel Daley Conklin
2. Margaret Strate
3. Helen Heglund
4. Marian Miller
5. Margaret Gjertsen
6. Harold Martinson
7. Sophie Gary
8. Dale Kilby
9. Kay Lund
10. Mel Hagerness
11. Earl Andersen
12. Ted Steeland
13. Harold Falls
14. Robert Carlson
15. Roy Lind
16. Kelly Neprud
17. Mrs. J. R. Petersen
18. Mrs. Elias Rachie
19. Elias Rachie
20. L. L. Johnson
21. Fred Mueller
22. Ruth Aasen
23. Dorothy Extrom
24. Eleanor Becker
25. Ella Gustafson
26. Louise Berger
27. Linnea Falley
28. Irene Johnson
29. Mildred Roan
30. Charlotte Johnson
31. Evelyn Hille
32. Marian Edblom
33. Evelyn Sundt
34. Eleanor Bersell
35. Helen Brandt
36. Al Konigson
37. Gladys Vogland
38. Mrs. C. O. Teisberg
39. Betty Wold
40. Ruth Neprud
41. Mrs. C. M. Roan
42. Elsie Fisher
43. Bertilla Wald
44. Solveig Grande
45. Dagmar Thompson
46. Ethel Hasselgren
47. Laura Williams
48. Evelyn Walters
49. Clarice Jensen
50. Mildred Ulvestad
51. Helen Olson
52. Gwen Torblee
53. Viola Nelson
54. Margaret Ebert
55. Harriet Nelson
56. Clarence Nelson
57. Ray Fischer
58. Dr. J. R. Petersen
59. Dr. C. M. Roan
60. William G. Fisher
61. Inga Holm Garthus
62. Mrs. Fred Mueller
63. Unidentified
64. Orville Jacobson
65. Roy Haugen
66. Chester Hagander
67. Ingolf Lee
68. David Zetzman
69. Helen Schuch
70. Ken Severud
71. Helen Ingvaldson
72. Jeanette Berge
73. Ann Hagen
74. Cliff Thompson
75. Lois Cedarstrand
76. O. M. Sando

This picture of the home office staff (and spouses) was taken in 1946 at the Columbia Chalet in Minneapolis. The photo appears in Chapter Three, pages 86-87.

1. Doris Tone
2. Elaine Nelson
3. Miriam Johnson
4. Dorothy Zetzman
5. Arlene Carlson
6. Virginia Mollan
7. Barbara Ness
8. Lillian Root
9. Phyllis Heggem
10. Jean Stinsky
11. Betty Westerlund
12. Yvonne Bredesen
13. Audrey Roufs
14. Genevieve Bobeck
15. Eleanor Tweeten
16. Lillian Reine
17. Harriet Martinson
18. Martha Severson
19. Marion Norrbom
20. Priscilla Lokkesmoe
21. Shirley Ramlet
22. Alice Krueger
23. Rosalie Nelson
24. Lila Hasse
25. Frances Miller
26. Darlene Sotobeer
27. Margaret Morth
28. Maxine Leighton
29. Josephine Hultman

30. Colleen Sutherland
31. Elizabeth Mork
32. Marilyn Benson
33. Muriel Erbes
34. Shirley Olson
35. Lorraine Bathen
36. Arlene Sigler
37. Elsie Fisher
38. Mrs. J. R. Petersen
39. Betty Anderson
40. Lorraine Knacke
41. Avis Munkberg
42. Helen Olson
43. Martha Boesche
44. Betty Schnabel
45. Janet Lien
46. Lorraine Ziegler
47. Betty Blesi
48. Margaret Ebert
49. Vera Forare
50. Maurine Bendickson
51. Arline Drange
52. Welden Ingvaldson
53. Lorenz Jost
54. Mrs. Al Holtan
55. Mrs. Harold Hoel
56. Al Holtan
57. Bernice Rohne
58. Mary Ann Westberg

59. Shirley Swanson
60. Mildred Hollinder
61. Verna Heinz
62. Bernadette Becker
63. Ethel Ann Johnson
64. Eleanor Haukeness
65. Olive Elliason
66. Carol Thompson
67. Elizabeth Dahl
68. Betty Uglem
69. Fred C. Mueller
70. Mrs. Fred Mueller
71. Ray Wolf
72. Jean Reinhardt
73. Mrs. O. R. Jacobson
74. Merrolyn Halvorson
75. Dagny Olson
76. Helen Hendrickson
77. Renee Sembrick
78. Jennie Lorentson
79. Martha Tiller
80. Evelyn Johnson
81. Mary Wilson
82. Arleen Lindstrom
83. Agnes Anderson
84. Kenneth Severud
85. William Steeland
86. Dr. J. R. Petersen
87. Elias Rachie

88. Mrs. Elias Rachie
89. Mrs. N. K. Neprud
90. Inga Holm Garthus
91. Margaret Dittes
92. Solveig Chambers
93. Mary Kolstad
94. Marjorie Beckey
95. June Holmen
96. Helen Pearson
97. Astrid Johnson
98. Leota Swanson
99. Ruth Johnson
100. Esther Kindvall
101. Ray Moore
102. Orville Jacobson
103. Charlotte Erickson
104. Cliff Thompson
105. William G. Fisher
106. Mrs. Cliff Thompson
107. Mrs. Arvid Carlson
108. Arvid Carlson
109. Margaret Halverson
110. Geraldine Dwinnell
111. Mona Ries
112. Genevieve Gladen
113. Verna Rosty
114. Irene Sather
115. Jane Fink
116. Harriet Aasgaard

117. Elsie Haroldson
118. Betty Gammelgaard
119. Jean Talso
120. Margaret Hanson
121. Kathrine Solstad
122. Bertilla Wald
123. S. H. Holstad
124. Genevieve Brooks
125. Harold Hoel
126. Marjorie Lee
127. Alan Peterson
128. Chester Hagander
129. Mrs. C. Hagander
130. Mrs. Al Konigson
131. Al Konigson
132. Mrs. Ingolf Lee
133. Ingolf Lee
134. Alice Ganske
135. Ellen Jacobson
136. Lois Gunderson
137. Harriet Anderson
138. Al Drawbert
139. David Zetzman
140. Herbert Mohr
141. Margaret Johnson
142. Elaine Gerber

Index